797,885 Books

are available to read at

Forgotten Books

www.ForgottenBooks.com

Forgotten Books' App
Available for mobile, tablet & eReader

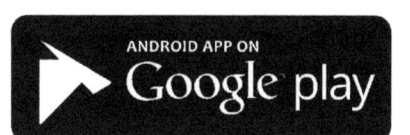

ISBN 978-0-282-39610-7
PIBN 10850134

This book is a reproduction of an important historical work. Forgotten Books uses state-of-the-art technology to digitally reconstruct the work, preserving the original format whilst repairing imperfections present in the aged copy. In rare cases, an imperfection in the original, such as a blemish or missing page, may be replicated in our edition. We do, however, repair the vast majority of imperfections successfully; any imperfections that remain are intentionally left to preserve the state of such historical works.

Forgotten Books is a registered trademark of FB &c Ltd.
Copyright © 2017 FB &c Ltd.
FB &c Ltd, Dalton House, 60 Windsor Avenue, London, SW19 2RR.
Company number 08720141. Registered in England and Wales.

For support please visit www.forgottenbooks.com

1 MONTH OF FREE READING

at

www.ForgottenBooks.com

By purchasing this book you are eligible for one month membership to ForgottenBooks.com, giving you unlimited access to our entire collection of over 700,000 titles via our web site and mobile apps.

To claim your free month visit: www.forgottenbooks.com/free850134

* Offer is valid for 45 days from date of purchase. Terms and conditions apply.

English
Français
Deutsche
Italiano
Español
Português

www.forgottenbooks.com

Mythology Photography **Fiction** Fishing Christianity **Art** Cooking Essays Buddhism Freemasonry Medicine **Biology** Music **Ancient Egypt** Evolution Carpentry Physics Dance Geology **Mathematics** Fitness Shakespeare **Folklore** Yoga Marketing **Confidence** Immortality Biographies Poetry **Psychology** Witchcraft Electronics Chemistry History **Law** Accounting **Philosophy** Anthropology Alchemy Drama Quantum Mechanics Atheism Sexual Health **Ancient History Entrepreneurship** Languages Sport Paleontology Needlework Islam **Metaphysics** Investment Archaeology Parenting Statistics Criminology **Motivational**

PREFACE.

The publication of an ancestral record has become an event of such frequent occurrence as to hardly call for excuse or comment. A few words of explanation will therefore suffice as my preface.

Several years since, while on a business trip to Hartford, Conn., I examined the *History of Simsbury, Granby, and Canton, Conn.*, published in 1845, by Noah A. Phelps, and *Sketches of West Simsbury*, published in 1856, by Abiel Brown. I found in these histories my own family tree, with but one omission, which I afterwards supplied from the probate office at Hartford. My attention was forcibly called to the rapidly approaching decay and obliteration of many of the earlier manuscript town records of the colonial period, and I realized that any further searches I might wish to make, for personal details concerning the "early fathers," should be prosecuted at once. I have since carried out a resolution then formed, to gather every attainable item which would throw any light on the life and pursuits of men of the first and second generations of the New England family bearing the Moses name. The results have been so fruitful that I have decided to preserve them in book form. Incidental to these researches I have obtained the names of many descendants. I therefore append a genealogical record, which, though not complete, should give to nearly all who claim New England descent, and who can trace back their ancestry for four generations, an opportunity to establish their lineage.

Many of the descendants of the forefathers will doubtless feel disappointed that I have not made search for them and placed them where they justly belong with the modern names in this book.

I can only say by way of apology for omissions and imperfections, that I have been but two years in gathering material, and have been able to give to this compilation no more than the occasional spare hours of an active business life.

I print this work for my personal satisfaction and also with the hope of gratifying the few friends and correspondents who have aided in the researches necessary to such an undertaking — who realize its difficulties, and have with myself found interest and pleasure in overcoming them.

Among others who have assisted me, I make especial mention of Rev. Vincent Moses of Patten, Maine; of Joshua Moses of Hoopeston, Ill., and of the Hon. Charles J. Hoadly, State Librarian at Hartford, Conn., from each of whom I have received valuable material.

The book is published for private circulation.

ZEBINA MOSES.

WASHINGTON, D. C., Dec. 24, 1889.

JOHN MOSES OF PLYMOUTH COLONY.

It is a matter of actual record that as far back as 1647 there were three New England colonists bearing the name of John Moses. Of these, the earliest mention is of John Moses of Plymouth.

There is nothing to indicate relationship between him and John Moses of Portsmouth; but family traditions and statements, as well as strong circumstantial evidence and the inherent probabilities of the case, seem to determine beyond reasonable doubt that he was the father of John Moses of Windsor. Several accounts in the possession of the older branches of the descendants of John Moses of Windsor state positively that he was the son of a John Moses of Plymouth.

From these accounts one is selected that has several times been in print. In a personal sketch of the late Schuyler Moses,[*] published several years since in *Mason's Semi-Centennial History of Rochester, N. Y.*, John Moses is mentioned as the "son of John Moses who came from England in 1632, and who is supposed to have been married before he emigrated to America." . . . .

"This John Moses was a blacksmith, and brought with him from England, in 1632, a set of tools which have remained in the Moses

---

[*] Schuyler Moses, after his removal from Connecticut to New York, lived for many years in the same house with his father, who died as late as 1847, aged 86, and also remembered his grandfather, Elisha, who was born in 1735.

This Elisha's grandfather was born in 1681. It will thus be seen that the story of the anvil, and of its original ownership, might have been handed down through but very few persons in reaching the venerable Schuyler Moses The New York *World* of March 14, 1880, contained the following notice: "Schuyler Moses died yesterday in his 91st year; he was the oldest Freemason in the State of New York, the oldest pioneer of Rochester; he voted for James Monroe in 1820, and for Harrison in 1888, and served as a juryman in 1888."

family down to the present time, a period of two hundred and fifty-two years."

A number of the *Iron Age*, published during the Centennial Exposition of 1876, gives a description of an anvil exhibited at Philadelphia in a building devoted to New England historical relics. Extracts from this article, printed thirteen years since, are as follows:

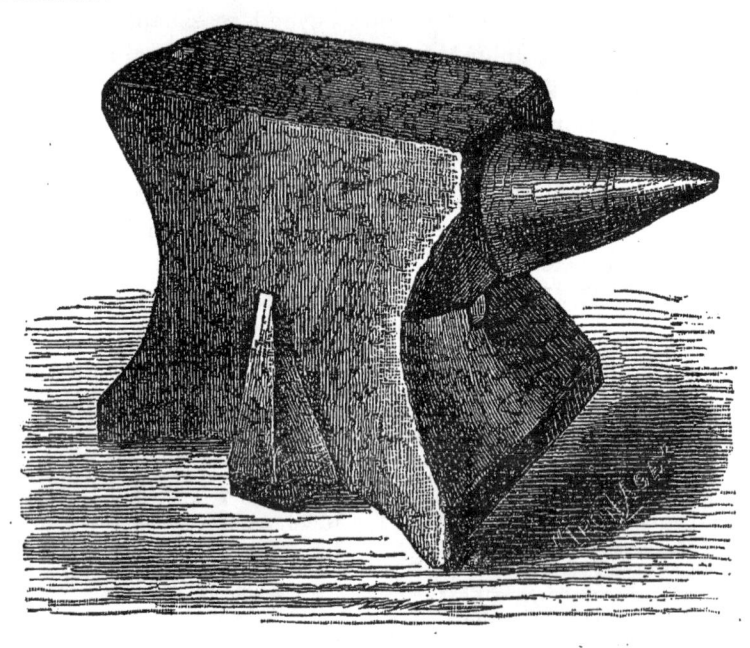

"AN ANVIL OF THE SEVENTEENTH CENTURY."

"The old anvil shown in the accompanying illustration has already been described in these columns, but some additional particulars concerning it will be of interest. It is 11 inches high, 16 inches long to horn, four inches wide, and weighs 126 pounds. Mr. Seymour says: 'I assure you it has seen hard service. There is no question as to its being made in 1632.'"

In the earlier article above alluded to, a letter, dated March 13, 1876, from Mr. Norman Seymour, Secretary of the Livingston County, N. Y., Historical Society, is published, from which is quoted: "Among the relics that have been brought out so far this centennial year, I have found in our town an old anvil, and marked on it in figures cut in the iron *1632*. This anvil was brought over from England about the year 1632 by John Moses."

JOHN MOSES OF PLYMOUTH COLONY. 11

Farther on, after tracing from John Moses of 1632 the genealogy of the Schuyler Moses family (which will be found in later pages of this work), the *Iron Age* adds: "The anvil is now at this date in possession of Miss Aurelia Moses, the oldest daughter of Elisha Moses, Jr., and of Rebecca, the daughter of Elisha Drayton Moses, who now resides at Mount Morris, Livingston County, N. Y. It is truly an old relic, and its battered condition proves that it has seen hard service during nearly 250 years."

The anvil was, sometime after the Exposition, removed to the residence of the late Schuyler Moses, at Rochester, N. Y., where the writer has lately examined it, and verified the above description.

From a letter from Schuyler Moses to Charles Moses of Brooklyn, N. Y., dated May 21, 1885, a full copy of which is in the writer's possession, the following extract is given: "I have traced the Yankee Moses family back to Plymouth, Mass., 1632."

In a letter written several years since to the Rev. Vincent Moses, and kindly furnished with other material for this history, Schuyler Moses distinctly makes the statement, that he once had in his possession a record showing that the first John Moses of his line was from Plymouth, Mass., and that he came to this country in 1632.

Marcus Moses, born 1800, brother of Schuyler, in a letter to Rev. Vincent Moses, April 4, 1872, also gives the story of the anvil as handed down from his father and grandfather.

His sister Aurelia Moses, born in 1803, and other members of the family, also confirm the account.

The writer deferred communicating with the late Schuyler Moses, considering that on account of his great age it would be better to visit him when business should lead in the direction of Rochester, N. Y. Unfortunately this purpose was too long delayed, and recent correspondence with his heirs and a personal call at his late home at Rochester, have not added any fresh particulars to the foregoing items of family history. The account of the "Moses Anvil" is given here as it has been handed down through the generations. The researches of the writer furnish considerable circumstantial evidence in favor of this tradition of the Mount Morris branch of the Moses family.

The Lechford account of John Moses of Plymouth, which will presently follow, was not published, and the book which contains it was not distributed to the few principal libraries where it can now be found, until 1886. In the opinion of the writer its existence is unknown to any of the Moses name besides himself at the date of this publication. It appears from the Lechford history that John Moses of Plymouth, though not properly a blacksmith, was a shipwright, and that he would have had use for an anvil. From what is given hereafter, it will also be seen that John Moses of Windsor, though not a blacksmith, had ownership in a cider mill, saw mills, and a grist mill, and had evidently a knowledge of mechanics. In the inventory of his estate, taken after his death, is enumerated "iron tools and old iron," which from the considerable valuation of £6 and 10s. might well have included an anvil.

Without reference to the anvil, it is clear that in several families the story has been inherited, that the father of John Moses of Windsor was a John Moses who landed on the New England coast in 1630 or 1632. These accounts, so carefully handed down from father to son, gather new force in view of the historical proof lately obtained by the writer that there was a John Moses of Plymouth, at least as far back as 1640, although none of those of the family with whom the writer has had correspondence with reference to the Moses traditions were informed as to his knowledge of such proof, which he purposely withheld, that no bias might be given through him to their communications. This proof is afforded by the Lechford historical sketch of John Moses of Plymouth, already referred to, and which is now given in full.

In the transactions of the American Antiquarian Society, Vol. VII, is published a "Note book kept by Thomas Lechford, Lawyer in Boston, Mass. Bay, from June 27, 1638, to July 21, 1641."

In the preface to the volume, the Rev. Edward Everett Hale, under date of September 17, 1885, speaks of the Society's determination to publish the Note book, and goes on to state that "it is one of the most valuable documents which have been preserved of the history of the first generation of Massachusetts. It is the daily record of the work done in the office of the only professional lawyer in the Colony. The present owner of the original manuscript is Samuel Jennison of Boston. . . . . . I have not been able to discover the time or place of Lechford's embarkation for New England, nor in which of the twenty ships which brought 3,000 passengers to Massachusetts in the summer of 1638, he came.

JOHN MOSES OF PLYMOUTH COLONY.   13

His Note book begins, 'Boston in New England-27-4-the day of my landing, 1638.'"

"In July, 1640," he wrote to England, "I do profess that I am of this mind and judgement. I thank God that Christians cannot live happily without Bishops as in England, nor Englishmen without a King." . . . . . Of Massachusetts, he writes, "I am not of them in church or commonweal — some bid me begone." . . . On the 16th of November, 1641, after his landing in England, he writes, that he "had returned humbly to the Church of England."

With this necessary introduction, quotation is now made from page 418 of the volume VII, above referred to.

IN THE QUARTER COURT HELD AT BOSTON — 4 — 2 — 1641 —

"JOHN MOSES of Duxbury, Shipwright, plt.   In an action of tres-
THOMAS KEYSER and JOHN GUY of Lynne, def[ts]   pass upon the case.

The said John Moses Complayneth against the Defendants for y[t] whereas in or about the third moneth Anno Domini 1640 they did retyne the said complaynent to make for them a pinnace in forme as followeth that is to say: thirty-foote by the keele and five foote and halfe in the hould deepe to be made proportionable according to the same with a deck and to be seeled throughout the said pinnace and to be finished the last of August then next following for which they the said defendants promised to pay the said plaintiffe 40£ and such other charges as are mentioned in the writing of agreement thereof at the finishing of the said pinnace under the hands of both the said defend[ts] and the said plt. And the said plaintiffe indeed saith that the said defend[ts] were by agreement also betweene them the said def[ts] and plt. to deliver to the said plt. divers materiells towards the finishing the said pinnace by the day aforesaid appointed in the said agreement but they the said defen[ts] fayled therein so that the said pinnace could not be finished by the said day appointed through the default of the said defend[ts], neither were they ready to satisfie the said plaintiffe for the said pinnace when it should be finished as was agreed as aforesaid. But the said plaintiffe was forced to sell the said pinnace away to Captain Edward Gibbons in the third moneth last and to finish the same for him whereby the said pinnace lay upon the plaintiffes hands in building from the said last of August Anno Dni 1640 till the midst of the third moneth last, being 9 moneths.   To the damage of the said pl[t] 19£ 19s 11d.

	£	s	d
The said pl[t] received in pitch okhum and nayles	5	3	
And in money or moneys worth		10	
And in pitch and okhum more		10	
And in nayles more		1	6
And in ready money at sight		3	

Philip De Lanoe of Duxbury, aged about 36 yeares sworne saithe that John Moses of Duxbury aforesaid shipwright having a pinnace in hand to build for one Thomas Keyser and his partner as this deponent hath heard he was intreated by the said John Moses to inquire at some house in Boston for pitch and oakhum that should be left there by the said Thomas Keyser and his partner for the use of said pinnace and this deponent did inquire two several times for the said pitch and oakum about the latter end of the fift moneth last or the beginning of the sixt moneth last but could not find where the same was left though he inquired at divers houses, but two or three who said they knew Keyser and his ptr. then told this depon. that the said Keyser intended not to have the said pinnace for that he was not able to pay for it nor his partner neither, whereof this deponent tould the said John Moses who thereupon borrowed this deponents boate who went therein with another man to seek said Keyser and his partner about the said pitch and oakhum and pinnace, and they were waiting with his said boate three weekes in the chiefe mackrell time in September which was above 4£ damage to this deponent."

"Will Latham of Duxbury planter aged about 32 yeares, sworne upon oathe, that in the seventh moneth last he went in a boate from Duxbury aforesaid with John Moses to seek Thomas Keyser and his partner about a pinnace that the said John Moses had in hand for them, and that this deponent and the said Moses were out about the said business for about three weekes."

Foot Notes by the Editor of *Lechford's Manuscript Note Book* made in 1885:

"Of John Moses and John Guy I can find no mention at all in Savage. Thomas Keyser was a seafaring man of whom little other remembrance was preserved. He has obtained a species of fame through his mention by Winthrop, Vol. 2, p. 231, where are related certain operations of one Smith and his mate Thomas Keyser in a voyage undertaken by them to the coast of Guinea."

"Philip Delano or Philip De La Noy as it was formerly written was said to have been a Frenchman, member of the Church at Leyden. He came over in 1621, was a freeman in 1622 and was one of the early settlers of Duxbury where he became a man of 'much respectibilitie' according to Windsor."

"Wm. Latham was a more obscure inhabitant of Duxbury whither he moved from Plymouth. He had come over in the Mayflower as servant to Governor Carver — see Bradford, p. 447—450."

In the *History of New England* from 1630 to 1649, by John Winthrop, Esq., first Governor of the Colony of the Massachusetts Bay, two quite lengthy accounts are given of this Thomas Keyser, who behaved so meanly in relation to the pinnace he had ordered of the shipwright, John Moses. Extracts are given as showing the character of Keyser, and as also showing peculiarities in the religious beliefs of the time.

Vol. I, p. 321, year 1639:

"There happened a memorable thing at Plimouth about this time. 'One Keysar of Lynn being at Plimouth in his boat and one Dickerson with him a professor, but a notorious thief, was coming out of the harbor with the ebb and the wind southerly, a fresh gale; yet with all their skill and labor, they could not in three hours get the boat above one league, so as they were forced to come to an anchor, and at the flood, to go back to the town, and as soon as they were come in, the said Dickerson was arrested upon suspicion of a gold ring and some other pieces of gold which upon search were found about him and he was there whipped for it."

In Vol. II, p. 243, year 1645,— Keyser appears as mate on a vessel owned by James Smith, "who was a member of the Church of Boston," also they together made a voyage to Guinea to trade for Negroes.

Quite a lengthy account is given of this slave-trading venture, and of a law suit brought by Smith against Keyser for bringing home the vessel, leaving him (Smith) at Barbadoes, also of their being brought to account for "murder," "Stealing negers," also "chacing the negers (as aforesayde) upon the Sabbath day, which (being a servile work and such as cannot be considered under any other heade), is expressly capitall by the law of God."

If any punishment was inflicted upon them it does not appear in the records.

It is stated that the pinnace was afterward finished and sold to Captain Edward Gibbons. On page 321 of *Prince's Chronology*, under date of October 19, 1630, appears a list* of 108 persons of the Massachusetts Bay Colony who "desired to be made freemen," among them "Edward Gibbons (afterward Major-General)."

The question naturally arises, why this ship-yard of John Moses was not mentioned by some of the historians of the Plymouth Colony. It must be confessed that this is somewhat surprising, yet it should be remembered that Duxbury, though but a few miles from Plymouth across the bay, was, in 1640, a separate township and had its own records. Winsor, in his *History of Duxbury*, page 82, says: "It is greatly to be regretted that the earliest

---

* Very curiously, in this list appears also the names of Henry Woolcot and the Rev. John Warham, who are mentioned in connection with John Moses of Windsor in the first paper concerning him.

records of Duxbury are lost. We have evidence that they were burned, as the existing records testify — the first entry on the leaf of the present records was made in 1666." It therefore follows that but for this discovery of the *Lechford Manuscript Note Book*, and its publication in 1886, which so strikingly confirms the old time traditions in the Moses family, we should have had but little actual knowledge of the shipwright John Moses. It borders on the marvelous that this manuscript and Governor Bradford's *Manuscript History of Plymouth Colony*, should both have come to light after having been lost for over two hundred years.

Considering the record of the law suit, the following deductions may fairly be made. That John Moses probably had his business established at Duxbury as early as 1639. He must also have had more than a merely local reputation, as indicated by the fact that his first and second order for the pinnace apparently came from Lynn and Salem. He may have worked as a shipwright at one of these towns. The fact that there is historical mention of Henry Moses, a mariner (possibly a son), who married in Salem in 1659, is corroborative of this deduction.

He must almost inevitably have been a settled man of middle age, to have learned his trade in England, and to have been possessed of wood-working and iron-working tools, some capital, and a knowledge of affairs to justify him in making contracts on his own account.

The fact that he employed Thomas Lechford, "the only lawyer of the Colony," (Massachusetts Bay Colony); whose practice was discouraged and occasionally stopped by the Puritans,* who hated him for his adherence to the Church of England, would, considering the times, give a fair inference that John Moses did not share in the Puritan dislike of Lechford or of his religious views. A reading of Lechford's book will confirm this inference.

There is nothing in the papers presented to the court or in any records now extant to show exactly where the John Moses ship-yard was located. From the local histories, it seems extremely probable that he must have bought or rented from one of the original proprietors, perhaps from Philip Delano, mentioned in the lawsuit, whose land in Duxbury we find described in *Plymouth*

---

*Lechford's Note Book. — " Quarter Court — 7th mo. 1639. — Mr. Thomas Lechford is debarred from pleading any mans cause unless his own and admonished not to presume to meddle beyond what he shall be called by the Court."

Colony Records, Vol. I, p. 67, as bounded on the south side by the lands of John Alden, and on the east side by the sea.

In *Winsor's History of Duxbury* a reference is made to Ralph Chapman, another ship carpenter, who might possibly have worked with John Moses on the pinnace, as it is almost certain that assistance must have been needed at some stage of the work. Chapman is mentioned as early as 1640, when he had a grant of "4 acres at Stoney Brook," and also, "more land to the north, towards Green's Harbor." John Josselyn, in his *"Account of Two Voyages to New England in the Year 1638,"* states that there is "excellent timber for shipping at Green's Harbor to eastward of Plymouth." So far as appears from the records of Plymouth Colony, their only shipwrights, up to the year 1660, may have been John Moses and Ralph Chapman. It is highly probable that John Moses did not come to New England to escape religious persecution, but rather to fill a demand for men who could build ships. It is certain that as far back as the time of this lawsuit the ship-building industry was a prominent one in New England, and that for several years previously it had been largely carried on by the Massachusetts Bay Colony, a very short distance to the north of Plymouth. If John Moses came to this country as far back as 1630 or 1632, it is in every way probable that he worked at the ship-yards of Lynn or Salem or other of the Massachusetts Bay ports, before going to Plymouth; and this would further appear from the fact that little ship-building was carried on at Plymouth, and that no mention is made of the sending over of John Moses or Ralph Chapman in the voluminous correspondence of the English Council, or of the partners in the Plymouth Colony Adventure.

Extended quotations are given below, showing the premises upon which the writer has based his inferences above stated.

Massachusetts Historical Collections, Vol. III, p. 160, with reference to Plymouth Colony:—"In 1624 the ship-carpenter Winslow died." Page 211:—In 1627, "They had no ship-carpenter neither knew how to get one at present."

With reference to Massachusetts Bay Colony:—*Records of Mass.*, Vol. I, p. 394. In letter of Council in England to the Governor in Mass., April 17, 1629, "We have sent six shipwrights of whom Robert Moulton is chief."

Chronicles of the First Planters of New England by Young: In 1629—

"This was probably the first vessel built in the Colony and preceded by at least two years the building of Winthrop's bark at Mistick called the *Blessing of the Bay*, of 30 tons, launched July 4, 1631. Cradock carried on ship-building at Mystick River, and in 1633 had a vessel on the stocks of 100 tons, and next year of twice the burden. In 1636, a ship of 120 tons, the *Desire*, was built at Marblehead. In 1640, Hugh Peters procured some to join for building a ship at Salem of 300 tons, and the inhabitants of Boston built one of 150 tons called the *Trial*. In the summer of 1642, five ships were built, three at Boston, one at Dorchester, and one at Salem."

The author of "*New England's First Fruits*" writes in 1642: "Besides many boats, hoys, shallops, lighters, and pinnaces, we are in the way of building ships of 100, 200, 300, or 400, tons. Five of these are already at sea."

In the *Colonial State Papers of Great Britain*, page 158, under date of 1638, — Communication of Emanuel Downing to Secretary Coke —

"He has made inquiries respecting the ship-carpenters, Mr. Winthrop the Governor has with him in New England. There is Will Stephens, who built the *Royal Merchant* of 600 tons, so able a shipwright as there is hardly another such to be found in the kingdom, and two or three others. . . . . The plantation will next year build ships of any burden."

From Lechford's *Note-book*, from notes in relation to a lawsuit —

"Nehemiah Bourne was a Charlestown ship-builder (1639). He also lived at Dorchester for some time, and a year or two after he moved to Boston."

In same case — Note : — "Thomas Hawkins was a shipwright, also a merchant and part owner of many vessels, owned land in Charlestown and lived in Dorchester and Boston."

Page 255 : — "Hassard may have been the ship-carpenter of Boston — (4–16–1640)."

Page 279 : — "The account of Thomas Robinson concerning particulars between him and John Swinforth ship-carpenter interested in one bark called the *Speedwell* — (5–29–1640)."

Page 350 : — "Walter Merry was a shipwright having his shipyard and wharf at the point bearing his name just to the north of Gallups Point — (10–2–1640)."

From *Plymouth Records*, published 1889, (township, *not* Colonial, records), quotation is made as follows:

"At a towne meeting the 10 of Desem. 1646. It was agreed that whosoever coms not to ye towne meeting being thereunto warned at ye time appoynted shall forfite to ye towns use for every shuch defalte 12d. exept he have a sufficient and lawfull excuse."

In the list of 77 persons which follows is the name "John Moses."

In the same volume, at a date in 1647, appears a list (which is unexplained) of 72 persons; 10 of the names are marked "absent," — among the absentees — "John Moses."

From the foregoing it may be assumed that the shipwright had taken up his domicil in Plymouth at some time previous to 1646.

A careful examination of the volume just quoted, covering all township proceedings from 1636 to 1705, will almost inevitably lead to the conclusion that John Moses must have carried on his occupation outside the township proper of Plymouth — perhaps across the bay at Duxbury, or Green's Harbor. In Plymouth township records are found grants of land to numerous inhabitants; also on pages 116 to 118 are enumerated taxes against every person having a trade or occupation, with no mention of "John Moses." Nor is there a mention of any ship or boat builder in all of the minute proceedings recorded during the period named.

In the same volume appears a list which is apparently under date of 1668, and has this heading: "The names of such as have voated in Towne meeting in the Towne of Plymouth." Ninety-eight names are given, among them, "John Moses."

Somewhat strangely, under date of February 15, 1668, appears the following:

"The towne . . . took an exact view of the list of the names of those that were formerly called and had voated in Town meeting and established such as were found to be Townsmen according to said order and admitted some few more unto them and Referred others to further consideration. The names of those who were found to be Townsmen of Plymouth according to the abovesaid order which Relates unto the time of the establishment of the Towne of Plymouth and the bounds thereof sett by the court which was in the yeare 1640."

Then follows 68 names, John Moses not among them.

In an unconnected list of townsmen of the date of May, 1676, are 82 names, and among them "John Moses."

In the preface to the volume it is stated that in some instances "entries have not been made in chronological order;" . . that in "some instances sheets were probably copied and entered wherever in any part of the original volume there was sufficient blank space."

Turning now to the COLONY *Records of Plymouth*, in 12 large volumes, by Shurtleff and Pulsifer, we find in Vol. III, in the "presentments by the Court," under date of Oct. 5, 1652: "We present James Cole of Plymouth, for entertaining townsmen in his house contrary to the order of the Court."

"We present Thomas Clarke and John Moses of Plymouth, for staying and drinking at James Coles' contrary to the order of the Court."

A verdict of "acquittal" was rendered on both presentments. From which we infer that our shipwright was of a somewhat convivial turn, and was perhaps not strictly a Puritan.

On page 30 of same volume it is stated that at a term of the General Court, on June 7, 1653, "Surveyors of the Hiewaies" were appointed for Duxborough, Plymouth, and other towns, — three surveyors for each town, and that the surveyors for Plymouth were; "John Moses, Christopher Winter, and Thomas Morton."

In *Plymouth Colony Records*, Vol. VIII, p. 181, is mentioned: "Such of the towne of Plymouth as have taken the oath of Fidelitie in the yeare 1657"— 23 persons, — among them "John Moses."

According to *Winsor's History of Duxbury* he must have become a member of one of the churches of the Colony in order to have been admitted a freeman. "*Lechford's Plain Dealing*," page 83: "Every freeman when he is admitted takes a strict oath to be true to the society or jurisdiction."

Quite possibly this "taking of the oath" was in some way connected with a new policy adopted by the Plymouth Colony in 1657. Commencing with that year, and continuing for several years, fines were imposed "for refusing to take the oath of fidelitie." The *Plymouth Colony Records* show that in two years, 1658 to 1660, forty-eight persons were fined for this refusal, the most of them 10 pounds each. Vol. VIII, p. 95: "For absenting themselves from the public worship of God" twelve persons were on March 1, 1658, fined 10 shillings each.

In Vol. III, p. 196, of the *Plymouth Colony Records*, is given the verdict, on July 15, 1660, of a jury "conserning the sudden death of James Pierse of Boston, late deceased." The verdict rendered was, that "he was struck by thunder and lightning in a boate in Plymouth Harbor." "John Moses" was one of the twelve jurymen.

The changed condition of John Moses' church relations does not appear to have greatly modified his social tendencies. Page 222 recites that on June 10, 1661, "Gyles Packard, Senior, for suffering men to drink in his house, fyned 10 shillings. John Moses, for being drunke the second time, fined 10 shillings."

As the most trifling offences were carefully noted in the *Plymouth Colony Records*, and as the old shipwright appears but twice before the court, we must conclude that his lapses were not frequent.

The last mention in the *Colony Records* of John Moses of Plymouth, comes to us from page 223 of the same volume, where he appears on July 23, 1661, to have been "summoned by Mr. John Alden, Assistant to the Governor, as the foreman of a jury of twelve men 'concerning the sudden death of John Bond of Plymouth.'"

Volume VIII of the *Plymouth Colony Records* is principally filled with lists of births and marriages. Very few deaths appear. There is no record of the death of John Moses, or of births of children bearing the name of Moses, from which it is evident that John Moses had no children after his settlement in Plymouth Colony, which appears to have been at some time prior to 1640.

CHAPTER II.

A CONNECTING CHAPTER OF HISTORY.

It is a part of the plan of this little work to give to the founders of the New England families of the Moses name an environment of history that will fit into, and with, the few personal items that can be gleaned from the records.

It is stated in the opening sentence of *Phelps' History of Simsbury* that "most of the inhabitants of Windsor left England in 1630, resided in Dorchester until 1635, from whence they moved to Windsor."

A very detailed history of Dorchester has been published by the Antiquarian Society of the town, in which probably more than a thousand names are given of early settlers, including most of those found afterward in Windsor; but nowhere is mention made of John Moses. *Matthew Grant's Record*, made in 1677, published in appendix of *Stiles' History of Windsor*, is also strong evidence that John Moses did not come from Dorchester. It would therefore seem to follow that the town of Windsor must have had other settlers. Let us see.

Both Stiles and Brown, in their published histories, give Plymouth, and even Mayflower ancestry to the Brown family of Windsor, and there is every reason to think that others of the early settlers on the Connecticut were from Plymouth. The Rev. Nathaniel Chauncey, the "colleague" of the Rev. Mr. Warham, was "born in Plymouth about 1639."

From *Prince*, page 433, under date of 1633, is quoted: "Those of Plymouth are the first English that both discovered this place and built the same. . . . We have a great new bark and a frame of a house with boards, nails, etc., ready . . . coming to our place since called Windsor."

From Governor Bradford's *History of Plymouth:* "On the 8th of June, 1633, the Dutch completed a fort named the 'Good Hope' about the place of the present town of Hartford." On passing the fort with the bark, Bradford goes on to relate that —

"The Dutch demanded what they intended." .... "They bid them strike and stay or else they would shoot them, and stood by their ordnance ready fitted." "They answered they had commission from ye Gov. of Plimoth to goe up ye river to such a place, and if they did shoote they must obey their order, and proceeded." . . . Coming to their place (on the site of the present town of Windsor) "they clapt up their house quickly," . . . "and palisadoed their house aboute."

From *Barber's Connecticut Historical Collection*, page 124:

"Plymouth House — This house stood about two miles southeast of the 1st Congregational Church, on the river bank, about twenty rods from a point of land extending down the river near the western shore. It was at the place that the Farmington or Windsor river entered the Connecticut. The mouth of the river is now about 60 rods above. The meadow lying in the vicinity of where the house stood is now called Plymouth Meadow. . . . ." 1634. "A party of 70 men, Dutch, under arms with banners displayed, assaulted the Plymouth House, but they found it so well fortified, and the men who kept it so vigilant and determined, that it could not be taken without bloodshed. They therefore came to a parley, and finally returned in peace."

From Doyle, "*The English in America*," page 207:

"In July, 1635, Bradford received a letter from Jonathan Brewster, who was at the head of the Plymouth settlers on the Connecticut, telling of the intrusion" (of the Massachusetts Bay settlers). "He would not apparently have objected to the occupation of vacant territory by the new comers, but they had specially set their affections on the very spot which the Plymouth Government had bought from the Mohicans, and had held so manfully against the Dutch. The difficulty, it is clear, was mainly caused by the emigrants from Dorchester."

From Jonathan Brewster's letter is also quoted:

"It was your will we should use their persons and messenger kindly, & so we have done & do daily to your great charge, for the first company had well nigh starved, had it not been for this house, for want of victuals."

We quote again from Doyle:

. . . . "The emigrants from Plymouth protested against the aggression. They finally accepted a compromise. They were to retain their house, with two parcels of land, making 1/16 of the tract purchased from the Indians. For the rest they were to be compensated."

Bradford states, "But the unkindness was not soon forgotten;" and on page 348:

"This yeare (1636) two shallops going to Coonigtecutt with goods from ye Massachusetts of such as removed hither to plant, were cast away; . . . . afterwards another boate of theirs going thither, likewise was cast away, and such goods as came ashore were preserved for them. Such crosses they mette with in their beginnings which some imputed as a correction from God for their intrution (to ye wrong of others into ye place). But I dare not be bould with God's judgments in this kind."

Doyle, in his "*English in America*," states that in "1636" "Fresh outrages by the Indians had been committed on the Connecticut and on a trading vessel from Plymouth."

Enough has been quoted in the foregoing to serve the purposes of this chapter, which is to show, that although Windsor may be said to have been settled from Dorchester, still it had some years previously been visited by pioneers from the more adventuresome Plymouth Colony, who had made a foothold if not a permanent lodgment. It was the "far West" of the New England of 1640 to 1650. What more likely than that the young and hardy spirits of Plymouth should seek their fortune there.

CHAPTER III.

JOHN MOSES OF WINDSOR AND SIMSBURY.

John Moses of Windsor, of whom the earliest record is 1647, was a young man full of enterprise and spirit. Apparently without relations in this new community and adhering to the Church of England, he nevertheless seems to have not been without friends. Important duties were early entrusted to him in spite of his youth and political and religious disabilities,— and from the outset and all through his life he appears as a negotiator between the colonists and the warlike tribes of Indians immediately around them. The Plymouth Colony was peculiarly a trading and adventuresome community, constantly pushing in all directions for traffic with the Indians, and it is likely that young John may have gone to Windsor in search of ship stores or in some way as the representative of his father's ship-building interests. He appears first in a business way as an agent or associate of John Griffin, the pioneer of Massacoe, afterwards Simsbury.

In the town records of Windsor is recorded the first Indian deed of the lands of Simsbury, afterward ratified by fuller deeds and covering about 100 square miles. It reads as follows:

"These present writing shows that we Pacatoco and Pamatacount and Youngcowet, Indians and owners of Massaco Friends to him that burnt John Griffins picth and tarre — We doe hereby declare our unability to make satisfaction for the said losses any way but by the giving up our right in the land at Massaco unto the said John Griffin; and in regard the said offender being resigned and delivered up now to us, and fully acquitted for all his miscariag to the said John Griffin.

"Wee the aforesaid Indians doe hereby promise to come, at any time or times to Coart or Coarts to passe over all our rights in all our lands at Massaco, only the named Indians do reserve two acres of land and will themselves fence it in and maintaine it; — And what writing John Griffin shall cause to be made, all we the aforesaid Indians do promiss to confirm it by our hand and sealls freely set thereto as we have come to this present writing this 28th June 1648.

witness hereunto	The sign of Pacatoco
JOHN MOSES	The sign of Pamatacount
GEORGE ABBET	The sign of Youngcowet"

For a full account of this deed and subsequent ratifications, see the *History of Simsbury*, published in 1845, by Noah A. Phelps, where also may be found further references to John Griffin. On page 12: "In 1643 John Griffin and Michael Humphrey commenced the manufacture of pitch and tar." Page 11: In 1663, "A grant of two hundred acres was made by the General Court to John Griffin in consideration 'that he was the first that perfected the art of making pitch and tar in those parts.' This tract of land including another grant made subsequently by the town was afterwards known by the name of Griffin's Lordship." On page 84 — petition for a grant, and as the third reason, in the prayer of the petitioners,

"Also for our encouragement in raising tar and turpentine for the supply for his Majesty's naval stores, and our only valuable commodity in foreign parts." Page 80: — "The manufacture of pitch and tar was commenced and carried on at this place by John Griffin and Michael Humphrey then of Windsor, though subsequently both of them became inhabitants of this town. At first, they had a partner of the name of John Tinker, who afterwards settled as a merchant at New London. These articles being in great demand for the uses of the British Navy, as well as for ship-building generally, commanded a ready sale at high prices and were nearly the only ones allowed by England to be exported."

Stiles speaks of "John Tinker," one of the partners, as of "Boston in 1654." Pitch and tar would naturally have been marketed at Boston, Plymouth, and Salem.

If we now go back to the record of the lawsuit in which John Moses, the shipwright of Plymouth, was plaintiff, we find that he had difficulty in obtaining a sufficient supply of "pitch and oakum." The trading voyages between Plymouth and Windsor and highly probable dealings between the shipwright and the manufacturers of "pitch and tarre," would easily explain the association of young John Moses with Griffin or with Tinker, the Boston partner.

As to George Abbet, who with John Moses procured the deed from the Indians, no reference to him is made in records of Dorchester, Windsor, or Simsbury.

In *Plymouth Colony Records*, Vol. VII, p. 118, is given an account for military stores allowed to Pelig Sandford by the Court held in June, 1628, and in this account appears this item: "1 c.– 3 q.– 16 lb.– of biskett delivered to John Abbet by General Cudworth's order." George Abbett does not appear in the history of the settlement, and he may have come from Plymouth Colony.

To be among the Indians on the extreme frontier at this time required a stout heart as well as tact in dealing with savages.

Dwight, in his *History of Connecticut*, p. 113, states that: "The Indians of Windsor were in a very hostile state at this time (1646). They burned a quantity of tar and turpentine, rescued by force one whom the officers had seized, and threatened messengers afterward sent to them."

To go a little backward, it is now proper to state that the very first historical mention that we have of young John Moses, is found in the records of the Particular Court at Hartford, Conn. As will be seen later on, he, and Michael Humphrey, already mentioned, considered themselves "members of the Church of England." John Griffin was made a freeman only by special action of the Court, and not until 1658.

Even a mild adherence to the Church of England or Cavalier party, in those days, included a belief in gay social customs, which were abhorrent to the strict Puritans.

From the *Colonial Records of Connecticut*, p. 160, is quoted under date of March 2, 1647, "John Moses acknowledgeth himself bound to this commonwealth in Recognizance of 20£ and Matthew Allen in 10£ pruided that he the said John Moses appeare at the next p ticular Court and keep good behauior in the meane tyme."

As illustrating the offences of the time : — At the same session of the Court, "Edward Chancill for diulging misreports agt Hide is fyned 40 s." Also "Nicholas Gunning for a miscaridge,— beating of a cow of Ralfe Keelers."

Something over a year later, June 1, 1648, the case came up for trial and on page 164, same book, we find : — "John Moses for miscaridges wth Dauid Wilton his daughter fyned 20 shillings." On the jury of twelve men who rendered this verdict we find the name of "Dauid Wilton," himself.

As will be observed from its use in the Gunning's case, and in the Indian deed — above mentioned — the word "miscaridge" was a general term in those days, corresponding very nearly to the present use of the word "misbehavior."

Very likely, in the flush of youth, he broke the following "Blue Law : " — (See Laws of New Haven.) " No man shall court a maid in person or by letter without first obtaining consent of her parents, 5£ penalty for the first offence, 10£ for the second, and for the third, imprisonment during the pleasure of the Court." As the young man was fined but 20 shillings, we must conclude that his offence was very trivial, or that he was for some reason treated with special consideration.

David Wilton afterward served in the same troop of horse with him, and also sold him land.

The association of Matthew Allyn, the bondsman for John Moses and his first friend of record, with the early Plymouth Colonists, is shown in the following quotation from the *Memorial History of Hartford County*:

"Plymouth House (1633) — Lot 43¾ acres Indian title. The material for the house was prepared in Plymouth, Mass., and landed here Oct. 16 (26), 1633. When the pioneers from Massachusetts came here in the early summer 1635, they were entertained at this house by Jonathan, son of Elder Brewster, and we find him here still in 1636. When the Plymouth Colony sold their claim to the Dorchester people, 1637 (which covered a larger tract than is shown in the accompanying map), they reserved this lot and house and certain other tracts of uplands. These were sold, 1638, to Matthew Allen of Hartford, who came here and occupied them. There is strong presumptive evidence in support of the tradition that Mr. Allen used the material of this house in the construction of the house that he built on the reserved 'acre on the hill.'"

From Stiles' *History of Windsor* we learn that Allen attempted to evade taxes levied by the town, on the ground, that having purchased from Plymouth Colony, the lands were not amenable to tax of Connecticut.

Stiles also states that on May 3, 1638, Lieutenant Wm. Holmes, "by power of attorney, sold to Matthew Allen of Hartford all the lands, houses, servants, goods, and chattels of the Plymouth Company in the town of Windsor."

Somewhat previously to the date when he befriended young John Moses, Matthew Allen had his own troubles with the extremists of that generation, as witness the following quotation from the *Memorial History of Hartford County*:

"He was excommunicated by the Church in Hartford, and June 3, 1644, he appealed to the General Court for redress; the records do not show how the affair was settled, but it may have been one cause of his removal to Windsor. Nevertheless, few men in the colony had more influence or received more honors from the people than Mr. Allyn."

The *Records of Plymouth Colony*, Vol. VIII, show that a Matthew Allen — Wm. Allen, (who married Priscilla Brown,) and several of the Allen family, were repeatedly fined for "attending Quaker Meetings" and for "refusing to take the oath of fidelitie." From Lechford's *Note Book*, p. 416, we learn that "Matthew Allen, . . . upon the river of Connecticot," had a brother, "Thomas Allen," in Plymouth Colony.

It will be noted that John Moses came into Court early in 1647. He had already been in the Colony long enough to make acquaintances and friends. Later on he is remembered by one of his friends in a will, which appears from Trumbull's *Colonial Records*, to have been one of the earliest recorded in the Colony. It was dated October 17, 1648, and reads as follows:

"The testament of Edward Chalkwell. Imp. I doe bequeathe vnto Nicholas Sension my gunn and sword and bandaleers and best hatt and 40 shillings. Item to John Moses, my best sute and coat and stockings and shoes. Item to Mr. Warham, 40 or 50 shillings according as my goods doe hold oute after my debts be paid. Item to George Phelps, 3 pounds and if anything be left I give it to the poor of the Church and I doe make George Phelps executor of this my will and testament. Witnesses Henry Woolcott, Nicholas Sension."

The inventory of the property shows that his "coate, jackett, and breeches" were 3£ out of a total of 13£ 7s. 8d.

Of the parties mentioned in the trial and in the will, four of them, Matthew Allyn, John Moses, George Phelps, and Henry Wolcott, are found previous to 1650, as owners of town lots close adjoining each other, and on the old Plymouth Colony property.

Proceeding in chronological order, we next hear of John Moses in a deed dated May 1, 1649, and recorded in the Windsor *Town Records*, Vol. I, p. 120. The record reads:

"John Moses hath purchased of Owen Tudor his house orchard and home lot and hopyard with all the appurtenances lying on the East side of the highway, being 2 acres more or less in length from the bounds of Plimouth Meadow East through the swamp to the upland west as it Lyes, bounded North by the land of Matthew Allyn, South by the land of Ambrose Fowler in part and Henry Wolcott the Elder the residue, and by the lands of James Loomis the Elder West, East by Plimoth Meadow also 20 acres in the woods bounded North by the land of Thomas Ford, Every way else by the Common."

For a better understanding of this first purchase of John Moses, a copy in part of the map of Windsor, 1633 to 1650, is here reproduced.

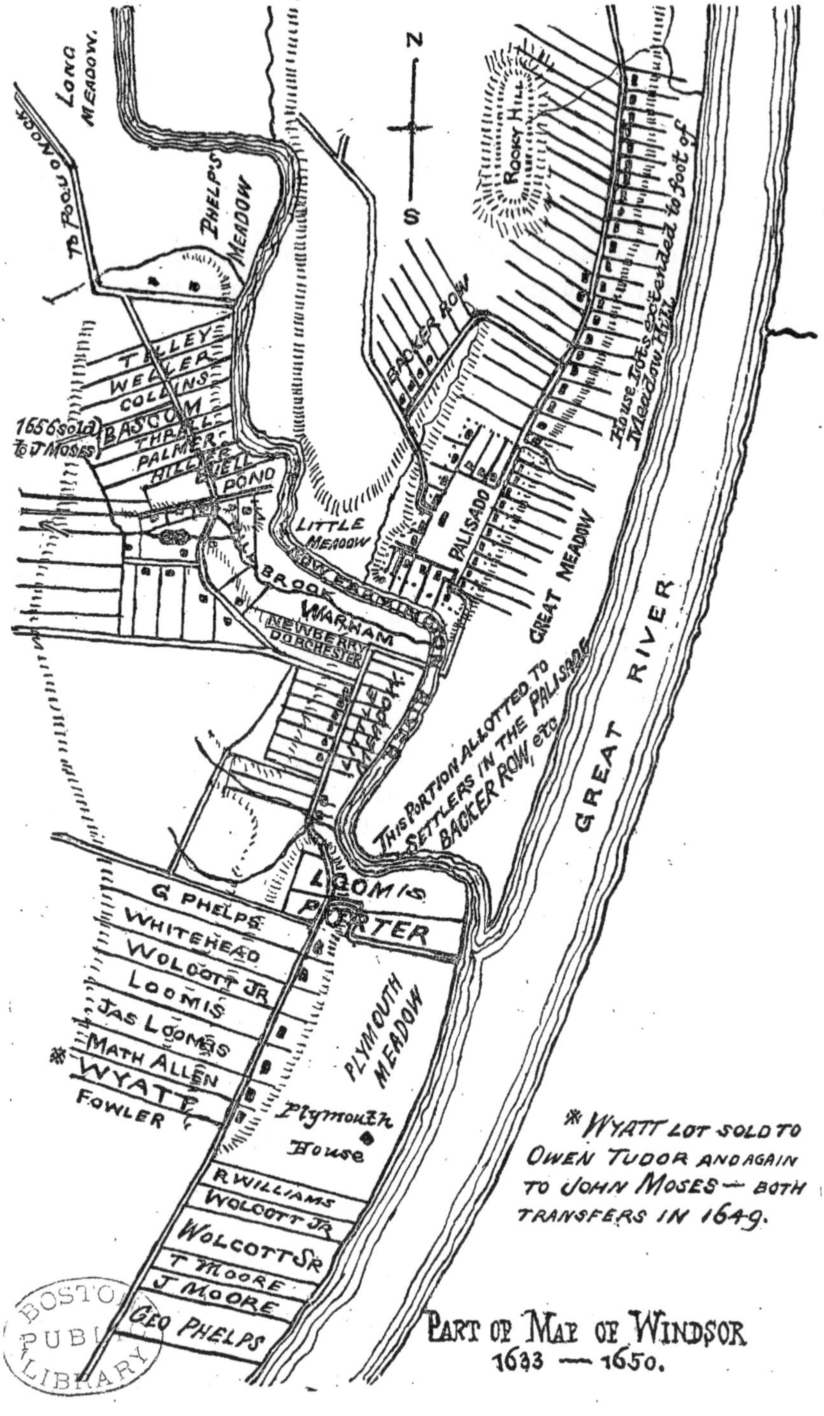

PART OF MAP OF WINDSOR
1633 — 1650.

BOSTON PUBLIC LIBRARY

If this map* was intended to show the actual owners of lots in 1650, then the name of John Moses should have appeared thereon in place of Wyatt. Owen Tudor must have sold the same year he bought, as it appears from the *Hartford County Memorial History* that "he (Tudor) bought the John Wyatt place 1649." The same history mentions that "John Wyatt only appears on record when his lot of two acres was sold to Owen Tudor, 1649." *Plymouth Records* give a Lieut. James Wyatt as a freeman of Taunton in that Colony in 1643. The name is unusual, and it may be that John Wyatt was a relative.

It will be noticed that the house purchased by John Moses in 1649 is the nearest to the old Plymouth House, and following the southern boundary in the description, we find that it must have come within a few rods of the first English house and fortification in Connecticut, built by the Plymouth Colony in 1633.

After the purchase of the Wyatt place, in 1649, we hear nothing of John Moses for more than two years. He may have been with John Griffin making and selling "pitch and tarre." It is unlikely that he, a young man, was permitted to live in the house he had bought, for the town records show that:

"Dec. 1, 1651, John Moses had allowance to sojourn with Simon Miller in his house."

The *Hartford County Memorial History* mentions, in connection with this entry that, in 1637, the General Court enacted that,

"No young man that is neither married nor hath any servant and be noe publick officer shall keep house by himself without consent of the Town where he lives first had, under pain of 20 shillings per week."

"No Master of a family shall give Habitation or entertainment to any young man to sojourn in his family but by the allowance of the Inhabitants of the Said Town where he dwells, under the like Penalty of 20 shillings per Week."

The same history gives other instances showing the watchful guardianship of the town authorities.

"Sept. 13, 1652,—It is assented that Isaac Shelden and Samuel Rockwell shall keep house together in the house that is Isaacs, so they carry themselves soberly and do not entertain idle persons to the evil expense of time by night or day." Also that, "John Bennet should be entertained by William Hayden in his family."

---

* A complete map of Windsor in 1650, is printed in *Stiles' History of Windsor*, and in *Hartford County Memorial History*.

Also, in 1656, — "That no person or persons whatsoever shall be admitted inhabitant in this town of Windsor without the approbation of the town. . . . . . Nor shall any man sett or sell any house or land so as to bring in any to be inhabitant into the town without the approbation of the townsmen, or giving in such security as may be accepted to save the town from damage."

John Moses having been quartered in the house of Simon Miller, we hear nothing further of him until the latter part of 1652, when he again appears before the Particular Court (see *Manuscript Records*, Vol. II, at office of Secretary of State, Hartford). "Sept. 7, 1652, In action between Job Drake plt. and John Moses Defdt. . . . Jury find for Defdt. — Costs of Court."

"Dec. 6, 1652, Owen Tudor plt. Contra John Moses Dfdt. in an action of slander to the damage 2 £. . . . Jury find for plaintiff."

The marrriage of John Moses is thus entered in the Windsor Church record:

"JOHN MOSES MARRIED MARY BROWN, MAY 18, 1653."

The writer has made careful search, and does not find the name of Brown among the early settlers of Windsor or adjoining towns, excepting, however, Peter Brown of Windsor, whose first child, Mary Brown, was born May 2, 1659. Stiles, Phelps, and Brown, in their respective histories, so frequently referred to in these pages, all mention the Peter Brown family of Windsor as of Mayflower descent.

After his marriage, John Moses may have commenced housekeeping in the Wyatt House, purchased from Tudor in 1649, or, if Stiles is correct, he may have lived on his other property in the immediate neighborhood. We read in *History of Windsor*, p. 136: "John Moses bought a part of Joseph Loomis' home lot on the west, opposite side of the highway, and sold it in April, 1655, to Nathaniel Loomis."

In the manuscript records of the town of Windsor, Book I of Deeds, the writer found entered under date of July 9, 1656, several parcels of real estate, and on the margin of the record the disposition made of the properties after the death of John Moses. These entries are: "July 9, 1656, John Moses has purchased of Thos. Bascom his dwelling house and home lot and $6\frac{1}{2}$ acres, more or less; also one parcel of $5\frac{3}{4}$ acres; also one parcel $\frac{3}{4}$

of an acre (afterward sold to Nicholas Palmer); also woodland (afterwards sold to Saml. Farnsworth); also butting against the lower end of Long Meadow, 32 acres; also in the 2^d or Long Meadow, 4 acres of meadow (afterward made over to Timothy Moses). John Moses has by purchase of Richard Sexton $2\frac{3}{4}$ acres of Long Meadow — (To Timothy). John Moses has purchased of Walter Lee his home lot, 10 acres, in Windsor — (To Timothy)."

Page 125, Dec. 31, 1660, — "John Moses hath purchased of George Phelps a parcel lying north of the fence of Plymouth Meadow — eight acres, more or less."

From these, and similar holdings acquired at subsequent dates; from town proceedings; from his death at Windsor and probate of his estate; it is evident that the principal residence of John Moses was in Windsor, and that his residence and operations in Simsbury were made for business purposes, and perhaps for the sake of establishing his eldest son.

He was of a bold and adventurous spirit, and four years after his marriage we find him enrolled under the then hero and idol of New England, Capt. John Mason of Windsor.

In the town acts, March 11, 1657-8, — "A troop of 30 horse, the first in the Colony, was organized by the general Court and placed under the command of Capt. John Mason." In the list of troopers are 17 Windsor names, and among them "John Moses."

It will be most convenient in the remainder of this sketch to write of John Moses in connection with leading characteristics of his life, and without reference to the chronological order of events. As a soldier he was for years subject to constant calls from other occupations to repress, and at times to fight the Indians, who, in the immediate neighborhood of Windsor, vastly outnumbered the whites. If we examine a picture of a soldier of the Cromwellian period, we can probably form a fair idea of the appearance of the Windsor troopers. In the account of "*Two Voyages to New England,*" 1638, John Josselyn gives the cost per man of equipping soldiers as follows: "Armor for one man 17 s — 1 long piece $5\frac{1}{2}$ foot 1L, 2s, — 1 sword 5s, 1 bandalier 1s 6d — 1 belt 1s — 20 lbs powder 18s, 60 lbs shot or lead, pistol and goose shot 5s." *Winsor's Duxbury* states: "The bandoleers were large leathern belts worn by ancient musketeers for supporting of their arms. It passed over the right shoulder and under the left arm."

Stiles, in his *History of Windsor*, page 157, speaks of the "steel cap and breastplate of Capt. John Mason." In King Philip's War, 1675-6, the hardships endured, and the sacrifices made, by the trooper, John Moses, were of the order that "try men's souls." His property near Mount Phylip (see old map of Simsbury) must have been swept away by the burning of Simsbury on March 26, 1676. The *Memorial History of Hartford County* describes it:

"It was a Sabbath day. A band of Philip's warriors rushed through the deserted town and applied the torch to the thatched roofs, and forty dwelling houses, with barns and other buildings, were consumed. Fences, farming utensils, furniture, farm produce, and provisions were gathered into heaps and burned. The ruin was complete; not a house or building was left."

Previous to this the different colonies had united to place an army in the field. In the campaign against the Indians, the close of the "Swamp fight," or "Storming of the Naragansett fort," in 1675, is thus described in Stiles' *History of Windsor:*

"Amid the shrieks of women and children and rattling of musketry . . . . the Indian defences were fired . . . . a dense column of smoke, which rose from the smouldering ashes, was all that was left of some 4,000 once brave and happy souls. It was a glorious victory for the English. but it brought sorrow as well as safety to their homes. 6 captains and 80 soldiers were killed or mortally wounded, and 150 wounded. Two days of exposure and three hours of hard fighting were followed by a distressing march through sleet and deep snows bearing with them their dead and wounded. The next morning the snow was exceedingly deep and the cold intense, and the jaded and frost bitten army could scarcely move. 400 troops were unfit for duty. Mason was so badly wounded that he died in a year after."

Says Hollister in his *History of Connecticut:*

"It would be idle for me to attempt to delineate the sufferings of the wounded soldiers. — A part of them as the night and storm advances become insensible. — The pulses grew feebler, the cheek paler, and the frame stiffened into its final repose."

Not only was John Moses in this battle, but we can fancy the feelings of a father when we know that he had two wounded sons with him on that terrible night march, boys of only 17 and 19 years.

How full of pathos is this entry, which the writer found at Windsor in the first volume of births and deaths:

"Here I set down the deaths of several persons that were against the Indians and were wounded that they dyed. — It was on 19 of December,

1675. — Thomas son of John Moses dyed July 29, buryed ye 30, 1681. — 22 years old. — Wm Moses son of John Moses dyed Nov. 27, 1681."

The *History of Windsor*, in speaking of King Philip's war says: "To all the numerous levies drafted during the war, Windsor contributed a large proportion of troops, having in the service at different times 125 mounted dragoons. These dragoons, from their greater facility of movement were constantly employed in rapid marches, bearing dispatches and scouting parties." — Among these troopers "in actual service and receiving pay on war account" we find the name of "John Moses."

On June 11, 1676 — "Contributions for the sufferers after the burning of Simsbury;" — among other names we find "John Moses £5–6s." His own house in Simsbury was of course destroyed.

In the genealogies which follow these sketches, it will be found that many descendants of John Moses have been soldiers in all wars. They have not proved themselves unworthy of the family crest and motto of their English progenitors. (See Appendix.)

John Moses exhibited a combative nature, not only as a soldier, but he also had the moral courage to stand out for his convictions in religious matters, though his position must have been costly to him and unpleasant in every way. He probably inherited from his father a belief in the tenets of the Church of England.* Under date of 1664 he appears as one of seven signers to a very remarkable and curiously worded document, which is given in full, having been copied by the writer from the original in the State Library at Hartford:

"To the Honored and General Assembly of the Corporation of Connecticutt and New England.

"The humble address and petition of sundry persons of and belonging to, the same corporation showeth:

---

* See Neal's *History of New England*, Vol. I, page 215, as to "thousands in New England" belonging to that Church in 1645.

Lechford's *Plain Dealing*, published in 1641, p. 106 : "Some late occurrences concerning Episcopacie — Master Wilson did lately ride to Green's Harbor in Plymouth Patent to appease a broyle between one Master Thomas and Master Blindman when Master Blindman went to the worst and was sent away to Coneticot." (Lechford was lawyer for John Moses ; Green's Harbor the probable location of John Moses' shipyard in 1641; and "Master" was the title given by Lechford and some others to clergymen.)

John Moses (1st) lived for more than seventeen years in Plymouth Colony before he "took the oath" as freeman in 1657 — which was the year that several were heavily "fyned for refusing to take the oath of fidelitie" and "for absenting themselves from the public worship of God."

Winsor's *History of Duxbury*, p. 84, "freemen were on special application admitted to those rights" . . . "church membership however being a necessary qualification."

"That whereas, we whose names are subscribed being Professors of the Protestant Christian Religion, Members of the Church of England and subjects to our Sovereign Lord Charles the Second, by God's Grace King of England etc., and under these sacred ties mentioned and maintained in our covenant sealed with our baptism, having seriously pondered on our past and present want of those ordinances which to us and our children as members of Christ's visible church ought to be administered. Which we apprehend to be to the dishonor of God and the obstruction of our own and our children's good (contrary to the pious will of our Lord the King, his main purpose in settling these plantations, as by the Charter and His Majesty's letter to the Bay June 26, 1662, and thereways is most evidently manifested) to our great grief, the sense of our duty towards God, the relation we stand in to our mother the Church, our grateful acceptation of His Majesty's Royal favor, the edification of our own and our children's souls, and many other good Christian and profitable ends (as also at a late session of this honored assembly having secured a favorable encouragement from the Worshipful Deputy Governor) hereunto moving us, we are bold by his own address to declare our aggreviance and petition for a redress of the same.

"Our aggreviance is, that we and ours are not under the due care of an Orthodox ministry, that will in a due manner administer to us those ordinances that we stand capable of, as the baptising of our children, our being admitted (as we according to Christ's order may be found meet) to the Lord's Table, and a careful watch over us in our way and suitable dealing with us as we do well or ill, with all whatsoever benefits and advantages belong to us as members of Christ's Visible Church, which ought to be dispensed by the officers of the same, of which being destitute, we humbly request, that the Honored Court would take into serious consideration our present state in this respect, that we are thus as sheep scattered having no shepherd and compare it with what we conceive you cannot but know, both God and our King would have it different from what it now is, and take some speedy and effectual course for redress therein, and put us in a full and free capability of enjoying those aforementioned advantages which to us as Christ's Visible Church do of right belong, by establishing some wholesome law in this Corporation, by notice whereof, we may both claim and receive of such officers, who are or shall be by law set over us in the Church or Churches where we have our abode or residence these forementioned privileges and advantages.

"Furthermore we humbly request that for the future, no law in this Corporation may be of any force to make us pay or contribute to the maintenance of any minister or officer of the Church that will neglect or refuse to baptise our children and to take care of us, as of such members of the Church as are under his or their charge or care.

"That in hopes that your careful and speedy consideration and issue hereof, will be answerable to the weight of the matter, and our necessities, and that matters of less moment may be omitted till this be issued. We

wait for a good answer, and for this Honorable Court we shall ever pray, etc. "Signed by WILLIAM PITKIN (Hartford).
"MICHAEL HUMPHREY (Windsor).
"JOHN STEDMAN (Hartford).
"JAMES ENO (Windsor).
"ROBERT REEVE ———
"JOHN MOSES (Windsor).
" Oct. 17, 1664. JONAS WESTOVER (Windsor)."

Facsimile of the signature of John Moses to the above petition.

It is probable that a similar paper was previously presented, for we find in the *Colonial Records*, under date of March 10, 1663, this entry:

"Mr. Clarke in behalf of the Church complaynes of James Eno and Michael Humphrey for a misdemeanor in offering violence to an established law of this Colony . . . . for several things contayned in a paper presented to the Court . . . The Court having seriously considered the case respecting James Eno and Michael Humphrey do declare such practice to be offensive."

. . . . . "The Court remits the sensure due, provided answerable reformation doth follow."

In the old Windsor Church record is given a full list of the members of the Church of Windsor in 1677. The name of John Moses is not found among them. *Stiles' History of Windsor* gives a petition of nearly 100 inhabitants on the east side of the river for a "Particular Worship," and among the signers John Moses. As this was May 13, 1680, and he died in Windsor three years thereafter, it is probable that he adhered to the Church of England all his life.

Although they signed papers and took part in church quarrels, it is reasonably certain that the sons of John Moses were not members of the Puritan Church. See a list of members of the Church of Simsbury in 1697 — (*Phelps' History*, p. 55), in which the sons of John Moses are not mentioned. As soon as an Episcopal parish was established some of the Moses children were baptized therein, and for several generations a considerable number of the Moses name are found with that church. The Rev. William Gibbs was the first rector of the St. Andrews Parish in Simsbury. If we are to credit an account given by Peters in his *History of Connecticut*, he was at times very badly treated by the Puritans. Phelps, in his *History of Simsbury*, says of him: "He was a missionary sent out by a society instituted in England for the propagation of the Gospel;" . . . . also . . . "Towards the close of his life ill health prevented his preaching, but it did not in the least diminish his ardor in the cause of Episcopacy, or his affection for his parishioners. Few clergymen have lived more beloved, or died more lamented. His good name yet survives, though nearly seventy years have passed since his decease."

The adherence of John Moses to the unpopular Church of England indicates a strong character, and we are therefore not surprised to find him leading in the settlement of Simsbury, where, indeed, he must have resided at different times without giving up his property and home in Windsor. *Phelps' History of Simsbury* is now quoted, page 13: "The first grants by the committee of which any record exists were made in 1667." Among the twenty-three names we find John Moses located in "Weatague east." . . . "These persons did not immediately remove their families from Windsor to Massacoe, though it is believed that by 1669 all of them had become inhabitants of the new plantation."

A tracing has been made by the writer, from the original in the State Library, Hartford, of a part of the map of Simsbury, made in 1730, and it is here reproduced. It will be seen that the location of John Moses in the mountain pass by Mount Philip peculiarly exposed him to attack from the Indians.

Very probably John Moses had some practical training in mechanics from his father, the shipwright of Plymouth. In the course of his business career he was connected with the building and operating of grist mills, saw mills, and cider mills; and the irons and tools in his house at his death indicate that he was familiar with the mechanics of milling. From *Phelps' History*, page 77:

"The first mills erected in town were situated on Hop Brook, near the present site of Tuller's Mills, and were built in 1679. These consisted of a grist and saw mill, and were put up by Thomas Barber, John Moses, John Terry, and Ephraim Howard, who contracted with the town to keep the mills in good repair, to grind grain for the tolls allowed by law, to sell to the inhabitants boards at four and six pence per hundred, and not to transport oak to any other town. * In consideration of which, the town allowed them the mill privileges, the right to take timber on the common lands, — a lot of good timber lands, and twenty pounds payable in town

In 1890 I published a book giving the history of John Moses, the shipbuilder of Plymouth, a Colonial settler of 1632; and of John Moses, of Portsmouth, a Colonial settler of 1639; with some account of their descendants.

I have this year published a second volume containing other historical items concerning the early fathers, and have added about 4,500 names to the record of their descendants. A list of soldiers of the Moses name who served in American wars is included. Many pages of the Appendix are devoted to biographical sketches of noted men of the Moses family who lived in England before the days of the Commonwealth.

The editions of each volume are small with no stereotyped plates. The few copies of the first volume yet remaining in my hands I have bound in with the second volume, which by reason of continual references to the earlier publication will be of little value to anyone not owning the first volume.

The greater part of the edition of the first volume was sent out free of cost to the recipients, but I shall not follow the same course with the combined volumes because they are limited in number, and since I can not distribute generally as before I do not wish to make discriminations. I shall, however, donate fifty of the books to leading libraries in this country and England, to insure the permanent preservation of the record.

As to the remainder, I will furnish the combined volumes (Nos. I and II) cloth bound, gilt lettering on sides and back, to early applicants at five dollars, remitted in Money Order or Draft on New York. When the stock of books approaches exhaustion I shall raise the price to ten dollars. Some copies of the second volume have been bound separately, but they will be useful only to those who already own the first volume. For the present the price of the second volume will be three dollars.

Address:

ZEBINA MOSES,
711 H Street, N. W., Washington, D. C.

rates. The place has been occupied as a mill seat up to the present time (1845) one hundred and sixty-six years."

The writer found the mill still in existence when he visited it in 1889, and it is yet known as Tuller's Mills. A grandson and a granddaughter of the John Moses, builder and miller as above, each married a Tuller. *Simsbury Rec.*, B. II, p. 150, is recorded, on April 13, 1716: "John Moses deeded to his son Thomas Moses a mill and privileges lying on the east side of the river against my old house lot, also on a line running to the end of Mount Philip." This is yet another mill, and was perhaps erected by John of Windsor, father of the John here mentioned.

Whenever negotiations with the Indians were to be conducted, the town of Windsor seems to have desired the services of John Moses. On page 109 of *Stiles' Windsor* we find that:

"In April, 1666, Jas. Enno and John Moses purchased from Nassahegan lands on both sides of the Rivulet from Windsor to Massacoe. This land extended on the south side of the Rivulet to the foot of Massacoe Mountain, and on the North side to the Mountain that answers to the foresaid Mountain — Eastward to a new way or road passing out of Pipestave swamp going to Westfield, and Southward from the Rivulet to the Mill Brook as it runs into the Wilderness and so to the Mountains. This tract, containing some 28,000 acres, was confirmed to the purchasers Dec., 1669, by Rippaquam and Seacet, excepting two islands in the rivulet." . . . . Enno and Moses the same year released this purchase to the town of Windsor, whose agents they were, and received 15 L — 14 s — 2 d — the amount expended by them, in lands situate under the Simsbury Mountain above Salisbury Plain, near the river, and known as Tillins Marsh."

The *Hartford County Memorial History* gives the facsimile of the signatures of John Moses and James Eno from the Indian deeds above mentioned.

Facsimile of the signature of John Moses on Indian Deed.

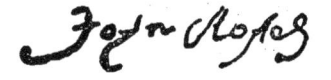

In Windsor, 2d Book of Town Acts, are two entries in relation to dealings of John Moses with the Indians, which time has nearly obliterated. They are as follows, p. 9: "This day (Feb. 3, 1667,) John Moses has . . . (undecipherable) . . . about Indian Yuxrgas, and now demands (undecipherable) pounds from ye town and relinquishes his demand of land." Page 46, May 3, 1677: "All of townsmen being together John Moses — (undecipherable)

he was at ti[
his *History of*
out by a soci(
Gospel;" .
life ill health
diminish his
his parishion
died more la]
seventy year
 The adher(
land indicate
prised to fin
indeed, he m
his property
is now quot
which any re
three names
 . . "Thes
from Winds
of them had
 A tracing
State Librar
in 1730, and
tion of John
exposed him
 Very pr(
mechanics 1
course of h'
and operati
irons and t
familiar wi
page 77:

"The first
present site (
a grist and s
John Terry,
the mills in
sell to the inhabitants boards at four and six pence per hundred, and not
to transport oak to any other town.* In consideration of which, the town
allowed them the mill privileges, the right to take timber on the common
lands, — a lot of good timber lands, and twenty pounds payable in town

MAP OF SIMSBURY—MADE ABOUT 1730.

(NOTE—This complete Map should have been placed opposite Map Index page 144.)

rates. The place has been occupied as a mill seat up to the present time (1845) one hundred and sixty-six years."

The writer found the mill still in existence when he visited it in 1889, and it is yet known as Tuller's Mills. A grandson and a granddaughter of the John Moses, builder and miller as above, each married a Tuller. *Simsbury Rec.*, B. II, p. 150, is recorded, on April 13, 1716: "John Moses deeded to his son Thomas Moses a mill and privileges lying on the east side of the river against my old house lot, also on a line running to the end of Mount Philip." This is yet another mill, and was perhaps erected by John of Windsor, father of the John here mentioned.

Whenever negotiations with the Indians were to be conducted, the town of Windsor seems to have desired the services of John Moses. On page 109 of *Stiles' Windsor* we find that:

"In April, 1666, Jas. Enno and John Moses purchased from Nassahegan lands on both sides of the Rivulet from Windsor to Massacoe. This land extended on the south side of the Rivulet to the foot of Massacoe Mountain, and on the North side to the Mountain that answers to the foresaid Mountain — Eastward to a new way or road passing out of Pipestave swamp going to Westfield, and Southward from the Rivulet to the Mill Brook as it runs into the Wilderness and so to the Mountains. This tract, containing some 28,000 acres, was confirmed to the purchasers Dec., 1669, by Rippaquam and Seacet, excepting two islands in the rivulet." . . . . Enno and Moses the same year released this purchase to the town of Windsor, whose agents they were, and received 15 L — 14 s — 2 d — the amount expended by them, in lands situate under the Simsbury Mountain above Salisbury Plain, near the river, and known as Tillins Marsh."

The *Hartford County Memorial History* gives the facsimile of the signatures of John Moses and James Eno from the Indian deeds above mentioned.

Facsimile of the signature of John Moses on Indian Deed.

In Windsor, 2d Book of Town Acts, are two entries in relation to dealings of John Moses with the Indians, which time has nearly obliterated. They are as follows, p. 9: "This day (Feb. 3, 1667,) John Moses has . . . (undecipherable) . . . about Indian Yuxrgas, and now demands (undecipherable) pounds from ye town and relinquishes his demand of land." Page 46, May 3, 1677: "All of townsmen being together John Moses — (undecipherable)

Indians — (undecipherable) and Jacob Drake and Thos Bissell to go out with him to Massacoe as soon as they can." This last entry evidently refers to an exploration, and the sending of an advance party with a view to the re-occupation of the abandoned homes, after the burning of Simsbury by the Indians. Very likely it was soon after this that John Moses rebuilt his home in the mountain pass (see map, opposite page 38), aided, no doubt, by his eldest son, who was at that time 23 years of age. This spot is described in the *Hartford County Memorial History* as follows:

"Mount Philip is scarcely distinguishable from Talcott Mountain, but from any standpoint in the Farmington valley it is a distinct and prominent mountain peak. . . . . From the summit the view is enchanting. There stand the Tower and the Summer-house. . . . . Mount Philip received its name from the first settlers on their return from their sad exodus at the burning of Simsbury. By that name only it has been known by their descendants for more than two hundred years. Every rod of land upon it is, and has been many times recorded as lying and being upon Mount Philip."

The writer visited Simsbury for the first time in the spring of 1889. The extensive meadows spreading for miles along the Farmington River (the ancient Tunxis); — the noble elms scattered over the whole length of the valley; — the absence of factories and and the noisy adjuncts of trade; — are features that combine to give to the Simsbury valley a charm which justifies all that has been said in its praise. For the information of those of the Moses name who may desire to make a pilgrimage to the home of their ancestors it is proper to add that no vestige of the old Moses house now remains. During his stay in the town the writer was greatly indebted to Jeffery O. Phelps, Esq., for information concerning Simsbury families and localities. He stated that the last of the Moses family to occupy the homestead were the widow and children of Michael Moses, who lived there as late as 1840 or 1845. The home was torn down in 1855; the stones have been removed from the cellar and the site leveled. The property is now owned by the heirs of Amon Latimer.

Returning from this description of the outlying plantation of John Moses at the base of Mount Philip to his home at Windsor, quotations are now given from the town records to show his locality and neighborhood in that first of Connecticut towns.

From Vol. I, p. 46, of *Windsor Town Acts:* — "Feby 18, 1660 — On this day complaint was brought in of some neglect among the neighbors that

should have made a sufficient ditch to drain the highway. It is now referred with the consent of Wm. Phelps, John Moses and James Enno to a committee . . . . . If it be judged meet to carry the water between the land of John Moses and Nicholas Omhorn their other neighbors shall joyne as the committee shall judge is to be beneficial to them."
. . . . "Also a difference has come between John Moses and James Enno about a piece of ground before the house of James Enno, John Moses has now agreed that James Enno shall have it to injoye it — Also John Moses is allowed to injoye that swell of land that lyes between the bounds of his first lot and the highway." Page 166, "Mar. 15, 1672. John Moses purchased 83 acres of Reuben Strong — 30 acres in a tryangle — also 13 acres John Moses has had bounded out to him by Samuel Grant at Greenfield." Page 188, "February 2, 1677 — Mary relict of Capt Saml Marshall deceased and Capt Benj Newberry, Capt. Daniel Clark, Lieut David Wilton and Lieut John Mandsly sell to John Moses of Windsor a parcel of marsh land lying towards the west bounds of Windsor, being of estimation ten acres."

We glean some further items from manuscript records in the archives of the Secretary of State at Hartford. Vol. II, — Particular Court,— Mar. 4, 1657 —

"Nicholas Palmer for letting some Indians more than once have Syder to drinke contrary to the law of this Commonwealth is fined forty pound, $\frac{1}{3}$ part to be paid to Josias Ellsworth and John Moses in equal proportion the other $\frac{2}{3}$ to the Public treasury."

May 12, 1660 — John Moses — a Juryman of the Particular Court.

June 4, 1663, and January 15, 1664 — John Moses a juryman of the Hartford Quarter Court.

Before the Quarter Court March 3, 1669 — "John Moses plaintiff Thomas Mascall Defdt. for breach of covenant — £12."

April 19, 1670. "John Moses complains against Edward Bartlett for attaching 18 bushels of corn at Massacoe. — Judgment against John Moses 10 shillings and costs."

June 1, 1670.— "William Alistone engageth his cowe, his horse and sowe to John Moses to answer what he shall be found to be truly indebted to him."

April 5, 1671 — John Moses collector of Rates.

March 7, 1671-2 — Estate of Timothy Plumb.— John Moses and Joseph Ellsworth constables sworn for Windsor.

Jany 20, 1673, March 2, 1675, and April 18, 1677 — John Moses served as juryman of the Quarter Court.

From 1677 to 1683 we hear little of John Moses. His residence during this period in all probability alternated between Simsbury and Windsor.

His life of great activity and usefulness to the settlers of both towns was brought to a close October 14, 1683, as recorded in 1st vol. of births and deaths of the town of Windsor. His age is nowhere given. He died without a will. The writer has obtained certified copies of all probate papers connected with the settlement of the estates of John Moses of Windsor, of his widow who died September 14, 1689, and of the eldest son John, who died August 3, 1714. These papers bear so strongly on the business and family relations of John Moses that no excuse is offered for their appearance in full:

Probate Records, v. 4, p. 75:—A County Court held at Hartford December 6. 1683.—

An inventory of the estate of John Moses was exhibited in Court & oath made by his relict that there was a true presentment of the estate of the deceased to the apprizers so far as at present is known, & if more comes to knowledg it shell be aded to the inventory.

1683. Vol. IV. pp. 141, 142:— An Inventory of the estate of John Moses whoe deceased October 14. 1683 :

	£	s	d
Imprimis, his dwelling house barne sider house and home lott.	70	00	00
To 11 acres of land on the other side of the way.	27	00	00
To 24 acres of woodland at 10s per acre.	12	00	00
To 32 acres of woodland neere second meadow.	13	00	00
To 6 acres 3-4 in second meadow.	20	00	00
To a home lott bought of Walter Lee containing 10 acres.	40	00	00
To 24 acres swamps & woodland by the mill brook.	10	00	00
To 13 acres of woodland purchased of Sarah Linsly.	13	00	00
To 10 acres of marsh near Massaccoe.	12	00	00
To 100 acres of woodland near Paquanock.	40	00	00
To 90 acres of woodland near Massengery.	30	00	00
To 25 acres of land at Massaccoe wth barne & house.	86	00	00
To 2 cider presses a mill tubs & a press chaine.	08	00	00
To lumber in the barne a fann & aples.	01	00	00
To hay wheat barley & flax in the barne.	10	00	00
To 32 barrells of cyder at 10s per barrell.	16	00	00
To 4 cowes one steer & a calfe.	19	15	00
To 2 horses 61. To 9 swine 71.	13	00	00
To an iron kettle 16s. An iron trowe 2s.	00	18	00
To an iron pott 4s. To a grindstone 1£.	1	04	00
To a horse collar traces cart & other tackling.	1	00	00
To cedar at home 10s. cedar payd for 30s.	2	00	00
To 2 payer of pistolls & houlsters.	2	05	00
To iron tools & old iron & chaines in the parlor.	6	10	00
To 3 gunns 31. To a sadle cloathe brest plate & crooper 25s.	4	05	00
To wearing apparell.	17	19	00
To a chasse bed boulster & 1 payer of sheets 2 coverleds 1 blanket.	3	00	00

JOHN MOSES OF WINDSOR AND SIMSBURY.

	£	s	d
To a feather bed & bolster payer old sheets 1 coverled.	5	05	00
To a bedstead curtaines & valents.	2	00	00
To trundle bedsted 6s. To 1 doz napkins 12s.	00	18	00
To 7 payer of sheets 5£. To 5 payer pillow beers 1£.	06	00	00
To a chest 3s. To 4 bags salt & a barill 13s.	00	16	00
To a piece of leather 10s. To lumber in the parlor 10s.	01	00	00
To 22 yds of tow cloth at 2s, 6p per yrd.	02	15	00
To 8 yds of cotton cloth at 4s per yard.	01	12	00
To 3 shott pouches & bulletts 8s. To a small pistoll 5s.	00	13	00
To 10 yds of duffler at 8s per yard.	04	00	00
To 23 yds of woolen cloath at 4s 6p per yard.	05	03	00
To 2 yards of lindsy woolsey 6s. To 3 yds woolen cloath 4s 6p per yard.	00	19	06
To books 12s. To one payer of stillyards. 12s.	01	04	00
To a croscott sawe 12s. To a mill saw 1£ 10s.	02	02	00
To 8 porring dishes & a bason 10s. 4 cups 2 dram cups 8s.	00	18	00
To 3 tramels 1 payer of cob iron tongs & slice.	01	00	00
To a cutlash 15s. To a cartroape 2s.	00	17	00
To an old pot & ketle 1£. To 5 pewter platters 1£.	02	00	00
To lastin ware 5s. To 7 glass botles & 3 juggs 8s.	00	13	00
To 2 earthen cups and a salt, an houre glas & candlestick.	00	02	06
To wooden ware & 5 spoones 6s. To 5 payles 5s.	00	11	00
To a great kettell 2£. another kettle 16s. another kettell 24s.	04	00	00
To 3 littell kettels & 2 skillets.	01	00	00
To a warming pan 5s. a frying pan 6s. A spitt 3s.	00	14	00
To 5 baggs 12s-6p. To 4 bush 1-2 corne 11s-3p.	01	03	09
To 3 payer of cardes 4s. To a table 10s. 4 chayers 4s.	00	18	00
To 3 sickles 5s. To a sith & snead 2s.	00	07	00
To tubbs & keelers & 2 small cask.	00	08	00
To 2 bedsteads & coardes 10s. a box 3s. A chest 2s.	00	15	00
To a bed 1 payer of sheets 2 coverleds & boulster.	03	15	00
To another bed boulster payer of sheets a coverlid ruggs & 2 pillows.	02	10	00
To 11 pounds hempe 5s-6p. To 12 pounds occom yarne 12s.	00	17	06
To 7 pounds of cotton & woolen yarne.	09	17	06
To 2 yards of flaxen cloath.	00	06	00
To an old sadle a pillion & cloath.	01	00	00
To 4 bush 1-2 corne 11s-3p. To a cradle 4s.	00	15	03
To 30 lbs of yarne at the weavers.	01	10	00
To 78 lbs of cotton & 3 lbs of flax.	06	00	00
To lumber in the chamber & a payer of old boots.	00	06	00
To 5 small caske.	00	10	00
To 2 old coverleds.	00	10	00
To 11 bush of oatmeale & 4 baggs sent to Boston.	04	00	00
To a thousand of board at Massacoe.	02	00	00
To a firkin of soape.	00	15	00

	£	s	d
To a cannoe.	00	15	00
To 1 spade & 2 broad howes.	00	10	00
To tobaccoe and hops.	00	10	00
To a pitch forke & hay knife.	00	05	00
To 6 barells of cyder.	03	00	00
To 50 aple trees.	02	10	00
To irons of a saw mill.	02	00	00
To one payer of oxen at Massacoe.	10	00	00
	575	01	00

Apprised by us,—HENRY WOLCOTT.
TIMOTHY PHELPS Seur.
DANIEL BIRGE.

	£	s.	d.
Debts due to John Moses a yoake of oxen.	10	00	00

The children are,—

John, 28 years of age.
Timothy, 14 " " "
Mary, 22 " " "
Sarah, 19 " " "
Margaret, 17 " " "
Martha, 12 " " "
Mindwell, 07 " " "

Vol. 4, p. 79:—A speciale Court held at Hartford December 18th. 1683.—This Court grants administration upon the estate of John Moses to the widdow and her son John, & distribute the estate as followeth:—to the widdow sixty fower pounds of the personal estate to be to her and her heirs forever & a third of the reall during her life:—to the eldest son one hundred & twenty fouer pounds:—to Timothy sixty six pounds:—to Mary the eldest daughter because of her weaknesse seventy pounds:—to the fouer youngest daughters sixty pounds apiece, to be payd to the children as they come of age & if any dye before they be of age their portions are to be divided among the survivors, & if the estate fall short by debts it is to be born proportionally by the legatees according to this division, & John Moore & Return Strong are appoynted to be overseers to assist the administrator, & to distribute the estate to the children as they come of age, the sons to have their portions in land part present & the rest in reversion after their mother.

Vol. 4, p. 85:—A County Court held at Hartford March 6. 1684:— Whereas this Court hath been informed that in John Moses inventory there is a parcele of land bought of Sarah Linsley thirteen acres valued at thirteen pound, which is judged worth sixty pounds, that parcele of land is by those appoynted to distribute the estate to be valued in proportion as the other land & what overpluss it makes is to help beare what the estate is fallen short since the inventory is taken.

JOHN MOSES OF WINDSOR AND SIMSBURY.

. Vol. 5, p. 7: — A County Court held at Windsor by adjournment November 11. 1689.

The last will and testament of Mary (widow) Moses was exhibited in Court and oath made to it by Job Drake & inventory of the estate, both which the Court accepted of & approved & order it to be recorded. This Court do appoynt Sargt Timothy Phelps & Josiah Gillet to distribute the estate to the children according to the will of the deceased & to secure the portions of the younger children till they be of age or deliver it into the hands of theire guardians.

1689. SEPT. 9TH. MARY MOSES LAST WILL WAS that her son John should have two barrels of cyder & Timothy should have the cyder mill and press & the rest of her estate should be equally divided amongst the rest of her children.

GEORGE NORTON.
JOBE DRAKE, June.

Vol. 5, pp. 32, 33 : — An Inventory of the estate of Mary Moses widdow deceased taken Sept. 23, 1689.

	£	s.	p.
Imprimis. 1 great ketle 21 5s. 1 small ketle 1L.	03	05	00
To a feather bed 2 pillowes 1 chafe bolster.	03	00	00
To 1 bed boulster pillow 30s. 3 ruggs 31. 15s. 1 rug 10s.	05	15	00
To 3 sheets 30s. 2 payre of sheets 30s. 2 payer of pillow best 6s.	03	06	00
To 1 bed sted & cord & curtains & valens	02	00	00
To 5 towels 5s. 5 yds linin & woolen cloth & 2 remnants of cloath 11s.	00	16	00
To her wareing aparell linin & woolen.	07	06	00
To 112 yds lining yarne 23s. 23 lbs of occum yarne 1 L–14s.–6p.	01	17	06
To 1 payer of cards 1s. 3 earthen pots. 2s.	00	03	00
To 1 pewter pint & beater 3s. 2 iron pots & pot hooks 24s.	01	07	00
To meale in the barne 6s. a payer of pillowes. 1s.	00	07	00
To payles 3s. 3 bush indian 7s–6p. 3 bush 1-2 rye meale 16s.	01	00	06
To salt 18p. 4 chairs 4s. 3 spoons 18p.	00	07	00
To 4 old barells 8s. 2 axes 8s.	00	16	00
To the mill & press.	06	00	00
To 5 swine 4£–10s. 2 cowes 8l. 1 heifer 2l. 2 calves 1L–10s.	16	00	00
To aples 4l. 2 acres of indian corn 1L. 10s.	05	10	00
To hay made in the 2nd meadow.	02	00	00
To hops on the ground.	00	05	00
To 3 old barells 6s. 1 chest 5s.	00	11	00
Totall.	62	12	00

Taken by JOHN MOSES.

Vol. 9, p. 28 : — (holograph) will of John Moses of Simsbury.

IN THE NAME OF GOD AMEN. —

I, John Moses, being of sound minds and memory, altho week of boddy, but calling to mind my own mortalite and knowing that it is appointed for all men once to die, do make and ordain this my last will and testament, that is to say, principally and first of all I give and recommend my soul into the hands of God that gave it, and my body I recomment to the Earth to be buried in decent Christian Burial att the discretion of my Exsecuteur, nothing doubting but att the General Resurection I shall receive the same again by the maity power of God, and as touching such worldly estate wherewith it has pleased God to bles me in this life, I give demise and dispose of the same in the following maner and forme after my funeral charge and other lawful dept ar paid.

In primis I give and bequeath unto Deborath my derly beloved wife a thirds of all my improvable lands during her natural live and the thirds of my mouvable estate for ever, with the halve of my buildings, halve the seller, a halve the wels during her natural live.

Item, I give unto John my beloved son five shelings seeing I have given him alredy fifty pounds.

Item. I gave unto my son Williaume the halve of lend lying upon the West River in the west montaigne seeing he have alredy receved forty pounds.

Item. to my son Thomas I give him a halow lying nex the river upon the Reiet hand of Sermenton Route souther of Thomas Humfryis botom, seeing he have alredy receved fourty pounds.

Item. I give my youngest son Caleb a double portion of the remainder of my estate.

Item. I give unto my son Jochua a equell portion with my three daughters, namely Deborah Mary and Martha, the rest of my Estate to be equaly diveided betuine them four of my children last mentioned, that is to be understod my undiveided estate.

Fardre, I do ordaine and appointe my well beloved frind James Cornish Seignieur and my loving wife Deborah to be the Exsecuteurs of this my last will and testament and I do hereby utterly disalow revoque and disabule all and every other former testament will legacies and bequests and exsecuteurs by me in any ways befour named willed and bequeathed, ratifaied and confirming this and no other to be my last will and testament.

In witnes whereof I have hereunto set my hand and seal this twinty first day of Agus, Seventeen hundre and fourteen, in the presence of the witnes her mentioned.

JOHN MOSES. (Seal).

Andrew Robe
Mary X Humphry
James Poisson.

Vol. 8, p. 257:—A Court of Probate holden at Hartford within and for the County of Hartford, July 5th. Anno Dom. 1715.

John Moses of Symsbury Administrator on the estate of John Moses Senior late of Symsbury deceased, exhibited now in this Court an Inventory of the estate of the said deceased upon oath in manner accustomed, which inventory the Court orders to be recorded and kept on file, namely an Inventory of such estate of said deceased found remaining upon the decease of the executrix.

Vol. 8, p. 258 : —
Caleb Moses* of Symsbury a minor aged about 16 years & ¼, — son of John Moses Senior late of Symsbury deceased, appeared now before this Court and made choice of his brother Joshua Moses of Symsbury to be his Guardian, whereupon this Court doth allow and confirm the said Joshua Moses to be Guardian of the said minor accordingly, and the said Joshua Moses before this Court acknowledged himself bound to the treasury of this County in a recognizance of fifty pounds lawfull money that he will truly and faithfully perform his trust of Guardian of the said minor according to law.

Mary Moses of Symsbury a minor aged about 13 years appeared now before this Court and made choice of her brother William Moses of Symsbury to be her Guardian, whereupon this Court doth allow and confirm him to be Guardian of the said minor accordingly. And the said William Moses before this Court acknowledged himself bound to the treasury of this County in a recognizance of fifty pounds lawfull money, that he will truly and faithfully perform his trust of Guardian of the said minor according to law.

This Court doth appoint and constitute Joshua Moses of Symsbury to be Guardian to Martha Moses a minor aged about 10 years, daughter of John Moses Senior late of Symsbury deceased, and the said Joshua Moses before this Court acknowledged himself bound to the treasury of this County in a recognizance of fifty pounds that he will truly and faithfully discharge his trust of Guardian of the said minor according to law.

Nearly all of the earlier Windsor and Simsbury town records contribute something to the family history. Space is afforded to the references, in the event that any Moses descendant should desire to make further searches.

Windsor Deeds, Vol. II. Dec. 16, 1683.— Set off of 100 a. from her father's estate to Mary Moses w. of Saml. Farnsworth. Dec. 16, 1683.— Set off 125 a. to Sarah Moses w. of Saml. Butler. Dec. 11, 1683. — Deed of John Moses and his mother Mary Moses Ad. of John Moses. Mar. 19, 1690.— Set off of her portion to Martha Moses now Martha Crow.

Windsor Deeds, Vol. V. Feby. 24, 1719.— Joshua and Caleb Moses to Sergt. James Eno, lands part in Simsbury and part in Windsor, between Turkey Hills and the River. May 5, 1725.— Deed to William Thrall,

---

* The writer has in his possession the original will of this Caleb Moses, who died in his 91st year. His second son was Daniel, who died a soldier in the Revolutionary war. For distribution of his estate see *Simsbury Probate Records*, p. 166. The third son of Daniel was Zebina Moses, the first of the name, and whose will is found in *Simsbury Probate Records*, Vol. VII, p. 539.

signed by Mary Tuller (alias Moses,) w. of Jacob Tuller, Richard Roberts and Deborah Roberts (alias Moses) and Martha Moses.

Simsbury Town Acts, Book I, page 17. Nov. 29, 1677. — Grant from the town to William Moses. This was the William "wounded 19 of Dec. 1675,"—"that he dyed,—Nov. 27, 1681," and it will be noted that the grant was made on his attaining his majority. Grants by the town of Simsbury to John Moses are found in the same volume, pages 30, 34, 39, 46 (two grants), and 57.

John, the son of John of Windsor, appears to have made over much of his property to his children before his death, and to have regretted it, in one instance at least. Vol. II of Deeds, Feb. 7, 1703: — "Land between the two Phillips, the northerly end bounded upon the lands of my father John Moses." Dec. 30, 1706, John Moses, Sr. gives to his sons John and William as part of their portion — April 18, 1710, to his son Thomas; April 22, 1710, to his son John; Nov. 8, 1710, to his son William. On a leaf of the *Simsbury Records* is found this entry,: "John Slater Reg. of Town of Simsbury. We give you notice not to record to my son John Moses that deed of land that he had of me,— to wit: of part of my meadow lot here in Simsbury at Weatogue until further orders from me and I pray you take notice of this my caution by me John Moses Sr. Ent. Jany. 14, 1708."

Vol. II of Deeds, May 30, 1709 — John M xwell to William Moses: — Nov. 11, 1712. Thomas Moses in deed mentions his "brother William and Honored father John."

In a town list (*Sims. Rec.*) of lands owned in Simsbury in 1723 we find: "John Moses 140 acres, Joshua Moses 150 acres, Caleb Moses 100 acres, William Moses 74 acres, and Thomas Moses 54 acres.

EXPLANATIONS.

The numbers at the left of names are for tracing purposes, and are so placed for convenience in subsequent references to a preceding ancestor.

When a name is not carried forward for an independent paragraph, all that is to be said concerning that name appears immediately following its first mention.

The small numeral above the name indicates the generation to which that name belongs. The following abbreviations are used: m. for married, b. for born, d. for died, bap. for baptized; (Pro. Rec.) for Probate Records; (Hart. Pro. Rec.) for Probate Records of Hartford; (H. of Wind.) for History of Windsor by Henry R. Stiles; (H. of Sims.) for History of Simsbury, Granby, and Canton, Conn., by Noah A. Phelps, published in 1845; (H. of W. Sims.) for Genealogical Sketches of the Early Settlers of West Simsbury, now Canton, Conn., by Abiel Brown, published in 1856; (Sims. Rec.) for manuscript records of the town of Simsbury, Conn.; (W. Rec.) for manuscript records of the town of Windsor, Conn.; (St. A. Ch. Rec.) for manuscript parish records of Saint Andrews Episcopal Church, Bloomfield, Conn.; (W. B. Ch. Rec.) for Old Wintonbury Parish Records; (Sims. Ch. Rec.) for manuscript records of Puritan Church of Simsbury; (Col. Hist. Conn.) for Colonial History of Conn. by Trumbull and Hoadly; (Bark. Rec.) for manuscript records of Barkhamsted, Conn.; (Farm. Rec.) for manuscript records of Farmington, Conn.; (Nor. Rec.) for manuscript records of Norfolk, Conn.; (Coll. Essex Ins.) for Historical Collections of the Essex, Mass., Institute.

CHAPTER IV.

SOME OF THE DESCENDANTS OF JOHN MOSES OF PLYMOUTH AND JOHN MOSES OF WINDSOR AND SIMSBURY.

1 JOHN[1] MOSES of Plymouth, Mass., shipwright, came to New England between 1630 and 1640.

CHILDREN :* John Moses of Windsor, d. Oct. 14, 1683.

2 JOHN[2] MOSES, son of JOHN (1), settled at Windsor, Conn., previous to 1647, soldier of Capt. John Mason's troop of horse, m. Mary Brown, May 18, 1653. He d. Oct. 14, 1683. She d. Sept. 14, 1689.

CHILDREN: (Wind. Rec. and Hist. Sims.): John, b. June 15, 1654, d. Aug. 31, 1714; William, b. Sept. 1, 1656, d. Nov. 27, 1681; Thomas, b. Jan. 14, 1658, d. July 29, 1681; Mary, b. May 13, 1661; Sarah, b. Feb. 2, 1662; Nathaniel, b. ——; Dorkis, b. ——; Margaret, b. Dec. 2, 1666; Timothy, b. Feb. 1670; Martha, b. March 8, 1672, d. Jan. 30, 1689; Mindwell, b. Dec. 13, 1676, d. Jan. 6, 1697. Windsor Church Record under date of Aug. 7, 1677, mentions that John Moses had then 9 children.

Mary was the second wife of Samuel Farnsworth, mar. in 1685, had son, Joseph, b. Aug. 20, 1705.

Sarah was the wife of Samuel Butler.

Martha, m. Samuel Crow, Jan. 30, 1689.

Mindwell, m. Sergt. John Thrall, Jan. 6, 1697, and had nine children John, b. Oct. 13, 1699; Moses, b. April 29, 1702; Aaron, b. Sept. 27, 1704, d. 1731; Amy, b. Jan. 10, 1706; Joseph, b. May 13, 1710; Daniel, b. Dec. 13, 1712; Joel, b. 1716; Charles, b. 1718; Jerusha, b. 1722.

3 JOHN[3] MOSES, son of JOHN (2), settled in Simsbury, Conn., on his father's farm near Mount Philip. Married Deborah Thrall, July 14, 1680. She belonged to Puritan Church — see list, (H. Sims.) Nov. 10, 1697, of 43 persons. She d. May 16, 1715.

CHILDREN: (Sims. Rec.) John, b. April 26, 1681, d. 1759; Deborah (1st), b. Oct. 1, 1682, d. 1683; William, b. March 25, 1684, d. July 14, 1745; Thomas, b. May 8, 1685; Joshua, b. Oct. 3, 1689, d. Feb. 6, 1773;

---

* Henry Moses, of Salem, Mass., who was married Feb. 1, 1659, and was a sea captain, was probably a son (see No. 144). Thomas Moses, of Dorchester, Mass., was possibly another son (see Chap. VI).

Deborah (2d), b. Jan. 12, 1691; Caleb (1st), b. Aug. 1, 1694, d. Nov. 23, 1697; Othniel, b. Jan. 10, 1696, d. March 18, 1697; (Sims. Ch. Rec.) — (undecipherable) "Moses, son of John, bap. Nov. 14, 1697." Caleb (2d), b. (Sims. Rec.) Jan. 4, 1698, d. Mar. 21, 1787. "This is ye 2d son of yt name." Othniel (Sims. Ch. Rec.), b. Sept. 6, 1701 — bap. 7th, d. Sept. 11, 1701. Mary, b. Sept. 1, 1702; Martha, b. 1705.

Deborah, m. Richard Roberts soon after death of her father.

Mary, m. Jacob Tuller, Jan. 27, 1721.

Martha, (Hist. Wind.,) "Martha, Aunt of Lieut. Timothy Moses, d. July 9, 1764, aged about 56." (Sims. Rec.) Mary Moses, daughter of Martha Moses, b. June 5, 1736.

4 WILLIAM^3 MOSES, son of JOHN (2), lived with his father in Windsor. Was a soldier in "Philip's War." At the age of 19, at the storming of the Narragansett fort, Dec. 19, 1675, "was wounded that he dyed." (See Wind. Rec., Vol. I.) "He died Nov. 27, 1681." The town of Simsbury made him a grant of land in 1677.

5 THOMAS^3 MOSES, son of JOHN (2), lived with his father in Windsor. Was a soldier in "Philip's War." At the age of 17, at the storming of the Narragansett fort, Dec. 19, 1675, "was wounded that he dyed." "He dyed July 29, buryed ye 30, 1681." (W. Rec.)

Quite probably both of these sons were wounded with arrows, and thus lingered for years before death put an end to their sufferings.

6 TIMOTHY^3 MOSES, son of JOHN (2), appears to have held property in Windsor for years. He was but 14 years of age at his father's death. About the time he arrived at his majority, it is seen from (W. Rec.), July 22, 1696, that he deeds his brother John certain lands called "Greenfield." Previously, July 24, 1690, portions of his father's estate had been set out to him. From (W. Rec.) he had 32 acres near Long Meadow, 2¾ acres in Long Meadow, 4 acres in the Second Meadow, and "Walter Lee's home lot" of 10 acres as purchased by his father. (From Col. Hist. Conn.) — Oct., 1736 — James Thrall administrator of Aaron Moses late of Windsor — debts more than property — petitions to sell land. (This Aaron Moses was probably a son of Timothy.)

The writer has made careful search for further records concerning Timothy Moses, and with almost no results.

7 JOHN[4] MOSES, son of JOHN (3,) lived in Simsbury, Conn.; m. (1st) June 14, 1705, Sarah Tuller, daughter of John Tuller. She d. (tombstone) June 18, 1712, aged 26; m. (2d) June 4, 1713, Hannah Hoskins of Windsor. She survived her husband. She and Zacheus Gillet were executors of his will, dated June 10, 1759, (Hart. Pro. Rec.) He mentions sons, Timothy, Benoni, John, Zebulon; daughters, Sarah, Zeruiah, Hannah. These with other children mentioned in town books at Simsbury make the record:

CHILDREN: Timothy, (Sims. Ch. Rec.) bap. July 14, 1706, d. Sept. 12, 1751; Sarah, (Sims. Ch. Rec.) b. Aug. 30, 1708, and baptized Sept. 5, 1708; Zeruiah; Benoni, b. 1711, d. 1787; Infant, b. March 23, 1714, d. 27th; John, "born of Hannah his 2d wife, July 5, 1715, d. 1768;" Deborah, "third daughter of John Moses, b. Nov. 3, 1718;" Hannah; Zebulon, b. May 21, 1721; Antony, b. Dec. 27, 1722.

Sarah, m. Mr. Johnson.

Zeruiah. m. June 5, 1740, Ensign Joseph Cornish.

Deborah, m. a Mr. Weed.

Hannah, m. William Roberts — (see the will, also p. 119 Brown's Hist. of Sims.) which states of William Roberts: His w. was Hannah ———, that they had several children — Anna, b. 1748, m. Abel Adams. About commencement of the Revolution, parents removed to Vermont. The Cong. Ch. Manual, W. Rutland, Vt., states he was "one of the founders of the church," that he gave ground for the graveyard, and was the first buried in it. He d. Nov., 1788.

8 WILLIAM[4] MOSES, son of JOHN (3), lived in Simsbury; m. (1st) about 1710, widow Elizabeth Reade, daughter of John Law of Concord. She d. (Sims. Rec.) May 13, 1738. He m. (2d) Nov. 20, 1738, Hannah Humphrey.

From the settlement of his estate (Hart. Pro. Rec.) it is inferred that he practiced medicine, for we find in the inventory of his effects: "A Doctor's Instrument, Doctor's Book, vials, glass bottles, quart glass, small scales and weights," also a good wardrobe, very necessary to a doctor in the olden time, as: "leather breeches and apron, tobacco box, looking-glass, several pairs of breeches, stockings, coat, great coat, hat, shoes, and cane, silver buckles, guns, etc." He had "2 Bibles, 1 book 'Deceitfulness of Man's Heart,' and a 'Service book';" from which last item he may have been an Episcopalian. He had also "5 acres of land in the meadow, and 40 acres in the West Woods." On March 6, 1753, the Court appointed Jabez Cornish guardian of David Moses, a minor, aged 11 years, son of William Moses, late of Simsbury."

CHILDREN: — perhaps not all — (Sims. Rec.) Bildad, b. May 6, 1727; Hannah, b. Oct. 12, 1739; David, b. May 29, 1742. There is no further record of these children.

9 THOMAS[4] MOSES, son of JOHN (3), m. Sarah Alderman, daughter of William Alderman, Jan. 5, 1709.

CHILDREN: — perhaps not all — (Sims. Rec.) "Amey the first daughter of Thomas Moses, bap. Sept. 13, 1713."

10 JOSHUA[4] MOSES, son of JOHN (3), m. (1st) Dec. 12, 1717, Hannah Strickland. She d. Jan. 16, 1718–19, leaving twins three days old; m. (2d) June 28, 1722, Mary Brook. He deeds lands in New Hartford in 1744 and 1745. We find in Norfolk Records, deed July 2, 1772, from "Joshua the elder to son Joshua." Also, he bought lands in Norfolk in 1769. From (Sims. Rec.) he d. Feb. 6, 1773, "of an eating cancer of the mouth, aged about 85." By his will, dated Sept. 18, 1772, he leaves property £354 to "sons Joshua, Othniel, and John; to daughters Hannah, Mary, and Rachel."

CHILDREN: — perhaps not all — (Sims. Rec.) Hannah and Mary, twins, b. Jan. 14, 1718–19; Rachel, b. July 16, 1724; Joshua (from his will probably eldest son); Othniel, b. July 1, 1730; John (probably youngest son).

Rachel, m. Nathaniel Wilcox, Dec. 23, 1748.

Hannah, m. (Sims. Rec.) Benjamin Mills, Dec. 30, 1747.

11 CALEB[4] MOSES, son of JOHN (3), lived to a great age in Simsbury, and died, according to the family Bible and (Sims. Ch. Rec.), on March 21, 1787. He m. Sept. 15, 1726, Hannah Beaman. — (Sims. Ch. Rec.) "The aged Mrs. Moses, wife of Caleb, buried Dec., 1779." He was under the guardianship of his uncle during his youth. (Sims. Rec.) "Nov. 2, 1719 — Agreement to settle a difference concerning bounds of land between James Hillyer, Jr., and Caleb Moses, Joshua Moses acting as guardian (said Caleb being present and acting for himself)" . . . . they "are now come to this loveing agreement.".

He was a man of note in the community, and among the family papers is a commission under the Crown of England showing him to have been a constable and collector.

The writer has in his possession some twenty original papers handed down through the generations from this Caleb. The oldest of these is a deed dated February 25, 1735–6, from Jacob Tullar, of certain lands in the town of Farmington. Aside from the interest these papers have for those, who, like the writer, have descended through Caleb, their peculiarities illustrative of the age in which they were written, make them worthy of somewhat extended quotations. Instance the following as showing the degree of thankfulness expected from a grown-up son:

"I, Caleb Moses, Jr., do acknowledge that I have received of my honored father, Caleb Moses, a deed of Land which I do acknowledge to be my full share of his estate. Except he give me something by his will, which if he Doth I shall be Thankful for it and look upon it an unmerited Bounty from my honored father, and always Look upon myself a Debtor to him for his kindness. Witness my hand.
Dated April 14, 1760.   (Signed)   CALEB MOSES, Jr."

Receipts for land deeded to them by their father in 1767, as their full share of his estate, and signed by Caleb's son Abel, and his daughter Lucy Humphrey, are found among the papers.

We now come to the will of Caleb, which is interesting as showing the old English plan of entailing an estate. From the papers in the writer's possesion it would seem that Caleb owned the old home farm of his grandfather, with additions on Mount Philip and in the valley, and we know that for many generations the "male heirs" of Caleb owned and lived at the old homestead. The will reads as follows:

"In the Name of God Amen. I, Caleb Moses, of Simsbury, in the County of Hartford, being of Sound mind and memory, and in a State of Health, Thanks be given to God. Therefor and knowing that it is apointed for all men once to Dye Do make and ordain this to be my Last will and Testament principally and first of all I give and Recommend my Sole unto the Hands of God That gave it and my Body I Recommend to the Earth to be Buryed in a decent and Christian manner at the Discretion of my Executors, and as Touching the worldly estate wherewith God hath blessed me with in this Life, I give in manner following:

"Item, I give to my Beloved wife The one third part of my movable estate I shall dye possest on and the use and Improvement of the One Third part of my Lands During her Natural Life.

"I also give to the Heirs of my Son Caleb Moses Deceased and to my son Daniel Moses and to my son Abel Moses the one half of my movable estate to be equally Divided after my Decease, viz: the Heirs of said Caleb one Third part, to my son Daniel one Third part, to my son Abel one third part and my Right at Susquehannah* my will is shall be

---

* A thorough search has been made of Hartford County histories for some explanation of the phrase, "my Right at Susquehannab." The only clue to this clause of the will is found in the *History of Connecticut* by the tory, Rev. Samuel Peters, from which is quoted:

"Having been in possession of that Country One hundred and forty years, the General Assembly, though unsupported either by law or justice, resolved to take up and settle their lands

equally Divided between the Heirs of my son Caleb Moses and all the my other equil, the Heirs of Caleb aforesaid one Third.

"I give to my son Michael all the Rest of my Estate both Real and personal which I have not Diposed of viz: all my Lands on the East Side of the River in Simsbury or Farmington to be an Estate to him and his Descendants to him & his male Heirs and not to be Disposed of by him or Them Either by Deed or Lease or Release for a Term of years, but only to his next nearest of kin and all the Land which given to my said son Michael and to the Rest of my said Sons whom I have conveyed by this will my will is They nor either of them shall sell Dispose of by Deed Lease or Purchase except to the Next of kin and a Reasonable Time of payment given for the purchasing the same and shall first offer the same to Them. I also give to my Daughter Lucy Humphrey five shillings over & above what I have given her in Lands and movable Estate within six months after my Decease and I do constitute and appoint my Beloved wife Hannah and my son Michael Moses to be executors to this my will, and I do pronounce & Declare this and no other to be my Last will and Testament.

"Signed sealed pronounced and Declared this 8th day of June 1776.
"Noah Humphrey   CALEB MOSES (seal)"
"Elisha Cornish
"Hez. Humphrey."
Fac simile of signature of Caleb Moses.

CHILDREN of Caleb Moses (Sims. Rec.): Caleb, b. May 18, 1727, d. Feb. 18, 1773; Daniel, b. June 22, 1729, d. in the army Sept. 8, 1776; Abel, b. June 24, 1733; Ashbel, b. Dec. 6, 1735; Michael, b. Sept. 12, 1737, d. (Bible and tombstone) Mar. 14, 1797; Lucy, b. May 9, 1740.

Lucy, m. Nathaniel Humphrey of Simsbury (family papers).

12   CALEB[5] MOSES, 2D, son of CALEB (11), m. Mary Adams, July 6, 1749. He was (Sims. Rec.) "found dead in his bed in morning Feby. 18, 1773." His will mentions sons Abraham, Reuben, Seba, James, and daughters Mercy, Phœbe, and Lydia.

Among family papers is one that reads "At a General Assembly of the Governor and Company of the Colony of Connecticut holden in New Haven on the Second Thursday of October 1773," and recites that the debts and charges "surmounts the movable estate of the deceased Caleb Moses, Jr." and empowers Caleb Moses 1st as executor to sell certain real estate of "said deceased."

West not Only of Hudson but Susquehanna River and extending to the South Sea. In pursuance of this resolution they with modesty passed over New York and the Jerseys because they are possessed by Mynheers and fighting Christians and seized On Pennsylvania claimed by Quakers who fight not for either wife or daughter."

CHILDREN (Sims. Rec.) Abraham, b. June 22, 1750, d. 1823; Reuben, b. Feb. 18, 1753; Mercy, b. Mar. 18, 1756; Mercy 2d, b. Sept. 16, 1758; Seba, b. April 26, 1760; Phœbe, b. Dec. 6, 1762; James, b. Feb. 8, 1766, buried (Sims. Ch. Rec.) Dec. 3, 1778,— "James, son of widow Moses;" Lydia, b.——

Phœbe, m. (Sims. Ch. Rec.) April 10, 1783, Asa Woodford.

Reuben, Soldier Col. Belden's 18 Reg.—prisoner retreat from New York, Sept. 15, 1776.

Seba (Brown's W. Sims.) m. Ardelice Graham. From Pension Office we learn that in 1777 he was a soldier in Col. Moseley's Reg., and while at Tiverton, R. I., Col. Barton, in a daring exploit, captured the offensive British General Prescott, over whom the next day Moses was placed as guard.

March, 1778, he volunteered under Capt. Burr, and was at Horse Neck, White Plains, and West Point.

June, 1779, he volunteered with Capt. Job Case, and at Horse Neck was in the force attacked by Col. Delancey's horsemen.

From Nov. 1779, was for two months under Capt. David Phelps and Lieut. Aaron Moses.

After the war he lived in New Hartford and Barkhamsted, and removed, about 1806, to New Lebanon, N. Y., where he was living in 1832.

13. DANIEL^5 MOSES, (H. W. Sims.,) "son of CALEB (11). With his wife Mary Wilcox (b. 1732 and d. 1816), (a dau. of Azariah Wilcox) came from the old Parish to West Simsbury about the year 1756, and settled on the farm now (1856) owned by Bethuel Case adjoining the farm of the late Capt. Robert Wilcox deceased in North Canton." Daniel Moses was a soldier and died in the army at New York, Sept. 8, 1776. (H. W. Sims., and gravestone North Canton.)

In Pro. Rec. of Sims., p. 166, is found the distribution of the estate on Mar. 8, 1779. The inventory shows an aggregate of £471–11s. Lands are set out as follows: To Daniel, eldest son (2 parts) 19$\frac{3}{4}$ acres, to Roger 9$\frac{3}{4}$ acres, Zebina 9$\frac{3}{4}$ acres, Lois 9$\frac{3}{4}$ acres, Hannah, 9$\frac{3}{4}$ acres, Charlotte 11$\frac{1}{4}$ acres, Sybil, wife to Martin Roberts, 9$\frac{3}{4}$ acres, Mary, wife to Hezekiah Andrews, 10 acres. The above subject to the widow's thirds during her life and her occupancy of one third part of dwelling-house and barn. To Daniel, eldest son, $\frac{2}{3}$ of house and barn. To Roger, Zebina, Mary, Sybil, Hannah, Lois, and Charlotte, to each $\frac{1}{3}$.

From the above, from *Brown's History*, and other sources, the record stands:

CHILDREN: Daniel (the 2d) d. Sept. 9, 1805, aged 46 years; Roger, b. (Bark. Rec.) Feb. 13, 1767, d. 1828; Zebina (the 1st) (monuments at Old Simsbury and at Marcellus, N. Y.), b. April 15, 1764, d. Nov. 23, 1815; Lois; Hannah; Charlotte; Sybil; Mary.

Roger (See No. 126).
Charlotte, m. Job Phelps.
Sybil, m. Martin Roberts.
Mary, m. Hezekiah Andrews (Andrews' Mem. Hist.).
Lois, m. (Sims. Ch. Rec.) in 1781, Andrew Roby.

14 ABEL[5] MOSES, son of CALEB (11), born (Sims. Rec.) June 24, 1733. In Hartland, Conn., is tombstone of Abel Moses, died June 14, 1785, aged 52. He was of the Episcopal Church, as we find this entry in the St. Andrew's Ch. Rec. "bap. at Hartland, June 3, 1764, male child of Abel Moses named Abner." Also in Vol. 13, Col. Hist. of Conn., petition of Abel Moses and five others that they were professors of the Church of England (Oct. 1771), and that they be exempt from certain taxes. From Marcus Moses and Maritta (Moses) Case, now (1889) living at Barkhamsted, Conn., we learn that their grandfather, Martin Moses, had brothers and sisters, Abel, Ashbel, Abner, and Lydia. The Pro. Rec. of Sims. give us under date of April 25, 1800, the distribution of the property of Lydia Moses, of Hartland, an intestate, to "heirs Abel, Ashbel, Abner, and Martin," presumably her brothers (as her nearest of kin).

CHILDREN (perhaps not all): Lydia Moses, b. about 1756, d. (tombstone Hartland) May 16, 1799, aged 42; Abel, b. 1757, d. (tombstone Hartland) Aug. 24, 1800, aged 43; Ashbel, b. ———; Martin, b. 1761, d. (tombs. Barkhamsted) Sept. 21, 1849, aged 88; Abner, bap. (St. And. Ch. Rec.) June 3, 1764. Mrs. Maritta Moses Case thinks there was an Azariah Moses who went to Ohio.

Lydia died unmarried; distribution of her estate April 25, 1800.
Abner, Mrs. Case states that he went to Genessee, N. Y.

15 ASHBEL[5] MOSES, son of CALEB (11). From the fact that Caleb Moses in his will in 1776 mentions all of his then living children and provides for the heirs of Caleb 2d, then deceased, it seems probable that Ashbel was at that time dead and without heirs.

16 MICHAEL[5] MOSES, son of CALEB (11), was a soldier in Col. Phelps' 18th Conn. Reg.; — lived and died on the old homestead at Mount Philip which his father willed should be entailed and "be an Estate to him and his male heirs and not to be disposed of by him or them." Michael's property at his death amounted to £1430; — a large sum considering the time and place; — and this he willed, (Sims. Rec.) on Aug. 12, 1796, to his wife Thankful, eldest son Michael, sons Collin, Caleb, Levi, Luther, Martin, and daughters Chloe Humphrey, Anna Case, Amy Wells, Lucy, and Rhoda. He m. July 2, 1764, Thankful Case. The widow m. in 1798 (Sims. Ch. Rec.) Capt. Bennett.

CHILDREN : (Bible) Michael, Jr., b. Jany. 30, 1766, d. (tombstone) Jan. 27, 1816; Chloe, b. Nov. 1, 1767; Anne, b. Nov. 1, 1769; Amy, b. May 30, 1776; Colin, b. Nov. 6, 1778; Levi, b. Nov. 13, 1783; Caleb, b. Feb. 9, 1785, d. (tombstone) April 12, 1806; Luther, b. Nov. 20, 1788, d. (tombstone) Jan. 21, 1830; Martin, d. 1833; Lucy, bap. Aug. 27, 1786; Rhoda, ———.

Amy, m. Horace Wells.
Chloe, m. Lot Humphrey (Sims. Ch. Rec.) Dec. 1, 1784.
Anna, m. Nathan Case.
Lucy, m. Benj. Case.
Rhoda, m. Asa Humphrey — *Children :* Flora; Marietta, m. a Sherwood; Amanda (m. Nathan Grimes).
Martin — *Children* (perhaps not all) — John ———; Delia (m. Apr. 13, 1840, Richard C. Humphrey) —; William.
Caleb, m. Hepzibah; — On Nov. 18, 1806 (Sims. Ch. Rec.) an allowance in goods amounting to $867.25 was made for her support as "Relict of Caleb."
Levi went to South Carolina and d. there. *Children :* Orville, d. in Hartford; Asenath, Jeanette, Hoyt.
Colin, unm., d. in Weatogue; was a soldier in Isaac Phelps' command, war of 1812.
Colin, *Levi*, and *Luther* are mentioned as having land near the "Cove," the "Meadow," and on the "Mountain," in a deed of Feb. 10, 1802, from Caleb to Michael.

17 TIMOTHY[5] MOSES, son of JOHN (7), was a soldier with rank of Lieutenant. He and his immediate descendants are given in Stiles' *History of Windsor*. The baptisms and deaths are also found on the church records of the old Wintonbury Parish, formerly in Windsor, and now in the town of Bloomfield. "At a meeting of the proprietors of Windsor, Oct. 23, 1740, (Windsor Rec.) for the purpose of setting off to several residents of Windsor certain undivided land," Timothy Moses was one of the grantees. His will, however, is recorded at Simsbury, Sept. 18, 1787. He gives sons Timothy, Aaron, and Elisha, and granddau. Susannah Trimble, £20 each, and to grandchildren Dorcas, Isaac, and Ambrose, heirs of his daughter Dorcas deceased, £5 each. He m. (1st) Sarah Phelps, she d. Sept. 12, 1751; m. (2d) Sarah, ———

(W. Ch. Rec.) "Sarah ye 2d wife of Lieut. Timothy Moses d. Nov. 19, 1759;" m. (3d) Elizabeth Humphrey "ye 3d wife of Lt. Timothy Moses, d. Oct. 6, 1763;" m. (4th) Anne ——— "ye 4th wife from ye first church of Christ in New Milford in 1764." His 3d w. Elizabeth, Sept. 13, 1761, wills property to her husband, Timothy Moses, sister Lydia Wilcox, and brother Ezekiel Humphrey.

CHILDREN: (Sims. Rec.) Timothy, b. Feb. 5, 1732, d. 1793; Aaron, b. Oct. 6, 1733, d. 1809; Elisha, b. Feb. 25, 1735-6, d. 1808; Sarah, b. Feb. 23, 1738-9; Zerviah, b. Nov. 2, 1740, d. 1763; Martin, b. July 13, 1743, "killed by felling of a tree, Jan. 27, 1766;" Keziah, b. May 31, 1746; Dorcas, b. Oct. 31, 1748; Lydia, b. Aug. 5, 1751.

"These children were born to Timothy Moses by his first wife, Sarah, whose maiden name was Sarah Phelps."

Sarah, (H. W. Sims.) m. Isaac Graham.
Zerviah, (H. W. Sims.) m. Daniel Graham (tombstone N. Canton).
Keziah, (Sims. Rec.) m. Joseph Adams, Apr. 24, 1766.

18 BENONI[5] MOSES, son of JOHN (7), was a soldier. His name is found in Lexington Alarm list. The H. W. Sims. states that he settled in the North District about 1744; — was a carpenter and a man of note. From Farmington records, he appears to have bought lands in that town previously to 1740. And also in same records is mentioned May 30, 1755, in deed to J. Hart, as of "Norfolk." From Sims. Rec. we have an inventory of his estate, taken April 9, 1787, by Capt. Aaron Moses, Elisha Graham, and Elisha Moses. An allowance is made to Asa Moses as one of the administrators. In St. Andrew's Episcopal Church Record, is the entry "Benoni Moses conformed Oct. 1, 1764." His burial is also recorded in same church record, from which we conclude he belonged to the Church of England. The town records of Farmington show that he m. (1st) Jan. 3, 1736, Phoebe Woodruff. He m. (2d) Susannah Humphrey, dau. of John Humphrey, on June 5, 1740, the same day his sister Zerviah m. Ensign Joseph Cornish. She (Susannah) d. June 12, 1774, and he m. (3d) Phoebe Brewer Oct. 27, 1775. She d. 1786.

CHILDREN: Phoebe, b. at Farmington July 9, 1737; Ezekiel, b. Jan. 7, 1741, d. Oct. 17, 1761, in the army, at Crown Point; Elnathan, b. Feb. 28, 1743, d. about 1827; Susannah, b. July 13, 1746; Lois, b. Dec. 5, 1749; Shubael, b. May 11, 1753, d. Mar. 9, 1823, at Ticonderoga; Sarah, b. Dec. 4, 1756; Ezekiel 2d, b. Feb. 5, 1762, d. Nov. 15, 1834; Elizabeth, b. Dec. 24, 1765.

Lois, m. Darius Hill, Mar. 31, 1768. From (H. W. Sims.) "The mother (Widow Lois Hill) and her three daughters left the town near the beginning of the present century."

19 JOHN[5] MOSES, son of JOHN (7). Brown's H. W. Sims. states that "He was among the earliest settlers of West Simsbury, probably as early as 1745. He with his wife Rhoda settled on the place now (1856) owned by Seymour D. Moses . . . . . near the North burying ground, which was on his premises. . . . . . . He erected a grist-mill on his last farm which bore his name. He left the town in the latter part of the last century." The Cong. Ch. Man. of W. Rutland, Vt., gives his name among fourteen who founded the church in 1773. In the list of members are (1785) Jonah, and Asa Moses, and (1788) Eunice, and Dorcas Moses. These may, or may not, have been his children. They are not otherwise accounted for. Asa was administrator of estate of Benoni Moses, and was a soldier, Col. Hooker's Reg., in 1777. (Rutland town Rec.) John Moses deeded Mar. 9, 1785, "south half of my home lot to my beloved son John Moses Jr." From *Brown's History*, John Moses m. Rhoda ———. She d. 1768, æ. 43.

CHILDREN: perhaps not all, as evidently Brown gives tombstone inscriptions only, and there are wide intervals. Eunice, b. 1752, d. 1754; Rhoda, b. 1756, d. 1761; Infant, b. 1768, d. 1768. From Rutland Rec., John Jr. lived in Rutland 1785.

20 ZEBULON[5] MOSES, son of JOHN (7). He appears to have lived at Turkey Hills, which is now in the town of East Granby. In Rutland deeds we find the name of "Zebulon Moses Jr." He was an Episcopalian, and nearly all we know of his family is gathered from the St. A. Ch. Rec., and is as follows:

CHILDREN of Zebulon Moses, all bap. at Turkey Hills. Reuben, bap. May 27, 1764; "Burial Turkey Hills Oct. 1768, a daughter to Zebulon Moses;" Charles, bap. April 12, 1767; Abiah, bap. July 16, 1775; Sybil, bap. July 16, 1775; (from Rutland Rec.) Zebulon Jr.

21 OTHNIEL[5] MOSES, son of JOSHUA (10). His father Joshua deeded him land in 1754. He was an Episcopalian.

From manuscripts in the State Library at Hartford we copy the following:

"Bond of Sept. 3, 1762. . . . That we whose names are underwritten will pay or caused to be paid to Roger Viets of Symsbury . . an annuity or yearly sum of 30£ — . . the condition is; that if the above named Roger Viets A. B. being a candidate for holy orders, shall as soon as conveniently may be transfer, or cause himself to be transferred, to

Great Britain and there receive holy orders according to the usage and ceremony of the Church of England, and as soon as conveniently may be after . . . shall return to Symsbury aforesaid and there officiate in the office of minister according to the rites and ceremonies of the Church of England, there so long and until orderly or providentially dismissed or removed from said charge. . . . (39 signatures — among them)

OTHNIEL MOSES,
ZEBULON MOSES."

Rev. Roger Viets succeeded Rev. William Gibbs as Rector of St. Andrew's Parish. From Hart. Co. Mem. Hist. we learn that, for "secreting" British officers and "holding traiterous correspondence with the enemy," Viets was "severely punished." He removed to Nova Scotia. . Othniel did not follow his rector politically. He was a soldier of Col. Woolcot's Reg. of. 1776 — (Adj.- General's Record of Conn.) From the St. Andrews Church Record we gather that he resided at different periods in different villages or parishes. That Record gives the following:

CHILDREN: At St. Andrew's Parish, Dorcas, bap. July 15, 1764. At Scotland (a parish now in Bloomfield), Linda, daughter of Othniel, bap. April 26, 1767, also on same date bap. "Rhoda, daughter of Othniel." At Suffrage (a parish now in Canton), Roxalana, daughter of Othniel, bap. April 30, 1769, and Isaac, bap. Sept. 29, 1771.

(Farm. Rec.) mentions Othniel as of Farmington in deed of 1773. In the Bristol, Conn., Records we find his name in deeds of 1785 and 1786, also in 1797 Othniel and Reuben Moses deed to Elijah Gridley. In 1798 Othniel, Othniel, Jr., and Reuben join in a deed, and in 1800 it appears that lands of Elihu Moses adjoin those of Othniel; also that the freeman's oath was taken at Bristol in 1880 by Othniel Jr. and Elihu; in 1805 by Chauncey; and in 1806 by Joshua.

From the foregoing and from statements of descendants we can add with reasonable certainty as:

OTHER CHILDREN of Othniel, the names of Othniel, Jr., b. Feb. 13, 1755, d. Oct. 8, 1841; Elihu, Chauncey, Joshua, and Reuben (see 131).

22 JOHN[5] MOSES, son of JOSHUA (10), m. (Sims. Rec.) Abigail Scott of Waterbury, Sept. 20, 1763. He was doubtless an Episcopalian, as witness the baptisms of most of his children (St. And. Ch. Rec.). Their birth dates are also given in Sims. Town Rec.

CHILDREN: Eunice, b. Dec. 7, 1764, bap. St. A., Feb. 17, 1765; Abigail, b. Aug. 23, 1766; John, b. Feb. 12, 1769, "bap. at Scotland, Easter, 1769;" Achsa, b. Sept. 13, 1770, bap. at Scotland,

July 14, 1771; Joshua, b. Dec. 14, 1772; Rue, b. Sept. 15, 1775, "bap. privately at Scotland, Nov. 5, 1775; Aruah, dau. of John Moses of Sims.;" William, b. May 15, 1778; Joseph, b. June 29, 1780; Sarah, b. May 15, 1774; Joab, b. Sept. 24, 1784; Abraham, b. June 1, 1786.

Eunice, from St. A. Ch. Rec. "Married at Scotland, Sept. 22, 1785, to Andrew Streever, both of Simsbury."

23 TIMOTHY[6] MOSES, son of TIMOTHY (17), lived in West Simsbury and Canaan, Conn., was a soldier, is spoken of in Colonial History as Ensign, in 1768, of trainband of Canaan, and Capt. 14th Reg., 1775, and is mentioned in Probate Records of Simsbury by title of Captain. Phineas Holcomb deeds lands in Canaan to Timothy, Jan. 20, 1749. The inventory of his estate taken June 5, 1793, shows his property to have amounted to £919, including 200 acres of land. He m. (1st) (H. W. Sims.) Thankful ———; she died in 1790, ae. 59; m. (2d) (Sims. Ch. Rec.) May, 1791, Bathsheba Canaday.

CHILDREN (perhaps not all): (Canaan Rec.) Timothy, b. May 13, 1755; Sarah, b. July 27, 1759; Thankful, b. May 9, 1760; Mary, b. Apr. 19, 1761; Levirah, b. Apr. 24, 1763; Keziah, b. Feb. 7, 1768.

Levirah, m. Rufus Bodwell, May 24, 1781.

24 AARON[6] MOSES, son of TIMOTHY (17), H. W. Sims. "came from Wintonbury to West Simsbury about 1757;" was a soldier — "Sergeant" — on the Lexington alarm list; also in Capt. Brown's Co., 1776; and was a Lieut. in 1779 under Capt. David Phelps; was also known, (H. W. Sims.) as "Deacon." By his will (Sims. Rec.) dated July 11, 1797, he leaves property to wife Rachel, sons Darius, and Seymour Aaron, and daughter Susannah Butolph. He m. (1st) Susannah Seymour; she d. 1783; m. (2d) Rachel Gilbert; she d. 1821.

CHILDREN: Darius, b. Nov. 11, 1758, d. (tomb N. Canton) Oct. 25, 1824; Asenath, b. Nov. 2, 1760; Aaron Seymour, b. July 29, 1762, d. 1772; Susannah, b. Sept. 13, 1764; Martin Levi, b. Dec. 20, 1766, drowned 1784; Seymour Aaron, b. Oct. 25, 1772; d. 1846.

Asenath, m. Mr. Adams.
Susannah, m. Joseph Butolph.

25 ELISHA[6] MOSES, son of TIMOTHY (17), m. Mercy Barber, dau. of Thos. Barber, June 21, 1759; she d. 1815.

CHILDREN: (Sims. Rec.) Mercy, b. May 22, 1760; Elisha, b. Nov. 8, 1761, d. Sept. 1847, at Mt. Morris, N. Y.; Infant, b. 1764, d. 1764; Frederick, b. May 31, 1770, d. 1824.

Mercy, m. Elihu Beach.

26 MARTIN[6] MOSES, son of Timothy (17), (H. of Wind.) m. Lydia ———, who had Martin born after his father's death, (Wby. Ch. Rec.) bap. April 30, 1766.

27 EZEKIEL[6] MOSES 1st, son of Benoni (18), (Sims. Rec.) was a soldier; died in the army, Oct. 17, 1761, at Crown Point.

28 ELANTHAN[6] MOSES, son of Benoni (18), with his brothers Ezekiel (2d) and Shubael, removed from the West Parish of Simsbury, Conn., to West Rutland, Vt.; m. Elizabeth ———, a French lady, who lived to the age of 96.

CHILDREN: Levi; William; Betsy, b. Oct. 23, 1773, d. July 4, 1814; Rufus, b. 1775, d. April 23, 1853; Seth, b. 1778, d. 1801; Stephen ———; Jeptha, b. 1784, d. May 17, 1834; Sybil, b. 1787, d. Jan. 18, 1808; Sylvia, b. 1787; Laura, b.———.

Levi — lived near his father "when Hiram attended school." *Children:* Alvah, "who lost an eye by an arrow;" Lydia; Betsey; Mary; Alice (m. Alonzo Gorham).

Betsy, m. Abel Phelps. *Children:* Moses, b. Aug. 25, 1803, d. Aug. 30, 1871, at Mapleton, Minn.; Elizabeth; Betsy, m. William Howlett, of Cattaraugus Co., New York.

Stephen died from bite of mad dog. His daughter Olive m. Mr. Daniels and went West.

Jeptha, m. Betsy Gorham, who afterward m. Rev. David Hascall, and d. 1866, ae. 81. Jeptha owned 600 acres in West Rutland. Had no children.

William — lived in Ohio and had two sons.

Sybil and *Sylvia* were twins. Sybil m. Barlow Gorham (living in 1881). *Children:* Sybil, Franklin, Hiram, and Dennis.

Laura, m. Fred Burgess, went West and joined the Mormons; was drowned on the way to Nauvoo, Ill.

29 SHUBAEL[6] MOSES, son of Benoni (18), was a soldier, enlisted May 6, 1775, in Conn. 2d, and was in 18th Conn. Reg., at New York in 1776; removed in 1777 from Simsbury in Conn. to West Rutland, Vt., where he was a church member in 1785. He afterward settled in Ticonderoga, N. Y., on the east side of the Outlet (Lewis place in 1881), and was one of the chief men of the Cong. Church.

30 EZEKIEL[6] MOSES 2d, son of Benoni (18), was a soldier; is mentioned in Levies of 5th Conn. Reg. in 1780. From Pension-Office papers: He served under Capt. Phelps; was in fort at Stonington; was with Capt. Burr at burning of Fairfield and Norfolk, in April, 1778; volunteered under Capt. Bradley; was at West Point and New Jersey under Col. Wells; detached by Baron De Kalb to serve in Chapman's Light Inf. After the war he removed to West Rutland, Vt.; was a church member in 1803. About 1816 he went to Ohio (probably Granville); he resided in Champaign Co. in 1829. His widow lived in Urbana in 1839. From Bible leaf in pension papers, he m. Mar. 17, 1790, Eunice ———. She d. June 4, 1834.

CHILDREN: Loice, b. Feb. 9, 1791; Anna, b. July 22, 1792; Phebe, b. Mar. 3, 1795; Loice Lorendy, b. Mar. 11, 1797; William B., b. July 26, 1799; Aaron, b. May 26, 1801; Eliza, b. June 9, 1803; Eunice, b. Dec. 6, 1806; Eliza, b. Sept. 19, 1809; Truman, b. June 5, 1810; Louis Curtis, b. Sept. 23, 1812; Eunice, b. June 23, 1814.

Above names attested by Truman Moses, who resided in Champaign Co. in 1839.

31 JOHN^6 MOSES, son of JOHN (22), lived in Simsbury; was probably an Episcopalian; m. Anna ———.

CHILDREN: (Sims. Rec.) Anna Maria, b. April 5, 1797; Martin, b. Feb. 26, 1799, bap. privately (St. And. Ch. Rec.) July 12, 1800; John, b. Mar. 19, 1802.

32 ABRAHAM^6 MOSES, son of CALEB 2d, (12). Brown, in his H. W. Sims., mentions that he resided on the East Hill; that he made a profession of religion in 1821; and that he died in 1823, having been found dead in his barn in a praying posture. He m. Mercy Case. She d. 1818. He was a soldier in Col. Belden's 18th Reg. at New York, in 1776.

CHILDREN: Loditha, Abraham, Jr., b. 1773, d. (tombstone) Dec. 9, 1802; Mercy, Dorcas, James; Thaddeus, b. 1784, d. 1828.

Loditha, m. Joab Barber.

Abraham, Jr., m. Charlotte Alford. By his will, April 20, 1802 (Sims. Rec.), he left property to his wife Charlotte, brothers James and Thaddeus, and sisters Dytha Barber, Mercy Rowland, and Dorcas Moses.

Mercy, m. William Rowland.

Dorcas, m. Job Talbot, of Avon, Conn.

James, m. Clarissa Wilcox, removed to the State of New York, and had a large family.

33 THADDEUS^7 MOSES, son of ABRAHAM (32), m. Merab Brockway.

CHILDREN: Candace, Terressa, Hosea; Lyman, b. in Canton, Conn., Sept. 12, 1816; Matilda, Abraham.

Candace, m. Reuben Loveland. She died in Milesburgh, Pa.

Terressa, m. Lucien Woodford. She d. in Collinsville, Conn.

Hosea, supposed to have died in Georgia.
Lyman T., b. in Canton, Conn., Sept. 12, 1816, removed to Ravenna, Ohio, in 1857; has daughter Laura S.
Matilda, m. Thomas H. Eddy; lives in Lamar, Pa.
Abraham, lives in Colebrook, Conn.

34 ABEL[6] MOSES, son of ABEL (14), lived in Hartland, Conn.; was a soldier and a prisoner on the retreat from New York, Sept. 15, 1776. His tombstone reads, "Lieut. Abel Moses, died Aug. 24, 1800." Under date of March 7, 1803, we find in *Probate Records* of Simsbury, that Daniel Beaman of Hartland was appointed guardian for minors in Hartland. (The grandmother of Abel, 2d, was a Beaman.) The minor *children* mentioned (presumably of Abel, 2d,) were William Moses, 9 years; Ambrose Moses, 5 years; George Moses, 12 years; Abel Moses, 7 years.

35 ASHBEL[6] MOSES, son of ABEL (14), of Hartland, Conn. He was a soldier of Col. Belden's Reg., and was engaged Mar. 26, 1777; was a pensioner at age of 79, in 1840, and his wife Esther was a pensioner same year, age 76. Married Esther ———; she d. (tomb New Hartford) Oct. 27, 1841, aged 78. From information derived from Marcus Moses and Mrs. Case, he had

CHILDREN: Ashbel, Jr., Barnabas, Nathan, Esther (Parry), Betsey, Clara, Julia, Savilla.
Ashbel, Jr., had a son Richard.
Barnabas, m. an Humphrey in Simsbury; he died in Providence, R. I. Was in Hezekiah Webster's command, war of 1812; had a son (Bark. Rec.) named Senator.

36 MARTIN[6] MOSES, son of ABEL (14), died at Barkhamsted, Conn., Sept. 21, 1849, aged 88 years and 5 months; m. Lydia ———; was a soldier, enlisted in 1777, and a pensioner of 1840.

CHILDREN: Martin, Jr., b. 1787, d. May 8, 1860; Elias, b. 1789, d. 1841; Asa, b. April 25, 1791, d. 1853; Erastus, b. August 11, 1793, d. aged 26; Anna, b. 1795, d. 1869; Miriam, b. June 3, 1798, d. Nov. 2, 1864; Lydia, b. Oct. 3, 1800, d. Aug. 5, 1854; Mercy, b. Sept. 27, 1802, d. ———; Rufus J., b. Sept. 20, 1807, d. Oct. 8, 1837; Marcus, b. April 25, 1805; Maritta, b. Dec. 26, 1809.

Martin, Jr., was in Phelps' Co., war of 1812; m. Hannah Rose, Granville, Mass. *Children* (according to Marcus) were Lucy, William; Oscar, who went to the war and d. after his return; Levi, Harriet, Orpha, and Mary, all born in Canton. Oscar, m. Jan. 2, 1858, Amelia Moses of Torrington; William's children were Frederick, Delia, Jennie.

Elias, m. Candace Humphrey of Canton; had child Elizabeth.

Asa, m. Almira Barber of Canton (see also H. W. Sims.); about 1840 went to Rootstown, O.; had children, Lorenzo, Loren, Edwin, Harvey, Henry, Hiram, Jane.

Anna, m. Ira Shepard of Farmington.

Miriam, m. Zera Hinman of Canton.

Lydia, m. Eli Case of Canton.

Mercy, m. Warner W. Hinman of Canton.

Rufus J., m. Eliza Ann Hinman of Canton. He lived at Collinsville, and had dau. Ellen, who d. Mar. 13, 1839.

Maritta, m. May 14, 1853, Wayne Case, and lives at Barkhamsted, Conn. He d. Oct. 1869, æ. 53.

37 MARCUS[7] MOSES, son of MARTIN, JR. (36), living (1889) at Barkhamsted, Conn., m. Fanny Case, Oct. 14, 1811.

CHILDREN: George, b. Jan. 31, 1837, d. April 28, 1853; Lucelia, b. Jan. 12, 1839, m. Albert Perry, has *children:* Wilbur Perry, b. Nov. 8, 1867; Anna L., b. Jan. 15, 1876.

38 ERASTUS[7] MOSES, son of MARTIN, JR. (36), was a cooper and d. at St. Jago de Cuba, in one of the West India Islands, aged 26. He m. Almira Grimes, and left *children:* Julia Ann, b. June 2, 1816; she m. Eli Case; Minerva, b. July 22, 1818; she m. John Murphy.

Hartford County carried on extensive dealings with the West Indies, "1750 to 1830," and, (Hart. Co. Mem. Hist.) "often youthful scions of old Hartford families . . . . succumbed to the yellow fever in Jamaica, Demerara, and other places in those southern seas."

39 DANIEL[6] MOSES, 2d, son of DANIEL (13), was a soldier with title of Lieutenant (see p. 130, Brown's W. Sims.); m. (H. W. Sims.) Anna Edgerton. His tombstone is in North Canton. From Sims. Prob. Rec., April 5, 1811, it appears that his estate was distributed to his widow Anna, and to children Daniel, Festus, Norman, Anna, and Auria Goddard.

CHILDREN: Daniel, 3d, b. April 17, 1791, d. Dec. 7, 1836; Festus; Auria; Norman, b. 1797, d. Feb. 10, 1861; Anna, d. Mar. 21, 1876, aged 83 (tombstone North Canton).

Auria, m. Grove Goddard. *Children:* Milton, Clymena, Sophrona, Jerome.

Anna, m. Jerome Case. *Children:* Corydon, Lucy, Ann Maria, Austria.

40 DANIEL[7] MOSES, 3d, son of DANIEL (39) (tombstone Old Simsbury).

CHILDREN: Daniel, 4th, b. June 25, 1811, d. Nov. 23, 1877; Miles, b. June 12, 1813, d. Aug. 19, 1864; Lydia, b. June 28, 1815, d. May 16, 1878; Marcus, b. Nov. 23, 1818; Uriah, b. Dec. 5, 1821, d. ——; Betsey, b. July 23, 1826; Celia A., b. May 1, 1832.

Lydia, m. David R. Shepard. *Children:* Miles D., Josephine S., Alfred M., Albert R., Amelia.

Celia A., m. Ebenezer A. Stoddard. *Children:* Lola H., b. 1862; Geo. A., b. 1866; Fred W., b. 1868; Lizzie C., b. 1869; Frank C., b. 1871.

41 DANIEL[8] MOSES, 4th, son of DANIEL (40), m. Elizabeth Hodge.

CHILDREN: Lucy, Randolph, Noel H.

42 MARCUS[8] MOSES, son of DANIEL (40), m. Jane Curtis.

CHILDREN: Uriah, Cora J., Burt R.

43 BETSEY[8] MOSES, daughter of DANIEL (40), m. N. W. Holcombe, M.D., of West Simsbury, Conn. He is a practicing physician, and is surgeon of the celebrated Putnam Phalanx. He has been elected by his fellow-citizens to the State Senate and to many other offices of trust and honor. They have no children.

44 FESTUS[7] MOSES, son of DANIEL (39), m. Amanda Miller.

CHILDREN: Lucius F., Solomon, Auria, Elbert S., Ellen R., Edwin B., Emily R.

45 NORMAN[7] MOSES, son of DANIEL (39), m. Ruby Hoskins. His tombstone is in North Canton.

CHILDREN: Monroe M., Jeanette.

46 ZEBINA[6] MOSES, son of DANIEL (13), lived in Simsbury, Conn.; m. (H. W. Sims.) Jan. 8, 1786, Theodosia, daughter of Eliphalet Curtis, who represented Simsbury in the General Assembly of 1780. She died at Marcellus, N. Y., Aug. 29, 1850. She was a woman of wonderful energy and ability. Brown, in his History, states that "the families that bore the name of Curtis were among the most prominent in West Simsbury the latter part of the last century." In Sims. Prob. Rec. we find that Zebina Moses, on April 18, 1817, willed property to sons Zebina, Linus, Curtis, Chester, Horace, Myron, and to daughters- Theodosia (St. John), Charlotte, Pluma, and Elvira.

CHILDREN: Zebina, 2d, b. Oct. 31, 1786, d. Dec. 30, 1843; Linus, b. Feb. 13, 1789, d. Mar. 24, 1834; Pliny, b. April 23, 1791, d.

Feb. 19, 1792; Curtis, b. Dec. 27, 1792, d. April 21, 1862; Theodosia, b. July 14, 1795, d. Sept. 27, 1863; Charlotte, b. July 19, 1797, d. July 8, 1844; Chester, b. Sept. 16, 1800, d. May 13, 1870; Horace, b. July 3, 1803, d. Jan. 3, 1840; Myron, b. May 11, 1805, d. ——; Pluma, b. Nov. 8, 1807, d. June 7, 1851; Elvira, b. Oct. 18, 1810, d. Nov. 27, 1883.

Theodosia, m. June 15, 1814, Elijah St. John of Simsbury. *Children:* Caroline (Ely), b. June 21, 1814, d. Feb. 25, 1859; Curtis, b. Mar. 1, 1820, d. Aug. 10, 1822; Moses E., b. May 7, 1823, d. Nov. 8, 1869; Nehemiah C., b. Feb. 9, 1830, d. Feb. 16, 1831.

Horace, m. Nov. 5, 1826, Juliette White, of Marcellus, N. Y. She d. Aug. 21, 1852. They had one son, Horace Myron Moses, b. in 1831, d. Mar. 2, 1859; monument in Marcellus, N. Y.

Elvira, m. (1st) Jan. 1, 1833, Ichabod Lawrence, of Marcellus, N. Y. He d. May 12, 1839. She m. (2d) Nathan H. Raymond, of Cambridge City, Ind. *Children:* Joab Lawrence, b. 1835, d. Jan. 28, 1889. He made a great fortune in Utah. Theodosia, b. May 13, 1837, m. John Lackey, d. at Cambridge City, Ind., Mar. 21, 1859.

Myron, m. Ann Jacobs of Canada, and resided at or near Newcastle, Canada. *Children:* Ann Eliza, Horace, George, Juliette, perhaps others. Little is known of the family. Horace Moses, when last heard from, lived near Pleasant Hill, Mo.

47 ZEBINA[7] MOSES, 2d, son of ZEBINA (46), removed from Simsbury, Conn., to Marcellus, N. Y., about 1816. He had been a blacksmith, and in company with his uncle Israel Curtis started a shop a few rods west of the mill in the village of Marcellus. Their principal work was the forging of plow irons. About 1824 he bought out the Holcombe farm. In 1837 he owned about 450 acres of farming lands. His house was the home for brothers, sisters, and several relatives, as they came from Connecticut, and until they had time to locate in homes of their own. His widowed mother lived with him for several years. He was six feet in height, weighed 210 lbs., was noted for his strength, was blue-eyed and of florid complexion. He was a generous liver, had arrangements for table supplies of shell-fish from old Connecticut, and was widely known for his readiness to purchase choice game, fish, or early vegetables. His farming operations required the employment of many men. Cider was the common drink of the time, and of that beverage fifty barrels were sometimes consumed in a single year at his long and hospitable table. On Sundays he dressed in the fashion of his day, in blue coat with brass buttons, and drove with his family in a handsome carriage to the Episcopal Church, of which he was a church warden. He was also a Freemason. Space has been given to this personal description because the subject of the sketch was of the old school, and undoubtedly a type of some of his ancestors. They, according to tradition and family papers, belonged to that class of New Englanders who, if blessed with prosperity, were not averse to the enjoyment of the good things of this life. He m. Nov. 1808, Jane Grimes. She was b. Mar. 22, 1791, and d. Nov. 13, 1865 ; she was the daughter of Capt. Moses Grimes, of Simsbury ; her mother was a Judson and her grandmother a Clark.

CHILDREN : Cynthia, b. Mar. 11, 1810, d. Apr. 22, 1811 (tombstone Simsbury) ; Gad, b. in Simsbury May 3, 1812, d. Mar. 9, 1890; Guy, b. in Simsbury Nov. 18, 1813 ; Job, b. in Simsbury Aug. 30, 1815, d. July 26, 1887 (tombstone Marcellus); Dan, b. in Marcellus Mar. 17, 1819, d. Aug. 27, 1889, buried at Marcellus; Amoret, b. Sept. 22, 1825 ; Rebecca Jane, b. July 23, 1828 ; Pluma Elvira, b. Dec. 2, 1830.

48 GAD[8] MOSES, son of ZEBINA (47), lived in Greenwood, Ill. ; m. (1st) Nov. 26, 1836, Delana Hovey ; she d. May 5, 1843 ; m. (2d) May 14, 1844, Catherine Fury.

CHILDREN : Mary A., b. in Marcellus Sept. 26, 1837 ; Grove, d. in infancy ; Delanie, b. in Greenwood, Ill., May 15, 1845 ; Grove 2d, b. June 21, 1847, d. Oct. 24, 1869 ; William H., b. Jan. 1, 1851 ; Frances, b. Dec. 25, 1853, d. Mar. 5, 1855 ; Jennie Belle, b. May 25, 1857, d. 1890.

Jennie Belle, m. June 12, 1883, Harry H. Chittenden.

49 MARY A.[9] MOSES, dau. of GAD (48), m. Aug. 29, 1854, at Marengo, Ill., Willard D. Paine.

CHILDREN : Ida May, b. Nov. 3, 1855; d. May 26, 1859 ; Charles W., b. May 6, 1860 ; Nellie, b. Mar. 3, 1868, d. June 9, 1868.

Charles W., m. Jennie E. Taylor. *Children:* Albert C., Delmer, Carribel, Mary Ethel.

50 DELANIE[9] MOSES, dau. of GAD (48), m. Feb. 26, 1863, Charles H. Rathbun, of Buffalo, N. Y., where she now resides. He d. July 28, 1879.

51 WILLIAM H.[9] MOSES, son of GAD (48), m. July 5, 1887, Maude Mason.

52 GUY[8] MOSES, son of ZEBINA, 2d (47), removed in 1868 from Marcellus, N. Y., to Washington, D. C. ; m. March 30, 1837, Lucina C. Bingham. She was b. Sept. 29, 1815, and was a daughter of Calvin and Betsey Scott Bingham. The Binghams and Scotts were old and notable families of Bennington, Vt.

CHILDREN: all born in Marcellus, N. Y.; Zebina, 3d, b. April 8, 1838; Margaret Isadore, b. July 3, 1839, d. Oct. 28, 1842; Robert Henry, b. Jan. 13, 1844; Louis Bingham, b. Jan. 16, 1846, d. at Washington, April 12, 1867; John Bingham, b. May 2, 1856.

53 ZEBINA[9] MOSES (third of the name, and compiler of this book) is the son of GUY (52). At the age of sixteen he removed from Marcellus to Michigan. Since 1861 he has been a Government officer at Washington; in the Interior Department; Cashier of the House of Representatives; Secretary to the Vice-President during most of General Grant's second term; Enrolling Clerk of the Senate; and Asst. Supt. of Railway Mail Service.

54 ROBERT H.[9] MOSES, son of GUY (52). Soldier 122d N. Y. Vols. Aug. 28, 1862, to June 23, 1865. 1st Lieut. July 9, 1864; Adjt. Nov. 23, 1864; Brevet Captain April 15, 1865, to rank from Oct. 19, 1864, "for meritorious conduct at the battles of Winchester, Fisher's Hill, and Cedar Creek, Va." At the close of the war he engaged in business at Syracuse, N. Y., and is now a manufacturer and merchant in New York, to which city he removed in 1867.

55 JOHN B.[9] MOSES, son of GUY (52), resides at Washington, D. C.; m. Dec. 18, 1885, Muriel Elizabeth Thornton.

56 JOB[8] MOSES, son of ZEBINA (47), m. (1st) Oct. 13, 1841, Frances Ann Greenman; she d. Dec. 12, 1864; and m. (2d) April 24, 1867, Lena Drake.

CHILDREN: Oscar Greenman, b. May 5, 1843; Francis Samuel, b. July 4, 1861; Sanford Byron, b. Mar. 13, 1863.

Sanford B., m. Aug. 4, 1885, Annie L. Bakes.

57 OSCAR G.[9] MOSES, son of JOB (56), resides in New York city; m. Jan. 10, 1864, Mary Sallie Lea.

CHILDREN: Oscar[10] Lea, b. Dec. 16, 1864; Frances Laura, b. Mar. 20, 1866, d. Sept. 3, 1866.

58 FRANCIS S.[9] MOSES, son of JOB (56), m. Aug. 15, 1883, Belle Saunders.

CHILDREN: Lena, b. Nov. 4, 1886.

59 DAN[8] MOSES, son of ZEBINA (47), m. July 6, 1846, Venette R. Sperry.

CHILDREN: Willis S., b. 1849; Alice M., b. about 1852.

60 AMORET[8] MOSES, dau. of ZEBINA (47), m. Sept. 22, 1847, John S. Wright. She resides at Palmyra, N. Y.

CHILDREN: Frank Moses, b. June 7, 1850, d. May 11, 1887; Mary, b. Nov. 9, 1852; John Herbert, b. Mar. 23, 1855; Arthur Zebina, b. April 12, 1860.

Frank M., m. Mary M. Conway. *Children:* Mary Amoret, b. 1880, d. 1880; John Herbert, b. 1884, d. 1885; Infant.

Mary, m. Geo. P. Stuppleben, Nov. 18, 1874.

J. Herbert, m. Matty W. Hersee, Oct. 6, 1881.

Arthur Zebina, m. Stella E. Moore, Nov. 2, 1887.

61 JANE R.[8] MOSES, dau. of ZEBINA (47), m. Mar. 21, 1855, William A. Chapman. She resides in Palmyra, N. Y.

CHILDREN: Ann Holiday, b. Dec. 22, 1855; Mary Jane, b. Dec. 6, 1857; Albert William, b. July 23, 1861; Ella Clara, b. Dec. 25, 1864, d. Dec. 26, 1886; Frances Susan, b. Feb. 28, 1868.

62 PLUMA ELVIRA[8] MOSES, m. George W. Newell, July 6, 1853. She resides at Corfu, N. Y.

CHILDREN: George Moses, b. April 3, 1854, d. Feb. 20, 1881; Jenny, b. July 9, 1857; Louis Seymour, b. July 13, 1867.

63 LINUS[7] MOSES, son of ZEBINA (46), m. Emily Grimes (tombstone Old Simsbury).

CHILDREN: Pliny, b. Aug. 3, 1810; d. Jan. 28, 1888; Emmeline, b. Dec. 1, 1812, d. Oct. 1, 1834 (tombstone Simsbury); Albert, b. Nov. 19, 1814, d. April 24, 1886; Jane, b. Mar. 17, 1817, d. Aug. 28, 1883; Flora, b. June 24, 1819; Paulina, b. April 5, 1824; John, b. July 22, 1826.

Jane, m. April 11, 1839, Charles Weller. *Children:* Sarah Jane, (Allen), b. Jan. 8, 1842; Flora Ann (Cropley), b. Nov. 15, 1843; Alpheus, b. Nov. 7, 1845, d. Aug. 13, 1847; Frank, b. Jan. 29, 1851; Jessie F., b. Jan. 1, 1857, d. Jan. 28, 1863.

Paulina, m. (1st) Nov. 25, 1843, Rollin P. Case; m. (2d) Feb. 6, 1849, Elijah Case. *Children:* Henry E., b. Feb. 14, 1850, d. April 16, 1890; Arthur E., b. Sept. 19, 1853, d. Dec. 27, 1858; Flora I., b. April 9, 1857; Albert, b. Mar. 4, 1862, d. Jan. 12, 1864.

64 PLINY[8] MOSES, son of LINUS (63), m. April 24, 1834, Rachel L. Holcomb of Granby, Conn.

CHILDREN: Linus A., b. April 27, 1835, d. Feb. 6, 1879; Dighton, b. Oct. 3, 1841.

65 LINUS A.[9] MOSES, son of PLINY (64), m. April 23, 1859, Mary Bowen. Soldier 10th Conn. Inf., War of Rebellion, from Aug. 23, 1862, to June 15, 1865.

CHILDREN: Lena M., b. April 16, 1862, d. Oct. 15, 1864; Mary L., b. Sept. 24, 1866; Horace Chester, b. Oct. 2, 1871.

66 DIGHTON[9] MOSES, son of PLINY (64), is a Congregational minister at Reynolds Bridge, Conn.; m. Mary Gates of Simsbury, Nov. 27, 1862.

CHILDREN: George Linus, b. April 9, 1866; Sadie Emmeline, b. Nov. 24, 1867, d. April 14, 1890; Hattie Alice, b. Jan. 9, 1871.
Sadie E., m. Nov. 29, 1887, S. A. Walker of Norwich, Conn.
George L., m. Oct. 9, 1889, Mary E. Backus.
Hattie A., m. May 1, 1890, Eugene Benson.

67 ALBERT[8] MOSES, son of LINUS (63), m. Oct. 4, 1840, Mary T. ——.

CHILDREN: Emmeline G., b. Dec. 9, 1845; Alfred E., b. Feb. 22, 1848.
Emmeline G., m. Mar. 10, 1861, Orra Carpenter of Wisconsin. Her children: Lena M., b. Feb. 6, 1865, d. April 13, 1865; Eva E., b. May 20, 1866; Etta A., b. Mar. 17, 1871; Winnifred M., b. Mar. 25, 1876; Alice M., b. Oct. 19, 1877; Dora I., b. Aug. 21, 1882.

68 ALFRED E.[9] MOSES, son of ALBERT (67), m. 1875, Mary Mitchell.

CHILDREN: Loly G., b. Oct. 25, 1876; Bertie, b. Nov. 5, 1879, d. July 4, 1881; Frederic, b. Aug. 21, 1882; Hattie, b. Aug. 23, 1884.

69 FLORA[8] MOSES, dau. of LINUS (63), m. Jan. 22, 1846, John W. Alderman of Simsbury.

CHILDREN: Mary Paulina, b. Jan. 6, 1847, d. Feb. 21, 1853; Flora Theodosia, b. April 27, 1849, d. May 26, 1861; John Franklin, b. Sept. 16, 1854.
John F., m. Feb. 24, 1878, Ida E. Allen of Richmond, Ill. *Children:* Jessie Ida, b. Sept. 22, 1880; Hazel, b. Feb. 5, 1884, d. May 7, 1888.

70 JOHN[8] MOSES, son of LINUS (63), m. (1st) April, 1858, Elizabeth Eno of Vernon, Wis.; she d. April, 1864; m. (2d) May, 1865, Mrs. Cynthia Neuman; she d. Oct. 1878; m. (3d) Nov. 15, 1883, Mrs. Mary Griswold of Spencer, Iowa.

CHILDREN: Frederic E., b. Mar. 15, 1859; Emily, b. June 9, 1863; Edwin D., b. July 21, 1866; Flora B., b. Aug. 28, 1870; Oscar, b. Oct. 15, 1873.
Edwin D., m. June 9, 1889, in Milford, Iowa.
Flora B., m. Nov. 14, 1887, Onus H. Dixon of Spirit Lake, Iowa.

71 FREDERIC E.[9] MOSES, son of JOHN (70), m. Mar. 12, 1884, Sylvia Krom.

CHILDREN: Frank P., b. April 12, 1885, d. July 2, 1887; Una I., b. May 28, 1886; Charles R.[10], b. June 24, 1889.

72 CURTIS[7] MOSES, son of ZEBINA (46), was a merchant in Marcellus, N. Y., and was later in life Secretary and Treasurer of the Gas Company at Syracuse, N. Y., in which city he resided for several years previous to his death. He m. July 9, 1817, Elizabeth Talmadge, dau. of Jos. Talmadge. She d. April 3, 1877.

CHILDREN: Charlotte, b. Nov. 20, 1818; Benjamin Franklin, b. Dec. 22, 1819, d. Aug. 1, 1875; Lucian, b. May 29, 1822; Girard, b. Jan. 23, 1832, d. Apr. 13, 1874; Irving, b. April 5, 1836.

73 CHARLOTTE[8] MOSES, dau. of CURTIS (72), m. June 17, 1846, James W. Herring, who was b. in Vermont Jan. 27, 1811. They have no children. They reside in Syracuse, N. Y.

74 BENJAMIN FRANKLIN[8] MOSES, son of CURTIS (72), was a merchant; m. (1st) June 20, 1845, Elizabeth Platt; she d. Sept. 3, 1847, leaving no children; m. (2d) Sept. 6, 1849, Harriet Webber of Vernon, N. Y.

CHILDREN: Fanny A., b. Oct. 20, 1856; Charles W., b. Nov. 16, 1858.

Charles W. resides at Detroit, Mich. His mother and sister also reside in that city.

75 LUCIAN[8] MOSES, son of CURTIS (72), has been a merchant and contractor; is now living (1889) retired, at Skaneateles, N. Y.; m. June 18, 1863, Mary E. Pardee of Skaneateles, N. Y., daughter of Ebenezer and Almira Pardee of Wooster, Ohio.

76 GIRARD[8] MOSES, son of CURTIS (72), m. Nov. 22, 1854, Ann Snedicor of Long Island.

CHILDREN: Charlotte E., b. Aug. 3, 1855; d. 1857; Edward Curtis, b. Feb. 3, 1859; he m. April 17, 1880, Louisa Henze. He is living in New York city, and his *children* are Charlotte, b. Feb. 26, 1881; Annie, b. Feb. 25, 1883; Louisa, b. July 1, 1888.

77 IRVING[8] MOSES, son of CURTIS (72), is a merchant at Rochester, N. Y.; m. (1st) June 17, 1857, Jennie L. Fenn of Syracuse, N. Y. She d. at Marcellus, N. Y., Sept. 5, 1867; m. (2d) June 10, 1869, Abbie Burch of Syracuse, N. Y.

CHILDREN: by first marriage, Howard Fenn, b. Dec. 6, 1859, d. May 18, 1877; Ernest Clarence, b. July 7, 1862.

78 ERNEST C.[9] MOSES, son of Irving (77), resides at Syracuse, N. Y.; m. Sept. 4, 1888, Catherine Comstock Ramsdell of Fairport, N. Y.

CHILDREN: Kenneth Ramsdell Moses,[10] b. June 7, 1889.

79 CHARLOTTE[7] MOSES, daughter of ZEBINA (46), m. (Sims. Rec.) Jan. 28, 1822, Chester Moses of Canton, Conn., son of Darius Moses. He m. Louisa B. Hill of Hartford on Dec. 13, 1847. They resided at Skaneateles, N. Y.

CHILDREN: Franklin C., b. at Canton, Dec. 19, 1826, d. Feb. 27, 1856; Helen Charlotte, b. at Canton, Sept. 14, 1824, d. in Cortland, N. Y., Aug. 7, 1886.

Franklin C., m. (1st) Susan Spencer, Sept. 1, 1852; she d. Jan. 26, 1853; m. (2d) Josephine Peck, of Skaneateles, Nov. 1, 1854.

Helen Charlotte, m. May 27, 1852, Rev. Ephraim Hoag, who d. Oct. 3, 1869. *Children:* Charlotte Josephine, b. at Norwich, N. Y., Sept. 26, 1856; Franklin C., b. Dec. 29, 1860, d. Oct. 5, 1862; Clara Helen, b. in Cortland, N. Y., July 24, 1863; she m. Feb. 15, 1888, David D. Sutphen.

80 CHESTER[7] MOSES, son of ZEBINA (46), resided at Marcellus, N. Y., and at one time owned several woolen factories; m. (Sims. Rec.) June 18, 1823, Salome Case; she d. April 11, 1865.

CHILDREN: (Sims. Rec.) Julia Ann, b. April 30, 1825, d. Oct. 11, 1826 (tombstone Old Simsbury); Curtis Hallock, b. (Sims. Rec.) July 12, 1826 (family record June 12, 1826); Henry L., b. July 21, 1827, d. Jan. 26, 1851; Lucius, b. Dec. 8, 1831; Julia Henrietta, b. Aug. 30, 1836, d. Mar. 10, 1868.

81 CURTIS H.[8] MOSES, son of CHESTER (80), m. Oct. 9, 1849, Amanda J. Cook; resides at Memphis, N. Y.

CHILDREN: Frankie, b. Nov. 27, 1857; Mortimer M., b. May 11, 1860.

Mortimer M. is married, and lives in Syracuse, N. Y.

82 LUCIUS[8] MOSES, son of CHESTER (80), was a soldier, Captain in the 122d N. Y. Vols.; is a manufacturer, and resides at Syracuse, N. Y.; m. June 20, 1866, Emma Richardson of Auburn, N. Y.

CHILDREN: Lucius Lawrence Moses, b. Nov. 26, 1868.

83 JULIA HENRIETTA[8] MOSES, daughter of CHESTER (80), m. July 14, 1852, Judson L. Thompson.

CHILDREN: Chester M., b. Jan. 17, 1867; Helen, b. Mar. 3, 1868, d. July 17, 1868.

Chester M. married, and resides at Syracuse, N. Y.

84 PLUMA[7] MOSES, daughter of ZEBINA MOSES (46), m. (Sims. Rec.) Nov. 9, 1830, Sanford Dalliba, "both of Simsbury." He was for many years a merchant in Marcellus, N. Y., and d. at Farmington, Ill., July 26, 1888.

CHILDREN: Maria (deceased); Ellen, b. Oct. 11, 1835, d. April 23, 1844; Henry (deceased); John, d. 1889; Charlotte E., b.——; Elmer, d. 1881.
Maria, m. Joseph Platt, of Marcellus, N. Y.
Charlotte E., m. J. B. Lamkin, of Chicago, Ill.

85 MICHAEL^6 MOSES, son of MICHAEL (16). As the oldest son of Michael, the son of Caleb, he inherited the original Mount Philip homestead; m. Dec. 25, 1797, Anna M. Crane, who was b. Mar. 28, 1781, d. May 21, 1858. Following is the record from family Bible:

CHILDREN: Polly, b. Feb. 28, 1799, d. Aug. 5, 1838; Ashbel, b. April 16, 1800, d. (tombstone) Jan. 7, 1849; Norman, b. Nov. 25, 1801, d. Feb. 8, 1803; Lydia, b. May 31, 1803, d. July 14, 1858; Nathan, b. Jan. 10, 1805, d. Dec. 2, 1873 (tombstone, Old Sims.); Fanny, b. June 15, 1807, d. Sept. 27, 1816; Norman Watson, b. April 27, 1809, d. April 2, 1867; Newton, b. Mar. 10, 1811, d. Sept. 7, 1871; Anna Oleva, b. Dec. 22, 1813, d. Mar. 26, 1882; Michael Ambrose, b. April 7, 1816, d. Sept. 26, 1865.

Polly, m. Zenas Brace, of West Hartford. *Children:* Everett, Fanny, Albert.

Ashbel, m. Corrinna Case, of Simsbury. *Children:* Waldron and Seth. None living 1889.

Lydia, m. Oct. 15, 1823, George H. Brockett of Canton; one son, Evelyn. None living 1889.

Norman Watson, m. (Windsor Rec.) Nov. 23, 1831, Huldah Caldwell, of Windsor. *Children:* Henry, Helen, Charles, and William. None living 1889.

Newton, Was an architect; built the Fourth Church, Hartford; m. Althea Riggs of Washington, Conn. Had one child. None living 1889.

Anna Oleva d. unmarried.

86 NATHAN^7 MOSES, son of MICHAEL (85), was the last survivor of the children of Michael. He and his brother Ashbel were the only sons that remained in their native town. His widowed mother survived her husband forty-two years, and after the death of her eldest son handed down to Nathan a number of old deeds and family papers and the family Bible, dated 1752, which belonged to the first Caleb Moses, and which had passed through the families of the eldest son of each succeeding generation. As Nathan left no son, they were held by his eldest daughter. Nathan m. Nov. 18, 1828, Martha Latimer. She was b. Aug. 6, 1803; d. Aug. 19, 1880.

CHILDREN: Hannah Maria, b. April 10, 1829; Harriet, b.

Dec. 14, 1830, d. Oct. 9, 1832; Harriet Elizabeth, b. Sept. 14, 1833, d. Feb. 3, 1884; Nathan Lucius, b. Nov. 1, 1835, d. Nov. 30, 1853.

Harriet Elizabeth, m. May 1, 1856, Leveret Franklin Webster of Avon, Conn. *Children:* Louis, b. Aug. 3, 1858; Helen, b. Sept. 15, 1860; Anna, b. Apr. 27, 1865; Ada, b. March 20, 1870.

87 HANNAH MARIA[8] MOSES, daughter of NATHAN MOSES (86), is the last descendant now residing in Simsbury of that branch of the Moses family that inherited the old Mount Philip homestead. She m. March 4, 1849, John Bowen Johns of Delaware, O. He d. Jan. 18, 1850.

88 MICHAEL AMBROSE[7] MOSES, son of MICHAEL (85), m. Mary Allen Munsell of Windsor.

CHILDREN: b. in Hartford, Geo. N. Moses, b. Oct. 12, 1837; Lewis Edward, b. Feb. 6, 1840, d. June 9, 1842; Albert Alonzo, b. Jan. 27, 1846.

Albert A., m. June 20, 1874, Mrs. Julia Sanford (*nee* Sperry); resides at New Haven.

89 GEORGE N.[8] MOSES, son of MICHAEL AMBROSE (88), was soldier in War of Rebellion, Sergeant 24th Conn. Vols.; now resides at New Haven, Conn.; m. (1st) Oct. 18, 1858, Jane E. Bacon; she d. Oct. 4, 1873; m. (2d) June 10, 1875, Mrs. Emma L. Russell (*nee* Wagner).

CHILDREN: Alice E., b. July 23, 1860, d. May 12, 1861; Mary E., b. July 18, 1862 (m. Luther D. Porter of Hartford, Oct. 17, 1883); Charles R., b. April 7, 1877, d. July 13, 1877; Wallace B., b. April 7, 1877, d. July 20, 1877.

90 LUTHER[6] MOSES, son of MICHAEL (16), m. Huldah Goodrich, May 2, 1809.

CHILDREN: Stephen G., b. April 27, 1818; Luther M., b. March 27, 1816, d. May 27, 1880; Alfred, b. May 4, 1820; Selina, b. Feb. 19, 1810; Celestia, b. Nov. 10, 1811, d. April 2, 1887; Morgan, b. Sept. 19, 1813, d. April 30, 1815.

Stephen G.[7], now (1889) living at Hartford, Conn., m. Nov. 27, 1843, Mary H. Atkins. *Children:* Stephen G., b. Feb. 21, 1847, d. Feb. 19, 1853; Mary C., b. Jan. 27, 1851, d. Feb. 25, 1877; Lilly H., b. April 24, 1852; Charles G., b. April 4, 1855. The youngest daughter, Lilly H., m. Oct. 20, 1885, Rev. D. W. Clark; the youngest son lives at Hartford.

Celestia[7], m. (Sims. Rec.) Nov. 25, 1831, Abiel Homer Pease. Has *children:* Moses H., b. Feb. 22, 1835; Sarah H., b. Sept. 30, 1836, d. Aug. 7, 1837; Francis M., b. May 22, 1839.

Selina[7], m. Mar. 25, 1834, Merrick Richardson. She resides at Hartford.

Luther M.[7], m. Nov., 1843, Mary P. Lampson. *Children:* Sarah H., b. Aug. 19, 1844, d. May 7, 1890; Luther M., b. ——— ; Sarah H. m. Sept. 20, 1869, Edwin J. Smith. *Children:* Gertrude C., Henry C., Edwin J., George A., and Martin T. Luther M., Jr., m. Jan. 17, 1877, Minnie C. Smith. *Children:* Maud S., b. July 6, 1878.

Alfred[7] resides at Hartford; unmarried.

91 DARIUS[7] MOSES, son of AARON (24), resided in the North District, Canton; was a soldier in 1777 in Col. Hooker's regiment; was known by the title of Captain; was a Representative in General Assembly in 1814; (see Hist. of W. Sims. for following record): m. Sarah Adams, dau. of Lieut. David Adams; she d. 1834.

CHILDREN: Sarah, b. 1780, d. 1854; Darius, 2d, b. 1782, d. Aug. 21, 1824; Ashbel, b. Jan. 31, 1784, d. Sept. 14, 1867; Roxy, b. 1786, d. 1788; Chauncey, b. 1789, d. April 27, 1851; Flora, b. 1791; Roxy, b. 1796; Chester, b. Mar. 13, 1798, d. July 11, 1862.

Flora, m. Elisha Sugden.
Roxy, m. Bela Squires.
Chauncey (see 138).
Chester, m. Charlotte Moses, dau. of Zebina (see 79).

92 DARIUS[8] MOSES, son of DARIUS (91), Representative in General Assembly, 1818, (tombstone Canton,) m. Sodema Holcomb, dau. of Jesse Holcomb.

CHILDREN: Elizur, Richard, James F., Abigail, Mary.

Elizur, m. (St. Andrews Church), Dec. 31, 1835, Rebecca Bates.

93 ASHBEL[8] MOSES, son of DARIUS (91), removed to Skaneateles, N. Y.; m. Candace Dyer, Sept. 2, 1806; she d. Mar. 31, 1877.

CHILDREN: Jane A., b. Nov. 11, 1807, d. May 13, 1837; Daniel D., b. May 2, 1809, d. Sept. 20, 1862; Cordelia, b. Oct. 14, 1810; Solon, b. Mar. 25, 1817, d. Mar. 20, 1818; Solomon, b. March 25, 1819, d. March 28, 1858; Henry, b. Aug. 12, 1823, d. June 12, 1882.

94 DANIEL D.[9] MOSES, son of ASHBEL (93), m. March 22, 1834, Lucia A. Grover.

CHILDREN: Jane (Parsons), b. Nov. 22, 1835; Lucia M., b. Aug. 22, 1839, d. June 2, 1873, m. Shelden Merrill.

95 CORDELIA[9] MOSES, dau. of ASHBEL (93), m. Nathaniel Miller, Oct. 14, 1868.

96 SOLOMON[9] MOSES, son of ASHBEL (93), m. Fidelia S. Pettibone.

CHILDREN: Isabel E., b. Aug. 10, 1853, d. Oct. 5, 1860.

97 HENRY[9] MOSES, son of ASHBEL (93), m. Nov. 26, 1850, Lucina W. Rudd.

CHILDREN: James Ashbel, b. July 30, 1854, d. Oct. 11, 1859; Franklin H., b. June 23, 1856; Clara Lucina, b. May 10, 1858, d. Sept. 25, 1886, (m. Frank Powell, Oct. 20, 1880;) Edith M., b. March 9, 1863, (m. Chas. Foote, Jan. 5, 1887.) *Child:* Clara Adele Foote, b. Dec. 9, 1887.

98 FRANKLIN H.[10] MOSES, son of HENRY (97), m. Dec. 17, 1884, Cornelia R. Briggs.

CHILDREN: Harry Briggs[11], b. May 8, 1887; Bessie C.[11], b. March 22, 1889.

99 SEYMOUR AARON[7] MOSES, son of AARON (24), resided at Canton, Conn., m. Rhoda Humphrey.

CHILDREN: Seymour, d. about 1847; Aaron.
Seymour had *children,* Gideon Humphrey, and Seymour.

100 ELISHA[7] MOSES, son of ELISHA (25), removed from Canton to Lenox, N. Y., in 1810, and to Mount Morris, N. Y., in 1818; m. Hannah Merrill.

CHILDREN: Hannah A., b. Aug. 1, 1788, d. April 16, 1866; Elisha D., b. Feb. 12, 1790, d. Oct. 19, 1871; Ormenta, b. March 22, 1791, d. March 1, 1825; Arden, b. Sept. 6, 1792, d. April 12, 1842; Timothy, b. Aug. 9, 1794, d. Sept. 4, 1823; Phoebe, b. Feb. 23, 1796, d. Jan. 18, 1820; Betsey, b. Aug. 6, 1797, d. June 8, 1857; Schuyler, b. Dec. 31, 1798, d. March 13, 1889; Marcus, b. Sept. 30, 1800, d. Dec. 8, 1880; Edmund, b. Nov. 11, 1801, d. Sept. 22, 1864; Aurelia, b. Sept. 23, 1803; Flavia, b. July 25, 1805, d. July 3, 1858.

Elisha Drayton lived in Mount Morris, N. Y. *Children:* Rebecca (Mrs. Jasper), Eliza, and America.

Arden, drowned in Saginaw Bay in 1841; left sons, and daughters, Virginia, and Missouri, in Michigan. One son was killed at Gettysburg.

Timothy died a bachelor in Hindoostan in 1823.

Marcus lived in Lockport. *Children:* William Quimby, b. 1837; Marcus E., b. 1842, d. a soldier in the late war; Alexander S., b. 1845, lives in Lockport; Harriet A., b. 1839; Sarah J. (Hotchkiss).

Edmund, a bachelor, d. in Buffalo, N. Y.

Aurelia lives at old homestead, Mt. Morris, N. Y.

Betsey, m. George Wilner. *Children:* Marcus, Merriman, and two daughters in Michigan.

101 SCHUYLER[8] MOSES, son of ELISHA (100), was one of the pioneers of Rochester, N. Y. Personal items concerning him are given in chapter I of this book. He m. (1st) July 6, 1824,

Elsie Carpenter; she d. July 16, 1836; m. (2d) Mar. 22, 1837, Mrs. Susan Morgan; she d. Nov. 9, 1838; m. (3d) Dec. 4, 1840, Bertha Callender; she d. May 24, 1871.

CHILDREN: William S., b. 1827; Elsie A., b. 1835; Martha A., b. 1848; Fred. A., b. 1856.

Elsie A., m. Sept. 27, 1856, Adolphus A. Hobe; resides at San Francisco, Cal. *Children:* nine in number, all living in 1889 except one son, who d. in 1864.

Martha A., living, in 1889, in the old homestead at Rochester, N. Y.

102 WILLIAM S.^{9} MOSES, son of SCHUYLER (101), lives in San Francisco, Cal.; m. Nov. 12, 1855, Addie Warren.

CHILDREN: Addie, b. Dec. 30, 1856; Elsie, b. June 25, 1860; both d. in infancy.

103 FREDERICK A.^{9} MOSES, son of SCHUYLER (101), resides at Rochester, N. Y.; m. Nov. 26, 1878, Mary Hibbard.

CHILDREN: Frederick C., b. 1882; George H., b. 1884.

104 HANNAH A.^{8} MOSES, dau. of ELISHA (100), m. about 1808, Henry Crane of Litchfield, N. Y.

CHILDREN: S. H.; Judge A. M. Crane of Oakland, Cal.; E. T.; Albert E.; Mrs. I. E. Scaddin; Amelia P.; D. E.; and Charles A.

105 ORMENTA^8 MOSES, dau. of ELISHA (100), m. 1818, Friend Barnard.

CHILDREN: Wellington, and Phœbe.

106 FREDERICK^7 MOSES, son of ELISHA (25), m. (Brown's W. Sims.) Delilah Mills.

CHILDREN: Milo, b. May 12, 1793; Clarissa, b. Sept. 1, 1795; Horatio, b. Sept. 1, 1795, d. Dec. 9, 1876; Lorenzo, b. June 2, 1797; Orestes, b. Sept. 30, 1798; Clarissa Paulina, b. July 7, 1800.

Milo. One tradition is that he was lost at sea, and another that he went to sea in one of Astor's fur vessels, and that the most of the Oregon family of the Moses name are his descendants. Papers in Pension-Office show that Milo Moses, b. in Simsbury, enlisted in 1819, aged 26, as soldier 6th U. S. Inf. Discharged in 1822; wounded by explosion, and pensioned.

Lorenzo, m. Mar. 13, 1824, Elizabeth Brush; was, in 1855, a contractor and builder in New York City.

Orestes, m. July 13, 1822, Emeline L. Griffin.

Clarissa P., m. Feb. 28, 1827, Peter Kemple.

107 HORATIO^8 MOSES, son of FREDERICK (106), m. Nov. 26, 1829, Nancy B. Creamer. Removed to California about 1858, from Paterson, N. J.

CHILDREN: John C., b. Aug. 27, 1830; Emma R., b. April

1, 1832; Julia A., b. Dec. 3, 1838; Horatio, b. Mar. 1835; Frederick, b. Mar. 6, 1839.

108 JOHN C.[9] MOSES, son of HORATIO (107), m. (1st) May 5, 1853, Charlotte G. Wilcoxson; m. (2d) Kate E. Brush.

CHILD (by 1st wife): Lorenzo, b. Aug. 23, 1856.

109 LORENZO[10] MOSES, son of JOHN C. (108), resides at New Haven, Conn.; m. April 12, 1882, Susan O. Bentley, dau. of Thomas Bentley.

CHILDREN: Bessie, b. Feb. 4, 1883, d. Aug. 11, 1883; Edna, b. July 8, 1883, d. Aug. 11, 1883; Carrie W., b. Jan. 1, 1888, at Derby, Conn.

110 EMMA R.[9] MOSES, dau. of HORATIO (107), m. (1st) May 4, 1853, Isaac C. Buckhout; m. (2d) Mr. Broadwell. She resides in New York city.

CHILDREN (by her first marriage): Jennie S., b. Dec. 18, 1854, (m. Charles A. Travis;) Geo. A., b. June 11, 1857; Craig E., b. Nov. 5, 1865.

111 JULIA ANN[9] MOSES, dau. of HORATIO (107), m. April 13, 1857, Watson A. Bray. Resides at Fruitvale, East Oakland, Cal.

CHILDREN: Emma, b. May 19, 1858, (m. Alfred H. Cohen;) John G., b. Mar. 24, 1860, d. Nov. 8, 1860; Mary G., b. Oct. 11, 1861, d. July 13, 1862; Robert A. and Edward M., twins, b. May 27, 1863; Mary and Julia, twins, b. Dec. 8, 1864; Mary d. Sept. 11, 1868; Howard W., b. July 11, 1871.

112 FREDERICK[9] MOSES, son of HORATIO (107), resides in Contra Costa Co., Cal.; m. Oct. 13, 1868, Mollie Reeder.

CHILDREN: Frederick A., b. Sept. 21, 1869; Robert T., b. June 3, 1873; Edward H., b. Sept. 12, 1880.

113 RUFUS[7] MOSES, son of ELNATHAN (28), removed from West Simsbury to West Rutland, to Ticonderoga, to Dayton, N. Y., and about 1847 to French Creek; is buried at Clymer, N. Y.; m. (1st) at West Rutland, Vt., Lydia Ramsdale; she d. Sept. 13, 1828; m. (2d) at Orwell, Vt., Mrs. (Rand) Simmons; she d. at the home of William Moses, Dec. 11, 1879, aged 95.

CHILDREN (by first wife): Hiram, b. Sept. 3, 1798, d. Oct. 27, 1880; Augustus, b. June 18, 1800, d. April 27, 1862; Laura, d. about 1844; Seth, b. 1804, d. Nov., 1878; Elnathan, d. about 1854; Alonzo, b. Dec. 22, 1808, d. April 15, 1857; Eliza; Betsey, d. about 1846, at Orleans Co., N. Y.

PLYMOUTH AND WINDSOR LINE.

Laura, m. Samuel Harwood in Orleans Co., N. Y.; several children.
Elnathan lived in Crawford Co., Pa., and had a large family; one or more of his sons were in the army.
Alonzo had child, Mary Ann Moses, living (1889) at Dayton, N. Y.
Eliza, m. Samuel Harwood in 1845, and lived in Orleans Co., N. Y.

114 HIRAM[8] MOSES, son of RUFUS (113), m. April 9, 1821, Betsey Campbell, dau. of Capt. John Campbell, soldier of the Revolution; she d. March 30, 1877. Removed from Ticonderoga to West Haven, Vt., in 1839; to French Creek, N. Y., 1843; to Wayne, Pa., 1866; and to Clymer, N. Y., 1871; was a deacon in the Congregational Church.

CHILDREN: Emmeline, b. March 28, 1822, d. Sept. 16, 1847; John C., b. Feb. 25, 1824; Amasa Cassius, b. Aug. 22, 1826, d. Feb. 9, 1887; Laura, b. Feb. 21, 1829, d. Sept. 11, 1864; William W., b. Dec. 17, 1831; Chauncey B., b. Sept. 18, 1834; Augustus F., b. May 29, 1838; Hiram E., b. March 25, 1841; Vincent, b. July 1, 1844.

Emmeline, m. March 23, 1842, Horace E. King. *Children:* Charles King, who is married and has children.

Laura, m. May 2, 1849, Lawyer S. Terry.

115 JOHN C.[9] MOSES, son of HIRAM (114), resides at Clinton, Iowa ; m. July 21, 1850, Catherine U. Terry.

CHILDREN: Eaton L., b. June 13, 1851; Mary E., b. Aug. 2, 1853, d. Feb. 22, 1861; Laura L., b. Aug. 10, 1857; Frank S., b. June 13, 1861; John H., b. Aug. 15, 1863.

Frank S., m. Elizabeth ———, June 23, 1886.

116 AMASA CASSIUS[9] MOSES, son of HIRAM (114), m. April 12, 1848, Naomi A. Terry.

CHILDREN: Arthur H., b. Feb. 21, 1851; Lawyer C., b. Jan. 19, 1853; Edward W., b. July 23, 1856; William A., b. Oct. 17, 1858; Lincoln E., b. Oct. 14, 1860; Cassius M. T., b. Jan. 31, 1865; Seward E., b. Dec. 27, 1868.

Edward W., m. Jan. 29, 1882, Annie J. Wood.
William A., m. Dec. 21, 1882, Grace M. Buckland.

117 ARTHUR H.[10] MOSES, son of AMASA C. (116), m. April 20, 1872, Ella Snowden.

CHILDREN: Mary E., b. Feb. 7, 1873; Clyde L.[11], b. March 2, 1878; William B.[11], b. Sept. 15, 1884.

118 LAWYER C.[10] MOSES, son of AMASA C. (116), m. Dec. 24, 1879, Clara J. Mitchell.

CHILDREN: Clara B., b. Nov. 5, 1880, d. Feb. 27, 1881; Earle C.[11], b. June 25, 1882; Lillian A., b. Nov. 25, 1885.

119 WILLIAM W.[9] MOSES, son of HIRAM (114), m. Oct. 19, 1870, Lucinda W. Crosby.

CHILDREN: Laura, b. Aug. 16, 1871; Amasa R., b. Jan. 7, 1873; Clementine, b. Nov. 17, 1880.

120 CHAUNCEY B.[9] MOSES, son of HIRAM (114), m. March 11, 1865, Mary J. Henderson.

CHILDREN: Laura A., b. Feb. 12, 1866; Edith M., b. Oct. 13, 1868; Clifford H., b. April 2, 1872; Dasie M., b. May 27, 1875.

121 AUGUSTUS F.[9] MOSES, son of HIRAM (114), was a soldier, Com. Sergt., 49th N. Y. Reg.; m. Jan. 1, 1868, Eunice C. Newton.

CHILDREN: Edward N., b. Oct. 5, 1870, d. March 2, 1871; Lillie V., b. July 27, 1872, d. Oct. 14, 1875; Josephine A., b. Aug. 28, 1874.

122 VINCENT MOSES, son of HIRAM (114), graduate of Amherst College in 1866 and Hartford Theological Seminary in 1871; engaged in business until 1887, when he was ordained a Congregational minister; resides (1889) at Patten, Me.; m. (1st) Aug. 25, 1874, Evelyn Alice Hazeltine of Medway, Mass.; she d. Aug. 6, 1875; m. (2d), on June 5, 1883; Mrs. Lucusta Jane Thomas, daughter of Dr. Luther Rogers, Patten, Me.

123 AUGUSTUS[8] MOSES, son of RUFUS (113), b. at Pittsford, Vt.; m. Jan. 11, 1826, Calista Harvey.

CHILDREN: Sarah J., b. May 26, 1827, d. Oct. 25, 1845; Caroline H., b. Dec. 24, 1830; Henry H., b. Oct. 9, 1832; Mary E., b. Feb. 13, 1835. Children and grandchildren living at Ticonderoga.

Caroline H., m. 1847 to Mr. Cook.
Mary E., m. Sept. 30, 1866, Martin H. Shattuck.

124 HENRY H.[9] MOSES, son of AUGUSTUS (123), m. April 30, 1857, Emily J. Rising.

CHILDREN: Francis M., b. April 13, 1858; Horace A., b. April 21, 1862; Jennie R., b. Sept. 1, 1864; Harvey H., b. Oct. 29, 1871, d. May 8, 1880.

125 SETH[8] MOSES, son of RUFUS (113), d. in Michigan.

CHILDREN: Martha, living, 1883, at Battle Creek, Mich.; Hiram, living, 1883; Seth, d. 1856, aged 19; Andrew, soldier, d. in the army at Hamburgh Landing, Tenn., 1863, aged 19; George, d. at Lawrence, Mich., 1871, leaving wife and three daughters; Judson J.

126 JUDSON J.[9] MOSES, son of SETH (125), soldier, enlisted Sept. 17, 1861, in 3d Michigan Cavalry.

CHILDREN: Minnie (married); son b. June 23, 1865; Maria, b. July 15, 1871; Mary, b. Feb., 1879.

127 ROGER[6] MOSES, son of DANIEL (13), lived in Barkhamsted. His estate was distributed March 10, 1828, to widow Patience T. and children Salmon, Mark, Matthew, Lois (Hart), Hannah (Andrews), Almira (Paine), Ruth (Pike), Mary (Case). From the town records it appears he m. Feb. 9, 1792, Patience Tatitha Barber, and had:

CHILDREN: Salmon, b. Aug. 10, 1792; Almira, b. Jan. 14, 1795; Mary, b. July 13, 1797; Matthew, b. July 17, 1799, d. Feb. 7, 1861; Ruth, b. Sept. 29, 1801; Hannah, b. March 4, 1804; Lois. b. June 12, 1806; Mark, b. June 18, 1808, d. (tombstone Bark.) July 23, 1848.

Salmon. Marcus Moses, aged 85, informs writer that Salmon went to Ohio, and had daughters Esther and Betsey.

Almira, m. (1st) Cromwell Paine, and (2d) Eben C. Payne (see Pro. Rec.).

Mary, m. Newton Case.

Ruth, m. Hiram Pike.

Hannah, m. Wm. T. Andrews.

Lois, m. Noah Hart.

128 MATTHEW[7] MOSES, son of Roger (127), m. (Bark. Rec.), June 10, 1821, Malista Wilcox.

CHILDREN: Elmer, of New Hartford; Harry E. (from tombstone Barkhamsted) was b. Aug. 5, 1824, d. March 29, 1888; Jane; Lucia.

129 MARK[7] MOSES, son of ROGER (127), (Bark. Pro. Rec.), distribution of his estate, Aug. 4, 1848, to his widow, Eliza, and to his "heirs at law, Ruth Pike, Hannah Andrews, Lois Hart, Mary Case, Matthew Moses, Salmon Moses, and Almira Payne, wife of Eben C. Payne."

130 HARRY E.[8] MOSES, son of MATTHEW (128), m. Caroline ———.

CHILDREN (not all): Clifford S., d. Feb. 23, 1862, aged 4; Homer, d. Sept. 7, 1864, aged 11; according to Marcus Moses, he had *children* named Ernest, Herbert, and Georgiana, who m. Curtis Warner.

131 ELMER F.[8] MOSES, son of MATTHEW (128), m. (Winchester Rec.) Jan. 6, 1850, Louisa McElroy.

132 OTHNIEL[6] MOSES, son of OTHNIEL (21), lived in Bristol and in Burlington, Conn.; m. Mary Dowd; she d. Oct. 8, 1841. Will of Othniel, in Prob. Rec. of Farmington, mentions wife and children by name.

CHILDREN: Chauncey, b. May 29, 1783; Joshua, b. Aug. 20, 1784, d. Nov. 10, 1863; Mary, b. July 20, 1786; Laura, b. June 2, 1788, d. Jan. 13, 1880; Betsey, b. June 20, 1790; Sophia, b. Mar. 13, 1792; Chloe, b. Feb. 17, 1794; Orrin, b. May 12, 1796, d. Nov. 10, 1853; Isaac, b. Dec. 9, 1797; Rhoda, b. June 12, 1800.

Chauncey lived in Farmington; m. (1st) Fannie Hinman; m. (2d) Harriet Williams; no children.

Mary, m. Chauncey Colton, and had *children:* Mary and Sophia.

Laura, m. Samuel Payne of Farmington, and had *children:* Harriet, Jeannette, Sidney, and Fannie.

Betsey, m. Colton Kellogg and removed to Ohio. They had *children:* Sophia, Sidney, Cyrus, and Chloe.

Sophia, m. Isaac Belden of Burlington. *Children:* Emeline, Mary, Washington, Levi, Sophia, Constant, Isaac, Sarah.

Chloe, m. Ambrose Hart of Farmington. *Children:* Betsey, Samuel, and Frederick.

Rhoda, m. Ruel Palmiter of Burlington. *Children:* Edward, Antoinette, Orasmus, Chloe, Diantha, and Riley.

133 JOSHUA[7] MOSES, son of OTHNIEL (131), lived in Burlington; was a soldier of War of 1812, under Captain Daniel Deming; m. June 27, 1811, Chloe Beckwith. She died May 8, 1876.

CHILDREN: Richard, b. July 16, 1812, d. July 28, 1860; Mary, b. Mar. 3, 1824.

134 ORRIN[7] MOSES, son of OTHNIEL (132), lived in Burlington; m. Polly Tuttle.

CHILDREN: John, Salina, Jane, Luther, Chloe, Laura, Julia, Eveline.

John lives at Unionville, Conn.; m. (1st) Armilla Upson; no children; m. (2d) Anna Judd. *Children:* Orrin, Luther, Frank, and Charles.

Salina, m. Robert Hughes; one son.

Luther, m. Louisa Barnes. *Children:* Agnes (m. Edwin Abbe), Celia (m. Edwin Mix), and Nellie. Luther d. in New Britain.

Chloe, m. Andrew Upson. *Children:* Dennis, William, Burton, Luther, Mary, and William.

Laura, m. Henry Milod; two children.

Julia, m. Thomas Brooks. *Children:* Bertha, Bessie, and Mabel.

Eveline, m. Hubert Hart. *Children:* Arthur, Ernest, William, Carlos, Frank, and Mary; resides at Unionville.

135 ISAAC[7] MOSES, son of OTHNIEL (132), m. Matilda Barnes, who d. in Avon, Conn.

CHILDREN: Martin, Chauncey, and Charles.

Charles resides in Avon; m. (1st) Juliette Fuller; m. (2d) Mary Colvin. A Charles Moses was a soldier of the late war, enlisting at Canton in the 1st Conn. Heavy Artillery. Possibly Charles, the soldier, was the grandson of Orrin (see 134).

136 RICHARD[8] MOSES, son of JOSHUA (133), m. at Bristol, Conn., April 19, 1836, Rachel Norton. She m. (2d) Henry Gridley of Bristol.

CHILDREN: Harriet E., b. Jan. 12, 1837; Adrian, b. Mar. 21, 1838; Sarah, b. Aug. 23, 1839, d. Nov. 14, 1845; Ellen, b. Dec. 14, 1840; Emerson, b. May 10, 1843; Bernard, b. Aug. 27, 1846; Dennison, b. Aug. 28, 1848, d. Feb. 15, 1853; Richard A., b. Aug. 13, 1850; Lucius H., b. Feb. 10, 1853.

Adrian lives in Unionville, Conn. *Children:* Arthur and Henrietta.

Ellen, in 1861, m. Asa Upson; is now a widow, residing at East Saginaw, Mich.

Emerson resides in Lake Crystal, Minn., and has sons, Oliver and Charles.

Bernard is a professor at Berkeley College, Berkeley, Cal.

Richard A. resides at Woonsocket, S. Dak., and has a dau., Ellen B.

Lucius H. resides at Lake Crystal, Minn.

137 MARY[8] MOSES, dau. of JOSHUA (133), m. Oct. 25, 1843, Lucius D. Pond of Unionville, Conn.

CHILDREN: Joshua M., b. Jan. 19, 1845; L. Bradford, b. July 14, 1847; Mary E., b. Aug. 3, 1853, d. Dec. 8, 1887.

138 CHAUNCEY[8] MOSES, son of DARIUS (91), was a Representative in the General Assembly from Canton, Conn., in 1843; m. Catherine Johnson.

CHILDREN: Harry, d. July 5, 1838, aged 21; Elizabeth; Flora A.; Rollin, b. Feb. 6, 1825; Seymour D.

Elizabeth (Farmington, Conn., Prob. Rec.) wills, Mar. 8, 1858, property to sister, Flora A. In the inventory are notes of Rollin and Seymour D.

Rollin resides (1889) at Manhattan, Kan. He has a fine estate just outside the town.

Seymour D. Mention is made in Hist. W. Simsbury of the place formerly owned by him.

139 JOSHUA[5] MOSES, son of JOSHUA (10), resided in Norfolk, Conn. From Norfolk town records we find that, on April 24,

1769, "Joshua Moses, of *Simsbury*, bought land in Norfolk of Matthew Phelps;" also a deed, July 2, 1772, from "Joshua, the elder, to son Joshua." In the distribution of the estate of Joshua, Nov. 4, 1795, Norfolk Pro. Rec., mention is made of wife Abigail, and the reservation of a "shop" to Jonathan; then further distribution is made to Joshua, Thomas, Jonathan, Abigail Palmer, and Jesse Moses, as "heirs of Joshua." Previous to this are recorded several deeds, Nov. 30, 1792, for "love and good will," to "son Jesse," "son Thomas," "son Joshua, Jr.," and on Sept. 17, 1794, to Jesse Moses "from his honored father." It seems a little singular that a son Jonah was left out of this distribution, as we find in Norfolk Records this entry: "Jonah Moses, son of Joshua Moses, and Abigail, his wife, b. Oct. 25, 1777." In the *History of the Terry Family* we learn that "Abigail Terry, b. Jan. 18, 1740, m. Joshua Moses of Norfolk."

CHILDREN: Joshua, Thomas, Jonathan, Abigail, Jesse, and Jonah.

Abigail[6], (Winchester Rec.), m. April 23, 1728, Reuben Palmer.

Joshua[6], (Norfolk Rec.), distribution of estate of Joshua Moses to Elizabeth, his widow, on June 13, 1822.

Jesse[6]. The "Terry History" states that Roxy Terry m. a son of Jesse Moses of Norfolk, and that they became Mormons. (Sims. Ch. Rec.) "James Moses m. Roxy M. Terry, April 9, 1833."

Jonah[6]. On Oct. 25, 1804, Jonah deeds to Jonathan land bounded north by Thomas Moses, south by land of Ruth Moses, now Ruth Sturtevant. On Oct. 17, 1805, "Nathan Sturtevant and Ruth, of Glover, Co. of New Orleans, Vermont," deed to Jonah of Norfolk. Jonah may have resided for a time in Vermont or elsewhere, and was thus omitted in the distribution of his father's estate.

Thomas[6], on Feb. 9, 1803, deeds land to Jonah and Jonathan. Sept. 15, 1824, administration granted to Thomas on estate of Ralph Moses, late of Norfolk. (Ralph was probably a nephew.) On Oct. 12, 1832, administration granted to Thomas on estate of Benjamin Moses of Norfolk on account of a widow Clarissa and a minor child, Abigail, 1 year old, for whom Michael T. and Thomas Moses are appointed guardians.

140 ORR_{IN} MOSES of Winchester, Conn. Estate probated at Norfolk. Orrin and many others were doubtless descendants of the sons of Joshua, above mentioned, all of whom have removed from Norfolk. Orrin's property was distributed to his "mother Hannah," "brothers Reuben, Rufus, Clinton, and Thomas, and to sisters Sally Eggleston, and Charlotte Moses." There are reasons for believing that this Orrin and the family mentioned removed to

Torrington, Conn. The following notes are from the *History of Torrington:* "Admitted freeman in 1818, Austin Moses, *Rufus* Moses." "Members of Masonic Lodge at Newfield in Torrington about 1823, *Orrin* Moses, and, many years later, *Thomas* Moses." One of the "members of a band of music at Wolcottville, in Torrington, in 1832, was *Thomas* Moses." "Married Nov. 12, 1826, *Thomas* Moses and Ann M. Bissell." Also, "Ellen E. Moses, member of church at Wolcottville in 1868." Wm. Moses m. July 6, 1857, Rogenia M. Case of Torrington. "Oscar Moses of Canton m. Jan. 2, 1858, Amelia Moses of Torrington." From Old Winchester Records: "Joshua B. Moses, of Harwinton, m. Sept. 21, 1828, Ruth Richards of Winchester."

141 JONAH[6] MOSES, probably the son of JOHN (19), or ZEBULON (20), both of whom had sons at Rutland, Vt., who are not recorded at Simsbury, Conn. The Congregational Church Manual of West Rutland gives Jonah as a "member" in 1785, and as "dismissed to another church" at a subsequent date. His name is also found in Rutland deeds. Judge John Moses of Chicago furnishes the following somewhat imperfect record of the descendants of Jonah:

CHILDREN: Erastus, b. at Rutland, Vt., Sept. 6, 1792, d. at Naples, Ill., Sept. 6, 1838; Enam, living in Illinois in 1830; Clarissa; Sarah.

Enam. This singular name may have been taken from a near relative and gallant soldier of Simsbury, Conn., whose connection has not been traced.*

142 ERASTUS[7] MOSES, son of JONAH (141). From the Conn. Adj.-Gen.'s Record, we learn that he was a soldier, enlisting as a Sergeant at Middletown, Conn., Feb. 5, 1815, in the 25th U. S. Inf., under Major Daniel Ketcham. At some time after the war he removed to Canada, and again, in 1837, to Naples, Ill. He m. (1st) Nancy ———; and (2d), in Canada, in 1824, Jemima Merritt.

CHILDREN (by first wife): Ambrose J., b. April 12, 1814; William, d. in Naples in 1838; Polly, b. Aug. 4, 1817; (by second wife):

---

* An Enam Moses enlisted at Simsbury, Conn., in March, 1780, for the war under Capt. Hoagland in Col. Selden's Regiment of Light Dragoons; was in the fight in repelling the attempt of the British to capture Tarrytown on the Hudson. He was attacked with small-pox, and was permitted to return home in April, 1782; m. Feb. 13, 1783, Catherine Dickinson, of Manchester, Vt. He d. at Middlebury, Genesee Co., N. Y.; Aug. 2, 1829. His widow was residing there in 1843, aged 79.

CHILDREN: (From a Bible leaf in pension papers) James, b. March 18, 1792; Enam, b. April 3, 1795; Amarilla, b. Jan. 15, 1797; Myranda, b. Sept. 29, 1798; Lucinda, b. June 1, 1805.

John, b. at Chippewa, Can., Sept. 18, 1825; Priscilla, b. Oct. 3, 1828, deceased; Charlotte, b. June 4, 1831; Nancy, b. Nov. 12, 1835, deceased; William E., b. February, 1838, deceased.

143 JOHN[8] MOSES, son of ERASTUS (142), has had a prominent political and literary career. He has filled the offices of Judge of Scott Co., Ill.; Private Secretary (with military rank) to Gov. Yates during the late war; Member of the Legislature of Ill.; and is now Secretary and Librarian of the Chicago Historical Society. He is the author of a comprehensive History of Illinois, in two octavo volumes of 500 pages each. He m. (1st) April 17, 1849, Sarah Louisa, dau. of Col. Chas. F. Keener; she d. April 14, 1857; m. (2d) June 15, 1859, Sallie M. Woods, dau. of Col. John R. Woods.

CHILDREN: Caroline, b. Mar. 17, 1850; Richard H., b. April 26, 1851; John F., b. Oct. 24, 1853; Charles K., b. July 31, 1855; Louis, b. April, 1857, deceased; Mabel L., b. May 14, 1860; Sadie A., b. July 17, 1862, deceased; Henry W., b. June 14, 1866; Philip G., b. Aug. 1, 1869; Christine T., b. Mar. 18, 1872.

144 JOHN[6] MOSES, son of JOHN (19), is mentioned in the Rutland, Vt., Records in a deed of land which he received from his father as "my beloved son, John Moses, Jr." This "John, Jr.," removed from Rutland to Williston, and afterward to Huntington, Vt., where he died. He m. Polly Bates of Rutland, Vt.

CHILDREN: Silas, Anna, Hannah, Jonathan, John, and Lucy.

Silas, m. Diana Peck, of Hinesburg, Vt., and removed to Stockholm, N. Y., where he died. They had five children, some of whom are said to be yet living.

Anna, m. Samuel Tucker, and lived and died in Huntington, Vt. They had six children — two living in 1890: Daniel B. Tucker of Essex Junction, Vt., and John Tucker of Huntington, Vt.

Hannah, d. unm. at Huntington, Vt.

Jonathan, m. Mercy Sinkler of Essex, Vt. He d. in Underhill, Vt. They had two children.

John, m. Kitty Wilcox. They lived in Huntington, Vt., and had two children.

Lucy, m. (1st) Calvin Wright. They settled in Canton, N. Y., where he d., leaving five children; m. (2d) Nathaniel Chaffee of Monkton, Vt., by whom she had also five children.

As stated in the first chapter of this work, the writer considers that the record of the lawsuit gives a fair presumption that John Moses, the shipwright, of Plymouth Colony, had an earlier residence in either Salem or Lynn, which towns are only about eight miles apart, and in early days had one probate jurisdiction. It will be remembered that Keyser, Guy, and Gibbons, who were interested in the "pinnace," came from Lynn and Salem. The record of the lawsuit also shows that John Moses employed a *Mass. Bay* lawyer and was familiar with methods of procedure in that Colony. In the Salem Records the births of Moses children and Keyser children are entered in close proximity. The age at which a Henry Moses of Salem married, and his occupation as a sea captain, also lend probability to the theory that he was a son of John Moses of Plymouth. In an apocryphal way we therefore give Henry Moses as of the second generation. The writer has personally searched the early manuscript records of Salem, and gives the following items gleaned therefrom:

145 HENRY[2] MOSES, and Remember Gyles (Coll. Essex Ins. Vol. II, in an extended record of the Very family, gives her name as Remember Very) were, "maryd by Major Hathorn, 1-2-1659. Their da. Hannah bo. 20-11-59 and deceased 2-8 mo. 61 — Son Henry bo. 8-12 mo. 61; Da. Eliza b. 8-12 mo. 63; John – 19 Nov. 1666; – Remember b. 14-9 mo. 1668; Edward bo. 10-9 mo. 70; Eleazer bo. 23, Mar. 167 2/3; son Samuel born 24 June 1677." On April 17, 1684, Henry Moses was appointed one of the appraisers of the estate of John Very. In Vol. 3 of Probate Records appears an "Inventory of the estate of Henry Moses lately deceased," taken on 19th of Nov. 1685. Among the effects are "1 gun, fishing lines, parcel of old books, quadrant and compass, and forestaufe * without vanes.'"

Remember Moses, m. John Follit, Nov. 1702.

146 ELEAZER[3] MOSES (spelled Moises), "son of HENRY (145), m. to Hannah Ward, June 24, 1697." Probably commanded a vessel, as the Probate Records of 1718 mention him as " Captain." Administration was granted to his widow, Hannah; his property amounting to £159. (Vol. VII, Coll. Essex Ins.) Hannah, dau. of Eleazer, bap. Oct. 6, 1700.

CHILDREN: Hannah (Coll. Essex Ins.), bap. October, 1700; Eleazer, b. Nov. 28, 1703, d. in 1786; Henry, b. Dec. 31, 1710; Samuel, b.

---

* Dyche's Dict. of 1758: "Forestaff. An instrument formerly much used at sea to make observation of the sun, moon, and stars, with the face toward the object, but now almost out of use." Encyclopedic Dict.: "The forestaff has a straight square staff and four crosses or vanes, which slide thereon."

Oct. 21, 1714. (Vol. VII, Essex Ins.,) mentions Hannah as dau. of Eleazer, and as selling land to bro. Eleazer, 1722-1732 and 1761. Hannah, m. Nov. 29, 1722, Benj. Ropes.

Samuel[4], m. Sarah Brown, July 20, 1755.

147 HENRY[4] MOSES, son of ELEAZER (146), m. Sarah Osgood, "both of Salem," May 8, 1735 (Vol. VIII, Essex Ins.). Sarah, dau. of Henry and Sarah, bap. March, 1737. She m. (Salem Rec.) Nov. 18, 1755, John Carwick.

148 ELEAZER MOSES. The probate of his estate makes it difficult to say from whom descended. Administration granted, 1727, on "estate of Eleazer Moses, mariner, late of Salem, to his son Eleazer." Estate inventories £141, and includes, "an instrument of gunnery, a quadrant, and sea chart."

149 ELEAZER[4] MOSES, son of ELEAZER (146). Probate Rec. mentions him as a sailmaker of Salem, and that administration was granted to son Benjamin. (Vol. VII, Essex Ins.) Eleazer, with others, signs bond, Feb. 14, 1773; m. Nov., 1730, Mary Henderson.

CHILDREN (see Vol. VIII, Hist. Coll. Essex Ins.): baptisms, "children of Eleazer and Mary": Samuel, December, 1733; Eleazer, January, 1734, buried Sept. 25, 1774; Benjamin, Feb. 6, 1736, d. July 16, 1803; Mary, April 15, 1739; Henry, Dec. 21, 1740; John, May 9, 1742; Joseph and Hannah, June 3, 1744; Joseph, Nov. 3, 1745; Hannah, Jan. 28, 1750, d. April 21, 1797; John, Jan. 19, 1751.

Hannah, m. (Salem Rec.) May 22, 1768, John Chipman.

Samuel, m. (Salem Rec.) June 22, 1788, Elizabeth Dunkley.

150 BENJAMIN[5] MOSES, son of ELEAZER (149). (Vol. III, Coll. Essex Ins.) During Revolutionary War was master of private armed vessel *The Creature*, afterwards called the *Oliver Cromwell*. The latter part of his life he commanded the sloop *Indian*, sailing as a packet between Salem and Boston. He was admitted to Essex Lodge of Free Masons, Apr. 9, 1779. (Vol. I.) He was a volunteer on the expedition, Aug., 1778, to expel the British General Pigot and army from Rhode Island. m. June 7, 1761, Sarah Caryll.

CHILDREN (Coll. Essex Ins.,) Salem bap. in First Church: Sarah, Mary, and Benjamin, bap. Oct. 26, 1766; Samuel, Feb. 15, 1767; Sarah, Sept. 3, 1769; William, Oct. 6, 1771; Abigail, Jan. 9, 1774; William, July 19, 1778; Betsey, Dec. 3, 1780.

Samuel, m. (Salem Rec.) Nov. 27, 1808, Eunice Cheever.

Sally, m. (Salem Rec.) Nov. 18, 1792, William Pitman.

Betsey, m. (Salem Rec.) Oct. 9, 1806, Benjamin Hale.
Mary, m. in 1781, John Kehoo (who was lost at sea).

151 BENJAMIN[7] MOSES, son of BENJAMIN (150), m. June 27, 1784, Rebecca Stevens.

CHILDREN (From Coll. Essex Ins.,) Salem bap. First Church: Edward Lister, bap. July, 1786; Benjamin, bap. May, 1788.

152 JOSEPH[5] MOSES, son of ELEAZER (149), m. Nov. 8, 1767, Hannah Kimball.

CHILDREN (from Coll. Essex Ins.,) Salem baptisms: Joseph, May 28, 1769; John, Feb. 3, 1771; Hannah, Dec. 27, 1772; Thomas, July 10, 1774; "3 children of Joseph," in June, 1782; "child of Joseph," in April, 1783; Samuel, Jan. 22, 1785; Rebecca, August, 1791; Polly, October, 1791. Inscription in burial-ground: Mary, dau. of Joseph and Hannah, d. Aug. 2, 1838, aged 58.

Rebecca, m. (Salem Rec.) May 19, 1814, James Norfolk.

The town records of Salem give several Moses names, some of which cannot be properly connected. They are as follows:

SAMUEL MOSES of Ipswich. (Vol. XIII, Essex Ins., mentions sale of land to him, 1684.) Probate inventory, in 1691, shows property amounting to £132. In 1706, there was an agreement between Grace Stevens (*alias* Moses), widow of Samuel Moses, and Hannah Allen (*nee* Moses), wife of John Allen, and Mary Moses, only surviving children of Samuel Moses. In 1709, there is a set-off of dower.

JOSEPH MOSES and Tamsin Beans, m. July 27, 1699. (Coll. Essex Ins.) Salem bap. in North Church, Dec. 27, 1742, Hannah, dau. of Joseph.

CHILD: Hannah, m. (Salem Rec.) April 21, 1793, James Crowell.

SARAH MOSES, m. Sept. 18, 1740, Peter Cheever.

SARAH MOSES, m. Feb. 1, 1767, Joseph Allen.

SARAH MOSES, m. Nov. 4, 1778, Edward Dutton.

NABBY MOSES, m. June 9, 1795, Moses Yell.

DELIVERANCE MOSES (widow), m. Dec. 4, 1799, John Robertson.

MARTHA W. MOSES, m. Sept. 5, 1858, James Ed. Chipman.

REBECCA MOSES (widow), m. Moses Yell, Sept. 12, 1813.

EUNICE MOSES, m. Samuel Balch, Aug. 27, 1819.

CORNELIUS MOSES (mariner), of Salem; estate probated in 1831.

MARY MOSES, "single woman, late of Salem;" estate probated in 1838. Henry Moses of Portland, Me., administrator, certifies that he is a brother of Mary Moses, and legal representative of Samuel Moses, deceased (a brother of said intestate). The property is divided, one part to Henry and one part to representatives of Samuel Moses. On Aug. 28, 1838, a receipt is filed, signed by Naum L. Lund and Mary Moses Lund for one-half of the estate. A careful search of the records of Salem revealed the name of no other Moses since 1838. As will be noted, the last of the Salem branch appears to have resided in Portland, Me.

CHAPTER V.

JOHN MOSES OF PORTSMOUTH, N. H., AND SOME OF HIS DESCENDANTS.

In searching the earliest records of the sparsely settled New England of 1640 to 1650, we find the uncommon name of John Moses making its appearance about the same time in different colonies, and naturally the theory is evolved that the two men bearing the same name must have been closely related. It will be seen, however, from the facts and circumstances that herein follow, that it is extremely improbable that they were of the same family. John Moses of Plymouth was by tradition a Welshman, was a shipwright, and was apparently a Churchman among Puritans; while John Moses of Portsmouth was a Scotchman, an agriculturalist, and a Puritan among Churchmen. For a better understanding of the general surroundings connected with the founder of the New Hampshire branch, historical quotations are given:

From Brewster's *Rambles About Portsmouth* it appears that Portsmouth was first settled in 1623 by the Laconia Company, and that the "most interested and active men of the Company were Sir Ferd. Gorges and John Mason." That a "Manor house" was erected at "Odiornes Point," that between "three and four thousand acres" were "attached to this branch of the plantation," and that "the provisions of the grant were ample for carrying out the idea of the proprietors, which was to establish a Manor here agreeably to the English custom, the occupants of the land to be held as tenants by the proprietors of the soil." The company had agents to manage the colony, and from Doyle's *English in America* we learn that, "in 1638, there were in the Colony more than 40 horses, 100 cattle, 200 sheep, 54 goats, 22 cannon, 250 small arms, 48 boats for fishing, 50 workmen, and 8 Danes to overlook saw mills and make potash, also 22 women were among the settlers . . . . also in the inventory, a set of Church furniture. This makes it likely Mason was a zealous Anglican." . . . .
After the division of territory between Gorges and Mason and the

death of Mason in 1634, "the settlement was now free to shape its own course. The colonists either elected Williams governor or acquiesced in his continuance in office." Five years later it is recorded that "Williams the Governor, Ambrose Gibbons Assistant, and 18 others, have built a chapel and parsonage and endowed them with 50 acres of glebe, and have elected two church wardens and an incumbent."

From Lechford's *Plain Dealing*, published January 17, 1641:

"At Northam *alias* Pascattaqua is Master Larkham pastor. One Master H. K. (Knowles) was also lately minister there. The two fell out about baptising children, receiving of members, burial of the dead. . . . And further Master Larkham flying to the Magistrate, Master K. and a Captaine raised arms. Master K. going before the troope with a Bible upon a poles top, and he or some of his party giving forth that their side were Scots and the other English. . . . . Master K. and the Captaine, their leaders, were fined £100 apiece which they were not able to pay."

From what we learn later on in the history of the colony, it is quite probable that the Scotchman, John Moses, was of Master Knowles' party.

Through transfers of the colonial grant, George Cleeve and Richard Tucker claimed and held a disputed agency and jurisdiction over certain lands. Gov. Winslow of Plymouth writes to Gov. Winthrop of Mass., in 1644: "Rigby has good hap to light on two of the arrantest known knaves that ever trod the New England Shore to be his agents in Cleeves and Morton. . . . . In 1645, Cleeves was exercising jurisdiction at Casco." From *Portland in the Past* is also quoted: "On June 8, 1637, Gorges gave Cleves a commission for the letting and settling all or any part of his lands or islands lying between Cape Elizabeth and the end of Sagadahock River, and so up the main land 60 miles."

With this introduction, we come to the first historical mention of John Moses of Portsmouth or Pascattaqua, as it was then called.

In folio 1 of York Deeds is the record of a grant which places the date of John Moses' settlement in the colony at least as far back as 1639. The document is interesting from its quaintness, and is given in full:

"Witness these presents that We Geo Cleeue and Richard Tucker of Cascoe Bay in New England gentlem for and in consideration of Seaven yeares Seruice as an apprentice pformed vnto vs by John Moses now of

Puchatag River we have given granted & conformed vuto him the s^d John Moses his heyres and assigns one hundred acres of land In Cascoe bay lyng & next Adjoyneing vnto the land formerly granted vuto Geo Lewis by vs wch s^d hundred acres of land is to beginn at the side of the Lott of the s^d Geo Lewis & soe to runne westwardly by the side of the bay one hundred pooles in length and eighty seaven pooles in breadth vnto the main land vntill the sayd hundred acres be ended togeather with soe much marsh ground as belongeth to every hundred acres of land in the grant or deed granted to the s^d Geo Cleeue and Richd Tucker in consideration of the yearly rent of 2S and 2 days work to be payd unto the longest liver of them or their assigns & during the term of nineteen hundred yeares to be fully compleated and ended. To have and to hold all the s^d lands and premises vuto him the s^d John Moses his heyres and assigns during ye s^d term of & from them to whom it shall belong vpon ye decission between them for the rent aforesaid for all seruices w'souer and he the s^d Geo Cleeue & Richd Tucker do further promise vnto him the s^d John Moses that wee or one of us will at all times hereafter make further assurance of the s^d lands & pmises herein specified vnto him the s^d John Moses his heyres & assigns as shall be requisite for the further conformation of the same according to ye counsell learned in the laws.

In Witness whereof we have herevnto set our hands & seales the sixth day of Aprill in the yeare 1646.

Memoranda. That ye two days work inserted in the deed is exempted & clearly taken off.

In the presence of   Geo Cleeue   (seal)
Jno Dauis   Richard Tucker (seal)"
Dav. J M Easter"

In the introduction to the printed volume of *York Deeds* it is stated that "all of the Gorges lands were to be granted on the feudal plan." From *Portsmouth Records*, by Frank W. Hackett, we quote from page 31 : " town meeting list of January, 1648 . . land granted to Robert Davis a lot on Saggamore Creek, next point west of John Moysis." Page 20 : "Jan. 13, 1652, granted to John Moysis 15 acres." Page 23 : "On Dec. 5, 1653, to John Moysis 5 acres." Brewster's *Rambles*, page 27, gives the record of a distribution in 1660 of lands to "all such as were reputed inhabitants and free comyuers unto the year 1657." In this distribution or confirmation of titles, John Moses received 83 acres. Brewster also gives the subscribers, 1658 to 1666, to "maintenance of ye minister." The first name on the list is John Moses. In the *Prov. Papers of N. H.*, Vol. I, p. 285, John Moses appears in 1665 as one of the signers of a petition favoring the jurisdiction of Massachusetts over New Hampshire. He is mentioned several times in the early histories as Sergt. Moses, and he may have been sent over as a soldier by Sir Ferd. Gorges, who was of high military rank in England. Brewster's *Rambles* gives a plan of the seating in the meeting-house in 1693. The first of the three seats "under the pulpit" is assigned to "Sergt. Moses." . . . "In the mens gallery fronting the pulpit" is "Aron Moses." . . . In the "women's seat in the gallery," "Aron Moses wife."

Aaron Moses and Sarah Moses were children of John Moses. Concerning them and their descendants, quotations from histories are given: From Brewster's *Rambles*, "Timothy Waterhouse early in 1700 married a Miss Moses." "Ruth, daughter of Henry Sherburne, born in 1660, married Aaron Moses 1677." The original will of the "widow of Aaron Moses," dated in 1732, now in the possession of the Moses family at Portsmouth, and personally examined by the writer, shows that her name was "Mary," and that she had married for a second husband John Sherburne. The *New England Hist. and Gen. Register*, Vol. XVII, p. 253, states that "Ruth Sherburne married Aaron Moses of N. H., June 1, 1676;" also another history uses the same language, evidently taken from some record. There is no other conflicting entry showing the marriage of a Ruth Sherburne, while we find that Ruth's sister Mary married a Richard Sloper. Furthermore, the John Sherburne who married the widow Moses was a brother of Ruth and Mary Sherburne. From the record, it may be assumed that Aaron married first, Ruth, a daughter of Henry Sherburne, and from the will of his widow, we infer that he had a second wife named Mary, family name unknown. A grandchild of Aaron was named Ruth. Brewster mentions that Henry Sherburne was descended from a noble family in England and came to Portsmouth in 1631, and on page 55 of his *Rambles About Portsmouth* he states as follows: "Henry Sherburne of Pascataway may have been a papist; he was church warden of our Church of England Chapel in 1640; is spoken of by Winthrop, in the only document left of the town records burnt by the Bay Puritans in the civil wars, when the church was broken up and they re-annexed Maine and New Hampshire to their empire. It would look as if he turned Puritan in the civil wars and went to meeting, and wouldn't again after the king was brought back." On page 161 is given a list of the tax-payers of 1727, among whom are James Moses, Mark Moses, Josiah Moses, and Joseph Moses. On page 176: "At the siege of

Louisburg in 1745; Col. Nath. Meserve rendered essential service in constructing sledges for cannon. . . . . In 1749 he was commissioned by the British Government to build a ship of war of 50 guns, called the *America*. The ship was built near where the present Raynes shipyard now is. As the bridge was not then constructed, it may have been built in the rear of the Moses house." Page 196: "Among those who have kept their first localities for over 200 years are the Odeorne, Pickering, Moses, Whidden, and other families." Page 206: "Next on the south of the creek comes the farm of James Moses, which has been in the family for two centuries." Page 215, Association Test, August 14, 1776: "We, the subscribers . . . will to the utmost of our Power at the Risque of Our Lives and Fortunes with arms oppose the Hostile Proceedings of the British Fleets and Armies agst the United American Colonies." Among signers: "Thomas Moses, Theodore Moses, Saml. Moses, James Moses, Nadab Moses, John Moses, Aaron Moses." Brewster gives two entire chapters of his book to sketches and anecdotes concerning Joseph, Samuel, and Thomas Moses. In Volumes VII to XXXVII of the *New England Hist. and Gen. Register*, are given items concerning many of the New Hampshire branch of the Moses family. In the State Library at Concord, N. H., may be found a creditable book of Poems by Thomas Moses of Portsmouth.

In passing through Portsmouth on a business trip in 1889, the writer visited the old homestead of the Moses family. It is located near the suburbs of the city on the Sagamore Creek, and can only be reached by a private road. The original "ancestral acres" are yet in the Moses family. A part of the original farm is owned by William Moses, aged 82, whose house was burned in 1884. The home of the first John Moses and the greater part of the first farm is now occupied by Martha J. Moses and her nephew, William E. Rand and family. Every deed and will, even the certificate of the first survey of the land, is in the possession of the family. The present house, though quite old, is the third over the original cellar. Although so near the city, it is located in a secluded and picturesque spot. It has been handed down in direct line in the Moses family from John Moses, who is mentioned in the deed of Cleeves and Tucker in 1646, as then located at Portsmouth. The writer believes that, except in the neighborhood of Portsmouth, there are very few instances in the United States where a property

OLD HOMESTEAD—OWNED AND OCCUPIED BY THE MOSES FAMILY 244 YEARS.

has remained continuously in the family name and been occupied by direct descendants of the first proprietor for 244 years. The historical associations of the place and natural beauty of the spot suggested to him the idea of a photograph of the old Moses homestead on the Sagamore, which he had taken and which is here reproduced. The gigantic old oak beneath which the children of so many generations have played, the grassy slopes, and a rocky bluff overhanging the water, are especial features, and are sure to make a strong and lasting impression on any pilgrim Moses who looks upon the home selected by the first of the New Hampshire line of the Moses name.

Mr. Alfred D. Moses, who died in 1888, had compiled from the family archives a manuscript sketch, a copy of which his widow and her brother, Mr. Joshua S. Moses of Hoopeston, Ill., have kindly furnished for publication. With slight changes and added material, it reads as follows:

*AGREEMENT BETWEEN SARGT. JOHN MOSES & HIS SON AARON:

This Indenture made ye 6th of January and in ye yeare of our Lord God One Thousand and six hundred Seventy-nine: Witnesseth yt John Moses of Saggamore Creek commonly so called & in ye county of Dover and Portsmouth & of ye one parte & Ann ye now other partie: unanimously have agreed & by these presents doe fully agree as followeth, Vis: ye Sd. John Moses with ye consent of his wife Ann as aforesaid as well severally as joyntly hath sett or made over unto their sonn Aaron so supposed as aforesaid ye one half of his ye said John Moses. his plantation farm or tenement as houses, outhouses, wood and woods belonging, meadows, marshes, with all and every convenient privilege or priveleges, yt. is, may or shall belong or appropriation to ye said premises: with his stock as followeth: Two oxen, two steers, three years old apiece, three cows, Three heifers, two yearlins and three calfs: to be managed as followeth. Vis. ye sd. Aaron is to manage, prove and improve ye whole of ye said plantation or farm: Receiving for ye same ye one half of ye profits, or increase of ye said land, or chattell, as of corn, hay, wood, for fireing or building, or anything else, shall or may be improved of ye sd John Moses' farm, as aforesaid, it as aforesaid whether growing above or under ground. with half of ye Butter & cheese. ye Sd John Moses & his wife Ann as aforesaid to have ye other half. they and every of them to make use of their several parts to their own behoof & benefit. them and every of them, by these presents binding themselves not to sell or dispose of any of ye fore-mentioned commodities, but to acquaint one ye other

---

* The writer found this document of 1679 in fair preservation, and had it photographed, but found that if reduced so as to be printed on a page of this work it could not be read without glasses.

thereof & likewise, ye parties aforesaid for themselfs severally & jointly consent & by these presents agree to pay equally all rates, taxes, other or any other publick charges ye one ye one half, & ye other ye other half. according to ye honest intent & meaning of this present instrument or writing: Further ye sd John Mosses with the consent of his wife Ann, they severally & jointly have consented, & by these presents agreed yt after ye decease of ye sd John Mosses ye sd Aaron ye sd John Mosses supposed sonn is to have and injoy ye said farm or tenement wholly to his owne propperty ys behoof & benefitt. To have and to hold to him his heirs, executors, Administrators or assigns for ever & ye Sd John Mosses with Ann his wife doe ingage for themselfs & either of them, their heirs or either of their heirs, Executors Administrators or assigns: to consolidatt conferm & make good ye aforesaid premises. to ye Sd Aaron to have and to hold, to him his heirs or assigns for ever, from all suit or suits, cause or causes in law yt may arise by, from or under them, their heirs or either of their heirs Executors, Administrators or assignes. As witness O E hand & Seales ye day & yeare first above written.

Signed sealed & delivered
in yt presence of   John ✶ Mosses his seal O
   John Sherburn   & mark
   Francis Huckins   Ann A Mosses her seal O
   Thomas Beck   & mark
   Polly Walker   Aaron Moses.

It is to be understood yt ye Stock within spoken is to be parted once in three years. It is here to be noted yt through forgetfullness in yt. within premises the vrs forgotten this as all here agree upon by themselfs that in this place it shall stand as firm in Law as if it was in the inclusive place yt is as followeth yt Sd Aaron within mentioned is out of his own part as within written to pay unto Sarrah his sister to ye value of five pounds in Currant pay of New England, to be paid in or upon ye marriage of ye said Sarrah as witness our hand ye 7th of January & in yt year One thousand six hundred Seventie nine, as within written.

                                                           his
Witness, polly Walker   John ✶ Mosses
                                             mark
     Francis Huckins
     Thomas Beck   Aaron Moses

Ports$_m^o$ In New Hampshire. John Moses and Aaron Moses came and acknowledged the above writing to be their act and Deed before me Wm Vaughn of the Counsell of Portsmouth

Agreement between Sergt John Moses and his Son Aron Recorded in the Records of Dou^s Portsmouth 2^d of Sept. 1681 — Book ye 3^d folio 163 per me Elias Hillman Recorder

(Fac simile of signature of Aaron Moses to above agreement.)

Aaron Moses

Copy of the Will of "Mary Sherburn" who was the "widow" of Aaron Moses (Son of John Mosses, or John Moysis), and married John Sherburn Oct. 20th, 1720:

In the name of God, Amèn. I, Mary Sherburn of Portsmouth in the Province of New Hampshire in New England, "Widow," being aged and infirm, though of a sound disposing mind and memory and not knowing how soon God in his providence may call me from hence, do make and ordain this to be my last will and testament

Impromise:—I heartily and sincerely recommend my soul into the hands of the Almighty God that gave it me hoping through the merits and intercession of Jesus Christ my Savior and Redeemer he will be graciously pleased to accept of it: and my body to be decently buried at the charge of my Executors hereafter mentioned.

Item 1. I give and bequeath to my sons James Moses, Joseph Moses and Josiah Moses, to each of them a sheep to be delivered them by my Executors.

Item 2. I give and bequeath to my Grand-daughter Mary Moses the daughter of my son Joseph Moses my feather-bed and bedding belonging to it: and my biggest Iron pot.

Item 3. I give and bequeath to my three Grand-daughters, Mary Moses the daughter of my son Joseph, Abigail the daughter of my son Josiah and Mary the daughter of my son James all my silver either wrought into plate or in money, to be equally divided amongst them.

Item 4. I give and bequeath to my four daughters, namely, Martha Moses, Hannah Moses, Abigail Moses and Sarah Scott, all my wearing apparel to be equally divided amongst them.

Item 5. I give and bequeath to my son Mark Moses all my household goods of what kind soever, not heretofore in this my last will disposed of, and also my oldest cow and one Steer and three hogs: he paying a small debt that I owe to Joshua Pierce, Mrs. Priest and Mr. Thomas Sibron:

Lastly I do hereby nominate, constitute, and appoint my sons James Moses and Joseph Moses to be my Executors to this my last will and testament. Dated this 9th October 1732. Signed, sealed and delivered by Mary Sherburn to be her last will and testament, before us.

Theodore Atkinson Mary Sherburn
Saml. Sherburn
Margaret X Hickett

The will of James Moses, June 3, 1772, gives to his children: Mary (Melcher), Aaron Moses, Sarah (Wallace), Martha (Stavers), and Ruth (Seavey), each twenty shillings; also, to his son, John Moses, one piece of land lying in Portsmouth, $\frac{1}{4}$ of an acre, on which John Moses' house and barn stands, and another piece, $\frac{3}{4}$ of an acre, occupied by John Moses; also the pasturing of a cow during the lifetime of John Moses on other lands of the estate. All the rest of the estate, real and personal, is given to his grandson Nadab, son of Aaron Moses, who is also executor.

The will of James Moses (2d), Feb. 12, 1861, gives to his children, Dorothy M. Rand, Eliza M. Odiorne, William Moses, Samuel W. Moses, James Moses, 4th, and Mary B. Wendell, each one hundred dollars; also to his children and to his grandson, William E. Rand, all the personal estate not given to his daughter, Martha J. Moses, and grandson, William E. Rand, to be equally divided among them all; to his daughter, Martha J. Moses, and grandson, Wm. E. Rand, the residue of estate, real, personal, and mixed in equal proportions, they, in equal proportions, to pay the legacy of $600, divided among six of his children. His son, Samuel W. Moses, is appointed executor.

FIRST GENERATION.

Among the first "planters" that came to the Piscataqua was JOHN MOYSIS (or Mosses) a Scotchman by birth; he settled on the south side of Sagamore Creek, taking up 42 acres of land, running back towards Bellahac Brook, to which was added by vote of the town, Feb. 3, 1660, 43 acres more, on the town record of March 30, 1664: "Land laid out to John Mosses, four skore and five acres" by "Sherburn and Cotton," Surveyors. He was a Deacon in the first church in the town. On the town record of 1658, at a meeting called to raise subscriptions for the maintaining of the ministry, he heads the paper with one pound. He had the title of "Sergeant;" from whence he derived it we know not. From old papers we find that his wife's name was "Ann," that they had two *children*, Aaron and Sarah. In the agreement made between "John Moses and his son Aaron," Aaron is to pay to his sister Sarah on her marriage five pounds. This, we presume, was to be her marriage portion.

SECOND GENERATION.

AARON MOSES, son of John, was b. at Sagamore Creek. Brewster, in his *Rambles*, says he was m. in 1677 to Ruth, daughter of Henry Sherburn; she was b. June 3, 1660. His widow's given name, written in her will, is "Mary." (We believe the "Ruth" to be an error.— *A. D. M.*)

There is no record of his death. The Town Tax-book of the year 1713 shows that the "Old Homestead" was taxed to the

"Widow Moses" and her son James. From town and provincial papers it appears that he was a public man, having held a number of offices in the town and State. He was Lieutenant in Capt. Tobias Langdon's company, and was one of the members of a court martial called by Gov. Usher at New Castle, Sept. 29, 1696.

CHILDREN were: James, Joseph, Josiah, Mark, Martha, Hannah, Abigail, and Sarah.

SARAH MOSES, daughter of John, was b. at Sagamore Creek. Brewster, in his *Rambles*, says: "About a third of a mile north of the Old Ham Mansion-house, on the Point, (Freeman's Point, North Portsmouth,) between the great elm and the shore, in a grove, is the cellar of the house of Timothy Waterhouse, the tanner. . . . His wife was Miss Moses." (From tradition, and what I heard from my Grandmother, this Miss Moses was Sarah, of Sagamore Creek, she being the only Miss Moses in or at Portsmouth at that time.— *A. D. Moses.*)

THIRD GENERATION.

JAMES MOSES, son of Aaron, was a farmer and cordwainer; born and died on the old homestead. He bought of his brothers and sisters all the title they had to their father's (Aaron Moses) estate. Jan. 7, 1728, he was received in the church. He m. Sept. 10, 1713, Martha Jaxon.

Children (Ch. Rec.) were: Mary, John, Aaron, Sarah, Martha, Ruth, Joseph.

JOSEPH MOSES, son of Aaron, b. at Sagamore Creek, was a house-joiner. Brewster, in his *Rambles*, says the Doctor was a native of England; in this he was in error; he was a brother of James, Josiah, and Mark.

["Oft when I was a child have heard my grandmother and father tell of his eccentric humor. He was a brother to my grandfather's grandfather, James Moses. Their mother, after the decease of her husband (Aaron Moses), married John Sherburn; they lived on the Rye road, near the Rye line (separating Rye and Portsmouth), in a field now owned by the heirs of Michael W. Tucker. The old cellar is still visible, about one-third of the way from 'Sherburn's Well' to Tucker's barn (on Rye line). The line runs southwest from Samson's Point on Sagamore Creek to

Bellahack Brook, and the above-mentioned place is on the Rye side of the line."— *A. D. Moses.*]

From *New Eng. Gen. Register*, Vol. XXII: "Joseph Moses m. Rebecca Ayres, Aug. 17, 1712." From Ch. Rec.: "Hannah, daughter of Joseph (Dr. Joe) and Hannah Moses, bap. Oct. 26, 1729" (from which we conclude he may have had a second wife).

JOSIAH MOSES, son of Aaron, was a tanner; was a constable 1736; m. Abigail ———.

Children (Ch. Rec.): George, bap. June 3, 1722; Daniel, bap. Mar. 21, 1728.

MARK MOSES, son of Aaron, was a farmer and cordwainer; moved to Epsom, N. H. From *N. Eng. Hist. Reg.*, it appears he m. Martha Williams, Oct. 29, 1724.

Children (Church Rec. of Portsmouth): Elizabeth, b. June 1, 1729; other children, (family record,) Samuel, Aaron, William, Sylvanus, James, and a daughter.

SARAH MOSES, daughter of Aaron, m. 1714, Sylvanus Scott, an Englishman and a weaver. The house in which they lived was situated in what is known as "Scott's Orchard," then a part of the Moses homestead (and later belonged to Michael W. Tucker, then his heirs, and now, 1889, to John W. Johnson, who purchased the same from the Tucker heirs).

March 9, 1732, they conveyed to James Moses (her brother) all the title they had to her father's effects, and removed to Scarborough, from thence to Machias, in Maine.

Children (from Ch. Rec. of baptisms): Sarah, 1716; Amos, 1718; Frances, 1720; Samuel, 1723.

FOURTH GENERATION.

MARY MOSES, daughter of James and Martha J., m. John Melcher, a weaver.

JOHN MOSES, son of James and Martha J., b. at Sagamore Creek, and was a shipwright by trade. In 1786 he sold the land his father gave him in the old homestead to Nadab Moses (his nephew), for 18 pounds, his real estate comprising the original two pieces of land,* and moved with his family to Epsom, N. H.

---

*The piece where his house was, has always retained the name of "Uncle Johnnie's garden"; the other as the "Big Pen." A large old apple tree now stands where once stood Uncle Johnnie's house, and each year furnishes a bountiful supply of sweet apples.— *J. S. Moses*, 1889.

Prov. Papers: The above-mentioned John Moses was with Capt. Nat. Meserve in the Crown Point expedition.

AARON MOSES, 2d, son of James and Martha J., bap. (Ch. Rec.) June 14, 1719.

From tradition, I should say he was the true type of a Moses. He was a shipwright; was at the siege of Louisburg in 1745 with Col. Nat. Meserve; and after his return worked for Meserve on a ship of war, the *America*. He seems to have possessed many of his Uncle Joe's eccentricities. His wife's maiden name was Fernald; they had three children — one son, Nadab, two daughters, Molly and Dorothy. Tradition says he was to have two sons, one to be called Nadab, the other Abihu; the last-named failed to put in an appearance.

SARAH MOSES, daughter of James and Martha, bap. Sept. 10, 1721; m. Samuel Wallace of Rye (Wallace Sands, Rye Beach).

Children: Sarah (Seavey); Hannah (Marden); Mary, (Tucker); Abigail (m. Nadab Moses her cousin); Samuel, Jr. (m. Parsons); Elizabeth (Jennings); Martha (Langmaid).

MARTHA MOSES, daughter of James and Martha J., bap. Aug. 14, 1726, m. Bartholomew Stavers, an Englishman; she d. Feb. 19, 1792. She was the mother of Capt. Wm. Stavers of Portsmouth.

RUTH MOSES, daughter of James and Martha J., bap. May 3, 1730; m. William Seavey of Rye; d. 1798, in Chichester, N. H.

FIFTH GENERATION.

NADAB MOSES, son of Aaron Moses, 2d, b. in Portsmouth (near south mill dam), in 1749. At about 8 years of age he went to live with his grandfather (James Moses), at Sagamore Creek, and by his grandfather's will he became heir to the Old Homestead. He m. Jan., 1776, Abigail Wallace (his cousin), his father and her mother being children of James and Martha J. Moses; was made a deacon in the old South Church, Portsmouth, in 1785; d. and was buried at the Homestead, Sagamore Creek, Jan. 21, 1792.

Children: Martha J., b. in 1777; James Moses, 2d, b. Jan. 21, 1779, d. Dec. 11, 1863; Aaron, 3d, bap. April 1, 1781, d. Dec. 30, 1831; Samuel and Sarah, twins, b. 1783; Elizabeth, b. May 12, 1785; Levi, b. Aug. 20, 1787, d. July 15, 1863; Dorothy, d. in infancy.

MARY MOSES, daughter of Aaron Moses, 2d, bap. Aug. 22, 1756, d. at Sandwich, N. H.; she m. Mar. 17, 1778, Daniel Moulton of Rye, N. H.

Children (Ch. Rec.): Polly, bap. Jan. 17, 1799, m. Dan Skinner.

DOROTHY MOSES, daughter of Aaron Moses, 2d, m. Amos Beck, Portsmouth, Oct. 4, 1764 ; she died of small-pox.

Children: Henry, of Goshen, N. H.; James, bap. 1772; Catharine, m. Nath. Walker; Aaron, bap. 1767; Molly, bap. 1777; Abigail, bap, 1780.

SIXTH GENERATION.

MARTHA J. MOSES, daughter of Nadab, m. Billy Rand of Rye, N. H.

Children: Samuel M., m. Dorothy (his cousin); Sarah, m. William Hall; Levi M., unm.

JAMES MOSES, 2d, son of Nadab, m. 1803, Mary Odiorne of Rye, N. H. Lived and died on the Old Homestead (at Sagamore Creek), which he inherited from his father, Nadab, by will.

Children: Dorothy, b. Jan. 9, 1804; Eliza B., b. July 9, 1805; William, b. Feb. 24, 1807; Mary Ann, b. April 3, 1809; Samuel W., b. April 10, 1811; James, 4th, b. July 14, 1813; Mary B., b. June 3, 1816; Martha Jaxon, b. May 28, 1818.

AARON MOSES, 3d, son of Nadab, lived in Portsmouth, was a house and ship joiner; m. (1st) Ruhama Mason of Rye; she d. Sept. 15, 1819, aged 34 ; m. (2d) Mary V. Floyd, on Nov. 17, 1820.

Children (by his 1st wife): Mary, b. Aug. 11, 1807; Aaron, 4th, b. Jan. 21, 1809, d. 1849; James, 3d, b. 1811; Leonard, b. 1814, d. 1857; Abigail W., b. 1818. (By second wife): Thomas F., b. 1821; Susan, b. 1823; Caroline, b. 1825; Charles, b. 1827; Elvira, b. 1829; William, b. 1831.

ELIZABETH MOSES, daughter of Nadab, b. at Sagamore Creek, May 12, 1785, d. May 6, 1876, aged 90 y. 11 m. 24 d., she being the last of the sixth generation of the "Nadab" branch of the Moses family. She married Michael W. Tucker (a cousin).

Children: Mary W., Adeline, Elizabeth, Joseph, Charles, Edward, Abagail M., Martha, James M., and Susan.

LEVI MOSES, son of Nadab, was a house and ship joiner, was kind hearted and genial, and known to all as "Uncle Levi;" m. Jan. 16, 1813, the "widow" Elizabeth Jackson.

Children: Edward, Alfred Davis, Henry Jackson, Sarah Elizabeth, Mary Abby, Martha Ann, Levi, Jr., Angelia Streeter, and Sarah Elizabeth.

SEVENTH GENERATION.

DOROTHY MOSES, daughter of James 2d and Mary Moses, b. Jan. 9, 1804; m. Samuel M. Rand, of Rye.

Children: Albert, James, William E., Amos, Abbie, Henry, Charles W., and Martha S., all of whom are married.

MARTHA J. MOSES, daughter of James 2d and Mary Moses, b. May 28, 1818.

ELIZA B. MOSES, daughter of James 2d, b. July 8, 1805; m. Simeon Odiorne.

Children: Mary, Elizabeth, Martha Ann, and James M.

MARY ANN MOSES, daughter of James 2d, b. April 3, 1809; d. young.

SAMUEL W. MOSES, son of James 2d, b. April 10, 1811, m. Olive Cate.

Children lived to grow up: Fred. F., Annie, Ettie, and Samuel W., Jr.

JAMES MOSES the 4th, was the son of James the 2d, and his wife Mary, was b. July 14, 1813; (James the 3d, b. 1811, was the son of Aaron Moses the 3d); James the 4th, m. (1st) Clara Ferguson; they had one child, who d. young; he m. (2d) Louisa Philbrick, who now survives him.

MARY B. MOSES, dau. of James 2d, b. June 3, 1816; m. Henry F. Wendell of Portsmouth.

EDWARD MOSES, son of Levi, b. Oct. 27, 1813; d. May 18, 1864.

ALFRED D. MOSES, son of Levi, b. July 3, 1815; d. Dec. 24, 1888; he m. Julia Ann Moses (a cousin), and they had one *child* named Clara Abby, b. May 30, 1874. He expended considerable labor in gathering material from the family archives, much of which is included in this sketch.

HENRY J. MOSES, son of Levi, b. June 6, 1817; d. Sept. 30, 1820.

SARAH ELIZABETH MOSES, dau. of Levi, b. June 16, 1820; m. a Mr. Goodrich.

MARY ABBY MOSES, dau. of Levi, b. April 17, 1822; d. Sept. 20, 1863.

MARTHA ANN, dau. of Levi, b. May 15, 1824; d. Feb. 22, 1825.

LEVI MOSES, JR., son of Levi, b. Aug. 17, 1826; d. Sept. 24, 1861.

ANGELIA S. MOSES, dau. of Levi, b. March 27, 1828; d. Aug. 12, 1887.

WILLIAM MOSES, son of James 2d, and Mary Moses, b. at Sagamore Creek, Feb. 24, 1807, is a farmer, and owns part of the Old Homestead, on which he built and resided from the time of his marriage in 1831 until his buildings and their contents were destroyed by fire, May 12, 1884, after which he bought a small place on Sagamore Road, about one mile from the Old Homestead, where he now (1889) resides. He m. Abàgail Atwood Seavey, dau. of Joshua Seavey, who was the son of Paul and Sarah (*nee* Wallace) Seavey. Sarah Wallace was the dau. of Samuel and Sarah (*nee* Moses) Wallace; and Sarah Moses Wallace was the dau. of James and Martha (*nee* Jaxon) Moses of Sagamore Creek.

EIGHTH GENERATION.

Children of William Moses: Julia Ann, b. Dec. 3, 1831; Augusta Olive, b. July 4, 1833; James William, b. Sept. 2, 1835, d. Oct. 21, 1847; George Henry, b. Nov. 29, 1838, d. Sept. 31, 1839; John Edward, b. April 10, 1840, d. Nov. 16, 1847; Clara Abby, b. May 29, 1843, d. July 18, 1846; Joshua Seavey, b. March 26, 1846.

JULIA A., m. Alfred D. Moses, and they had one *child.* Clara Abby, b. May 30, 1874.

AUGUSTA O., m. Wm. W. Seavey of Lee Co., Ill.; they have one *child,* Albion M.

JOSHUA S., m. Hattie L. Bixby of Lee Center, Lee Co., Ill., Feb. 14, 1870, at Amboy, Ill., by the Rev. Geo. H. Wells.

Child: Fred. Wallace, b. June 26, 1871, at Lee Center, Ill.

Fred. Wallace of the Ninth Generation is the son of Joshua S., son of William, son of James 3d, son of Nadab, son of Aaron 2d, son of James, son of Aaron, son of John and Ann Moses. Aaron, b. in 1655, was the first, and Joshua S., b. in 1846, was the last Moses born on the old Moses farm.

There was one house burned near where the one built by Nadab Moses now stands. The old family burying ground is just east of the buildings on quite a high point of land overlooking the placid Sagamore. In this burial place now lie the ashes of the past generations of our ancestors, who certainly chose for a home in the wilderness a very picturesque spot.

WILLIAM RAND, son of Saml. M. Rand and Dorothy (Moses) Rand, went to live with his grandfather. (James Moses 2d), when quite young and with his maiden aunt (Martha J., daughter of James 2d, and Mary Moses), inherited the old homestead on Sagamore Creek, where they now reside, he having m. Emily Bell of Portsmouth, and reared an interesting family of five children, the youngest of which is now (1889) thirteen years old.

MARTHA J. MOSES, daughter of James 3d and Mary Moses, b. May 28, 1818, is the only one of her father's family who has undertaken to sail out on life's stormy ocean without a mate. She has always lived at the old homestead, and in the same house with the past five generations; namely, her grandmother, Abigail W. Moses, her father and mother, her brothers and sisters, her nephew, and nephew's children.

The present house at the Old Homestead, built by Nadab Moses, is the third house placed over the same cellar.

This we believe to be as nearly a correct record of the Moses family of Sagamore Creek, Portsmouth, N. H., as any one has ever been able to produce; all we know of where the first John Moses came from is from tradition, which says he came from Scotland, and we presume he was among the very first settlers of New Hampshire.—[A. D. M.]

DESCENDANTS OF MARK MOSES, THE SON OF AARON, WHO WAS THE SON OF JOHN MOSES OF SAGAMORE CREEK.

MARK MOSES of the third generation, m. Oct. 29, 1724, Martha Williams, and moved to Epsom, N. H. He d. Feb. 2, 1789, aged 86.

Children: Elizabeth (Ch. Rec. Portsmouth), b. June 1, 1729; Samuel, b. ———; Aaron, b. 1742, d. at Gilmanton, N. H., Mch. 20, 1816, aged 74; William, b. ———; Sylvanus, b. at Epsom, Aug. 25, 1754; James, b. Feb. 27, 1758, d. Aug. 17, 1819; another daughter, name unknown.

FOURTH AND SUCCEEDING GENERATIONS.

SYLVANUS[4] MOSES, son of Mark[3], m. Aug. 22, 1776, Mariam Young of Danvill; served in the war; was at White Plains under Capt. Emery for nine months; after his discharge settled on farm next his brother James.

Children: Sarah, John, Joseph, David, Mariam, Joshua, Elijah, Polly.

Sarah[5] lived at Epsom; m. Richard Locke; and had children.

John[5] lived in Chichester; m. Susan French of Stratham; had four sons, all dead.

Joseph[5] lived in Concord; m. Lydia Gould of Amesbury, Mass.; had eleven children, none living.

David[5] lived in Stewardstown; m. Hetty Rand of Epsom; had five children, one living.

Mariam[5], m. Mark French of Epsom; had two sons, both deceased.

Joshua[5], m. Hannah Downs of Berwick, Me.; settled in Allenstown; had eight children, none living; he d. in Pittsfield.

Elijah[5], m. Ruth Parker of Lyman; had six children, none living.

Polly[5], m. Robert S. Cochran of Pembroke; settled in Deerfield; had one child, Sallie T. Cochran who was b. Feb. 3, 1814, and who m., in 1835, Samuel Brown of Epsom, and had *children:* Sarah M.[7] (Fowler), Robert C.[7], Thomas M.[7] (was a soldier, d. 1865), Walter H.[7]

SAMUEL[4] MOSES, son of Mark, was the eldest son; settled in Meredith; m. twice; his first wife — a Weeks — had several children; the eldest son was Samuel, d. 1847.

SAMUEL[5] m. Mary Trickey.

Children: Thomas[6] (dead), Willis[6], James E., lives in Haverhill; Elizabeth C. (Haines), lives in Concord.

WILLIS[6] MOSES, son of Samuel, m. (1st) 1875, Maria Staples; and (2d) 1887, Susan E. Griffin.

Children: Charles H., George A., Elizabeth.

JAMES[4] MOSES, son of Mark, settled on the home place at Epsom; m. Mch. 9, 1780, Elizabeth Sherburne of Northwood.

Children: Mark, b. Jan. 19, 1781, d. Mch. 11, 1811; James, b. Jan. 7, 1783, d. Oct. 30, 1812; Jane, b. Oct. 9, 1784; Betsey S., b. Dec. 15, 1786; Mary, b. Nov. 28, 1788, d. Dec. 2, 1864; Sarah, b. Aug. 27, 1792.

MARK[5] MOSES, son of James, m. June 19, 1802, Betsey Cate.

Children: Joseph J., b. Oct. 30, 1803, d. Mch. 30, 1889; Dearborn B., b. Aug. 3, 1805, d. Aug. 23, 1881; Mark S., b. July 7, 1808, d. Jan. 4, 1865.

JOSEPH J.[6] MOSES of Manchester, N. H., son of Mark[5], m. Apr. 9, 1829, Hannah Cate.

Children: Elizabeth S.[7], who m. Mch. 29, 1857, Sherburn D. Cass of Byfield, Mass.; and has child Myrtle E., b. Jan. 19, 1866, m. Aug. 3, 1889, to D. H. Hill.

DEARBORN B.[6] MOSES of Epsom, son of Mark, m. Feb. 13, 1839, Sally H. Locke.

Child: Sarah L., b. Nov. 25, 1841; m. June 19, 1869, James H. Tripp. *Her child:* Walter H., b. Apr. 24, 1875.

MARK S.[6] MOSES, son of Mark, m. (1st) May 29, 1835, Elvira Dolbear; (2d) Jan. 1, 1854, Mary A. Towle.

Children: John M., b. Aug. 2, 1855; lives at Northwood Ridge, N. H.; Cyrus S., b. Aug. 28, 1860, d. Apr. 30, 1864.

JAMES[5] MOSES, son of James, m. Feb. 26, 1817, Betsey Chesley.

Children: Hannah P., b. Sept. 25, 1807, d. Jan. 27, 1885; Lucinda ———.

HANNAH P.[6] MOSES, dau. of James; m. May 5, 1825, Benjamin L. Locke.

Children: Lucinda M., Henrietta C., Almira E., James L., Marianna J., Ann L., Adela A., Sarah M., W. F. Estes.

BETSEY[5] MOSES, dau. of James, m. Nov. 25, 1807, David Sherburne.

Children: William, James Moses, Eliza, David, Sarah Jane Moses, b. Mch. 22, 1821 (m. John S. Cate), William, Mary Ann, Lucinda R.

MARY[5] MOSES, dau. of James, m. May 26, 1814, John Morrison.

Children: John, b. May 30, 1815 (m. Mehitable Bartlett); James, Betsy, Jane (m. James Knowlton).

SARAH[5] MOSES, dau. of James, m. Nov. 8, 1814, John Lake.

Children: Moses, Aaron, James, Mary J., Sarah A., Lovina S., Orlando H., Elmira E.

AARON[4] MOSES, son of Mark[3], m. about 1765, Dorothy Sanborn, who d. at Gilmanton, N. H., June, 1820, aged 75.

Children: William, d. at Gilmanton, Feb. 21, 1825, aged 51, George, Abiather, Aaron, and probably a daughter, Susan.

George[5] had a son named Dyer.

Abiathar[5] had sons, John, William, and Sanborn (who moved to Iowa); also dau. Olive, who m. her cousin, Nathaniel Moses, son of William.

WILLIAM[5] MOSES, son of Aaron[4], m. Oct., 1797, Susan Boynton, b. at Rowley, Mass., and d. Apr. 17, 1856, aged 83.

Children (all b. at Gilmanton, N. H.): Charles, b. Feb. 22, 1799, d. at Brooklyn, N. Y., May 13, 1866; Nathaniel, b. May 24, 1801, d. at Campton, N. H., June 20, 1886; Susan, b. June 19, 1803, d. at Gilmanton, Oct., 1805; Aaron, b. July 4, 1805, d. at Hackensack, N. J., Sept. 24, 1883; David Boynton, b. Sept. 29, 1809; Hiram W., b. Jan. 6, 1812; John M., b. Jan. 6, 1812, d. at Flemington, N. J., June 12, 1877; William, b. May 7, 1814.

CHARLES[6] MOSES, son of William, m. (1st) Apr. 15, 1830, Phebe Wyman; she d. Jan. 17, 1855, at New York; m. (2d) Susan Fox.

Children: Charles H., b. at Boston, Mass., Mch. 3, 1831; Elizabeth W., b. July 4, 1834.

CHARLES H.[7] MOSES, son of Charles, m. Sept. 15, 1863, Emma J. Ask, who was b. at New York, Oct. 11, 1837.

Children: Charles E., b. at New York, Nov. 17, 1872; Henry M., b. Feb. 17, 1875, at Brooklyn, N. Y.

ELIZABETH W.[7] MOSES, dau. of Charles, m. Nov. 25, 1855, Otis B. Davis.

Child: Charles O., b. at New York, June 14, 1857.

NATHANIEL[6] MOSES, son of William; m. June 13, 1831, Olive Moses, who d. at Campton, N. H., Oct. 23, 1857.

Children: Dorothy J., b. Nov. 20, 1834, d. at Franklin Falls, N. H., Jan. 13, 1879; Abigail K., b. June 28, 1839; Olive M., b. Jan. 16, 1842.

DOROTHY J.[7] m. Albert A. Marden.

Child: Mabel D., b. at Franklin Falls, N. H., July 28, 1872.

ABIGAIL K.[7] m. Martin Silver.

Child: Olivette, b. at Lynn, Sept. 9, 1860, who m. David G. Bartlett.

AARON[6] MOSES, son of William, m. Dorothy Rollins.

Children: Susan F., b. Apr. 1, 1831, at Campton, N. H., d. Aug. 2, 1883, at Hackensack, N. J.; John M., b. at Pittsfield, N. H., Aug. 16, 1834, d. May 17, 1872.

Susan F. m. George N. Brown.

JOHN M.[7] MOSES, son of Aaron, m. Ellen M. Brown.

Children: Nellie F., b. Aug. 6, 1857 (m. J. P. Story); Dolly M., b. Oct. 20, 1859 (m. Samuel Lozier); Carrie L., b. Jan. 1, 1867 (m. James Black).

DAVID BOYNTON[6] MOSES, son of William, after a boy's life on a farm, spent a few years in Boston, then with his brother William came to New York in 1834 and started in the provision business. The firm "D. B. & W. Moses" packed largely in New York and the West, and cured and sold the first bacon that was ever sent to Europe. Three other brothers, Charles, Aaron, and John M., afterwards came to New York and embarked in the same business. David B. retired from active business in 1864, and spends his time between his country seat at Sing Sing, N. Y., and his city home in New York. He m. May 28, 1840, Jeanette A. Campbell, who was b. in 1819, and d. Dec. 20, 1877.

  Children: Isabel, b. Mch. 6, 1847, at New York; she m. Duplessis M. Helm, who d. Dec. 30, 1889, at New York.

HIRAM W.[6] MOSES, son of William, m. Feb. 4, 1835, Lavinia A. Connor; she d. May 15, 1884.

  Children (b. in Gilmanton, N. H.): Hiram W., b. May 20, 1837; Valeria C., b. Aug. 28, 1838.

  Valeria C. m. Oct. 5, 1865, Luther Sargent. *Child:* George J., b. Nov. 19, 1866.

HIRAM W.[7] MOSES, son of Hiram W., m. (1st) May 5, 1860, Elizabeth J. Carr; she d. Nov. 10, 1864; m. (2d) June 30, 1867, Arvilla A. Edgerly.

  Children: Isadora, b. Dec. 27, 1862 (m. Alvah S. Rand on Oct. 24, 1883); William W., b. May 20, 1873; Susan R., b. Feb. 7, 1878.

JOHN M.[6] MOSES, son of William, m. (1st) Olive C. Foss, who d. at New York, Dec. 30, 1865; m. (2d) Mrs. Sarah O. Somerby; she d. at Flemington, N. J., Apr. 28, 1880.

WILLIAM[6] MOSES, son of William, m. Feb. 22, 1844, Susan A. Ranlet, who was b. at Gilmanton, N. H., Apr. 1, 1821.

WILLIAM[5] MOSES, son of Aaron[4], m. Oct., 1797, Susan Boynton, b. at Rowley, Mass., and d. Apr. 17, 1856, aged 83.

Children (all b. at Gilmanton, N. H.): Charles, b. Feb. 22, 1799, d. at Brooklyn, N. Y., May 13, 1866; Nathaniel, b. May 24, 1801, d. at Campton, N. H., June 20, 1886; Susan, b. June 19, 1803, d. at Gilmanton, Oct., 1805; Aaron, b. July 4, 1805, d. at Hackensack, N. J., Sept. 24, 1883; David Boynton, b. Sept. 29, 1809; Hiram W., b. Jan. 6, 1812; John M., b. Jan. 6, 1812, d. at Flemington, N. J., June 12, 1877; William, b. May 7, 1814.

CHARLES[6] MOSES, son of William, m. (1st) Apr. 15, 1830, Phebe Wyman; she d. Jan. 17, 1855, at New York; m. (2d) Susan Fox.

Children: Charles H., b. at Boston, Mass., Mch. 3, 1831; Elizabeth W., b. July 4, 1834.

CHARLES H.[7] MOSES, son of Charles, m. Sept. 15, 1863, Emma J. Ask, who was b. at New York, Oct. 11, 1837.

Children: Charles E., b. at New York, Nov. 17, 1872; Henry M., b. Feb. 17, 1875, at Brooklyn, N. Y.

ELIZABETH W.[7] MOSES, dau. of Charles, m. Nov. 25, 1855, Otis B. Davis.

Child: Charles O., b. at New York, June 14, 1857.

NATHANIEL[6] MOSES, son of William; m. June 13, 1831, Olive Moses, who d. at Campton, N. H., Oct. 23, 1857.

Children: Dorothy J., b. Nov. 20, 1834, d. at Franklin Falls, N. H., Jan. 13, 1879; Abigail K., b. June 28, 1839; Olive M., b. Jan. 16, 1842.

DOROTHY J.[7] m. Albert A. Marden.

Child: Mabel D., b. at Franklin Falls, N. H., July 28, 1872.

ABIGAIL K.[7] m. Martin Silver.

Child: Olivette, b. at Lynn, Sept. 9, 1860, who m. David G. Bartlett.

AARON[6] MOSES, son of William, m. Dorothy Rollins.

Children: Susan F., b. Apr. 1, 1831, at Campton, N. H., d. Aug. 2, 1883, at Hackensack, N. J.; John M., b. at Pittsfield, N. H., Aug. 16, 1834, d. May 17, 1872.

Susan F. m. George N. Brown.

JOHN M.[7] MOSES, son of Aaron, m. Ellen M. Brown.

Children: Nellie F., b. Aug. 6, 1857 (m. J. P. Story); Dolly M., b. Oct. 20, 1859 (m. Samuel Lozier); Carrie L., b. Jan. 1, 1867 (m. James Black).

DAVID BOYNTON[6] MOSES, son of William, after a boy's life on a farm, spent a few years in Boston, then with his brother William came to New York in 1834 and started in the provision business. The firm "D. B. & W. Moses" packed largely in New York and the West, and cured and sold the first bacon that was ever sent to Europe. Three other brothers, Charles, Aaron, and John M., afterwards came to New York and embarked in the same business. David B. retired from active business in 1864, and spends his time between his country seat at Sing Sing, N. Y., and his city home in New York. He m. May 28, 1840, Jeanette A. Campbell, who was b. in 1819, and d. Dec. 20, 1877.

Children: Isabel, b. Mch. 6, 1847, at New York; she m. Duplessis M. Helm, who d. Dec. 30, 1889, at New York.

HIRAM W.[6] MOSES, son of William, m. Feb. 4, 1835, Lavinia A. Connor; she d. May 15, 1884.

Children (b. in Gilmanton, N. H.): Hiram W., b. May 20, 1837; Valeria C., b. Aug. 28, 1838.

Valeria C. m. Oct. 5, 1865, Luther Sargent. *Child:* George J., b. Nov. 19, 1866.

HIRAM W.[7] MOSES, son of Hiram W., m. (1st) May 5, 1860, Elizabeth J. Carr; she d. Nov. 10, 1864; m. (2d) June 30, 1867, Arvilla A. Edgerly.

Children: Isadora, b. Dec. 27, 1862 (m. Alvah S. Rand on Oct. 24, 1883); William W., b. May 20, 1873; Susan R., b. Feb. 7, 1878.

JOHN M.[6] MOSES, son of William, m. (1st) Olive C. Foss, who d. at New York, Dec. 30, 1865; m. (2d) Mrs. Sarah O. Somerby; she d. at Flemington, N. J., Apr. 28, 1880.

WILLIAM[6] MOSES, son of William, m. Feb. 22, 1844, Susan A. Ranlet, who was b. at Gilmanton, N. H., Apr. 1, 1821.

WILLIAM[5] MOSES, son of Aaron[4], m. Oct., 1797, Susan Boynton, b. at Rowley, Mass., and d. Apr. 17, 1856, aged 83.

Children (all b. at Gilmanton, N. H.): Charles, b. Feb. 22, 1799, d. at Brooklyn, N. Y., May 13, 1866; Nathaniel, b. May 24, 1801, d. at Campton, N. H., June 20, 1886; Susan, b. June 19, 1803, d. at Gilmanton, Oct., 1805; Aaron, b. July 4, 1805, d. at Hackensack, N. J., Sept. 24, 1883; David Boynton, b. Sept. 29, 1809; Hiram W., b. Jan. 6, 1812; John M., b. Jan. 6, 1812, d. at Flemington, N. J., June 12, 1877; William, b. May 7, 1814.

CHARLES[6] MOSES, son of William, m. (1st) Apr. 15, 1830, Phebe Wyman; she d. Jan. 17, 1855, at New York; m. (2d) Susan Fox.

Children: Charles H., b. at Boston, Mass., Mch. 3, 1831; Elizabeth W., b. July 4, 1834.

CHARLES H.[7] MOSES, son of Charles, m. Sept. 15, 1863, Emma J. Ask, who was b. at New York, Oct. 11, 1837.

Children: Charles E., b. at New York, Nov. 17, 1872; Henry M., b. Feb. 17, 1875, at Brooklyn, N. Y.

ELIZABETH W.[7] MOSES, dau. of Charles, m. Nov. 25, 1855, Otis B. Davis.

Child: Charles O., b. at New York, June 14, 1857.

NATHANIEL[6] MOSES, son of William; m. June 13, 1831, Olive Moses, who d. at Campton, N. H., Oct. 23, 1857.

Children: Dorothy J., b. Nov. 20, 1834, d. at Franklin Falls, N. H., Jan. 13, 1879; Abigail K., b. June 28, 1839; Olive M., b. Jan. 16, 1842.

DOROTHY J.[7] m. Albert A. Marden.

Child: Mabel D., b. at Franklin Falls, N. H., July 28, 1872.

ABIGAIL K.[7] m. Martin Silver.

Child: Olivette, b. at Lynn, Sept. 9, 1860, who m. David G. Bartlett.

AARON[6] MOSES, son of William, m. Dorothy Rollins.

Children: Susan F., b. Apr. 1, 1831, at Campton, N. H., d. Aug. 2, 1883, at Hackensack, N. J.; John M., b. at Pittsfield, N. H., Aug. 16, 1834, d. May 17, 1872.

Susan F. m. George N. Brown.

JOHN M.[7] MOSES, son of Aaron, m. Ellen M. Brown.

Children: Nellie F., b. Aug. 6, 1857 (m. J. P. Story); Dolly M., b. Oct. 20, 1859 (m. Samuel Lozier); Carrie L., b. Jan. 1, 1867 (m. James Black).

DAVID BOYNTON[6] MOSES, son of William, after a boy's life on a farm, spent a few years in Boston, then with his brother William came to New York in 1834 and started in the provision business. The firm "D. B. & W. Moses" packed largely in New York and the West, and cured and sold the first bacon that was ever sent to Europe. Three other brothers, Charles, Aaron, and John M., afterwards came to New York and embarked in the same business. David B. retired from active business in 1864, and spends his time between his country seat at Sing Sing, N. Y., and his city home in New York. He m. May 28, 1840, Jeanette A. Campbell, who was b. in 1819, and d. Dec. 20, 1877.

Children: Isabel, b. Mch. 6, 1847, at New York; she m. Duplessis M. Helm, who d. Dec. 30, 1889, at New York.

HIRAM W.[6] MOSES, son of William, m. Feb. 4, 1835, Lavinia A. Connor; she d. May 15, 1884.

Children (b. in Gilmanton, N. H.): Hiram W., b. May 20, 1837; Valeria C., b. Aug. 28, 1838.

Valeria C. m. Oct. 5, 1865, Luther Sargent. *Child:* George J., b. Nov. 19, 1866.

HIRAM W.[7] MOSES, son of Hiram W., m. (1st) May 5, 1860, Elizabeth J. Carr; she d. Nov. 10, 1864; m. (2d) June 30, 1867, Arvilla A. Edgerly.

Children: Isadora, b. Dec. 27, 1862 (m. Alvah S. Rand on Oct. 24, 1883); William W., b. May 20, 1873; Susan R., b. Feb. 7, 1878.

JOHN M.[6] MOSES, son of William, m. (1st) Olive C. Foss, who d. at New York, Dec. 30, 1865; m. (2d) Mrs. Sarah O. Somerby; she d. at Flemington, N. J., Apr. 28, 1880.

WILLIAM[6] MOSES, son of William, m. Feb. 22, 1844, Susan A. Ranlet, who was b. at Gilmanton, N. H., Apr. 1, 1821.

CHAPTER VI.

OTHER EARLY NEW ENGLAND FAMILIES OF THE MOSES NAME.

In the compilation of this work, evidence has been presented showing that there were, previous to the Revolution, other emigrants to New England bearing the Moses name, who also founded families. The few items concerning them which have been gathered, are published for the benefit of their descendants who may wish to make a more thorough investigation. Referring to the last pages of Chapter IV, it is proper here to call attention to SAMUEL MOSES, whose estate was probated in 1691. He was, most probably, closely related to Henry Moses of Salem; was possibly a brother.

The Joseph Moses of Salem, who married Tamsin Beans, was of the generation of Henry's children.

In the *New England Hist. and Gen. Register*, Vol. XXI, we find, among the marriages, births, and deaths, in Dorchester, Mass., "Mary, daughter of THOMAS MOSES, b. May 2, 1665."

As already stated in Chapter II of this work, the detailed and apparently exhaustive histories of Dorchester, in their numerous "lists," give no person of the name of Moses. The stay of Thomas Moses within that town may have been brief. He was of the generation of Henry Moses of Salem and John Moses of Windsor, and was possibly their brother and a son of John Moses of Plymouth, coming with the latter from England to his first landing and temporary home in Massachusetts Bay Colony. The surviving children of Samuel Moses were daughters, and the unconnected Moses names in the list of marriages, at close of chapter, may have been other descendants of Thomas Moses.

In the *New England Hist. and Gen. Register*, Vol. VII, we find, under head of general items, relating to the early settlers of Dover, N. H.: "TIMOTHY MOSES had wife Mary and *children*, Martha, b. 5 May, 1700; Timothy, b. 2 Sept., 1707." "TIMOTHY had wife and *child*, Martha, b. 5 May, 1732."

The original papers presented in Chapter V negative any theory that Timothy was descended from John of Portsmouth.; neither is the name Timothy perpetuated in the Portsmouth family. It is a little singular that this Timothy appears at Dover at the date that we lose all trace of Timothy (1st), of Windsor. In the *N. H. Prov. Papers,* Vols. IX, XI, and XII, the name of Timothy of Dover appears several times between 1732 and 1787.

William V. and Oliver Moses, formerly ship-builders of Bath, Me., and many other Moses families of Maine and New Hampshire, notably in Portsmouth and Exeter, N. H., are descended from a family of brothers that settled, about the middle of the eighteenth century, in Scarborough, Me. The writer has letters from W. F. Moses of Bath, Me., from Eliza (Moses) Barry (aged 73), of Buxton Centre, Me., and George Moses (aged 83), of Freedom, N. H., who substantially agree on the following table of lineage:

FIRST GENERATION.

Three brothers came from England, JOHN MOSES, WILLIAM MOSES, and GEORGE MOSES, or, as one has it, Amos, William, and George; that John or Amos (whichever his name) was a doctor, and returned to England; that William settled in Portsmouth or Exeter, and George in Scarborough, Me. Rufus Moses, now living (1890), at the age of 95, at Cape Elizabeth, Me., states that he was informed that his grandfather George was from the Isle of Jersey.

SECOND GENERATION.

GEORGE MOSES of Scarborough was a farmer, and had:
Children: Nathaniel, b. Oct. 13, 1758, d. about 1840; Josiah, Daniel, and George.

Josiah, m. a Millekin, and lived at Windom, Me.
Daniel lived at Windom, Me.

THIRD GENERATION.

NATHANIEL MOSES d. in Scarborough, Me.; m. Elizabeth Millekin, who was b. Sept. 10, 1765.

Children: Rebecca, b. Dec. 19, 1784; Sarah, b. Dec. 29, 1786; Benjamin, b. Jan. 16, 1788; Elizabeth, b. Dec. 16, 1790; Silas, b. Jan. 16, 1792; Rufus, b. June 28, 1795, and living at Cape Elizabeth, Me.; Hannah, b. Aug. 11, 1798; William V., b. Jan. 30, 1801, d. Dec. 10,

1878; Oliver, b. May 12, 1803, d. Feb. 14, 1882 ; Phœbe, b. Jan. 25, 1807; Ebenezer, b. Aug. 24, 1809.

GEORGE MOSES m. a Harmon.

Children: John (m. a Tenderson), Josiah (m. a Whitney); William, Annie, Abigail, Effie.

FOURTH GENERATION.

WILLIAM MOSES, son of George, was b. Oct. 29, 1772, and, according to one account, m. a ·Rice ; according to another, m. Annie Millekin, b. Dec. 31, 1774, and had :

Children: Cyrus, Fanny, William, George, b. 1803, living 1889; Horace, Mary, Eliza A., b. Jan. 30, 1817, living, 1889, at Buxton Centre, Me. (m. a Berry); Edward, living, 1889, at Malden, Mass.

WILLIAM V. and OLIVER MOSES commenced business together about 1825, in Bath, Me. They soon had one of the largest iron foundries of the State. They afterwards commenced ship-building, which they carried on for about forty years, building and sailing their own ships, under the different firm names of W. V. & Oliver, W. V. & Sons, and Oliver Moses & Sons. At one time they owned more shipping than any other concern in Bath.

WILLIAM V. MOSES, son of Nathaniel.

Children: William F. and Albert T. (twins), living, 1890, at Bath, Me.; Sarah E.; Thomas F., living, 1890, at Urbana, Ohio; Fanny E.; George F. and Alice D., both living at Cape Elizabeth, Me.

OLIVER MOSES, son of Nathaniel.

Children: Francis O., living, 1890, at Bath, Me.; Galen C., living, 1890, at Bath, Me.; Harriet S. (Knight), living, 1890, at Portland, Me.; Annie P. (Harris), living, 1890, at Portland, Me.; Wealthy C. (Hines), living, 1890, at San Francisco, Cal.

FIFTH GENERATION.

WILLIAM MOSES, the son of William, living, 1889, at Buxton Centre, Me.

Children: Almond, Frank, Mary, Austin, Horace W.

GEORGE MOSES, the son of William, living, 1889, at Freedom, N. H.

Children: Annie E. (Beach), Mary Jane (Pease), William R. of Freedom, Rose F. (Hayes), George W. of Lynn, Mass., Olen E. of Bradford, Mass.

SIXTH GENERATION.

HORACE W. MOSES, son of William, lives in Geneseo, Ill.

Children: Howard W.[7], Harry[7], Nellie[7], Drusilla[7].

The writer has failed in his attempts to obtain a connected genealogical line of descent from that William Moses, who settled in Portsmouth or Exeter, probably about 1730 to 1740. Among the Moses names mentioned in the Portsmouth Association Test of 1776 (*Brewster's Rambles, 1st series*), Thomas, Theodore, and Samuel, evidently belong to this line. From the *Rambles* we learn that Theodore and Samuel 2d were sons of Samuel 1st, and on p. 188 is a letter, dated Exeter, 1858, from Theodore Moses in his 93d year. He removed from Portsmouth to Newmarket in 1779, and 8 years thereafter to Exeter. "Samuel, Thomas, and William," petition from Newmarket, in 1785.

JOHN G. MOSES, living, 1889, in Portsmouth, N. H., states that he was b. 1809, his brother William in 1805, and his sisters Abbie, 1810, and Martha (Moses) Twing, in 1811. His father's name was William, and his father had three brothers, Benjamin (father of J. Woodman Moses, now living at age of 79, at Portsmouth), Thomas, and John, also one sister, Mary.

As already remarked, men of the Moses name appear to have responded promptly to the call to arms in all American wars. Among the soldier lists we find the following (Vol. VIII, *Coll. Essex Ins.*) quotation from *George's Almanac* of 1776,— An account of the "bloody battle of Bunker Hill": "Among the killed of the Provincials* was":

"MAJOR MOSES of Holden." Holden is in Worcester Co., Mass., and Major Moses was doubtless descended from one of the Moses families of Salem, who, at an early date, removed from their native town. The same may be said of:

ABRAHAM MOSES, who enlisted March, 1782, under Capt. John Fowle, in the 3d Mass. Reg., and was discharged by Gen. Knox, at New York, in 1784. In June, 1820, he was living in Rutland, aged 59 years. In his family, whom he supported at that time (pension papers) was a daughter, Lydia, aged 22, and a son, John, aged 20. Pensions were also issued to Revolutionary soldiers,

---

*The Almanac is authority for the statement that the total loss of the Provincials in killed, of field officers at the battle, was one Major-General, one Colonel, two Lieut.-Colonels, and two Majors.

Daniel Moses, Col. Marshall's Reg. Mass. line ; to Martha, widow of *Josiah Moses*, Mass. line ; and to Polly, widow *John Moses*, Mass. line.

ISAIAH MOSES enlisted at Wallingford, Conn., in 1776, in Capt. Bunnell's Co., Col. Douglass' Reg. The regiment was raised from counties west of the Connecticut River.

JESSE MOSES enlisted at same time and place.

JONAS MOSES enlisted at New Haven in the 6th Conn. Reg., Mar. 10, 1777.

The three names last mentioned probably belong to scions from the Simsbury tree. The Probate Rec. of New Haven, under date of Jan. 3, 1783, mention that Edward Crafts was appointed administrator of the estate of Jonas Moses, late of Derby, Conn.

JOHN MOSES, "late of Derby," had his estate administered upon July 2, 1804.

PHILIP MOSES. Petition to General Assembly, May, 1810, of Philip Moses and Hesther Frank, for sale of land at Humphreysville (part of old Derby), was acted on by Probate Court.

HENRY MOSES, MEHITABLE MOSES ET AL. of Derby. Petition of same for sale of land in New Haven acted on by Probate Court, Jan. 23, 1841.

JOHN C. MOSES, soldier of 1st Ill. Reg., in Mexican War. Pension issued to Polly, his widow.

No attempt has been made to make a list of Moses names of soldiers in the War of the Rebellion. Probably not one-fourth of such names entitled to a war record are so entered in this work.

APPENDIX.

A drawing in colors showing the coat of arms of the MOSES family, of which the above is an India ink copy, was procured by David B. Moses of New York, when making a tour through Europe in 1872, and is accompanied by the usual certificate from Cullerton, an authority on Heraldry, at 25 Cranbourn Street, London. That this blazon or device has considerable antiquity is proved from its description in a work published in 1780 by Joseph Edmonston, *Mowbray Herald Extraordinary*, which reads as follows :

    MOSES

        Gules — a chevron between three cocks — *Or*

The same description of the "Moses" coat of arms is given in the *Encyclopedia Heraldica*, also in *Burke's Heraldry*, and in *Burke's General Armory of England, Scotland, and Wales*.

From an authority on the subject, we learn that crests were added to coats of arms at a later period, and in *Robson's British Herald*, Vol. II., published in 1830, we find the following :

    MOSES — *gules* — a chevron between three cocks, — *Or*

    MOSES *Crest* — a cock reguard — *ppr.*

From Volume III. of same work it appears that the Moses heraldic motto, "*Dum Spiro Spero*" ("While I breathe I hope"), is also the motto of the following named Houses: The Viscount Dillon, Ascotti, Auchmuty, Bannatyne, Compton, Carlton, Sherman, Elrich, Glazebrook, Symonds, Pearson, Thompson, Sharp, and some other families.

In the *Dictionary of Heraldry*, by Coats, published in 1725, and in Evan's *Grammar of Heraldry*, we read:

"The Cock is the emblem of Strife, of Quarrels, of Haughtiness, of Victory, — because he rather chooses to die than yield, for which reason Aristophanes calls him the bird of Mars. Of the Cock, Guillim says as follows : 'As some account the Eagle the Queen, and the Swallow or Wagtail the Lady, so may I term this the Knight of birds, being of noble courage and also prepared evermore to the Battle — having his comb for a helmet, his long hooked bill for a falchion — he hath his legs armed with spurs, giving example to the valiant soldier to expel danger by fight rather than flight. Of all birds he may be best said in Blazon to be armed — that is, thus furnished and prepared to the encounter. Cocks are borne in Coat armor by many families both in England and other parts.'"

The writer has made some attempts to connect the founders of the New England families of the Moses name with their respective ancestors. The short time given to the compilation of this work, and the considerable expense which it was found would be involved, have precluded a thorough examination of the English records. There can be little doubt that John Moses of Portsmouth was a Scotchman. As already stated, there is a strong family tradition that John Moses of Plymouth was a Welshman. The histories of Plymouth make no mention of Scotchmen in that Colony. Several of the vessels bringing emigrants to Plymouth sailed from Bristol * near the borders of Wales.

---

* *Bradford's History of Plymouth*, p. 261 — Mr. Allerton (1630) had taken up some large sums at Bristol at 50 per cent. p. 298 — In 1632 — "Mr. Allerton little regarded his bond, for he carried her" (the ship *White Angel*, bought for the Plymouth Colony at Bristol) "to Bristol again, from whence he intended to set her out again, and so did three times into these parts, as will after appear." p. 304 — In 1632 — "Ship called the *Lyon*" landed at Boston "with 123 passengers, whereof 50 children all in health."

Prince's Chronicles. In 1631 — "The *Lion* set sail from Bristol and brought 20 passengers."

Richard Mather's Journal. In 1635 — Shipped for New England from Bristol in the *Mary and Bess* — mentions other ships from Bristol for New England — The *Angel Gabriel* and the *James*.

APPENDIX.

As the nearest considerable shipping port for Welshmen, it is likely that John Moses may have learned or worked at his trade of shipwright at Bristol, and possibly he there made the acquaintance of that John Guy, a party to the lawsuit (see p. 13), and concerning whom there is no other historical record. The Guys were a family of standing and note in Bristol.* Bayliss' *Memorial Plymouth Colony* mentions a Rev. John Myles, and many of his congregation of Swansea, Wales, as settlers of the town of Swansea, Plymouth Colony. *The Massachusetts Historical Coll., 4th series*, Vol. VI., p. 172, contains a letter of Nov. 28, 1640, from Edward Winslow of Plymouth Colony, to Gov. John Winthrop, in which he states that he has a "friend who has an estate in Wales" (name not stated), and asks advice concerning it. (Gov. Winslow and John Moses were fellow townsmen, of Duxbury, in 1640.)

So far as can be ascertained from any records, John Moses and Ralph Chapman were the only shipwrights of Plymouth Colony during the period between 1640 and 1660. At a time when these men were growing old, another shipwright arrives, and it is a fair presumption that he was a friend and correspondent of John Moses. From Winsor's *History of Duxbury*, we learn that "John Drew, a Welshman and ship carpenter, arrived in Plymouth in 1660, and had five sons, of whom three settled in Plymouth and two in Duxbury." The first purchase of land made by John Moses of Windsor, in 1649, was from Owen Tudor, a Welshman.† In answer to inquiries, Hon. Evan R. Jones, U. S. Consul at Cardiff, Wales, states that, "The use of Scripture names as surnames is comparatively common in this Principality; for example: we have families whose surnames are David, John, Joseph, Jeremiah, Jacobs, etc., and, of course, Moses." Concerning the Hon. William Abraham, who has represented the Rhondda District of Glamorganshire, Wales, in Parliament, as a Gladstone Liberal for more than ten

---

* In the *State Papers of Great Britain — James I*, we find in a petition for suppression of pirates, a mention, under date of Feb. 28, 1619, of John Guy as Mayor of Bristol. Also, in same papers, that a John Guy was Governor of Newfoundland in 1611. Also, under date of Nov., 1638, that Edwin Guy was a patentee with Gorges and others for New England land grants.

Doyle — *The English in America*, p. 34. Date of 1621 — "Guy, a Bristol merchant, who had under a patent settled a colony in Newfoundland." The name was unusual on this side of the Atlantic, and not preserved in Massachusetts Colonial records, and it seems probable that the John Guy of Lynn, who had dealings with John Moses, may have been connected with the Bristol family of Guys, who, as we have seen, were interested in shipping and colonization.

† In the *History of Windsor*, by Stiles, it is stated that William Buell and John Owen, also early settlers of Windsor, were Welshmen.

years, he writes that, "Mr. Abraham is a Welshman and speaks Welsh with more fluency than he does English."

Lower's work on *English Surnames*, Vol. I., mentions "Moses" as among the Scripture surnames of England; and in volume II., under the head of *Scottish Family Names*, he writes: "Of old Worthies we have Moses, Joseph, Samuel, Sampson, Daniel, Solomon, Jacob, Amos, Paul, Matthew, Mark, Luke, James, and Peter."

An acquaintance with Mr. D. H. Moses, an official of the St. Paul & Milwaukee Railroad, led to a correspondence with his father, the Rev. John Moses, a Presbyterian clergyman at Mineral Point, Wis. Extracts from his letters are given herewith. The lawsuit concerning the title to estates, which were very likely entailed, and which lawsuit is so clearly described by him, makes it certain that the Moses family of Monmouthshire and Wales is more than five hundred years old. Monmouthshire was once a part of Wales, and Rhymney and Ebbw Vale are on the eastern boundary line of the Wales of modern times.

MINERAL POINT, WIS., July 9, 1889.

To Z. MOSES, ESQ.:

Dear Sir:—In reply to your request through my son David, I will answer you as briefly as I can. In the year 1842, there was a test case of the family rights to my grandfather's real estate. He was what is called in the old country, a "State Freeholder." About one hundred years ago he went to law, and to carry that through he raised a mortgage on his estate, and in one way or another he could not redeem it. The estate was in the hands of Brown and Bailey, Ironmasters, in Sirhowy, Ebbw Vale, Monmouthshire. In 1842 they were going to dissolve partnership on account of some difficulty among themselves, so they advertised for heirs to come forward to claim the estate. One of my cousins, John Moses, a lawyer from London, came down to Rhymney, Monmouth, to investigate the estate. When Bailey and Brown saw that we were in earnest about our title, they settled among themselves to hold on to the estate at any cost. My cousin the lawyer, searched the records in the County of Monmouth, and found that the estate had been in possession of the Moses family over *five hundred years*, or back to the year 1342, and that the title was good and clear, only that there was a heavy mortgage against it. As we had no money to contend with these wealthy ironmasters, everything was dropped; and so it is to this day.

My grandfather's estate was, as I have said, in Monmouthshire, and in different parishes. His occupation was a farmer. His name was Edmund Henry Moses, a man of sanguine temperament, and so were all of his children. To three of his sons he gave a good education, and he gave them a good start in life, one a lawyer, another a gunsmith, and the third an ironmonger. Their names were Lewis, William, and Henry. One of them lived in Bristol, England, and the other two went to London, and were there in business on Market Street, and Blackfriars Street, as late as 1850. My uncle John was also in London for thirty years as a gunsmith. He paid us a visit in Rhymney, Monmouth, in 1840. Thomas, David, (my father), and Daniel, were all raised as farmers and after that mechanics. And they are all dead, and all of them but uncle Daniel Moses died in England and Wales. Uncle Daniel came to Canada in 1828, and from there went to Carbondale, Pa., where he was buried about twenty years ago. He has three sons, Ebenezer Moses in Ohio, Daniel in Scranton, and David in Wilkesbarre.

Before closing this letter, I will give an account of my parents. My father died from inflammation of the bowels in Rhymney, in 1844, 48 years of age. He was a very large and strong man; and so was uncle John, the gunsmith, from London. He was almost a giant, weighed 220 pounds when he was eighteen years old. I came to this country, to Carbondale, in 1850, and my wife with me. My mother, four brothers, and one sister, came after me in a few years. My mother was buried seven years ago in Scranton; she was 81. I am the oldest of seven children; was born Sept. 29, 1827; I have been in the ministry 34 years. My second brother, Daniel, lives in Victoria, B. C., and is well off. Evan Moses lives in Columbus, Ohio; his daughter, Miss Emma Theresa Moses, is in Leipzic, Germany, studying music as a pianist and organist. She has been teaching in Governor Foraker's family in Columbus, Ohio. David is in Washington Territory. Edmund, my brother, lives in Scranton, and my sister lives there also.
Yours truly,
JOHN MOSES.

MINERAL POINT, WIS., July 29, 1889.
MR. Z. MOSES, Washington, D. C.:

My Dear Sir: — I have received your last two letters, but happened to be at Monona Lake Assembly, at Madison, Wis., and only returned Saturday night.

My grandfather's estate was in different parishes, which I could not name, except the parish of Bedwellty, in which is Rhymney. . . . . . . The records may be found in different places. Of births, marriages, and deaths, a good many can be found in the Bedwellty Parish Church, Mon. . . . . The principal place for the records of the county is Monmouth. There are some records in the parish church of Gelly Gaer, Glamorganshire; this is very near Bedwellty. Some records may be found in the Episcopal Church of Llandaff, Glamorganshire. These are the only places I can mention now; but I am certain they could also be found in London, because the family lived there up to the year 1850. . . . . As to my own family, D. H. is the oldest, 37; Evan, in Milwaukee, 33; Albert, in school, 17; Miriam (Mrs. Bowen), 35; Annie is in Minneapolis, 28. As to the religious sentiments of the Moses family, they have been connected with the Church of England, Baptist, Methodist, and Presbyterians; and the same with respect to my own family.

I think our family tree is an honorable one, and will compare with the best I know. We are not all saints, but I think I can say one thing certain, there is not a scoundrel nor a mean man or woman among them for four generations. And most of us are good singers and musicians. . .
. . . .
Hoping this will give you an outline of our history, with kind respect,
I remain, yours,
JOHN MOSES.

In an interview with Morris Moses of Trenton, N. J., who was born in Wales, some particulars concerning his extraction were gathered. He is the son of John Edmund Moses, who with a brother were left orphans, and were taken care of and educated by an uncle, who was an Episcopal minister in Wales. After John Edmund had attained his majority he went to England and married Martha Kirke, near Nottingham, in Lincolnshire. He lived several years in that vicinity as an inn-keeper, and then emigrated in 1830 to Trenton, N. J. After two years he sent for his family. He spoke the Welsh language, and was an Episcopalian. His children (1889) may be recorded as follows: Martha, Mark, and Mary, all deceased; Morris, aged 63; Martin, aged 61; Matthew, aged 56; John, aged 36; Margaret, aged 40.

Had the publication of this book been delayed for several months, it is probable that inquiries set on foot across the ocean concerning the Scotch and Welsh families of the Moses name would have borne fruit.

A Moses family of Scotch origin has long resided in Buffalo, N. Y., and correspondence has been opened by them with relatives in Scotland.

James Moses of Trenton, N. J., is the owner of the great Mercer Pottery Company, is president of the Electric Light Company, of the Villa Park Company, and director in various other trusts and companies in Trenton, N. J. His brother, John Moses, is owner of the Glasgow Pottery Company in the same city; and both brothers are, or have been, wardens of the Episcopal Church.

James Moses writes:

"My father and grandfather were farmers in County Tyrone, North of Ireland. I left home when quite a boy, and before I took much interest in family history, but I understood that my grandfather came from Lanark, above Glasgow, in Scotland. Our family is the only one of the name I ever heard of in Ireland. William Moses of Louisville, Ky. (a son of my father's eldest brother), I think knows more of our family history than I do."

William Moses writes under date of February 24, 1890:

"The writer, William Moses, born in Ulster County, State of New York, was the son of Robert Moses, who was born at Six Mile Cross, County Tyrone, Ireland, who was the son of John Moses, who had an older brother, Robert, who held or inherited some property or titles, which at his death would have come to my grandfather, as his brother left no heirs. There was considerable correspondence about it at the time, as my father was the oldest son of the junior brothers. It seems, or was my understanding at the time, that my father, not being a subject of Great Britain, forfeited his title by descent. This correspondence took place between 1825 and 1830. So I only know from memory, and I was quite small at the time. Personally I do not know anything of this Scotch ancestry; but my grandfather's brother, Robert, inherited something from, or in Scotland. I never heard that he ever lived in Ireland. . . . . . I believe that the entire Moses family, or our part of it, held to the creed of the Church of England. I do not know what the occupation of my grandfather and his brother Robert was; but there were merchants, doctors, manufacturers, and farmers in the family, for I have seen some of my uncles and their cousins. My father was of a ruddy blonde complexion, and would pass anywhere for a Scotch-Irishman. I left home in 1834, and have only been a casual visitor to my relations since 1838. I came to Louisville in March of that year. . . . . . I once endeavored to get some facts from my oldest brother, who always lived in New York until my father died, and I felt knew more than I did. He went to New Orleans, and died there, so I am the only one living out of eight brothers. I will be 73 years old in April, and the oldest of the kindred that is living."

As the book goes to press a letter is received from a correspondent in Buffalo, N. Y., with enclosure as follows:

Extracts from letter from Miss Jane C. Moses of Glasgow, Scotland, to Miss Anna R. Moses of Buffalo, N. Y.:

113 Victoria Road, Crosshill,
Glasgow, 11th October, 1890.

. . . .

We can get no definite information further back than the year 1810. Our grandfather and great-grandfather were then living in Milngavie, a little place about ten miles out of Glasgow.

Our great-grandfather, as far as we can make out, was born about 1760, in a place called Shettleston, about six miles out of Glasgow, in quite an opposite direction from Milngavie. But how long they were in Shettleston, or where they came from, we cannot find out, nor when or why they left there and went to Milngavie. In those days registers were not kept as they are now. I went to Shettleston and saw the burying-place, but the sexton had no books or registers, so nothing could be found out there. Then I went to the Milngavie cemetery and saw several tombstones with the name of Moses on them, but could not find out who they were or in what relationship they stood to us. There is an estate called *Mosesfield* a few miles out of Glasgow, in an opposite direction to either of the two places I have named. I have heard my father and the other members of the family who are now dead say that it belonged to our branch of the family. People of a different name live in it now. We do not know when it went out of the family, unless a daughter of the house got or took possession; but we know nothing of a certainty. On one of the stones in Milngavie cemetery a death was recorded of ", William Moses of *Mosesfield*" in 1797, which shows that the estate must have been in the family at that time. Whether at the death of this William Moses it went out of the family, we have nothing, and can find out nothing to show. By writing to the Register House in Edinburgh, if information can be found anywhere, it will be there.

Extracts from a letter from Mrs. Mary Anne Maud (Moses) Jones, giving further particulars concerning the Moses family of Wales:

GELLIFAHAREN, LLANDYSSIL
CARDIGANSHIRE, SOUTH WALES,
October 20, 1890.

MR. Z. MOSES, Washington, D. C.:

Major Jones of Cardiff has written to me, as he has found out my maiden name was Moses, and I fancy and believe I must be a member of the same family as yourself. My late father's name was Edwin Moses. He was a civil engineer, and a son of Moses Moses, Tondu House, Bridgend, Glamorganshire. He (Moses Moses) was a mining engineer and mineral agent to Sir Robert Price, who owned vast estates in that county. My grandfather, Moses Moses, I know hailed from Monmouthshire and Merthyr Tydvil and neighborhood,* where he spent his younger days. . . . . . I am not in a position to tell you whose son he was. My grandfather held an important appointment under Sir Robert Price, and received £1,000 a year with a beautiful house, which fifty years ago was considered a very handsome income. He gave each of his eight children a liberal education, my aunt Jane being a clever historian and an accomplished woman, and my uncles were men of minds. Many years ago two or three of the brothers, my father being one of them, brought out a small book upon the coal basin of South Wales, which proved an authority upon

---

* Bradshaw's *Handbook*. "Besides the large and small works in and about Merthyr Tydvil, there are those at Aberdare, Brynmawr, Ebbw-Vale, Tredegar, Rhymney, Sirhowy, etc., nearly all seated at the head of valleys and many of them being in the neighboring county of Monmouth, which, though reckoned part of England, is essentially Welsh in its minerals, scenery, and people."

mining matters. My grandfather had a brother named William Moses, who wrote a book of poems called "*Cân-y-Gôg*," of course in the Welsh language. Some of his poems have been set to music, and one in particular is sung now at "Hunting Dinners" and such places. It is advice to his son who is about being married, how he is to live and how he is to treat his wife and the inmates of his household. I find the book is out of print, but I have heard of one copy, which I am trying hard to get into my possession, but I am asked a high sum for it, not for its value, but owing to its scarcity.

I have been anxious for a long time to assist you, in being able to send you some particulars of the family; but I find a great difficulty in procuring information. Day by day I have been expecting some particulars, but they have not come. I trust to be able to enclose a few particulars in this letter before closing same; however, if I am unable to do so I will write again in a few days, as soon as they have reached me. . . . . .

I was my father's only child. I was named after his favorite sister, "Mary Anne Maud Moses." Frederic emigrated to America. The brothers and sisters are now all dead. The last that died was Edmund Moses. He was a manager at some works in Glamorganshire, and died about ten years ago.

I have friends who are now visiting the churches in Bedwellty for me, but it takes a great deal of time, owing to my not being able to give any dates, and owing to the vast population of the different districts, the burials being so numerous.

. . . .

Yours most sincerely,
MARY ANNE MAUD JONES.

From another letter it appears that the ancient seat of the Moses family of Wales (now held by Brown and Bailey) is at the present day in the parish of Aberysbrath, in the neighborhood of Nant-y-glo or Abertillery.

The Vicar of the parish of Bedwellty states that the church registers in his possession fill a very large iron chest, and that it would take a week or more to examine them, even hurriedly.

In the event that any Moses descendant of New England lineage should desire further knowledge concerning the ancient Welsh and Scotch families, from which the Plymouth and Portsmouth Lines have sprung, the foregoing papers will furnish a basis for his future investigations. The localities are indicated where the records of the parent stock of both the Welsh and Scotch Houses may be found. The name is uncommon, and with patient search of the baptismal records of a few parishes, very probably a lineal connection for the founders of the New England Moses families could be established.

INDEX.

MOSES NAMES.

Aaron, 51, 56, 58, 59, 62, 64, 78, 96, 97, 99, 100, 101, 102, 103, 104, 105, 106, 109, 111, 112, 113.
Aaron S., 62.
Abbie, 117.
Abel, 54, 55, 57, 65.
Abiah, 60.
Abiathar, 111.
Abigail, 61, 77, 86, 90, 101, 103, 104, 105, 106, 116.
Abigail K., 112.
Abigail W., 106.
Abihu, 105.
Abner, 57.
Abraham, 55, 56, 62, 64, 65, 117.
Achsa, 61.
Addie, 79.
Adrian, 85.
Agnes, 84.
Albert, 71, 72, 123.
Albert A., 76.
Albert T., 116.
Alexander S., 78.
Alfred, 76.
Alfred D., 99, 106, 107, 108.
Alfred E., 72.
Alice, 63.
Alice D., 116.
Alice E., 76.
Alice M., 70.
Almira, 83.
Almond, 116.
Alonzo, 80, 81.
Alvah, 63.
Amarilla, 87.
Amasa Cassius, 81.
Amasa R., 82.
Ambrose, 58, 65.
Ambrose J., 87.
Amelia, 65, 87.
America, 78.
Amey, 53.
Amoret, 69, 70.
Amos, 104, 115.
Andrew, 82.
Angelia S., 107, 108.

Anna, 64, 65, 66, 88.
Anna M., 64.
Anna O., 75.
Anna R., 125.
Annie, 107, 116, 123.
Annie E., 116.
Annie P., 116.
Antony, 52.
Arden, 78.
Arthur, 85.
Arthur H., 81.
Aruah, 62.
Asa, 59, 60, 65, 66.
Asenath, 62.
Ashbel, 55, 57, 65, 75, 77.
Augusta O., 108.
Augustus, 80.
Augustus F., 81, 82.
Aurelia, 11, 78.
Auria, 66, 67.
Austin, 116.
Azariah, 57.
Benjamin, 86, 90, 91, 115, 117.
Benjamin F., 73.
Benoni, 52, 59, 63.
Barnabas, 65.
Bernard, 85.
Bertie, 72.
Bessie C., 78.
Betsey, 63, 65, 67, 78, 80, 83, 84, 90, 91, 111.
Betsey S., 110.
Bildad, 53.
Burt R., 67.
Caleb, 46, 47, 48, 51, 53, 54, 55, 57, 58, 64, 75.
Candace, 64.
Caroline, 88, 106.
Caroline H., 82.
Carrie L., 112.
Carrie W., 80.
Carver, 14.
Cassius M. T., 81.
Catherine, 106.
Celia, 84.
Celia A., 67.

17

INDEX.

Celestia, 76.
Charles, 11, 60, 84, 85, 106, 112, 113.
Charles E., 112.
Charles F., 78.
Charles G., 76.
Charles H., 110, 112.
Charles K., 88.
Charles R., 72, 76.
Charles W., 73.
Charlotte, 56, 57, 67, 68, 73, 86, 88.
Charlotte E., 73.
Chauncey, 61, 77, 84, 85.
Chauncey B., 81, 82.
Chester, 67, 68, 73, 74, 77.
Chloe, 84.
Christine T., 88.
Clara, 65.
Clara A., 107, 108.
Clara B., 81.
Clara Lucina, 77.
Clarissa, 79, 87.
Clarissa P., 79.
Clementine, 82.
Clinton, 86.
Clifford H., 82.
Clifford S., 83.
Clyde L., 81.
Colin, 58.
Cora J., 67.
Cordelia, 77.
Cornelius, 92.
Cyrus, 116.
Cyrus S., 111.
Cynthia, 69.
Curtis, 67, 68, 72, 73.
Curtis H., 74.
Dan, 69, 70.
Daniel, 47, 54, 55, 56, 66, 67, 104, 115, 118, 123.
Daniel D., 77.
Darius, 62, 74, 77.
Dasie M., 82.
David, 52, 53, 110, 123.
David B., 112, 113, 119.
David H., 122, 123.
Deborah, 46, 48, 50, 51.
Delanie, 69.
Dearborn B., 110, 111.
Delia, 65.
Deliverance, 91.
Dennison, 85.
Dighton, 71, 72.
Dolly M., 112.
Dorcas, 50, 58, 59, 61, 64.
Dorothy, 105, 106, 107.
Dorothy J., 112.
Drusilla, 117.
Dyer, 111.
Earle C., 81.

Eaton L., 81.
Ebenezer, 116, 123.
Edith M., 78, 82.
Edmund, 78, 123, 127.
Edward H., 80.
Edmund Henry, 122.
Edna, 80.
Edward, 89, 106, 107, 116.
Edward C., 73.
Edward L., 91.
Edward N., 82.
Edward W., 81.
Edwin, 126.
Edwin B., 67.
Edwin D., 72.
Effie, 116.
Elbert S., 67.
Eleazer, 89; 90.
Elias, 65, 66.
Elijah, 110.
Elisha, 9, 11, 58, 59, 61, 62, 78, 79.
Elisha D., 11, 78.
Elisha, Jr., 11.
Eliza, 64, 78, 80, 81, 89, 115.
Eliza A., 116.
Eliza B., 106, 107.
Elizabeth, 59, 84, 104, 105, 106, 109, 110, 115.
Elizabeth C., 110.
Elizabeth S., 111.
Elizabeth W., 112.
Elizur, 77.
Ellen, 85.
Ellen B., 85.
Ellen E., 87.
Ellen R., 67.
Elmer, 83.
Elnathan, 59, 63, 80, 81.
Elsie, 79.
Elsie A., 78, 79.
Elvira, 67, 68, 106.
Emma R., 79, 80.
Emma Theresa, 123.
Emerson, 85.
Emily, 72.
Emily R., 67.
Emeline, 71, 81.
Emeline G., 72.
Enam, 87.
Erastus, 65, 66, 87.
Ernest, 83.
Ernest C., 73.
Esther, 65, 83.
Ettie, 107.
Eunice, 60, 61, 62, 64, 92.
Evan, 123.
Eveline, 84.
Ezekiel, 59, 63.
Fanny, 75, 116.

Fanny A., 73.
Fanny E., 116.
Festus, 66, 67.
Flavia, 78.
Flora, 71, 72, 77.
Flora A., 85.
Flora B., 72.
Frances, 69, 104.
Frances L., 70.
Francis M., 82.
Francis O., 116.
Francis S., 70.
Frank, 84, 116.
Frank P., 72, 78.
Frank S., 81.
Frankie, 74.
Franklin C., 74.
Franklin H., 77, 78.
Fred F., 107.
Fred W., 108.
Frederick, 62, 65, 72, 79, 80, 127.
Frederick A., 78, 79, 80.
Frederick C., 79.
Frederick E., 72.
Gad, 69.
Galen C., 116.
George, 65, 66, 82, 104, 111, 115, 116.
George A., 110.
George F., 116.
George H., 79, 108.
George J., 113.
George L., 72.
George N., 76.
Georgiana, 83.
Gideon H., 78.
Girard, 73.
Grove, 69.
Guy, 69, 70.
Hannah, 53, 55, 56, 83, 88, 89, 90, 91, 103, 104, 105, 115.
Hannah A., 78, 79.
Hannah Maria, 75, 76.
Hannah P., 111.
Harriet, 65.
Harriet A., 78.
Harriet E., 75, 85.
Harriet S., 116.
Harry, 85, 117.
Harry B., 78.
Harry E., 83.
Harvey H., 82.
Hascall, 63.
Hattie, 72.
Hattie A., 72.
Hayes, 116.
Helen C., 74.
Henrietta, 85.
Henry, 50, 77, 89, 90, 92, 106, 114, 118.

Henry H., 82.
Henry J., 107.
Henry L., 74.
Henry M., 112.
Henry W., 88.
Herbert, 83.
Hester, 118.
Hiram, 63, 80, 81, 82.
Hiram E., 81.
Hiram W., 112, 113.
Homer, 83.
Horace, 67, 68, 116.
Horace A., 82.
Horace C., 71.
Horace Myron, 68.
Horace W., 116, 117.
Horatio, 79.
Hosea, 64, 65.
Howard F., 73.
Howard N., 117.
Irving, 73.
Isaac, 59, 61, 84.
Isabel, 113.
Isabel E., 77.
Isadora, 113.
Isaiah, 118.
James, 55, 56, 64, 86, 87, 96, 97, 101, 102, 103, 104, 105, 106, 107, 108, 109, 110, 111, 124.
James A., 77.
James E., 110.
James F., 77.
James W., 108.
Jane, 71, 77, 83, 84, 126.
Jane A., 77.
Jane C., 125.
Jeanette, 67.
Jennie, 65.
Jennie Belle, 69.
Jennie R., 82.
Jennison, 12.
Jeptha, 63.
Jesse, 86, 118.
Joab, 62.
Job, 69, 70.
John, 50, 51, 52, 53, 58, 60, 61, 64, 72, 84, 87, 88, 89, 90, 91, 93, 94, 97, 99, 100, 103, 104, 105, 108, 110, 111, 115, 116, 117, 118, 120, 121, 122, 123, 124.
John B., 70.
John C., 79, 81, 118.
John E., 108.
John Edmund, 124.
John F., 88.
John G., 117.
John H., 81.
John M., 111, 112, 113.
Jonah, 60, 86, 87.

INDEX.

Jonas, 118.
Jonathan, 86, 88.
Joseph, 62, 90, 91, 96, 101, 103, 104, 110, 114.
Joseph J., 110, 111.
Josephine A., 82.
Joshua, 46, 47, 48, 50, 53, 60, 61, 62, 84, 85, 86, 110.
Joshua B., 87.
Joshua S., 99, 108.
Josiah, 96, 101, 103, 104, 115, 116, 118.
Julia, 65, 84.
Julia A., 74, 79, 80.
Julia Ann, 66, 107, 108.
Julia Henrietta, 74.
Judson J., 82, 83.
J. Woodman, 117.
Keziah, 59, 62.
Kenneth R., 73.
Laura, 63, 80, 81, 82, 84.
Laura A., 82.
Laura L., 81.
Lawyer C., 81.
Lena, 70.
Lena M., 71.
Leonard, 106.
Levi, 58, 63, 65, 105, 106, 107, 108.
Levi M., 106.
Levirah, 62.
Lewis, 123.
Lewis E., 76.
Lillian A., 81.
Lillie V., 82.
Lilly H., 76.
Lincoln E., 81.
Linda, 61.
Linus, 67, 71.
Linus A., 71.
Loditha, 64.
Loice L., 64.
Lois, 56, 57, 59, 60, 64, 83.
Louis, 88.
Louis B., 70.
Louis C., 64.
Loly G., 72.
Lorenzo, 79, 80.
Lucelia, 66.
Lucia, 83.
Lucia M., 77.
Lucian, 73.
Lucinda, 87, 111.
Lucius, 74.
Lucius F., 67.
Lucius H., 85.
Lucius L., 74.
Lucy, 55, 58, 65, 67, 88.
Luther, 58, 76, 84.
Luther M., 76.
Lydia, 55, 56, 57, 59, 62, 63, 65, 66, 67, 75, 117.
Lyman, 64, 65.
Mabel L., 88.
Marcus, 11, 57, 65, 66, 67, 68.
Marcus E., 78.
Margaret, 44, 50, 124.
Margaret Isadore, 70.
Maria, 83.
Mariam, 110.
Maritta, 57, 65, 66.
Mark, 83, 96, 101, 103, 104, 109, 110, 124.
Mark S., 110, 111.
Martha, 44, 47, 48, 50, 51, 82, 103, 105, 107, 114, 117, 124.
Martha A., 78, 79, 107, 108.
Martha J., 97, 102, 104, 105, 106.
Martha W., 91.
Martin, 57, 58, 59, 63, 64, 65, 85, 124.
Martin Levi, 62.
Mary, 44, 47, 50, 51, 53, 57, 62, 63, 65, 77, 83, 84, 85, 90, 91, 92, 101, 103, 104, 105, 106, 110, 111, 114, 116, 117, 124.
Mary A., 69.
Mary Ann, 81, 106, 107, 108.
Mary Ann Maud, 126, 127.
Mary B., 106, 107.
Mary C., 76.
Mary E., 76, 81, 82.
Mary Jane, 116.
Mary L., 71.
Matilda, 64, 65.
Matthew, 83, 124.
Maud S., 76.
Mehitable, 118.
Mercy, 55, 56, 62, 64, 65, 66.
Michael, 40, 55, 57, 58, 75.
Michael T., 86.
Michael Ambrose, 75, 76.
Miles, 67.
Milo, 79.
Mindwell, 44, 50.
Minerva, 66.
Minnie, 83.
Miriam, 65, 66, 123.
Missouri, 78.
Molly, 105, 106.
Monroe M., 67.
Morgan, 76.
Morris, 124.
Mortimer M., 74.
Moses, 126.
Myranda, 87.
Myron, 67, 68.
Nadab, 97, 102, 104, 105, 108.
Nancy, 88.
Nathan, 65, 75.

INDEX. 133

Nathan L., 75.
Nathaniel, 50, 111, 112, 115.
Nellie, 84, 117.
Nellie F., 112.
Newton, 75.
Noel H., 67.
Norman, 66, 67, 75.
Norman W., 75.
Olen E., 116.
Olive, 111.
Olive M., 112.
Oliver, 85, 115, 116.
Orestes, 79.
Ormenta, 78, 79.
Orpha, 65.
Orrin, 84.
Oscar, 65, 72, 87.
Oscar G., 70.
Oscar Lea, 70.
Othniel, 51, 53, 60, 61, 83, 84.
Philip, 118.
Philip G., 88.
Phoebe, 55, 56, 59, 64, 78, 79, 116.
Paulina, 71.
Pliny, 67, 71.
Pluma, 67, 68, 74.
Pluma E., 69, 71.
Polly, 75, 87, 91, 106, 110, 118.
Priscilla, 88.
Rachel, 53, 62.
Ralph, 86.
Randolph, 67.
Rebecca, 11, 78, 91, 115.
Rebecca Jane, 69, 71.
Remember, 89.
Reuben, 55, 56, 60, 61, 86.
Rhoda, 58, 60, 61, 84.
Richard, 65, 77, 84, 85.
Richard A., 85.
Richard H., 88.
Robert, 125.
Robert H., 70.
Robert T., 80.
Roger, 56, 57, 83.
Rollin, 85.
Rose F., 116.
Roxy, 77.
Roxalana, 61.
Rue, 62.
Rufus, 63, 80, 86, 87, 115.
Rufus J., 65, 66.
Ruth, 86, 96, 103, 105.
Sadie A., 88.
Sadie E., 72.
Sallie, 86.
Salina, 84.
Salmon, 83.
Samuel, 89, 90, 91, 92, 97, 104, 105, 109, 110, 114, 117.

Samuel M., 106.
Samuel W., 102, 106, 107.
Sanborn, 111.
Sanford B., 70.
Sarah, 44, 50, 52, 59, 62, 77, 85, 87, 90, 91, 96, 100, 102, 103, 105, 106, 110, 111, 115.
Sarah E., 107, 116.
Sarah H., 76.
Sarah J., 78, 82.
Sarah L., 111.
Savilla, 65.
Schuyler, 9, 11, 78, 79.
Seba, 55, 56.
Selina, 76.
Senator, 65.
Seth, 63, 80, 82.
Seward E., 81.
Seymour A., 62, 78.
Seymour D., 60, 85.
Shubael, 59, 63.
Silas, 88, 115.
Solomon, 67, 77.
Solon, 77.
Sophia, 84.
Stephen, 63.
Stephen G., 76.
Susan, 106, 111, 112.
Susan F., 112.
Susan R., 113.
Susannah, 59, 62.
Sybil, 56, 57, 60, 63.
Sylvanus, 104, 109, 110.
Sylvia, 63.
Terressa, 64.
Thaddeus, 64.
Thankful, 62.
Theodore, 97, 117.
Theodosia, 67, 68.
Thomas, 35, 39, 46, 48, 50, 51, 53, 86, 87, 91, 97, 110, 114, 117, 123.
Thomas F., 106, 116.
Timothy, 33, 34, 50, 51, 52, 58, 59, 62, 78, 114, 115.
Truman, 64.
Una I., 72.
Uriah, 67.
Valeria C., 113.
Vincent, 11, 81, 82.
Virginia, 78.
Wallace B., 76.
Wealthy C., 116.
William, 35, 46, 47, 48, 51, 52, 62, 63, 65, 87, 90, 97, 102, 104, 106, 108, 109, 111, 112, 113, 115, 116, 123, 125, 126, 127.
William A., 81.
William B., 64, 81.
William E., 88.

134   INDEX.

William F., 115, 116.
William H., 69.
William Q., 78.
William R., 116.
William S., 78, 79.
William V., 115.
William W., 81, 82, 113.

Willis, 110.
Willis S., 70.
Zebina, 47, 56, 67, 68, 69, 70, 71, 72, 73, 74, 77.
Zebulon, 52, 60, 61, 87.
Zeruiah, 52.
Zerviah, 59.

OTHER NAMES.

Abbe, 84.
Abbet, 25, 26, 27.
Abraham, 121, 122.
Adams, 52, 55, 59, 62, 77.
Alden, 17, 20.
Alderman, 53, 72.
Alistone, 41.
Allen, 27, 28, 29, 30, 71, 72, 91.
Allerton, 120.
Alford, 64.
Andrews, 56, 57, 83.
Ascotti, 120.
Ask, 112.
Atkins, 76.
Atkinson, 101.
Auchmuty, 120.
Ayres, 104.
Bacon, 76.
Brown and Bailey, 122, 127.
Balch, 92.
Bakes, 70.
Bannatyne, 120.
Barton, 56.
Barnes, 84, 85.
Bartlett, 41.
Barnard, 79.
Barber, 38, 62, 64, 83.
Bascom, 30, 32.
Bates, 77, 88.
Beaman, 53, 65.
Beans, 91, 114.
Beach, 62, 116.
Beck, 100, 106.
Beckwith, 84.
Bell, 109.
Bennett, 31.
Bentley, 80.
Belden, 64, 65, 84
Berry, 116.
Bingham, 69.
Birge, 44.
Bissell, 40, 87.
Bixby, 108.
Black, 112.
Blindman, 35.
Bond, 20.
Bourne, 18.

Bowen, 71, 123.
Boynton, 112.
Brace, 75.
Bradley, 63.
Bray, 80.
Brewer, 59.
Brewster, 23, 28.
Briggs, 78.
Broadwell, 80.
Brockway, 64.
Brockett, 75.
Brook, 53.
Brooks, 84.
Brown, 29, 32, 50, 62, 90, 110, 112.
Brush, 79.
Buckland, 81.
Buckhout, 80.
Buell, 121.
Bunnell, 118.
Burch, 73.
Burgess, 63.
Burr, 56, 63.
Butler, 47.
Butolph, 62.
Caldwell, 75.
Callender, 78.
Campbell, 81, 113.
Canaday, 62.
Carpenter, 72, 78.
Carr, 113.
Cariton, 120.
Carwick, 90.
Caryll, 90.
Case, 56, 57, 64, 65, 66, 71, 74, 75, 83, 87.
Cass, 111.
Cate, 107, 110, 111.
Chaffee, 88.
Chesley, 111.
Cheever, 90, 91.
Chipman, 90, 91.
Chalkwell, 29.
Chancill, 27.
Chapman, 17, 64, 71, 121.
Chauncey, 22.
Chittenden, 69.
Clark, 41, 69, 76.

INDEX. 135

Clarke, 20, 37.
Cleeve, 94, 95, 97.
Cochran, 110.
Cohen, 80.
Coke, 18.
Cole, 20.
Colton, 84.
Colvin, 85.
Compton, 120.
Cook, 74, 82.
Conway, 71.
Cornish, 46, 52, 55, 59.
Crane, 75, 79.
Cradock, 18.
Creamer, 79.
Cropley, 71.
Crosby, 82.
Crow, 47.
Cudworth, 27.
Cullerton, 119.
Curtis, 67, 68.
Dalliba, 74.
Davis, 95, 112.
DeKalb, 64.
Delano, 14, 16.
Delancey, 56.
Deming, 84.
Dickinson, 87.
Dillon, 120.
Dolbear, 111.
Douglass, 118.
Dowd, 84.
Downing, 18.
Downs, 110.
Drake, 32, 40, 45, 70.
Drew, 121.
Dunkley, 90.
Dutton, 91.
Dyer, 77.
Easter, 95.
Eddy, 64.
Edgerton, 66.
Edgerly, 113.
Eggleston, 86.
Ellsworth, 41.
Elrich, 120.
Ely, 68.
Emery, 110.
Eno, 37, 39, 41, 47, 72
Farnsworth, 33, 47.
Fenn, 73.
Ferguson, 107.
Fernald, 105.
Floyd, 106.
Follit, 89.
Foss, 113.
Fowle, 117.
Fowler, 29, 30, 110.
Fox, 112.

Frank, 118.
French, 110.
Fuller, 85.
Fury, 69.
Gates, 72.
Gibbons, 13, 15, 89, 94.
Gibbs, 37, 61.
Gilbert, 62.
Gillet, 45, 52.
Glazebrook, 120.
Goddard, 66.
Goodrich, 76, 107.
Gorham, 63.
Gorges, 93, 95, 96.
Gould, 110.
Graham, 56, 59.
Grant, 22, 41.
Greenman, 70.
Gridley, 85.
Griffin, 25, 26, 27, 31, 79, 110.
Grimes, 66, 69, 71.
Griswold, 72.
Grover, 77.
Gunning, 27.
Guy, 13, 14, 89, 121.
Gyles, 89.
Hale, 12, 91.
Hall, 106.
Haines, 110.
Harmon, 116.
Harris, 116.
Hart, 59, 83, 84.
Harwood, 81.
Harvey, 82.
Hassard, 18.
Hathorn, 89.
Hawkins, 18.
Hayden, 31.
Hazeltine, 82.
Helm, 113.
Henderson, 82, 90.
Henze, 73.
Herring, 73.
Hersee, 71.
Hibbard, 79.
Hickett, 101.
Hide, 27.
Hill, 60, 74, 111.
Hillman, 100.
Hillyer, 53.
Hines, 116.
Hinman, 84.
Hoag, 74.
Hoagland, 87.
Hobe, 79.
Hodge, 67.
Holcombe, 62, 67, 68, 71, 77.
Holmes, 28.
Hooker, 77.

INDEX.

Hoskins, 52, 67.
Hotchkiss, 78.
Hovey, 69.
Howard, 38.
Howlett, 63.
Huckins, 100.
Hughes, 84.
Humphrey, 26, 27, 37, 46, 52, 54, 55, 59, 65, 78.
Jackson, 106.
Jacobs, 68.
Jasper, 78.
Jaxson, 103.
Jennings, 105.
Johns, 76.
Johnson, 85, 104.
Jones, 121, 126, 127.
Judson, 69.
Judd, 84.
Keelers, 27.
Keener, 88.
Kehoo, 91.
Kellogg, 84.
Kemple, 79.
Ketcham, 87.
Keyser, 13, 14, 15, 89.
Kimball, 91.
King, 81.
Kirke, 124.
Knight, 116.
Knox, 117.
Knowles, 94.
Krom, 72.
Lackey, 68.
Lake, 111.
Langmaid, 105.
Lamkin, 75.
Lampson, 76.
Langdon, 103.
Larkham, 94.
Latham, 14.
Lattimer, 40, 75.
Law, 52.
Lawrence, 68.
Lea, 70.
Lee, 33, 42.
Lewis, 95.
Linsley, 42, 44.
Locke, 110, 111.
Loomis, 29, 30, 32.
Loveland, 64.
Lozier, 112.
Lund, 92.
Marden, 105, 112.
Marshall, 41, 118.
Mascall, 41.
Mason, 33, 34, 50, 93, 106.
Mandsly, 41.
Maxwell, 48.

McElroy, 83.
Melcher, 101, 104.
Merrill, 77, 78.
Merritt, 87.
Merry, 18.
Meserve, 97, 105.
Millekin, 115, 116.
Miller, 31, 32, 77.
Mills, 53, 79.
Milod, 84.
Mitchell, 72, 81.
Mix, 84.
Moore, 44, 71.
Morgan, 78.
Morrison, 111.
Morton, 20, 94.
Moseley, 56.
Moulton, 17, 106.
Munsell, 76.
Murphy, 66.
Myles, 121.
Neuman, 72.
Newberry, 41.
Newell, 71.
Newton, 82.
Norfolk, 91.
Norton, 45, 85.
Odiorne, 93, 97, 102, 106, 107.
Omhorn, 41.
Osgood, 90.
Owen, 121.
Packard, 20.
Paine, 69, 83.
Palmiter, 84.
Palmer, 33, 41, 86.
Pardee, 73.
Parker, 110.
Parry, 65.
Parsons, 77, 105.
Payne, 84.
Pease, 76, 116.
Pearson, 120.
Peck, 74, 88.
Perry, 66.
Pettibone, 77.
Phelps, 29, 30, 33, 40, 41, 44, 45, 56, 57, 58, 59, 62, 63, 86.
Philbrick, 107.
Pickering, 97.
Pierse, 20, 101.
Pigot, 90.
Pike, 83.
Pitman, 90.
Pitkin, 37.
Platt, 73, 75.
Plumb, 41.
Poisson, 46.
Pond, 85.
Porter, 76.

Price, 126.
Priest, 101.
Prescott, 56.
Ramsdell, 73, 80.
Rand, 80, 97, 102, 106, 107, 109, 110, 113.
Ranlet, 113.
Rathbun, 69.
Raymond, 68.
Reade, 52.
Reeder, 80.
Reeve, 37.
Richards, 87.
Richardson, 74, 76.
Rice, 116.
Riggs, 75.
Rippaquam, 39.
Rising, 82.
Robe, 46.
Roberts, 48, 52, 56.
Robertson, 91.
Robinson, 18.
Rockwell, 31.
Rogers, 82.
Rollins, 112.
Ropes, 90.
Rose, 65.
Rowland, 64.
Rudd, 77.
Russell, 76.
Sanborn, 111.
Sandford, 26, 76.
Seacet, 39.
Scott, 61, 69, 101, 104.
Seavey, 101, 105, 108.
Selden, 87.
Sexton, 33.
Seymour, 10, 78.
Sharp, 120.
Shattuck, 82.
Shelden, 31.
Shepard, 67.
Sherburne, 96, 100, 101, 102, 110, 111.
Sherman, 120.
Shurtleff, 19.
Sibron, 101.
Silver 112.
Sinkler, 88.
Skinner, 106.
Slater, 48.
Sloper, 96.
Smith, 14, 15, 76.
Snedicor, 73.
Snowden, 81.
Somerby, 113.
Spencer, 74.
Sperry, 70, 76.
Squires, 77.
Staples, 110.

Stavers, 101, 105.
Stedman, 37.
Stephens, 18.
Stevens, 91.
St. John, 67, 68.
Story, 112.
Stoddard, 67.
Streever, 62.
Strickland, 53.
Strong, 41, 44.
Stuppleben, 71.
Sturtevant, 86.
Sugden, 77.
Sutphen, 74.
Swinforth, 18.
Symonds, 102.
Talbot, 64.
Talmadge, 73.
Taylor, 69.
Tenderson, 116.
Terry, 38, 81, 86.
Thomas, 82.
Thompson, 74, 120.
Thrall, 47, 50, 51.
Tinker, 26.
Towle, 111.
Travis, 80.
Trickey, 110.
Trimble, 58.
Tripp, 111.
Tucker, 88, 94, 95, 103, 104, 105, 106.
Tudor, 29, 30, 31, 32, 121.
Tuller, 38, 39, 48, 52, 53.
Tuttle, 84.
Twing, 117.
Upson, 84, 85.
Usher, 103.
Very, 89.
Viets, 60, 61.
Wagner, 76.
Walker, 100, 106.
Wallace, 101, 105.
Ward, 89.
Warham, 15, 29.
Warner, 83.
Warren, 79.
Waterhouse, 96, 103.
Webber, 73.
Webster, 65, 75.
Weeks, 110.
Weller, 71.
Wells, 64.
Wendell, 102, 107.
Westover, 37.
Whidden, 97.
White, 68.
Whitney, 116.
Wilcox, 53, 56, 59, 64, 83, 88.
Wilcoxson, 79.

Williams, 84, 94, 104, 109.
Wilner, 78.
Wilson, 35.
Wilton, 27, 28, 41.
Winslow, 17, 121.
Winter, 20.
Winthrop, 121.
Wood, 81.
Woodford, 64.
Woodruff, 59.
Woods, 88.
Woolcot, 15, 29, 30, 44, 61.
Wright, 70, 88.
Wyatt, 30, 31, 32.
Wyman, 112.
Yates, 88.
Yell, 91.
Young, 17, 110.

HISTORICAL SKETCHES

OF

JOHN MOSES, OF PLYMOUTH,

A SETTLER OF 1632 TO 1640;

JOHN MOSES, OF WINDSOR AND SIMSBURY,

A SETTLER PRIOR TO 1647;

AND

JOHN MOSES, OF PORTSMOUTH,

A SETTLER PRIOR TO 1640.

ALSO

A Genealogical Record

OF SOME OF THEIR DESCENDANTS.

VOL. II — 1906.

BY

ZEBINA MOSES.

HARTFORD, CONN.:
PRESS OF THE CASE, LOCKWOOD & BRAINARD COMPANY.
1907.

Williams, 84, 94, 104, 109.
Wilner, 78.
Wilson, 35.
Wilton, 27, 28, 41.
Winslow, 17, 121.
Winter, 20.
Winthrop, 121.
Wood, 81.
Woodford, 64.

Woodruff, 59.
Woods, 88.
Woolcot, 15, 29, 30, 44, 61.
Wright, 70, 88.
Wyatt, 30, 31, 32.
Wyman, 112.
Yates, 88.
Yell, 91.
Young, 17, 110.

HISTORICAL SKETCHES

OF

JOHN MOSES, OF PLYMOUTH,

A SETTLER OF 1632 TO 1640;

JOHN MOSES, OF WINDSOR AND SIMSBURY,

A SETTLER PRIOR TO 1647;

AND

JOHN MOSES, OF PORTSMOUTH,

A SETTLER PRIOR TO 1640.

ALSO

A Genealogical Record

OF SOME OF THEIR DESCENDANTS.

VOL. II — 1906.

BY

ZEBINA MOSES.

———•◆•———

HARTFORD, CONN.:
PRESS OF THE CASE, LOCKWOOD & BRAINARD COMPANY.
1907.

*CS71
.M91
1890

PREFACE.

The Japanese venerate and even worship their ancestors, and judging from the numerous societies in this country based on ancestry, as well as from family histories now multiplying so rapidly, the West will in its own way and erelong rival the far East, in preserving and glorifying the names and deeds of its founders and pioneers.

Our mental as well as our physical characteristics ; — our successes, or our failures in life ; — are not these dependent on a mysterious blending of the traits of many families, and upon a combination of qualities which we inherited at our birth ?

In other words, do we not owe what we are to the capital we started with; — to the worth of our ancestors, rather than to the circumstances and opportunities along life's pathway, which only an inherited aptitude makes us turn to our advantage ?

Is it then surprising that we want to learn about these ancestors, and about their places in life, that we may judge therefrom the average of their abilities and of their successes in their undertakings? Yet many persons wonder that any one can become interested in genealogical research. For myself, I will acknowledge that some persons give the historian of the family a great deal of needless trouble, and that it is a tax on one's patience to write letters that are not answered ; nevertheless there is to me a fascination in the work and I have found great satisfaction in discovering and recording personal items gathered in America and the British Isles, concerning the men of my own name who lived in the far distant past.

In looking over the American roster it is worthy of remark · 1st : That in all our wars the Moses family has furnished a notable proportion of its members as soldiers ; 2d : That there are comparatively few of the Moses name at the present time : and 3d : That taking into account the smallness of our genealogical group, a good showing has been made, and distinction has been given to

PREFACE.

the name, by the professional and literary achievements of several members of the later generations.

Much of the material gathered during the sixteen years that have elapsed since my first volume was issued, belongs to a remote period. It was likely to be lost if I did not publish it. Important corrections in the earlier volume have been made, and many names, previously omitted because unknown, have been brought to my notice and are now added to the records. An active search would probably give me more names. I have decided, however, to wait no longer, and accordingly publish a small edition of a second volume for circulation among a limited number of correspondents and friends.

On later pages I have made especial mention of those who have most aided me with valuable material. I thank them, and also others not mentioned, who have encouraged me by their work, their interest, and their enthusiasm.

ZEBINA MOSES.

WASHINGTON, D. C., Nov. 20, 1906.

CONTINUATION OF CHAPTER IV.

SOME OF THE DESCENDANTS OF JOHN MOSES OF PLYMOUTH AND JOHN MOSES OF WINDSOR AND SIMSBURY.

No discoveries have been made adding to our knowledge of John Moses the shipwright of Plymouth and Duxbury.

The loss of the records previous to 1666, of Duxbury, his business home, shuts out the possibility that we shall learn more of him or of his family. He lived until after 1661, at which date he was summoned by the famous John Alden, Assistant to the Governor of Plymouth, to be the foreman of a jury. He must have been of middle age in 1639, when we know he had his shipyard established, and he may have brought a family from England in 1632, or some of them may have been born after his arrival, probably at Lynn or Salem, where three of his customers lived.

His anvil of 1632, described on page 10, an heirloom handed down in the family, has since the death of Schuyler Moses at 91, remained in the possession of his son Fred A. Moses.

John[2] who went to Windsor when quite young, and who was "not permitted to live by himself until he married," had numerous descendants, many of whom are added in the present supplement.

The previous volume gives the reasons and the circumstances supporting the conjecture that Henry Moses of Salem, a mariner, who was young, and who married six years later than John[2], was also a son of John the first.

The estate of Samuel Moses of Ipswich was probated in 1691, eight years later than the death of John[2]. In the final settlement of the estate in 1706, it appears that his children were daughters only.

A Mary Moses, daughter of Thomas Moses, was born in Dorchester March 2, 1665. The mystery as to the subsequent life of father and daughter is still unsolved.

PREFACE.

the name, by the professional and literary achievements of several members of the later generations.

Much of the material gathered during the sixteen years that have elapsed since my first volume was issued, belongs to a remote period. It was likely to be lost if I did not publish it. Important corrections in the earlier volume have been made, and many names, previously omitted because unknown, have been brought to my notice and are now added to the records. An active search would probably give me more names. I have decided, however, to wait no longer, and accordingly publish a small edition of a second volume for circulation among a limited number of correspondents and friends.

On later pages I have made especial mention of those who have most aided me with valuable material. I thank them, and also others not mentioned, who have encouraged me by their work, their interest, and their enthusiasm.

ZEBINA MOSES.

WASHINGTON, D. C., Nov. 20, 1906.

CONTINUATION OF CHAPTER IV.

SOME OF THE DESCENDANTS OF JOHN MOSES OF PLYMOUTH AND JOHN MOSES OF WINDSOR AND SIMSBURY.

No discoveries have been made adding to our knowledge of John Moses the shipwright of Plymouth and Duxbury.

The loss of the records previous to 1666, of Duxbury, his business home, shuts out the possibility that we shall learn more of him or of his family. He lived until after 1661, at which date he was summoned by the famous John Alden, Assistant to the Governor of Plymouth, to be the foreman of a jury. He must have been of middle age in 1639, when we know he had his shipyard established, and he may have brought a family from England in 1632, or some of them may have been born after his arrival, probably at Lynn or Salem, where three of his customers lived.

His anvil of 1632, described on page 10, an heirloom handed down in the family, has since the death of Schuyler Moses at 91, remained in the possession of his son Fred A. Moses.

John[2] who went to Windsor when quite young, and who was "not permitted to live by himself until he married," had numerous descendants, many of whom are added in the present supplement.

The previous volume gives the reasons and the circumstances supporting the conjecture that Henry Moses of Salem, a mariner, who was young, and who married six years later than John[2], was also a son of John the first.

The estate of Samuel Moses of Ipswich was probated in 1691, eight years later than the death of John[2]. In the final settlement of the estate in 1706, it appears that his children were daughters only.

A Mary Moses, daughter of Thomas Moses, was born in Dorchester March 2, 1665. The mystery as to the subsequent life of father and daughter is still unsolved.

In the Norfolk County Records appears the marriage of Philip Eastman of Haverhill, Mass., to Mary Moses of Newbury, on Aug. 22, 1678.

There is little room for believing that she was the daughter of John[2] or Thomas, or Samuel, or Henry.

In a general way it may be assumed that young unmarried people, especially girls, came to this country with parents or guardians.

Strong circumstantial evidence favors the idea that prior to the known residence of John Moses the shipwright at Plymouth, he had a home and family in Salem or Lynn. (See pages 17 and 89;) but it does not appear with certainty, that the Moses name has been perpetuated to the present time through any of the above contemporaries of John Moses the 2d. Whether Henry, Samuel, Thomas, or the two Marys, were descendants of John the 1st is therefore of little importance to the Moses family of the present day.

The writer has regretted that he did not, in Vol. 1, publish the entire map of Simsbury, coarsely drawn in 1730, a tracing of which he made from the original in the State Library at Hartford, Conn.

Successive generations of the Moses family, dating from 1647 to 1906, have resided in the town; and in Granby and Canton, townships set off from Simsbury, since the date of the map. It is believed that it will be found useful in placing the families, parishes, and localities, mentioned in this history, and both halves of the map are now printed. A map index is given for convenience of readers.

MAP OF SIMSBURY, CONN., 1730.

Adam G.
Adams.
Alvords.
Bacon old.
Bacon.
Barber.
Barndore Hills.
Bare Hill.
Bever Dam Marsh.
Bissell.
Bissells Brook.
Buel.
Butolphs.

Case W.
Clark S.
Coocks.
Copper Hill.
Cornish Dea.
Dunkster.
Eno J.
Fort.
Grate Marsh.
Great Pond.
Griffins Marsh.
Griffins Plain.
Grist Mill.

Griswold Lieut.	Phelps Amos.
Hannover.	Phelps J.
Hatchet Hill.	Phelps N.
Higleys.	Phelps T.
Higley J.	Porters.
Higleys Marsh.	Reeds.
Higley S.	Robards.
Hillyer James.	Salmon Brook.
Holcomb.	Saw Mill (twice)
Holcomb Cap.	Saxtons.
Holcombs Island.	Scotland.
Holcomb David	Shaws Fort
Hopkins.	Sifers.
Hop Meadow.	Slater.
Hubbard.	Slater Widow.
Huffmans.	Slater S.
Iron Works.	Stevens
Lampson J.	Storer W. E.
Luis J.	Strickland J.
Messenger J.	Terreys Meadow,
Meeting House.	Tuller.
Mile Swamp.	Turkey Hills.
More Amos.	Weatogue East.
More Jonat.	Weatogue West.
More W.	Welshs Hill.
Moses.	Wenchels T.
Mount Phylip.	Whortleberry Hill.
Owens.	Wilcocks W.
Pearl Marsh.	Winchels.

Page 52, No. 7 JOHN[4] MOSES. In the land records of Goshen, Conn., Vol. 2, pages 117 and 119, appear deeds from John Moses of Simsbury to Samuel Thompson of New Haven, of land rights in "New Bantam, so called," also his deed to Aaron Cook of Wallingford; both deeds May 25, 1738.

Page 53, No. 8 DAVID[5] MOSES (son of WILLIAM), b. May 29, 1742. In the Hartford *Courant* of August 31, 1824, appears a notice of the death at Simsbury on August 21, 1824, of David Moses, Jr., aged 42.

From this accidental discovery of a "junior" David, of middle age in 1824, it seems possible that David and Bildad, sons of William[4], may have had families in Simsbury, where we know they had farms, and that the few Moses names of the Revolutionary period which cannot be placed, were their descendants.

Nor is it probable that the births of all of the children of Thomas and Joshua, brothers of William[4], were entered on the Simsbury town records. Page 53 shows wide intervals between the birth dates.

Page 53, No. 11 Caleb[4] Moses, son of John[3], in his will, (see pages 54 and 55,) bequeaths as one portion of his property, "my right at Susquehannah." To explain this phrase we must recall a fact often overlooked, that Connecticut, under her Charter, claimed lands now within the states of Pennsylvania and Ohio.

Quotation is made from an address made at Scranton, Pa., Dec. 22, 1903, by F. C. Johnson, M.D., as follows:

"Separated from Connecticut by the projecting lower portion of New York State, Westmoreland County, seventy miles square, had (during the Revolution), a population of about 2,000 souls. It was a part of the nearest Connecticut County, and its Members of the Legislature had to go on horseback nearly 200 miles. . . . In the Wyoming massacre out of 400 Connecticut men in the fight only 100 came out alive."

Caleb Moses must have been something of a land speculator in the territory which Connecticut sought to annex, and the following, copied from the original paper owned by George E. Hoadley of Hartford, Conn., shows dealings in undivided land shares, closely resembling modern syndicate operations:

"Know all men by these presents, that I John Owen of Simsbury in the County of Hartford, and colony of Connecticut, am holden and firmly stand Bound and Obliged unto Caleb Moses of Said Simsbury in said County and Colony in the full and Just Sum of One Hundred Pounds lawful money, to be paid unto him the Said Caleb Moses or to his heirs Executors and Administrators, To the which payment well and truly to be made, I Bind myself and my heirs and Executors and Administrators firmly by these presents. Sealed with my Seal, Dated this 24th Day of February Anno Domini 1761.

The Condition of the within written obligation is Such that whereas the above bounden John Owen, and the above named Caleb Moses have been at equal Cost and Charges in carying on and purchasing of the Indian Natives heads of the six nations so called, one whole Share or Right in a large Tract of Land Lying greatly on Susquehannah River in North America, as it is butted and bounded in a Deed of Sale from ye Sachems heads of the Six Nations or Tribes of Indians So called, and whereas the Said Caleb Moses his name is inserted in Said Deed to have and to hold one whole Share in Said Large Tract of Land, which said whole Right or share Contains One Eight Hundredth part of said Large Tract of Land, and the said Caleb Moses hath by one Deed of Conveyance of even date with these presents conveyed one half of said Share of Land to him the Sd John Owen with this Intent of each party that they shall for the future bear equal charges in carying on the affair relating to Said Share of Land. Now provided he the Said John Owen, his heirs or assigns, shall well and truly pay his equal proportion with him the said Caleb Moses from Time to Time Relating to said whole Share or Right of Land untill Sd Share can be Divided, and the affairs Relating thereto fully settled, then the above written obligation shall be void, otherwise Remain in full force and Virtue —— —— ——

Signed Sealed and Delivered   John Owen . . . . . Seal.
In the presence of ——
Judah Holcomb
Jon^a Pettibone."

Page 53, No. **10** RACHEL MOSES, m. Dec. 23, 1748, Nathaniel Wilcox of New Hartford, Conn. The Hist. of Hillsdale, N. Y., says: "She was a woman of great fortitude and during the French War, while her husband and sons were in the army, rendered important services as nurse and physician in her own town."

Page 56, No. **12** SEBA^6 MOSES: From pension papers. He lived in Simsbury, New Hartford, and Barkhamsted.; and in 1832 swears he had lived in New Lebanon, N. Y., for twenty-five years. (From N. Eng. Hist. Reg., Vol. 24.) Orra, dau. of Seba Moses, m. Feb. 28, 1796, Roger Stevens at Canaan, N. Y.

Page 56, No. **13** DANIEL MOSES, son of CALEB (11). From the Connecticut Historical Society Collections (1901), Vol. VIII, page 27, is quoted:

"An Ammunition Return of Capt. Ebenezer Fitch Bissell's Company ye 17th Reg., New York, May ye 15th, 1776.—Mens names that Got Guns and other Ammunition." Seventy-two names are given and among them *Daniel Moses*.

In "Conn. Men in the Revolution," (Report of Adjt.-Genl. State of Conn. 1889), we have a brief history of Col. Huntington's 17th Continental Regiment:

" Huntington's Regiment of 1775 as reorganized for service in the Continental Army for the year 1776. After the siege of Boston it marched under Washington to New York, (by way of New London and the Sound in schooners), and remained in that vicinity from April to the close of the year. Assisted in fortifying the City :-Ordered Aug. 24 to the Brooklyn front; Engaged in the battle of Long Island August 27 in and near Greenwood Cemetery; was surrounded by the enemy and lost heavily in prisoners; moved with the main army until after the battle of White Plains;

disbanded under General Heath near Peekskill Dec. 31, 1776. Rolls incomplete."

The Report of the Adjutant-General of Conn. rescues from oblivion about 100 names only, of the entire regiment; and the writer would never have known the regiment in which his ancestor served, except for the discovery of the Ammunition Return of one company of the regiment, and that, fortunately, the Company in which the name of Daniel Moses was enrolled. He died at New York, or Harlem. Heights, twelve days after the battle of Long Island; (See Hist. of West Simsbury and gravestone to his memory at North Canton, Conn., cemetery.)

On Sept. 2d, Washington wrote to Congress of the "distressing condition of his army;— filled with apprehension and despair;— dismayed and intractable."

A historian described the troops as "half clad and unsheltered, without tents or blankets," and the weather of early September on Harlem Heights as "cold driving rain at night succeeded by sultry heat." On one of these gloomy days of the Revolution, on Sept. 8, 1776, Daniel Moses gave his life for his Country. Whether wounded, or sick unto death, without shelter or care, we shall never know. Possessed of a competency according to the times, as shown by the probate of his estate, with a wife and large family, he yet at the mature age of forty-seven, enlisted as a private in the regular army at the first call to go to the siege of Boston and to fight it out wherever duty should lead him. All honor to the self-sacrificing private soldier, my patriot ancestor, Daniel Moses. (Z. M.)

Page 57, No. **13** Mary[6] Moses, wife of Hezekiah Andrews. Deed from Zebina Moses to Hezekiah Andrews of one fourth of a cider mill and several pieces of land on Simsbury Mountain for £60. (See Andrews Memorial.)

Page 58, No. **17** Timothy Moses. From Inscriptions on tombstones in Bloomfield, Conn., Cemetery:

"Timothy Moses, d. Aug. 25, 1787, aged 81.
Sarah, his wife, d. Sept. 12, 1751, aged 38.
Sarah, his 2nd wife, d. Nov. 19, 1759, aged 52.
Elizabeth, his 3rd wife, d. Oct. 3, 1763, aged 47.
Amey, his 4th wife, d. Mar. 18, 1786, aged 76.
Mrs. Mary ye 5th wife survives."

Sarah, dau. of Timothy, m. Jany. 12, 1756, Isaac Graham (Hist. Wethersfield).

Page 60, No. 19 JOHN MOSES, JR., (see 144) (and later in this Vol.), d. Mar. 6, 1842.

Add ASA MOSES as, with great probability, a son of John (19), in W. Rutland, Vt., in 1796 (See later pages of this Vol.).

Page 60, No. 20 ZEBULON JR. MOSES, b. 1754, d. 1808; also see later pages of this Vol. for other circumstantial evidence, that Jonah (No. 141), was a son of Zebulon (20).

Page 61, No. 22 JOHN[5] MOSES, son of JOSHUA (10), m. (Sims. Rec.) Abigail Scott of Waterbury, Sept. 20, 1763.

The Conn. Mirror of Feb. 24, 1823, gives the death of John Moses, at Waterbury, at the age of 94.

John Moses had a son JOSEPH, b. June 29, 1780; and the History of Waterbury, Vol. 2, p. 426, records the marriage of JANE AMELIA, dau. of JOSEPH MOSES of Waterbury on Nov. 28, 1844, to J. C. White. On page 154 it is stated that RICHARD P. MOSES was a post rider and proprietor of an overland stage, Waterbury to New Haven, from 1845, to the death of Mr. Moses in 1857. On page 92 we find BETSEY MOSES was married in 1840 to Mills P. Ford. On the same page are the marriages at Waterbury of SARAH MOSES in 1733 to Silas Johnston; DEBORAH MOSES, in 1740, to James Weed; and SALINA MOSES, in 1835 to F. A. Bailey.

For two of these marriages see page 52 of this book. SARAH and DEBORAH were cousins of JOHN[6]. The rector of St. John's Episcopal Church, Waterbury, states that the church records were burned about 30 years ago. This makes it impossible to give a complete record of the Waterbury family. A portion of the Church record was copied by the late Rev. J. L. Clarke, and from this copy we learn, that on July 3, 1831, was baptized: Lucretia Moses and Emeline Moses (both adults); and on Oct. 22, 1837, JANE AMELIA Moses, dau. of Widow Mary Moses. From this we can say that JOSEPH MOSES[6], of Waterbury, son of JOHN (22) m. Mary ———; (family name unknown.) CHILDREN: Jane Amelia (m. J. C. White); and that probably the other Moses names given above were descendants of the said Joseph.

Page 62, No. 23 Daughters of Captain TIMOTHY MOSES: MARY m. Dec. 7, 1780, Benjamin Benedict; KEZIAH m. Joseph Adams.

Page 63, No. 29 SHUBAEL[6] MOSES, Rev. Soldier. From Pension Papers it appears that he m. Oct. 5, 1774, Elizabeth Seager. She moved from Ticonderoga, N. Y., to Westport, N. Y., and states that she was 82 in 1840. They had two children who died young.

Page 63, No. 28 SIBYL and SILVIA MOSES, twins, daughters of Elnathan. Sibyl d. at the age of 21, after she had m. Barlow Gorham. Sylvia m. David Jackson and had the children mentioned on page 63, viz: Sibyl, Franklin, Hiram, and Dennis.

Page 64, No. 33 LYMAN T.[8] MOSES, m. Laura Scripture. No children.

Page 69, No. 52. GUY[8] MOSES, son of ZEBINA, 2d (47) removed in 1868 from Marcellus, N. Y., to Washington, D. C.; m. March 30, 1837, Lucina C. Bingham. She was b. Sept. 29, 1815, and was a daughter of Calvin and Betsey Scott Bingham. The Binghams and Scotts were old and notable families of Bennington, Vt. Guy Moses died March 10, 1893.

CHILDREN: all born in Marcellus, N. Y.; Zebina, 3d, b. April 8, 1838; Margaret Isadore, b. July 8, 1839, d. Oct. 28, 1842; Robert Henry, b. Jan. 13, 1844; Louis Bingham, b. Jan. 16, 1846, d. at Washington, April 12, 1867; John Bingham, b. May 2, 1855.

Page 69, No. 53 ZEBINA[9] MOSES (third of the name, and compiler of this book), is the son of GUY (52). At the age of sixteen he removed from Marcellus to Michigan. Since 1861 he has been a Government officer at Washington; in the Interior Department; Cashier of the House of Representatives; Secretary to the Vice-President during most of General Grant's second term; Enrolling Clerk of the Senate; and Asst. Supt. of Railway Mail Service. Resigned from office July, 1901, after forty years continuous Government service. Resides in Washington, D. C.

Page 70, No. 54 ROBERT H.[9] MOSES, son of GUY (52). Soldier 122d N. Y. Vols. Aug. 28, 1862, to June 23, 1865. 1st Lieut. July 9, 1864; Adjt. Nov. 23, 1864; Brevet Captain April 15, 1865, to rank from Oct. 19, 1864, "for meritorious conduct at the battles of Winchester, Fisher's Hill, and Cedar Creek, Va." (See Moses Soldier List.) At the close of the war he engaged in business at Syracuse, N. Y., and later was a manufacturer and merchant in New York, to which city he removed in 1867. Retired from business in 1905, and resides in New York.

PLYMOUTH AND WINDSOR LINE. 151

Page 70, No. **55** JOHN B.[9] MOSES, son of GUY (52) resides at Washington, D. C.; m. Dec. 18, 1884, Muriel Elizabeth Thornton.

Page 70, No. **56** SANFORD B.[9] MOSES, son of JOB (56), m. 1st, Aug. 4, 1885, Annie L. Bakes; m. 2d, July 11, 1895, Wilhelmina E. Neumuth.

CHILDREN: Frances Ernestine, b. July 29, 1896: Evelyn Louise, b. Nov. 24, 1900.

Page 70, No. **57** OSCAR GREENMAN[9] MOSES, son of JOB (56), m. Jan. 10, 1865, Mary Sallie Lea. She d. Sept. 21, 1906.

CHILDREN: Oscar Lea, b. Dec. 16, 1865; Frances Laura, b. Mar. 20, 1867, d. Sept. 3, 1867.

Oscar Lea[10] *Moses*, resides in New York City, m. April 22, 1896, Effie Dongan.

Page 73, No. **78** ERNEST C.[9] MOSES.

CHILDREN: Kenneth Ramsdell, b. June 7, 1889; Muriel Comstock, b. Aug. 13, 1892; Helen Catherine, b. July 24, 1894.

Page 72, No. **71** FREDERICK E.[9] MOSES, son of JOHN (70), has now (1906) a successful stock and grain farm of 960 acres at Ethan, S. Dak.

CHILDREN: Since 1890, are: John E., b. Apr. 23, 1891; Marion Elizabeth, b. Sept. 9, 1894.

Page 79, No. **103** FRED A.[9] MOSES, son of SCHUYLER (101), resides in Rochester, N. Y., and has in his possession since the deaths of his father and sister, Martha A., the heirloom described by the Livingston Co., N. Y. Historical Society, the anvil of John Moses, the shipwright. (See illustration on page 10.) Fred A. m. Nov. 26, 1878, Mary Hebard.

CHILDREN: Fred C., b. July 12, 1882; George H., b. July 27, 1884; Dorothy M., b. Oct. 20, 1892; Richard Schuyler, b. July 26, 1897.

Page 81, No. **117** CLYDA YORKE[11] MOSES, died suddenly July 4, 1905. She was the dau. of Arthur H. Moses, m. Aug. 10, 1904, Alva B. Adams.

MARY EMILY,[11] dau. of ARTHUR H. (117), m. Oct. 17, 1904, Fred T. Briggs.

Page 82, No. **121** AUGUSTUS F. MOSES, who was a gallant soldier of the 49th N. Y. Reg. in the Civil War, is still living in Jamestown, N. Y., and occasionally writes for the newspapers.

He describes a very old number of the Boston Gazette owned in Jamestown and dated Mar. 12, 1770, which with mourning border and illustrated with coffin, skull and cross bones, gives minute details of the "Boston Massacre." An advertisement in the same paper reads:

"Drifted from Point Shirley, about a Fortnight ago, a *Moses built Boat*. Whoever will bring her to John Baker, Store in Back Street, shall be satisfied for their trouble."

This Moses, builder of boats in Boston in 1770, has not been traced. Evidently his workmanship was highly esteemed.

Page 82, No. **123** CAROLINE H.[9] MOSES, dau. of AUGUSTUS, m. 1847, a Mr. Cook, and resided in Ticonderoga, N. Y. She d. Mar. 2, 1906.

CHILDREN : William ; Carrie.

MARY E.[9] MOSES, dau. of AUGUSTUS, m. Sept. 30, 1866, Martin H. Shattuck, and resided in Ticonderoga, N. Y.; she d. Mar. 14, 1906, and by her will left to the town of Ticonderoga, a fine building and grounds, (described by a local newspaper as "an ideal spot,") for a hospital; also a bequest of $500, annually, towards its maintenance.

Page 82, No. **124** FRANK M.[10] MOSES, son of HENRY H. (124), m.

CHILDREN : Ellen, b, Nov. 28' 1886 ; Luther, b. Nov. 16, 1888; Charles, b. Oct. 17, 1892; Marjorie, b. June 14, 1897; Harvey, b. May 25, 1899.

PAGE 82, HORACE A.[10] MOSES, son of HENRY H. (124), m.

CHILDREN : Madeline, b. Mar. 4, 1897.

PAGE 82, JENNIE R.[10] MOSES, dau. of HENRY H. (124), m. Irwin Stafford, M.D.

CHILDREN: Bradley E., b. June 14, 1900.

Page 84, No. **134** JOHN O.[8] MOSES, son of ORRIN[7], d. Oct. 14, 1906, at Unionville, Conn. His wife, Anna, d. Oct. 13, 1901.

CHILDREN : Frank E., b. Mar 9, 1878; Orrin J., b. Mar. 15, 1880; Charles R., b. Dec. 1, 1882; George L., b. Mar. 17, 1883.

Page 89, No. **145** HENRY[2] MOSES of Salem.

The descendants of Henry in the male line can be positively traced about one hundred and fifty years only. The Moses families appearing at interior towns in Massachusetts cannot be connected with certainty.

The reader who is interested in seeing a complete presentation of the Salem Moses group is referred to the "Driver Family," compiled by Mrs. Henry C. Cooke, who has courteously permitted extracts from her book as follows: The wife of Henry Moses was Remember Giles, bap. Jan. 20, 1638. Her mother, Bridget Very, was a widow when she married Edmond Giles and had four children by Giles. Remember was the second daughter.

Eleazer,[2] son of HENRY died in 1718.

Joseph,[3] is mentioned as a son of HENRY[2]. He married July 27, 1699, Tamosin Bean — see page 91 of this book.

Page 90, No. 149   ELEAZER[4] MOSES, son of ELEAZER (146).

Probate papers give him the title of "master mariner known as Captain" and the value of his property 237L.

SAMUEL[5], son of Capt. ELEAZER[4], bap. Dec. 10, 1733, m. July 30, 1755, Sarah Brown (on page 90 of this book, Sarah Brown is erroneously recorded as the wife of Samuel[4], son of the first Capt. Eleazer).

CHILDREN of Samuel[5]:

Samuel[6], m. June 22, 1788, Elizabeth Duncklee. (On page 90 of this book this Samuel is erroneously recorded as child of Eleazer[4])

Sarah[6], m. Nov. 4, 1778, Edward Dalton, who came to Salem in 1776 and was in the Navy in the Revolution. They had one daughter and six sons, one of whom, Eleazer Moses Dalton, died in Salem, May, 1886, in his 92d year.

Page 90, No. 150   BENJAMIN[5] MOSES, son of ELEAZER (149).

From Coll. Essex Ins., Vol. 11, page 177, it appears that Benjamin Moses m. 1st, Sarah Carroll, by whom he had a daughter, Abigail, who m. Moses Yell (see Nabby Moses, page 91); m. 2d, Rebecca Stevens, who as a widow m. Moses Yell (see last entry on page 91). While the 2d wife of Benjamin Moses, she had a daughter Mary, who m. John Kehoo (see page 91).

The foregoing makes it certain that Benjamin[6], mentioned on page 91, as 150, did not marry Rebecca Stevens. There is no record to show who was the mother of his two children, Edward Lister, bap. July, 1786, and Benjamin, bap. May, 1788.

Page 91, SARAH MOSES, m. Sept. 18, 1740, Peter Cheever:

The "Driver Family" states she was the widow of Henry[4] Moses (see No. 147).

Page 91, SARAH MOSES, m. Nov. 4, 1778, Edward Dutton. This should be Edward Dalton.

CORRECTIONS AND ADDITIONS.

Page 9, "The New York World of March 14, 1880," should read 1890.

Page 50, MARTHA MOSES, erase death Jan. 30, 1689.

Page 51, OTHNIEL MOSES, change birth to Jan. 10, 1696–7.

Page 51, DEBORAH (MOSES) ROBERTS, d. Mar., 1777. CHILDREN; Richard; Penelope; John.

Page 53, JOSHUA MOSES (son of Joshua), b. Feb. 24, 1727.

Page 55, CALEB MOSES, 2d wife, Mary Adams; change to Mercy Adams.

Page 58, MARTIN[6] MOSES, b. June 29, 1794; Rhoda, b. Apr. 2, 1791.

Page 78, No. 100 BETSEY (MOSES) WILNER, had a son, Malcolm, in addition to children mentioned.

Page 79, No. 104 HANNAH A. (MOSES) CRANE, had a son, Sherburne, in addition to children mentioned.

Page 79, No. 105 ORMENTA (MOSES) BARNARD, had a daughter, Charlotte, in addition to children mentioned.

Page 72, No. 66 HATTIE A. (MOSES) BENSON, has a daughter, Jessica L. Benson.

Page 76, No. 90 LILY H. (MOSES) CLARK, has a son, Paul Alexander Clark, b. Oct. 6, 1889.

Page 86, RALPH MOSES was a son of Thomas and not a nephew.

Page 18, BENONI MOSES, for £800 on Dec. 2, 1755, sold to Joshua Whitney, 100 acres in Norfolk.

Page 68, THEODOSIA (MOSES) ST. JOHN; erase date of birth of first child. The correct date not now at hand.

Page 86, No. 139 JESSE MOSES, d. April, 1860, at North Canaan, aged 90 (*Courant* Apr. 13, 1860).

Page 76, No. 87 HANNAH MARIA (MOSES) JOHNS, d. July, 1897, at Simsbury, Conn.

Page 83, No. **132** OTHNIEL MOSES, d. —, aged 74 (Hartford *Courant*, Apr. 7, 1829).

Page 58, No. **16** LEVI MOSES, d. Nov. 12, 1824, aged 40, at Washington, N. C. (*Courant*, Jan., 1825).

Page 58, No. **16** HOYT MOSES, d. in 1893, aged 72, in Bloomfield, Conn.

Page 66, No. **37** FANNY (CASE) MOSES, d. Feb. 11, 1903, at the home of her daughter, Mrs. Perry.

Page 67, No. **41** NOEL H. MOSES, b. Jan. 10, 1855, d. Apr. 19, 1904.

Page 81, No. **115** JOHN C. MOSES, d. Mar. 7, 1897.

Page 82, No. **119** WILLIAM W. MOSES, d. Nov. 30, 1904.

Page 72, No. **70** JOHN MOSES, d. Feb. 17, 1905.

Page 70, No. **57** OSCAR GREENMAN MOSES, d. Mar. 21, 1900.

Page 70, No. **60** AMORET (MOSES) WRIGHT, d. May 5, 1901.

Page 77, No. **95** CORDELIA (MOSES) MILLER, d. June 18, 1901.

Page 74, No. **82** LUCIUS MOSES, d. Jan. 12, 1896.

Page 73, No. **73** CHARLOTTE (MOSES) HERRING, d. Jan. 27, 1894.

Page 73, No. **75** LUCIAN MOSES, d. March 27, 1893.

Page 73, No. **77** IRVING MOSES, d. Feb. 8, 1895.

Page 65, No. **34** ABEL MOSES, d. Aug. 1, 1833, buried in Scotland cemetery.

Page 76, No. **90** SELINA (MOSES) RICHARDSON, d. Aug. 30, 1895.

Page 70, No. **59** WILLIS S. MOSES, d. Feb. 2, 1906.

Page 79, No. **101** MARTHA A. MOSES, d. Oct. 9, 1896.

Page 72, No. **66** SADIE E. (MOSES) WALKER, d. Oct. 14, 1890.

Page 77, No. **92** JAMES F. MOSES, d. Feb. 24, 1897, at Bucksport, Me.

200 MARTIN[7] MOSES, son of MARTIN (26), was baptized Apr. 30, 1766 (Wb'ry Ch. Rec.), and m. Roxy Haskell, Mar. 3, 1773. He removed from Windsor Locks to Whitestown, N. Y., where he died, and his two sons and one daughter returned to Windsor Locks about 1798.

CHILDREN: Martin, b. Dec. 16, 1793, d.——; Jabez Haskell, b.——, d. between 1825 and 1830, in Illinois; Roxa (Collins).

201 JABEZ HASKELL[8] MOSES, son of MARTIN (200), resided in Connecticut, and in Cayuga Co., N. Y., was associated with a Mr. Avery on a contract for the Erie Canal at Lockport, N. Y. He m. Betsy Abbott, who d. about 1837.

CHILDREN: Jabez H., b. in Ira, Cayuga Co., N. Y., Oct. 7, 1825; a son d. in infancy; Sidney d. about 1860, unmarried, at Reading, Mich.

202 JABEZ H. MOSES, son of JABEZ H. (201), was a soldier in 2d Michigan Cav.; was educated at Michigan University, and Rush Medical College, graduated 1867; was appointed an Ass't Surgeon of the Navy. Has practiced medicine at Half Rock, Mo., and at Galt, Mo., where, retired from practice, he now resides; m. Feb. 16, 1864, Maria Van Bryck.

CHILDREN: Sidney B., b. Mar. 25, 1867; Loula, b. June 19, 1878.

Sidney B.[10], resides in Kansas City, Mo., m., Mar. 19, 1890, Clara Bonner. Children: Haskell[11], b. Dec. 26, 1891; Franklin[11], b. July 31, 1896.

Loula[10], m. Feb. 16, 1898, Guy W. Todd, and resides in Kansas City, Mo.

203 MARTIN[8] MOSES, son of MARTIN (200), lived in Somers 14 years, and in Peekskill 39 years, learned his trade in Worcester and Springfield. He d. May, 1893; m. 1st, Dec. 8, 1820, Phebe L. Baldwin; 2d, Dec. 16, 1823, Elizabeth A. Hastings; 3d, Dec. 16, 1835, Maria Fisher.

CHILDREN: Sarah Baldwin, b. Feb. 14, 1823; Harriet Newall, b. Dec. 9, 1834, d. May 15, 1879; Clarinda Roberts, b. Sept. 19, 1826; Ozial Hastings, b. Oct. 30, 1828; Ruth Ann, b. ———, d. Feb 19, 1852; Harrison; Elizabeth, b. May 30, 1838, d. Dec. 2, 1901; Roxana C., b. Aug. 28, 1840, d. Dec. 17, 1872; Augusta M., b. Aug. 20, 1843, d. Nov. 21, 1876; Martin Jr., b. Sept. 11, 1846; Jabez H., b. Mar. 23, 1849; Frederick C. S., b. Jan. 3, 1852, d. Mar. 17, 1854; Charles Alfred, b. July 14, 1857, d. Oct. 5, 1882.

Clarinda R., m. May 9, 1855, Robt. E. Clark, resides at Peekskill, N. Y.; *dau.* Alida E., b. Nov. 11, 1856.

Roxana C., m. Oct. 9, 1861, John C. Purdy of Croton Falls, N. Y.; *children:* Fred A., b. July 17, 1862; Irving E., b. Nov. 16, 1866.

204 OZIAL H.[9] MOSES, son of MARTIN (203), lives in Chicago, Ill., m. Margaret Tompkins.

CHILDREN: Madge, George, Abby.

205 HARRIET N.[9] MOSES, dau. of MARTIN (203), m. July 17, 1842, Robert Ames, lived at Peekskill, N. Y.

CHILDREN: Elizabeth, b. June 16, 1843; Sarah L., b. Jan. 19, 1845; Melinda L., b. July 17, 1847; Mina I., b. Mar. 21, 1850, d. Apr. 17, 1865; Charles E., b. May 28, 1855, d. May 14, 1893; Harriet I., b. Nov. 6, 1856; Robt. M., b. Aug. 27, 1859; Claribel, b. Apr. 28, 1862.

206 MARTIN[9] MOSES, Jr., son of MARTIN (203), resides in Peekskill, N. Y., m. Sept. 6, 1871, Mary A. Porter.

CHILDREN: Gertrude H., b. Apr. 25, 1873; Walter C., b. July 8, 1874; Martin, Jr., 2d, b. June 11, 1876, lives in New York; Alice R., b. May 31, 1879; Mary A., b. Apr. 4, 1881.

207 JABEZ H.[9] MOSES, son of MARTIN (203), resides at Croton Falls, N. Y., m. July 16, 1873, Elizabeth Hitchcock.

CHILDREN: Helen E., b. Apr. 14, 1875; Ethel E., b. May 25, 1888; Edwin P., b. May 13, 1884.

Helen E., m. May 23, 1906, Henry Westcott.

208 WALTER C.[10] MOSES, son of MARTIN (206), lives in New York; m. Oct. 11, 1904, Bertha Lancaster.

209 MARTIN[10] MOSES, son of MARTIN (206), lives in New York; m. May 7, 1897, Ada Reynolds.

CHILDREN: Helen Porter, b. Apr. 6, 1898; Edna May, b. July 4, 1899.

210 ASHBEL[6] MOSES, son of ABEL (34) (see page 65 for personal paragraph); m. Esther Olivia Truman.

CHILDREN: Ashbel, b. Feb. 20, 1788; Esther, b. June 3, 1790; Barnabas, b. Mar. 21, 1792; Nathan, b. Aug. 14, 1794; d. at Barkhamsted, aged 50; Elizabeth Griswold, b. April 16, 1796, d. at 79; Parrizade, b. April 10, 1798; Clarissa Hatch, b. Nov. 13, 1799; Almira, b. June 15, 1800; Sevilla, b. Aug. 2, 1805; Julia, b. Mar. 4, 1810, d. at 88.

Esther, m. Henry Cooley of Granville and had *children:* Franklin and Floretta, who d. in Homer, Ohio.

Parrizade, m. Truxton Birge of Chatham, N. Y., and both are buried at Utica, Ohio.

Almira, m. Edmund Campbell of Winsted, Conn.; had *children:* James W. and Charles B.

Sevilla, m. Willard Murdock of Chicago, Ill., and had *children:* Juliet and Emily.

Julia, m. Evelyn Kilbourn and had *children:* Jane, Elizabeth, Alice.

211 BARNABAS[7] MOSES, son of ASHBEL (35), was in Hezekiah Webster's Command, War of 1812, m. Rachel Humphrey. They lived in Providence, R. I.

CHILDREN: Senator, Orator, Adaline, Sophronia, Pluma, Ann, Janet.

Sophronia, m. Willard Knight of Providence, R. I., and had *children:* Seril, Willard, Edgar, Adelaide.

212 ELIZABETH GRISWOLD[7] MOSES, dau. of ASHBEL (35), m. John Gibbs Williams, b. at Albany, N. Y., buried at Hudson, N. Y., aged 69.

CHILDREN: John Edward, b. 1825, d. young; Chester Ashbel, b. 1827, d. young; Esther Augusta Williams, b. at West Troy and m. 1st, a Mr. Rice and 2d, a Mr. Nash, who was a soldier in the Civil War and d. in California, Jan. 14, 1898. Mrs. Nash, in 1901, furnished much of the corrected data as to the descendants of Ashbel, and the writer greatly regrets that in 1906 he can learn nothing about her at her former residence at Auburn, California.

213 CLARISSA HATCH[7] MOSES, dau. of ASHBEL (35), m. 1st, John Parsons, of Spencertown, N. Y., and 2d, his brother, Chester Parsons.

CHILDREN: Whiting, Roswell, Elizabeth, Catherine, Chester, Jr.

214 ASHBEL[7] MOSES, son of ASHBEL (35), m. Sally Hughes. He was a mechanic and in 1829 he went to Georgetown, District of Columbia, to construct houses for workmen on the Chesapeake and Ohio Canal. His wife was killed through the blasting of a rock the same year, and he died of a fever two months thereafter.

CHILDREN: Eliza, b. at New Hartford, Conn., Sept. 24, 1811, d. at Spring Lake, Wis., Oct. 14, 1900; Richard, b. at New Hartford, Dec. 25, 1814, d. at Milton Junction, Wis., Dec. 29, 1896.

Eliza, m. Jan. 9, 1831, Thomas Joslin, who was a soldier of the Civil War and d. at Spring Lake, Wis., Oct. 14, 1900.

215 RICHARD[8] MOSES, son of ASHBEL (214), was a cabinet maker, carpenter, and contractor; was buried in Fort Atkinson, Wis. He m., April 12, 1835, Emeliza Pritchard of Litchfield, Conn.

CHILDREN: Marshall Stanley, b. at Wolcottville, Conn., Feb. 18, 1836; Richard James, b. at Herkimer, N. Y., Dec. 6, 1838, d. Oct. 1, 1874; De Witt Smith, b. at Morrisville, N. Y., Oct. 10, 1853.

216 MARSHALL STANLEY[9] MOSES, son of RICHARD

PLYMOUTH AND WINDSOR LINE. 159

(215), was a soldier of the 81st N. Y., 1861 to May 9, 1864, when he lost his leg.

He settled in Wisconsin, where he worked as a carpenter; m. Oct. 15, 1854, Katherine E. Kellar of Oriskany Falls, N. Y.

CHILDREN: Agnes A., b. Jan. 24, 1856; Cora E., b. Dec. 1, 1858; Marshall R., b. July 2, 1869.

217 RICHARD JAMES[9] MOSES, son of RICHARD (215), was a soldier of the Iron Brigade 1861; was a locomotive engineer, and was killed by his engine on the Union Pacific R. R.; m. at Madison, Wis., Louisa Rhodes. *Children:* one daughter, name unknown.

218 DEWITT SMITH MOSES, son of RICHARD (215), has been connected with the Hamilton Manuf. Co., Two Rivers, Wis., for 20 years; m. at Fond du Lac, Wis., Dec. 23, 1879, Delia Muth. She d. Sept. 27, 1898.

219 MARSHALL RICHARD[10] MOSES, son of MARSHALL S. (216), resides at Aniwa, Wis.; m. Oct. 24, 1888, Augusta B. Windau.

CHILDREN: Marshall Richard, Jr.[11], b. at Fort Atkinson, Wis., Aug. 3, 1891.

220 MARTIN[7] MOSES, son of MARTIN (36), was b. 1780, d. 1860; was in Phelps Co., War of 1812; m. in 1813, Hannah Rose of Granville, Mass. She was b. 1794, d. 1879.

CHILDREN: Lucy, b. 1814, d. 1832; William, b. 1815, d. 1889; Harriet, b. 1816; Orpha Ann, b. 1818, d. 1905; Lydia Lavina, b. 1821, d. 1881; Levi Rose, b. 1823, d. 1902; Mary, b. 1826, d. 1867; Oscar, b. 1829, d. 1862.

Lucy, m. Edward Strong; *Children:* Helen, Harlin.

221 WILLIAM[8] MOSES, son of MARTIN (220), m. Ann Doolittle.

CHILDREN: Fred, b. 1851; Jennie, b. 1853; Clara, b. 1855, d. 1884; Selah, b. 1859, d. 1882; Della, b. 1865.

Fred, m. Rosa Barnes. *Children:* Lillian, Lila, Edith, George.

Jennie, m. Edgar Yoemans.

Della, m. Charles Houghtaling.

222 ORPHA ANN[8] MOSES, dau. of Martin (220), m. Nov. 7, 1844, at Springfield, Mass., John McKay Warriner, who d. Nov. 28, 1886.

CHILDREN: James Franklin, b. 1846, d. 1849; Fannie Jane, b 1849. Emma Ann, b. 1852, and m. Russell Whitcomb.

kiah Webster's Command, War of 1812, m. Rachel Humphrey. They lived in Providence, R. I.

CHILDREN: Senator, Orator, Adaline, Sophronia, Pluma, Ann, Janet.

Sophronia, m. Willard Knight of Providence, R. I., and had *children:* Seril, Willard, Edgar, Adelaide.

212 ELIZABETH GRISWOLD[7] MOSES, dau. of ASHBEL (35), m. John Gibbs Williams, b. at Albany, N. Y., buried at Hudson, N. Y., aged 69.

CHILDREN: John Edward, b. 1825, d. young; Chester Ashbel, b. 1827, d. young; Esther Augusta Williams, b. at West Troy and m. 1st, a Mr. Rice and 2d, a Mr. Nash, who was a soldier in the Civil War and d. in California, Jan. 14, 1898. Mrs. Nash, in 1901, furnished much of the corrected data as to the descendants of Ashbel, and the writer greatly regrets that in 1906 he can learn nothing about her at her former residence at Auburn, California.

213 CLARISSA HATCH[7] MOSES, dau. of ASHBEL (35), m. 1st, John Parsons, of Spencertown, N. Y., and 2d, his brother, Chester Parsons.

CHILDREN: Whiting, Roswell, Elizabeth, Catherine, Chester, Jr.

214 ASHBEL[7] MOSES, son of ASHBEL (35), m. Sally Hughes. He was a mechanic and in 1829 he went to Georgetown, District of Columbia, to construct houses for workmen on the Chesapeake and Ohio Canal. His wife was killed through the blasting of a rock the same year, and he died of a fever two months thereafter.

CHILDREN: Eliza, b. at New Hartford, Conn., Sept. 24, 1811, d. at Spring Lake, Wis., Oct. 14, 1900; Richard, b. at New Hartford, Dec. 25, 1814, d. at Milton Junction, Wis., Dec. 29, 1896.

Eliza, m. Jan. 9, 1831, Thomas Joslin, who was a soldier of the Civil War and d. at Spring Lake, Wis., Oct. 14, 1900.

215 RICHARD[8] MOSES, son of ASHBEL (214), was a cabinet maker, carpenter, and contractor; was buried in Fort Atkinson, Wis. He m., April 12, 1835, Emeliza Pritchard of Litchfield, Conn.

CHILDREN: Marshall Stanley, b. at Wolcottville, Conn., Feb. 18, 1836; Richard James, b. at Herkimer, N. Y., Dec. 6, 1838, d. Oct. 1, 1874; De Witt Smith, b. at Morrisville, N. Y., Oct. 10, 1853.

216 MARSHALL STANLEY[9] MOSES, son of RICHARD

(215), was a soldier of the 81st N. Y., 1861 to May 9, 1864, when he lost his leg.

He settled in Wisconsin, where he worked as a carpenter; m. Oct. 15, 1854, Katherine E. Kellar of Oriskany Falls, N. Y.

CHILDREN: Agnes A., b. Jan. 24, 1856; Cora E., b. Dec. 1, 1858; Marshall R., b. July 2, 1869.

217 RICHARD JAMES[9] MOSES, son of RICHARD (215), was a soldier of the Iron Brigade 1861; was a locomotive engineer, and was killed by his engine on the Union Pacific R. R.; m. at Madison, Wis., Louisa Rhodes. *Children:* one daughter, name unknown.

218 DeWITT SMITH MOSES, son of RICHARD (215), has been connected with the Hamilton Manuf. Co., Two Rivers, Wis., for 20 years; m. at Fond du Lac, Wis., Dec. 23, 1879, Delia Muth. She d. Sept. 27, 1898.

219 MARSHALL RICHARD[10] MOSES, son of MARSHALL S. (216), resides at Aniwa, Wis.; m. Oct. 24, 1888, Augusta B. Windau.

CHILDREN: Marshall Richard, Jr.[11], b. at Fort Atkinson, Wis , Aug. 3, 1891.

220 MARTIN[7] MOSES, son of MARTIN (36), was b. 1780, d. 1860; was in Phelps Co., War of 1812; m. in 1813, Hannah Rose of Granville, Mass. She was b. 1794, d. 1879.

CHILDREN: Lucy, b. 1814, d. 1832; William, b. 1815, d. 1889; Harriet, b. 1816; Orpha Ann, b. 1818, d. 1905; Lydia Lavina, b. 1821, d. 1881; Levi Rose, b. 1823, d. 1902; Mary, b. 1826, d. 1867; Oscar, b. 1829, d. 1862.

Lucy, m. Edward Strong; *Children:* Helen, Harlin.

221 WILLIAM[8] MOSES, son of MARTIN (220), m. Ann Doolittle.

CHILDREN: Fred, b. 1851; Jennie, b. 1853; Clara, b. 1855, d. 1884; Selah, b. 1859, d. 1882; Della, b. 1865.

Fred, m. Rosa Barnes. *Children:* Lillian, Lila, Edith, George.

Jennie, m. Edgar Yoemans.

Della, m. Charles Houghtaling.

222 ORPHA ANN[8] MOSES, dau. of Martin (220), m. Nov. 7, 1844, at Springfield, Mass., John McKay Warriner, who d. Nov. 28, 1886.

CHILDREN: James Franklin, b. 1846, d. 1849; Fannie Jane, b. 1849. Emma Ann, b. 1852, and m. Russell Whitcomb.

223 LYDIA LAVINA[8] MOSES, dau. of MARTIN (220), m. 1854 at Winsted, Conn., Philo M. Goodwin.

CHILDREN: Abijah Martin, b. 1855, d. 1883; Lucy Amelia, b. 1856; Mary-Eliza, b. 1858, d. 1863; George Augustus, b. 1860, d. 1902; Minnie J., b. 1862; Alice Eliza, b. 1865, d. 1872. Of these George m. Louise Kaeser, and Minnie m. Collis Messenger, both residing in Hartford, Conn.

224 LEVI ROSE[8] MOSES, son of MARTIN, Jr. (220), son of MARTIN (36), was born in Canton, Conn., Nov. 25, 1827, was a builder and contractor, m. April 24, 1854, Martha N. Foster of Wentworth, N. H.

CHILDREN: Frank Foster, b. June 21, 1859, d. young; Jessie Frances, b. June 5, 1862; William Lindsley, b. July 11, 1865; Louis Howard, b. Apr. 16, 1867.

Jessie Frances[9], m. Oct., 1892, Waldo Lincoln Upson.
William Lindsley[9], m. Mar. 17, 1891, Teresa Antonette Zelke.

225 HARRIET W.[8] MOSES, dau. of MARTIN, Jr. (220), son of MARTIN (36), was b. Nov. 18, 1818, in Canton, Conn., m. Henry Willis, Nov. 23, 1842. He was born in Springfield, Mass., and there resides.

CHILDREN: Elenora E. (Goodman), of Gardner, Mass.; Henriette A. (Wilcox), of Springfield, Mass.; Caroline P. (Firmin), of Wichita, Kans.

226 ABNER[6] MOSES, son of ABEL (14), b. about May 20, 1764, d. at Vernon, O., March 8, 1808. He was a soldier of the Revolution, Col. Swift's 2d Conn. Reg. About three years after the war he m. Ruhama Johnson, and lived for a while at East Hartland, Conn.

CHILDREN: Polly, b. Feb. 13, 1786, d. Feb. 10, 1867, at Hartford, O.; Abner, b. about 1789; Azariah Wilcox, b. Sept. 21, 1791, d. Feb. 21, 1879, at Orangeville, O.; Nancy Moses, b. July 16, 1793, d. July 22, 1862.

In May, 1800, Abner Moses started with his family with an ox team for the Western Reserve of Ohio, then called New Connecticut. The way lay through New York State, crossing the Hudson at Fishkill and on to Easton, Pa., then through Penn. to Pittsburg, down the Ohio to Fort McIntosh, thence up several rivers and creeks to Vernon, then called Smithfield.

Some distance west of Easton, in the night, the wife, Ruhama, was taken suddenly ill, and at dawn the four children were motherless. The authorities refused to permit the body to be buried in the town, and it

PLYMOUTH AND WINDSOR LINE.   161

was buried, no one knows where. The father and motherless children continued on their way, arriving about June 18, 1800, at their new home in an unbroken wilderness. The sketch is given, to show the contrast between this luxurious age, and the "times that tried men's souls".

Polly, m. Oct. 22, 1810, Hosea Mowry of New Hartford, O., *Child*: Lucy R. Mowry, b. June 27, 1826, d. May 11, 1827.

Azariah Wilcox, unmarried, known as "Uncle John," was a soldier of Col. Richard Hay's Reg. in the War of 1812; was a pensioner; was buried with military honors.

227 ABNER[7] MOSES, son of ABNER (226), lived in Vernon, Ohio, Orangeville, O., and d. at Plattsville, Wis. He m. Nabby Jones, b. Dec. 20, 1791.

CHILDREN: Selden; Polly, b. Oct. 25, 1815, d. Oct. 20, 1827; Jesse; John; Alfred and Albert (twins); Mary, b. June 6, 1829, d. June 10, 1892; Wilber, b. 1835, d. 1835; Cordelia (married a Richards).

228 NANCY[7] MOSES, dau. of ABNER (226); m. about 1812, Jesse Brockway, who was b. Oct. 11, 1792, and resided near Orangeville, Ohio.

CHILDREN: Azariah, b. Feb. 7, 1814, d. Apr. 9, 1895; Chloe, b. Mar. 16, 1815; Fidelia, b. Mar. 16, 1817, d. May 31, 1901; Harriet, b. June 28, 1819, d. Feb. 17, 1904; Moses, b. Aug. 11, 1821, d. Sept. 25, 1847; Eliza, b. Feb. 27, 1824; Betsy, b. Sept. 27, 1827, d. Feb. 12, 1886; Olive, b. May 9, 1829, d. Nov. 1, 1887.

229 AZARIAH[8] BROCKWAY, son of NANCY MOSES (228), m. Jan. 25, 1838, Jane Green and resided in Orangeville, Ohio.

CHILDREN: John Emery, b. Jan. 14, 1843; has four children, resides at Pittsburg, Pa.; Alice Belinda (McFarland), b. Jan. 18, 1845, d. Oct. 20, 1899; Abigail Swift, b. May 4, 1848; Ferris Wade, b. May 5, 1851, has two children at Orangeville, Ohio; Abner Moses, b. Aug. 12, 1854; Mary, b. July 3, 1862, d. Feb. 2, 1863.

230 ABNER MOSES[9] BROCKWAY, received a legacy, because of, and with, the name of Abner Moses; he is greatly interested in genealogy and is himself compiling one; to him the writer is indebted for all the data relating to the descendants of the pioneer Abner Moses. He m. Margaret A. Chambers, who d. Nov. 11, 1888. He resides at Binghamton, N. Y.

231 LUCIUS LAWRENCE[9] MOSES, son of LUCIUS (82), resides at Syracuse, N. Y., m. Jan. 4, 1893, Oril Brown Colvin.

CHILDREN: Lucius Colvin Moses, b. Feb. 20, 1894.

223 LYDIA LAVINA[8] MOSES, dau. of MARTIN (220), m. 1854 at Winsted, Conn., Philo M. Goodwin.

CHILDREN: Abijah Martin, b. 1855, d. 1883; Lucy Amelia, b. 1856; Mary-Eliza, b. 1858, d. 1863; George Augustus, b. 1860, d. 1902; Minnie J., b. 1862; Alice Eliza, b. 1865, d. 1872. Of these George m. Louise Kaeser, and Minnie m. Collis Messenger, both residing in Hartford, Conn.

224 LEVI ROSE[8] MOSES, son of MARTIN, Jr. (220), son of MARTIN (36), was born in Canton, Conn., Nov. 25, 1827, was a builder and contractor, m. April 24, 1854, Martha N. Foster of Wentworth, N. H.

CHILDREN: Frank Foster, b. June 21, 1859, d. young; Jessie Frances, b. June 5, 1862; William Lindsley, b. July 11, 1865; Louis Howard, b. Apr. 16, 1867.

Jessie Frances[9], m. Oct., 1892, Waldo Lincoln Upson.

William Lindsley[9], m. Mar. 17, 1891, Teresa Antonette Zelke.

225 HARRIET W.[8] MOSES, dau. of MARTIN, Jr. (220), son of MARTIN (36), was b. Nov. 18, 1818, in Canton, Conn., m. Henry Willis, Nov. 23, 1842. He was born in Springfield, Mass., and there resides.

CHILDREN: Elenora E. (Goodman), of Gardner, Mass.; Henriette A. (Wilcox), of Springfield, Mass.; Caroline P. (Firmin), of Wichita, Kans.

226 ABNER[6] MOSES, son of ABEL (14), b. about May 20, 1764, d. at Vernon, O., March 8, 1808. He was a soldier of the Revolution, Col. Swift's 2d Conn. Reg. About three years after the war he m. Ruhama Johnson, and lived for a while at East Hartland, Conn.

CHILDREN: Polly, b. Feb. 13, 1786, d. Feb. 10, 1867, at Hartford, O.; Abner, b. about 1789; Azariah Wilcox, b. Sept. 21, 1791, d. Feb. 21, 1879, at Orangeville, O.; Nancy Moses, b. July 16, 1793, d. July 22, 1862.

In May, 1800, Abner Moses started with his family with an ox team for the Western Reserve of Ohio, then called New Connecticut. The way lay through New York State, crossing the Hudson at Fishkill and on to Easton, Pa., then through Penn. to Pittsburg, down the Ohio to Fort McIntosh, thence up several rivers and creeks to Vernon, then called Smithfield.

Some distance west of Easton, in the night, the wife, Ruhama, was taken suddenly ill, and at dawn the four children were motherless. The authorities refused to permit the body to be buried in the town, and it was buried, no one knows where. The father and motherless children continued on their way, arriving about June 18, 1800, at their new home in an unbroken wilderness. The sketch is given, to show the contrast between this luxurious age, and the "times that tried men's souls".

Polly, m. Oct. 22, 1810, Hosea Mowry of New Hartford, O., *Child*: Lucy R. Mowry, b. June 27, 1826, d. May 11, 1827.

Azariah Wilcox, unmarried, known as "Uncle John," was a soldier of Col. Richard Hay's Reg. in the War of 1812; was a pensioner; was buried with military honors.

227 ABNER[7] MOSES, son of ABNER (226), lived in Vernon, Ohio, Orangeville, O., and d. at Plattsville, Wis. He m. Nabby Jones, b. Dec. 20, 1791.

CHILDREN: Selden; Polly, b. Oct. 25, 1815, d. Oct. 20, 1827; Jesse; John; Alfred and Albert (twins); Mary, b. June 6, 1829, d. June 10, 1892; Wilber, b. 1835, d. 1835; Cordelia (married a Richards).

228 NANCY[7] MOSES, dau. of ABNER (226); m. about 1812, Jesse Brockway, who was b. Oct. 11, 1792, and resided near Orangeville, Ohio.

CHILDREN: Azariah, b. Feb. 7, 1814, d. Apr. 9, 1895; Chloe, b. Mar. 16, 1815; Fidelia, b. Mar. 16, 1817, d. May 31, 1901; Harriet, b. June 28, 1819, d. Feb. 17, 1904; Moses, b. Aug. 11, 1821, d. Sept. 25, 1847; Eliza, b. Feb. 27, 1824; Betsy, b. Sept. 27, 1827, d. Feb. 12, 1886; Olive, b. May 9, 1829, d. Nov. 1, 1887.

229 AZARIAH[8] BROCKWAY, son of NANCY MOSES (228), m. Jan. 25, 1838, Jane Green and resided in Orangeville, Ohio.

CHILDREN: John Emery, b. Jan. 14, 1843; has four children, resides at Pittsburg, Pa.; Alice Belinda (McFarland), b. Jan. 18, 1845, d. Oct. 20, 1899; Abigail Swift, b. May 4, 1848; Ferris Wade, b. May 5, 1851, has two children at Orangeville, Ohio; Abner Moses, b. Aug. 12, 1854; Mary, b. July 3, 1862, d. Feb. 2, 1863.

230 ABNER MOSES[9] BROCKWAY, received a legacy, because of, and with, the name of Abner Moses; he is greatly interested in genealogy and is himself compiling one; to him the writer is indebted for all the data relating to the descendants of the pioneer Abner Moses. He m. Margaret A. Chambers, who d. Nov. 11, 1888. He resides at Binghamton, N. Y.

231 LUCIUS LAWRENCE[9] MOSES, son of LUCIUS (82), resides at Syracuse, N. Y., m. Jan. 4, 1893, Oril Brown Colvin.

CHILDREN: Lucius Colvin Moses, b. Feb. 20, 1894.

232 OSCAR F.[9] MOSES, son of JOHN (70), resides in Ethan, S. Dak., m. Sept. 14, 1895, Delia E. Breer.

CHILDREN: Flora B., b. Aug. 20, 1896; Harold A., b. Dec. 27, 1899.

233 EMILY (EMMA)[9] MOSES, dau. of JOHN (70), resides at Perry, Okla., m. May 22, 1893, John Allen Price, M.D.

CHILDREN: John Paul, b. Oct. 12, 1895; Mary Winnifred, b. June 12, 1897; Virginia Elizabeth, b. June 22, 1903.

234 EDWIN D.[9] MOSES, son of JOHN (70), resides at Mt. Vernon, S. Dak., m. July 6, 1889, Nora E. McCreery.

CHILDREN: Ninna M., b. June 20, 1890; Beulah F., b. Mar. 30, 1892; Jessie M., b. Sept. 18, 1894; Frank D., b. Sept. 28, 1897, d. Oct. 4, 1898; Frederick E., b. Nov. 21, 1899.

235 FLORA B.[9] MOSES, dau. of JOHN (70), resides at Mt. Vernon, S. Dak., m. Nov. 14, 1887, Oness H. Dixon.

CHILDREN: Oness H., Jr., b. Dec. 21, 1891; Clyde L., b. Dec. 30, 1893; William B., b. Dec. 17, 1896; Sylvia G., b. Apr. 19, 1900; Fairy R., b. Sept. 1, 1905.

236 CHARLES W.[9] MOSES, son of BENJAMIN FRANKLIN (74), resides at Detroit, Mich.; m. Nov. 29, 1894, Rena Arlyle Traver, b. Nov. 26, 1869, at Newton, Iowa.

CHILDREN: Curtis Lee, b. June 20, 1899.

237 HORACE CHESTER[10] MOSES, son of LINUS A. (65), resides in New York City; m. June 12, 1906, Marion, dau. of William Graham of New York.

238 SYBIL MOSES, dau. of DANIEL (13), was born 1762 or 3, and m. Martin Roberts, who removed from Conn. to the state of New York. He served in the Revolutionary War, as Forage-master, collecting stores for General Lafayette's Army (see New York in the Revolution Appendix).

CHILDREN: Among others, Sybil.

Sybil (Moses) Roberts, m. Ephraim Blodgett, and had a daughter, Buelah Roberts Blodgett, who m. Henry Smith, and had a daughter Mary Smith, wife of Henry C. Lockwood. Mrs. Lockwood, a lineal descendant of the Revolutionary patriot, Daniel Moses, is one of the founders of the Daughters of the American Revolution; is an eloquent speaker, and has given almost her entire time for the last ten years to the advancement of the Society. Her daughter, Lilian Lockwood, is the Business Manager of the American Magazine, the organ of the D. A. R. Society.

239 RANDOLPH[9] MOSES, son of DANIEL (41), resides in West Simsbury, Conn.; m. Apr. 27, 1887, Linda Sackett of Westfield, Mass.

CHILDREN: Daniel Roland, b. May 20, 1890; Elizabeth Mary, b. Aug. 13, 1892.

240 ADRIAN[9] MOSES, son of RICHARD (136), resides at Unionville, Conn.; m. May 5, 1863, Clarinda V. Beckwith.

CHILDREN: Henrietta Augusta, b. Mar. 19, 1864; Arthur A., b. Jan. 21, 1867.

Henrietta Augusta, m. Jan. 4, 1899, Edwin Mathews. *Children:* Charles Arthur, b. Dec. 15, 1900; Adrian, b. Aug. 3, 1902.

241 ARTHUR A.[10] MOSES, son of ADRIAN (240), m. June 25, 1890, Mary Fellows.

CHILDREN: Arthur Emerson, b. Oct. 17, 1892; Clara Augusta, b. Apr. 18, 1898; Robert Adrian, b. Dec. 25, 1903.

242 BERNARD[9] MOSES, son of RICHARD (136), has had a brilliant political and literary career. Quotation is made from a newspaper article of many years since, at the time he had been elected President of Berkeley University, Cal. "Professor Moses, the successful candidate, is generally recognized as a man of marked individuality and strength of purpose. He graduated at Ann Arbor (Michigan University); went to Europe, taking up history as a specialty, going through a course at Leipsic University. At the Berlin University he enjoyed the intellectual direction of Professors Mommsen, Droyen, and Von Freitzke. He afterward went to Heidelberg, where in 1874 he received his degree of Ph.D. On his return to this country he accepted the Chair of history and political economy at the University of California. He is the author of many historical and political works." From the Authors Catalogue Cards in the Congressional Library, the following list is compiled:

THE CASA DE CONTRACTION OF SEVILLE.
DATA OF MEXICAN AND UNITED STATES HISTORY.
THE ECONOMIC CONDITION OF SPAIN IN THE SIXTEENTH CENTURY.
THE ESTABLISHMENT OF SPANISH RULE IN AMERICA.
THE ESTABLISHMENT OF MUNICIPAL GOVERNMENT IN SAN FRANCISCO.
THE RAILWAY REVOLUTION IN MEXICO.

THE CONSTITUTION OF COLUMBIA, TRANSLATED IN 1893.
THE CONSTITUTION OF MEXICO, TRANSLATED IN 1892.
FEDERAL GOVERNMENT IN SWITZERLAND.
DEMOCRACY AND SOCIAL GROWTH IN AMERICA.
THE GOVERNMENT OF THE UNITED STATES (1906).

On Mar. 16, 1900, President McKinley appointed him one of the Commissioners to govern the Philippine Islands; he remained there from 1900 to 1902; after his return he resumed his former position at the University of California.

He m. June 15, 1880, Mary Edith Briggs, Professor of History at Albion College.

CHILDREN: Auria, b. Jan. 12, 1893.

243 EMERSON[9] MOSES, son of RICHARD (136), resided before his death, June 26, 1901, at Lake Crystal, Minn.; m. Sept. 10, 1865, Alice W. Colvin.

CHILDREN: Oliver E., b. Feb. 19, 1872; Charles R., b. Sept. 30, 1876.

244 OLIVER E.[10] MOSES, son of EMERSON (243), m. Jan. 1, 1898, May Beebe.

CHILDREN: Bernard, b. Oct. 20, 1898; Jay E., b. Jan. 27, 1900; Bertha May, b. Jan. 27, 1901.

245 LUCIUS H.[9] MOSES, son of RICHARD (136), resides at Lake Crystal, Minn.; m. June 22, 1896, Bridget McGiveny.

CHILDREN: Adrian L., b. July 13, 1897; Gertrude E., b. Nov. 16, 1898; George F., b. Sept. 18, 1900.

246 RICHARD A.[9] MOSES, son of RICHARD (136), is an attorney at Cedar Rapids, Iowa; m. Feb. 11, 1877, Florence M. Russell.

CHILDREN: Ellen B.

247 MYRON[7] MOSES, son of ZEBINA (46), resided at Marcellus, N. Y., at Newcastle, Canada, and at Mt. Carroll, Ill., where he died March 26, 1863. He m. Ann Isabelle Jacobs, Nov. 20, 1831.

CHILDREN: Ann Eliza, b. June 1, 1834, d. Jan. 10, 1902; Horace Curtis, b. April 30, 1836, d. Jan. 2, 1895; George Annesley, b. Jan. 8, 1838, d. Jan. 12, 1842; Juliette, b. May 24, 1841, d. Jan. 16, 1842; Charlotte Elvira, b. Aug. 16, 1844; Mary Elizabeth, b. Jan. 17, 1847; Myron Joseph, b. May 10, 1849; Franklin Chester, b. Sept. 24, 1851.

Horace Curtis, d. unmarried at Independence, Kans.

Ann Eliza, d. unmarried at Independence, Kans.

Charlotte Elvira, m. Oct., 1865, Judson Allen, resides at Hannibal, Mo., and has one daughter.

Mary Elizabeth, m. Mar. 30, 1866, William Cooley, of Savanna, Ill., and has one child, a daughter.

Myron Joseph, resides at Everett, Mo., m. Dec. 23, 1890, Sarah E. Brown.

248 FRANKLIN CHESTER[8] MOSES, son of MYRON (247), by election and re-election, held the offices of Clerk, Deputy Sheriff, and Sheriff of Montgomery Co., Kansas, from 1885 to 1895. In 1899 he was elected Councilman of Independence, Kans., a city of 14,000 inhabitants. In 1901 he was elected its Mayor, declined to run again, and is at present in the City Council.

He m. April 28, 1878, Frances Ann Dobson at Everett, Mo.

CHILDREN: Lula Isabelle, b. Sept. 25, 1883; Gertrude Edna, b. Nov. 4, 1888; Robert Elmer, b. Aug. 10, 1895.

Lula Isabelle, m. Mar. 15, 1905, Alva E. Robley; has one child named Kenneth.

249 ASA[7] MOSES, son of MARTIN (36), about 1840, removed from Canton, Conn., to Rootstown, O.; m. Nov. 11, 1819, Almira Barber. She d. Nov. 8, 1853.

CHILDREN: Asa Lorenzo, b. Oct. 20, 1820, d. Apr. 30, 1846, James E., b. Nov. 21, 1822, d. about 1872; Lauren Newton, b. Jan. 15, 1825; Jane Elizabeth, b. Jan. 5, 1827; Hector, b. Oct. 17, 1828, d. about 1885; Harvey W., b. Jan. 29, 1830, d. about 1860; Henry, b. Nov. 29, 1832; Francis Hiram, b. Mar. 23, 1835.

Asa Lorenzo, m. Jan. 1, 1845, Elizabeth Heriff. *Children:* Asa d. in the Army.

Jane Elizabeth, m. Sept. 23, 1848, Andrew Jones; resides in Williamstown, Ohio.

Francis Hiram, m. Clara Ream. *Children:* Elmer, resides in Toledo, Ohio.

250 JAMES EDWIN[8] MOSES, son of ASA (249), m. Belinda White.

CHILDREN: Emma, m. William Shaweeker of Canton, Ohio; Edwin.

251 LAUREN NEWTON[8] MOSES, son of ASA (249), resides at Jefferson, O.; m. 1st, Oct. 2, 1851, Mary Kridler; m. 2d, Aug. 3, 1871, Kate C. Woods.

CHILDREN, by 1st marriage: Cora Ellen, resides in Boston, Mass.; Loren Sherman, resides at Hillsboro, Texas: by 2d marriage: Richard Woods, b. Aug. 25, 1872; Jessie Lenore.

Jessie Lenore, m. J. F. Craven, a contracting engineer of Pittsburg; they reside, however, at Jefferson, Ohio.

Richard Woods, resides at Coraopolis, Penn.; m. and has *Children:* Walter Lauren, b. Dec. 13, 1905.

252 HARVEY W.[8] MOSES, son of Asa (249), m. Rebecca Lynch.

CHILDREN: Charles, resides in Dunkirk, O., and has one child. Helen; Jennie, m. and residing in Williamstown, Ohio; Frank, deceased.

253 HENRY[8] MOSES, son of Asa (249), m. Nov. 12, 1857, Harriet Wheeler. He is now Mayor of Manson, Iowa.

CHILDREN: Hattie, m. William Wise; Harry; another son, deceased.

Page 85, No. **138** CHAUNCY[8] MOSES, Representative in the General Assembly from Canton, Conn.; m. Catherine Johnson.

CHILDREN: Henry, b. Oct. 22, 1817; Elizabeth, b. Oct. 27, 1819, d. in 1861; Flora A., b. Feb. 17, 1822, lives in Manhattan, Kansas; Rollin, b. Feb. 26, 1825, d. Aug. 30, 1895; Seymour Darius, b. June 2, 1828

Rollin, m. Adaline Mead, who d. Aug. 30, 1895.

254 SEYMOUR DARIUS[9] MOSES, son of CHAUNCY (138), was born in Canton, Conn., June 2, 1828, removed from West Simsbury to Manhattan, Kans., where he is still living; m. Sept. 18, 1852, in Canton, Harriet Mills.

CHILDREN: George Chauncey, b. at Canton, Nov. 29, 1856; Mary Elizabeth, b. at Unionville, Conn., Jan. 1, 1866, resides at Manhattan, Kans.

255 GEORGE CHAUNCEY[10] MOSES, son of SEYMOUR DARIUS (254), is a contractor and builder, engaged on Government work; has also a large business at Junction City, Kans.; m. Jan. 15, 1880, at Milford, Kans., Alice Jane Streator, b. in Lowell, Vt.

CHILDREN: Clyde Everett, b. June 27, 1882; Flora E., b. June 13, 1884, d. May 8, 1892; Abbie Ruth, b. June 9, 1887.

256 CLYDE EVERETT[11] MOSES, son of GEORGE CHAUNCEY (255), is associated with his father in business at Junction City, Kans.; m. July 24, 1902, Ethelyn Sylvester Geminy.

CHILDREN: George Geminy[12] Moses, b. at Junction City, Kans., Sept. 20, 1903. This boy has the distinction of being one of the earliest (probably the earliest), born child of the *twelfth* generation of Moses American lineage.

Page 77, No. **92**   Darius[8] Moses, Representative in the General Assembly from Canton, Conn.; m. Sodema Holcomb.

Children: Elizur; Richard; James F., b. Sept. 12, 1823, d. 1897; Abigail; Mary Elizabeth, b. about 1822, d. July, 1852, at Elmira, N. Y.

Elizur, m. at St. Andrew's Church, Simsbury, Dec. 1835, Rebecca Bates. He lived at Waterbury, Conn. He mysteriously disappeared, starting from his home one day to mail some letters, was never seen again.

Richard, resided in Waterbury, Conn.; was a carpenter; m. Nancy Wells; had one son, who d. young.

Abigail, m. Rev. William H. Frisbie, an Episcopal minister. They had three children, who died young. She had the rearing of three young children of her sister, after the death of Mrs. Bidwell at Elmira, and was much beloved by them. She herself died at Hartford, Conn.

257 MARY ELIZABETH[9] MOSES, dau. of Darius (92), m. about 1846, George Harvey Bidwell of Hartford, Conn.

Children: George Franklin, b. at Danville, N. Y., June 27, 1847; Charles Eli, b. at Bath, N. Y., Sept. 3, 1849, d. 1898; Mary Abigail, b. at Elmira, N. Y., July 4, 1852, m. Isaac F. Foote, New Haven, Conn.

George F. Bidwell is the Manager of the Neb. & Wyo. Div. of the Chi. & N. W. R. R.; resides at Omaha, Neb.; is married and has children.

258   JAMES F.[9] MOSES, son of Darius (92), was a member of the Ancient and Honorable Artillery Co. of Boston; and also of the Boston City Guards. He resided for several years before his death at Bucksport, Me. He m. Harriet Porter Buckley. She was b. in Berlin, Conn., in 1824, and d. at East Orland, Me., in 1903.

Children: born in Boston, Mass.; Frederick Holcomb, b. July 21, 1849; Nellie Hart, b. Dec. 7, 1853.

Nellie Hart, m. 1874, Charles G. Atkins, and resides in East Orland, Me.

259 FREDERICK HOLCOMB[10] MOSES, son of James F. (258), is a florist and landscape gardener at Bar Harbor, Me.; m. Oct. 23, 1873, Isabel Barnard of Bucksport, Me.

Page 88, No. **144**   John[6] Moses, son of John (19). Was pensioned as a Revolutionary soldier, Sept. 13, 1832. From pension papers it appears that he was b. at Simsbury, Jan. 9, 1761, d. at Huntington, Vt., Mar. 16, 1842; m. Polly Bates at Rutland, Vt., Dec. 18, 1785.— Of the children mentioned in Vol. 1, Hannah was

62 in 1849; Lucy, wife of Nathl. Chaffee, was 57 in 1848; Jonathan was 49 in 1844; Anna was an adopted child.

To give the reader an idea of the service of a Vermont soldier in the Revolution, extracts are made from the pension affidavits:

"Served one month from Rutland June 1777, under Capt. Smith; In Aug. 1777, enl. at Mulbery, Mass., for three months; — at Bennington and Saratoga. From Apr. to Nov. 1778, enl. at Rutland under Capt. Sawyer, (only four companies of rangers); employed in scouting and guarding. From Feby. to April 1779, called to guard continental stores. In Nov. 1779 under Col. Cleyhan called to meet enemy at Brandon, Vt.; thence to Pittsfield, thence to Rutland. In March 1780, to Ticonderoga: In June 1780, to Crown Point. In Oct. 1780, to Carleton. In 1781, called as a minute man several times on sudden expeditions. In 1782, went to Clarendon as guard two weeks. In Oct. called to Pellsford, took three tories, gone four days."

260 SILAS[7] MOSES, son of JOHN (144); was b. in 1789, d. in Stockholm, N. Y., in 1876, m. at Hinesburg, Vt., Diana Peck.

CHILDREN: Joel P., b. Jan. 8, 1825, d. June 17, 1896; Mandana, b. Mar. 24, 1826; Hiram, b. Feb. 28, 1828; Sarah Ann, b. Aug. 17, 1830; Rufus, b. Dec. 12, 1832; Louisa E., b. April, 1835; Lucretia, b. June 9, 1842, d. 1847; John, b. Oct. 25, 1844, d. Sept. 1847.

Mandana: m. 2d, a Lamson, lives in Edwards, N. Y.
Hiram lives at Sylvan Falls, N. Y., m. Mar. 13, 1853, Louisa Powers.
Sarah Ann lives at Parishville, N. Y., m. Jan. 29, 1853, John W. Wait.
Rufus, now deceased, m. July 1859, Lucinda Lyon.
Louisa E., m. Lester C. Manzer.

261 JOEL P.[8] MOSES, son of SILAS (260); lived in Parisville, N. Y., m. Sept. 6, 1853, Laura Clark.

CHILDREN: Owen, b. Feb. 14, 1865; Silas, b. Mar. 7, 1867; Ferdinand J., b. Feb. 16, 1869; Bernie O., b. Aug. 4, 1870; Ethel, b. May 3, 1872; George H., b. Aug. 15, 1874, d. Oct. 15, 1891; Harry, b. Dec. 30, 1878.

Owen, resides at Auburn, Kings Co., Washington. *Children:* Bessie Mertin Joel; George E.; Mildred L.; Andy.
Silas, resides at Parishville, N. Y. *Children:* George H.; Gerald L.; Susie; Fred; Rolly.
Ferdinand J., resides at Potsdam, N. Y. *Children:* Jay A.; Myfred M.; baby.
Bernie O., resides at Parishville, N. Y. *Children:* Lena A.
Ethel, m. ———, resides at Parishville, N. Y. *Children:* Eva M.; Roy L.; Eugenia; Lucy L.; Viola L.; Laura E.; Bennie S.

262 ASA[6] MOSES, probably son of JOHN (19). Asa was a Revolutionary Soldier, and was an administrator of the estate of

Benoni Moses, brother of John (19). He appears at West Rutland about 12 years after John had removed there; and in 1785 joined the Congregational Church which John and John's sister and brother-in-law had helped to found. Note also, that Asa's grandchild was named Asa Benoni. As stated on page 60, there are wide intervals between the births of three of John's children recorded on tombstones found in the West Simsbury burying ground, and in any event we can say with certainty, that Asa was a descendant of John of Plymouth and John of Simsbury. He died in West Rutland, Vt., in 1796. His wife's name is unknown. She married 2d a man by the name of Woods, by whom she had a son, Hiram Woods, who died at Batavia, N. Y.

CHILDREN OF ASA: Asa; Amasa, d. 1820; Artemas; Dorcas; Oren, b. West Rutland, Vt., 1791, d. at Malone, N. Y., 1864.

Asa: No information; but his widow lived in Highgate, Vt., after his death.

Dorcas, m. a Mr. Mead of Medina, N. Y. *Children:* Harry; Worthy.

263 ARTEMAS[7] MOSES, son of ASA (262), died at Champlain, N. Y. He signed deeds and mortgages at Middlebury, Vt., between 1813 and 1825. He m. Lydia Bump of Salisbury, Vt.

CHILDREN: Andrew J.

264 ANDREW J.[8] MOSES, son of ARTEMAS (263), m. Martha Nichols of Champlain, N. Y.

Children: Albert; Fannie.

Fannie, m. William Berri of Champlain, N. Y.

265 OREN[7] MOSES, son of ASA (262), m. Betsey Lawrence Stickney of Middlebury, Vt. She was b. July 10, 1791, at Weybridge, Vt., and d. March, 1868. He removed to Malone, N. Y.

CHILDREN: Oren, b. Mar. 6, 1820, at Malone, N. Y., living 1906; Myron, b. Oct. 5, 1823, d. Feb. 9, 1879.

266 OREN[8] MOSES, son of OREN (265), resides at Malone, N. Y.; m. Mary Ann Holley of Bristol, Vt., Nov. 11, 1851; she d. Feb. 23, 1899.

CHILDREN: Mary E., now the widow of Newcomb H. Munsill; Willis H.

Willis H., resides at Brooklyn, N. Y.

267 MYRON[8] MOSES, son of OREN (265), resided at Malone, N. Y.; m. Feb. 19, 1846, Harriet D. Phelps. She d. May 23, 1873.

CHILDREN: Myron L., b. Dec., 1846, d. Nov. 12, 1868; Laura M., b. Mar. 20, 1848, d. May 30, 1868; Millard F., b. Dec. 1, 1849,

d. May 26, 1905; Hattie L., b. May 26, 1851; Orson P., b. Aug. 1, 1853, d. Oct. 12, 1853; Ida F., b. Oct. 9, 1855, d. Dec. 26, 1875; Albert P., b. Dec. 27, 1857; George, b. Mar. 26, 1862, d. June 11, 1883; Orson E., b. Nov. 8, 1863, d. May 28, 1885; Fred, b. Oct. 23, 1869, d. Sept. 2, 1898; Catherine M., b. June 8, 1871, d. Aug. 21, 1871.

Hattie L., m. Aug. 18, 1872, David T. Hebart of Malone, N. Y.

268 MILLARD F.[9] MOSES, son of MYRON (267), resided at Malone, N. Y.; m. Oct. 14, 1876, at Malone, Catherine McDougall.

CHILDREN: Carrie Bell, b. Sept. 21, 1877, d. Jan. 25, 1879; William, b. Mar. 19, 1879; Baby, b. Sept. 16, 1880, d. Mar. 30, 1881; Jessie, b. Dec. 23, 1882; Mable, b. May 5, 1884; Lillian, b. Dec. 12, 1885, d. Aug. 18, 1903; Grace M., b. Mar. 25, 1894.

269 ALBERT P.[9] MOSES, son of MYRON (267), resides at Malone and Mountain View, N. Y.; m. Dec. 15, 1882, E. C. Nickelson, of Malone, N. Y.

CHILDREN: Jennie Grace, b. Sept. 19, 1883, d. Sept. 23, 1884; Ethel A., b. April 4, 1893; George A., b. June 29, 1894.

270 AMASA[7] MOSES, son of ASA (262), m. Electa Pond of Vermont.

CHILDREN: Hiram, b. at Shoreham, Vt., d. at Boulder, Colo.; Asa Benoni, b. May 2, 1815, at Shoreham, Vt., d. July 12, 1889, at West Stockholm, N. Y.; Lydia Belden, b. Mar. 12, 1818, at Shoreham, Vt.; d. at DeKalb, N. Y., Oct. 1893.

271 ASA BENONI[8] MOSES, son of AMASA (270), m. Apr. 19, 1852, Mary A. Foster, of Stockholm, N. Y.

CHILDREN: Emma L., b. Jan. 31, 1853, resides at Kingsley, Mich.; Amasa Foster, b. Oct. 6, 1855; Albert Pond, b. Sept. 16, 1857, at Potsdam, N. Y.; Elmer Ellsworth, b. May 1, 1861; Maryette, b. Dec. 15, 1863; Edwin Lincoln, b. Jan. 30, 1866, at Pierpont, N. Y.

Elmer Ellsworth, resides at Union City, Pa.; m. Apr. 9, 1904, Villa Taylor, of Grand Rapids, Mich.

Maryette, resides at Erie, Pa. The writer is indebted to her for data concerning her grandfather and his descendants.

272 AMASA FOSTER[9] MOSES, son of ASA BENONI (271), m. Dec. 27, 1877, at Cambridge, Pa., Anna Barbara Hanson.

CHILDREN: LeRoy H., b. Nov. 27, 1878; Ernest H., b. Jan. 30, 1881; Gerald, b. July 4, 1885; Mildred Elizabeth, b. June 18, 1888.

Ernest H., resides at Youngstown, Ohio.

Gerald, resides at Newcastle, Pa.

273 LeROY H.[10] MOSES, son of AMASA FOSTER (272), is in

Government office at Washington, D. C. Is at the present time, 1906, Private Secretary to the Secretary of the Navy.

274 ALBERT POND[9] MOSES, son of Asa Benoni (271), m. Jan. 1, 1892, Charlotte Dygert, of West Stockholm, N. Y.

CHILDREN: Dorothy May, b. May 2, 1905.

275 EDWIN LINCOLN[9] MOSES, son of Asa Benoni (271), m. Apr. 29, 1895, Anna Beatrice Coughlan, of Conneautville, Pa.

CHILDREN: Ethel May, b. May 29, 1897; Herbert Allan, b Apr. 16, 1902.

276 FRANK S.[10] MOSES, son of John C. (115), resides in Clinton, Iowa; m. June 23, 1886, Elizabeth Constance Shethar.

CHILDREN: Mary Constance, b. 1888; John Vincent, b. 1894; Katherine, b. 1898.

277 LINCOLN E.[10] MOSES, son of Amasa Cassius (116), is a merchant at Los Angeles, Cal.; m. May 12, 1891, Gertrude Jucker of Three Rivers, Mich.

CHILDREN: Edward Walter, b. June 8, 1894, at Pueblo, Colo.; Margaret, b. May 1, 1899, at Pueblo, Colo.

278 EDWARD W.[10] MOSES, son of Amasa Cassius (116), in 1871 removed with his parents from Chautauqua Co., N. Y., to a farm near the present location of the City of Great Bend, Kans. Has with his brothers been extensively engaged in merchandising, milling, grain buying, and the herding of cattle. He was elected Mayor of Great Bend, in 1884, 1885, 1893, and again in 1903 and 1905; m. Jan. 29, 1892, Anna J. Wood.

279 Page 81, CLAYTON LAWYER[10] MOSES; he has been President of the Moses Bros. Mill and Elev. Co., Vice-president Farmers and Merchants Bank, Councilman of Great Bend, Kans., and Commissioner of Barton Co., Kans. (Other particulars see No. 118.)

280 SEWARD EARL[10] MOSES, son of Amasa Cassius (116), is a merchant miller and otherwise interested with his brothers; m. Aug. 14, 1899, Edith Georgia Balcom, of Pueblo, Colo.

281 WILLIAM A.[10] MOSES, son of Amasa Cassius (116), is the Kansas City, Mo., member of the Moses Bros. Grain Co.

In 1891 he was elected Sheriff of Pueblo Co., Colorado, and through re-election served four years; m. Dec. 31, 1882, Grace M. Buckland; she d. July 5, 1906.

CHILDREN: Arthur C., b. Dec. 11, 1889; Alan, b. Nov. 13, 1894, d. July, 1899; Elinor, b. Jan. 7, 1901.

282 CASSIUS M.[10] MOSES, son of AMASA CASSIUS (116), resides at Los Angeles, Cal. Was Major of 2d Colo. Reg. during Cripple Creek riots in 1894; was Adjutant-General and Quartermaster-General of Colorado Jan. 1, 1895, to May 1, 1898; was in command in the field during the Leadville insurrection from Aug. 1896 to Mar. 1897, a campaign carried on 12,000 feet above the sea in a severe winter. On May 1, 1898, was enrolled as Major 1st Colorado Inf., promoted to Lieut.-Colonel Sept. 6, 1898, at Manila, mustered out with Reg. Sept. 8, 1899. Engaged at the fall of Manila and general assault of Aug. 13, 1898; on Mar. 25, 1899, commanded battalion in several engagements in advance on Malalos; was recommended for brevet Colonelcy for gallantry on the field; on June 10th commanded advance guard in the movement by General Lawton on Paranaque; was dangerously wounded and remained in hospital until regiment embarked for San Francisco. Was recommended by General Lawton to be Brevet Brigadier-General U. S. Vols. for gallantry at the battle of Guadaloupe Heights.

Married Oct. 14, 1890, Betsey Baldwin Coningham.

CHILDREN: Donna, b. Dec. 13, 1894, at Pueblo, Colo.; John Campbell, b. Aug. 20, 1896, at Denver, Colo.

Page 60, No. 21 OTHNIEL[5] MOSES (see personal paragraph, Vol. 1). Some of the following particulars are gleaned from the Hist. of Hillsdale, N. Y. Othniel was a soldier of the French War and of the Revolution (see Soldier List). He resided in Simsbury, Farmington, and Burlington, Conn., and d. at Burlington, Conn., in 1822. He m. in 1816, Sarah Pinney of Windsor, Conn.

CHILDREN: Othniel, Reuben, Elihu, b. in Burlington, 1730, d. Dec. 22, 1814; Isaac, Polly, Dorcas, Roxany, Olive, Rhoda, Cynthia.

Othniel, m. Mary David (see 132).
Isaac, d. in the Florida War.
Polly, m. Hezekiah Richards of New Hartford, Conn.
Dorcas, m. Joel Dorman of Burlington, Conn.
Roxanna, m. Mark Hamline.
Olive, m. Mr. Walker, and settled in Homer, N. Y.

Rhoda, m. a German, who was lost at sea.
Cynthia, m. John Talbot of Hartford Co., Conn.

283 ELIHU[6] MOSES, son of OTHNIEL (21). The Hist. of Hillsdale, N. Y., states that he served in Perry's fleet, Battle of Lake Erie. Mr. A. L. Moses states that the inscription on a tombstone in the East Cleveland, O., Cemetery, records that he was a Captain under Commodore Perry. He d. Dec. 22, 1814, of fever on shipboard while en route Detroit to Cleveland; m. at Burlington, Conn., Elizabeth Talbot (said to have been a descendant of Lord John Talbot of England), and settled in Farmington, Ohio, in 1804. Elihu handed down to his son, Luther, the tradition that the first Moses in this country was of Welsh descent.

CHILDREN: Ardolissa, b. 1799, d. Aug. 25, 1857; Charles, b. Nov. 31, 1800, d. Apr. 1, 1877; Elizabeth, b. 1823, d. May 5, 1846; Elihu, b. 1806, d. Jan. 8, 1861; Philo P., b. 1809, d. 1886; Roxana, b. 1813, d. 1877; Luther, b. 1811, d. Dec. 24, 1895.

Elizabeth, m. John P. Coleman.

284 ARDOLISSA[7] MOSES, dau. of ELIHU (283), b. at Farmington, Conn., m. July 13, 1817, A. H. Avery.

CHILDREN: Harriet Maria (Gardner), b. Apr. 23, 1818, d. Feb. 20, 1888; Betsey (Sorter), b. May 3, 1821; Mary, b. Oct. 28, 1824, d. June 28, 1825; Hezekiah, b. June 15, 1828, m. Harriet Welch; Charles, b. Sept. 11, 1835, d. July 13, 1850; Julia (Gates), b. Feb. 11, 1843, d. Jan. 14, 1887.

285 CHARLES[7] MOSES, son of ELIHU (283), resided at Euclid, O., d. at Nottingham, O. He was large and muscular, and was a farmer, carpenter, ship builder, and merchant; m. 1st, Sept. 18, 1825, Polly Atkins; she d. 1869; m. 2d, Mary Ann House.

CHILDREN: all b. at Euclid, O., Henry, b. Jan. 11, 1827, d. Aug. 30, 1861; George, b. Oct. 19, 1828, d. Apr. 22, 1853; Betsey M., b. Apr. 21, 1831, d. Apr. 19, 1893, John Nelson, b. May 16, 1833; Martha Ann, b. Nov. 8, 1835; Charles W. (twin), b. Mar. 17, 1840, d. June 27, 1904; Caroline A. (twin), b. Mar. 17, 1840, d. Apr. 7, 1901; William, b. July 19, 1842, d. Aug. 6, 1843; Augustus L., b. Sept. 29, 1844.

286 HENRY[8] MOSES, son of CHARLES (285), m. Oct. 14, 1847, Margaret Gawne.

CHILDREN: Irwin H., Ella L., Carrie M.

Irwin H., m. Ann Cheesborough of Toledo, Ohio, and had *Children:* Alonzo and Sylvester.

Ella L., m. Louis Dawes of Lorain, O.

Carrie M., m. W. H. Bregenzer of Nottingham, O.

287 BETSEY M.[8] MOSES, dau. of CHARLES (285), m. Nov. 4, 1852, James H. Currier, a Civil Engineer; left one son, Frank R.

288 JOHN NELSON[8] MOSES, son of CHARLES (285), has always been active in commercial, railroad contracting, and lumber business; is the senior member of the firm of N. Moses & Bros. of Cleveland, O.

289 MARTHA ANN[8] MOSES, dau. of CHARLES (285), m. Nov. 1, 1857, Rev. C. H. Warren and resided in New York. Mr. Warren was the editor of the Northern Christian Advocate for many years. He d. Nov. 23, 1901.

290 CHARLES W.[8] MOSES, son of CHARLES (285), was a retail merchant, then with the firm of N. Moses & Bros., and later engaged in handling his real estate holdings in and near Cleveland, O., m. Feb. 16, 1887, Mamie C. Hull, of Maumee, O.

291 CAROLINE A.[8] MOSES, dau. of CHARLES (285), m. Jan. 31, 1867, Warren F. Wolworth, a graduate of Oberlin, and a lawyer.

CHILDREN: Willie F., b. Oct., 1874, d. Nov. 3, 1897.

292 AUGUSTUS L.[8] MOSES, son of CHARLES (285), was, until the death of Charles W. Moses, the junior member of the firm of N. Moses Bros., Cleveland, O., dealers in ship timber, railroad ties, etc., contractors, etc.; m. July, 1868, Mary E. Dille, of Nottingham, O.

CHILDREN: Louis A., b. Oct. 3, 1876.

293 LOUIS A.[9] MOSES, son of AUGUSTUS L. (292), now living in Nottingham, O., is of the firm of N. Moses Bros., of Cleveland, O.; m. Oct. 3, 1899, Olive T. Crane, of Springfield, Mo.

CHILDREN: Marian Crane, b. Nov. 30, 1903; Marjorie Dille, b. Aug. 24, 1905.

294 ELIHU[7] MOSES, son of ELIHU (283), m. Nov. 5, 1829, Ann Grove.

CHILDREN: Harriet, b. May 5, 1831, d. July 11, 1841; Charlotte A., b. Apr. 2, 1833; m. Morris Stockman; Roxana M., b. Aug. 10, 1835, m. E. B. Spring; Catherine M., b. Feb. 15, 1837, d. Oct. 22, 1868; Eliza A., b. Dec. 2, 1838, m. C. F. Gawne; Candace T., b. Apr. 12, 1840, d. Oct. 19, 1899, m. E. M. Perkins; Martin L., b. Dec. 15, 1841, d.

Dec. 18, 1887; Celia, b. June 6, 1843, d. July 16, 1875, m. Archie Buttars; Sarah, b. Aug. 12, 1845, d. May 17, 1882, m. George Granger; Elihu B., b. May 30, 1847; George W., b. Apr. 27, 1849, d. Nov. 26, 1898; John E., b. Sept. 3, 1851.

Martin L., m. Apr. 2, 1865, Carrie Whittern.

George W., m. Sept. 18, 1874, Alice McGrath. *Children:* one son, living in Collinwood, O.

John E., m. Nov. 24, 1875, Ida Hendershot. *Children:* one son, who is married, lives in Collinwood, O.

295 PHILO PINNEY[7] MOSES, son of ELIHU (283), d. in Pine Grove, Nevada. In early days he built canal boats that plied upon the Ohio Canal. He and his brother, Luther Moses, built and owned several large propellers, which ran between Buffalo and Chicago. He went to California in 1861. He built the first quartz mill in Aurora, Nev.; m. Mary C. McIlrath.

CHILDREN: Samuel A., b. in 1836; Eliza A., b. 1838, resides in Oakland, Cal.; Julia A., b. 1840, m. W. H. Gray in Cal.; Betsey L., b. 1842, m. W. A. Morris; Elihu, b. 1843, d. 1850; Othniel, b. 1845; Philo P., b. 1847; Harriet A., b. 1855, d. 1881, in San Francisco.

Samuel A., m. Mary Bartlett of Cleveland, O., resides in Perry, O.

Othniel, m. Amanda Fish in Nevada.

Philo P., m Fannie Elling in Cleveland, O.

296 ROXANA[7] MOSES, dau. of ELIHU (283), m. 1834, Charles Munson.

CHILDREN: Philo, Robert, Luther, Ira, George, Arvilla, b. Mar. 31, 1850, d. Apr. 7, 1894; Ardolissa, b. Apr. 1852, d. Sept. 14, 1906.

Arvilla, m. Nov. 30, 1871, James C. Kellogg. *Children:* Roxana E. Kellogg, now residing in Cleveland, O.

297 LUTHER[7] MOSES, son of ELIHU (283), b. in Euclid, O., died while on a visit to San Diego, Cal.; was a builder of vessels and steamboats. He constructed, near White Fish Point, Mich., the first steamboat built upon Lake Superior, and between 1845 and 1857 was one of the most important builders and owners of sail vessels and steamboats upon the chain of great lakes. He had as a partner, Ira Lafrinier, and later, Philo Moses, his brother, though most of his enterprises were conducted by and for himself.

He was eccentric and bluff, but with the kindest and tenderest of hearts, he was often the prey to the designs of those who knew his temperament. He largely dispensed of his wealth during his lifetime, to relatives and friends; m. 1st, Arvilla Stockman, who

d. May 25, 1872;. m. 2d, June 30, 1873. Georgiana Caley, who d. Dec., 1894.

Page 84, No. 134 ORRIN[7] MOSES, son of OTHNIEL (See paragraph, Vol. 1), m. March 22, 1826, Mary Tuttle, of Bristol, Conn.

298 JOHN OTHNIEL[8] MOSES, son of ORRIN (134), was b. Sept. 10, 1829, d. Oct. 3, 1906; m. first, Armilla Upson; 2d, Ann Eliza Judd, who was b. July 21, 1847, d. Oct. 13, 1901.

CHILDREN, by 2d mar.: Frank Edwards, b. Mar. 9, 1878; Orrin Judd, b. Mar. 15, 1880; Charles Reade, b. Dec. 1, 1882; George Lyman, b. Mar. 17, 1884.

299 LUTHER[8] MOSES, son of ORRIN (134), m. Louisa Barnes.

CHILDREN: Agnes; Celia; Nellie; Luther.

Agnes, m. Edwin Abbe. *Child:* Luther (now in Yale University).
Celia, m. Edward Mix; resides in Cleveland, O.
Nellie, m. Emerson F. Harrington, of Hartford.

300 LAURA[8] MOSES, dau. of ORRIN (134), m. Henry Mylod, and resides in Norwood, Mass.

CHILDREN: Cora M.; Byron W.

Cora M., m. Arthur Parker, has dau., Hazel.
Byron W., m. and has son, Byron W., Jr.

301 CHLOE[8] MOSES, dau. of ORRIN (134), m. in Farmington, Conn., Oct. 2, 1859, Andrew S. Upson. He is an important manufacturer of Cleveland, O.

CHILDREN: Dennis Andrew, b. July 14, 1861; Willis, b. May 1, 1864, d. Feb. 6, 1869; Burton A., b. Oct. 2, 1865, d. Aug. 24, 1880, Luther Moses, b. Dec. 7, 1868, d. May 26, 1897; Mary Chloe, b. July 13, 1870; William Jewell, b. Dec. 30, 1877.

Dennis Andrew, m. Aug. 20, 1885, Nettie Louise Dunbar. *Children:* Elizabeth Hazel, b. Apr. 14, 1887; Dorris Adele, b. July 13, 1894.

Mary Chloe, m. Jan. 31, 1900, Frederick Holland Rose. *Children:* Burton Upson, b. Dec. 15, 1900; Helen Mary, b. Dec. 22, 1903.

302 EVALINE M.[8] MOSES, dau. of ORRIN (134), b. May 12, 1842, m. Aug. 1862, Hubert C. Hart, manufacturer at Unionville Conn.

CHILDREN: Arthur H., b. Aug. 20, 1863; Ernest M., b. Oct. 12, 1868; Willis O., b. June 24, 1875; Carl J., b. July 23, 1879; Edison W., b. Dec. 3, 1881; Nellie Mae, b. Apr. 20, 1885.

Arthur H., is an M.D. of Rye, N. Y.; m. Gertrude Nelson.
Ernest M., m. Ida Allen. *Children:* Leon; Nathaniel.
Willis C., m. Carrie Hart.

303 JULIA W.[8] MOSES; dau. of ORRIN MOSES (134), m. Jan. 14, 1869, Thomas B. Brooks. He was a soldier of the Civil War in 1st Mass. Cav., 1861 to 1865, resides at Unionville, Conn.

    CHILDREN: Bertha M. Brooks (Woodford), b. May 5, 1872, resides at Hartford, Conn.; Bessie M. Brooks, b. Mar. 5, 1874, d. Mar. 16, 1879; Mabel W. Brooks, b. Jan. 18, 1876.

304 ZEBULON[6] MOSES, son of ZEBULON (20), and his wife Sibyl, dau. of Amos Moore of Simsbury. The name, "Zebulon Jr., " is found in a Rutland, Vt., deed. He was a soldier of the Revolution in 1780, in Col. Allen's Vermont Reg.

The History of Livingston Co., published in 1905, contains the following: "Zebulon Moses came to Lima, N. Y., from Rutland, Vt., in 1791, and acquired the tract of land in Lima Village, on the northwest corner of which now stands the American hotel. Two years later he sold this tract and purchased the property which his great-grandson now occupies. His son Luther was a soldier in the War of 1812, and participated in many notable engagements along the Niagara frontier. "

In an old cemetery, a mile from the farm on which he died, is a marble slab, broken, and on the ground, on which is inscribed:

Zebulon Moses d. Aug. 30, 1808, aged 54; Hannah, his wife, d. Mar. 23, 1860, aged 92.

Zebulon was twice married, and almost certainly in Vermont. He had, "three sons by his first wife: Samuel; Reuben; Jonah."

Zebulon m. 1st, Phoebe ———; 2d, Hannah, dau. of a Thomas Lee, who settled in Lima about the time of Zebulon's arrival.

    CHILDREN: (From Bible records) by the first marriage: Samuel; Reuben, b. Oct. 17, 1780, d. Mar. 21, 1837; Jonah. By the 2d marriage: Luther, b. Sept. 28, 1787, d. 1876; Phoebe, b. Sept. 8, 1789; Katherine, b. Feb. 15, 1791; Charles, b. Nov. 27, 1892; Esther, b. Apr. 20, 1795; Ira, b. Sept. 12, 1799; Daniel, b. July 11, 1801, d. 1868; Wells, b. Sept. 4, 1806.

Jonah is recorded in Lima about the date of Zebulon's settlement in the town. His movements thereafter have not been traced.

William, lived and died in Michigan; had children.
Esther, m. and removed to Ohio.
Wells, removed to Michigan.
Charles, m. and removed to Ohio.
Ira, m. Marianna Goodrich of Lima, N. Y., and removed to the West.

305 SAMUEL[7] MOSES, son of ZEBULON (304), lived on a part of his father's homestead in Lima, until his house burned, when he removed to Allegany Co., N. Y.; m. Sarah Booth of Granger, N. Y.

    CHILDREN: Jonah, b. 1805, d. 1889; Erastus; David B., b. Apr. 2, 1824; Samuel; Maria; Lavina; Roxana; Sibyl.

  Erastus, went to California in 1853; was never heard from.

306 JONAH[8] MOSES, son of SAMUEL (305), resided in Lima, N. Y., and then in Michigan, where he died; m. 1st, Betsey Pender; m. 2d, ———; m. 3d, 1847, Lucia Benson, she d. 1855; m. 4th, 1856, Eunice Clark Osborne.

    CHILDREN by 1st m.: Reuben G., b. 1844: by 2d m., Sarah J., deceased; Charles, d. 1902; by 3d m.: Nelson David, b. Sept., 1847; Roxana, b. May, 1851; Mary Maria, b. June, 1855; by 4th m.: Esther J., b. May, 1857.

  Charles, has a son Edwin at Olean, N. Y.

  Nelson D., resides at Benton Harbor, Mich., and has *Children:* Owen T. of Chicago, Ill.; Ovid.

  Roxana (Harman), of Twining, Mich., has dau. Ella.

  Mary Maria, resides at Castile, N. Y., and furnished much information as to her father's family.

  Esther J. (Patterson), of Twining, Mich., has *Children:* Pearl; Eunice; Ivian; Carlton.

307 DAVID B.[8] MOSES, son of SAMUEL (305), resides in Marshall, Mich.; m. 1st, Sarah Templeton. She d. July 5, 1867; m. 2d, May 31' 1877, in Utica, N. Y., Delight M. Stockwell.

    CHILDREN, by 1st m.: Anna C., b. Mar. 2, 1851; James M., b. Oct. 4, 1854; May, b. July 22, 1860; by 2d m.: Florence C., b. Feb. 27, 1878.

  Anna, m. Nov. 1, 1876, Charles R. Bentley. *Children:* John F.; Sarah L.; Francis; Joseph; Jerome.

  May, m. July 27, 1887, Henry E. Holton. *Children:* Louise Moses; Harriet.

  Florence C., m. July 2, 1896, Perry Brooks of Marshall, Mich.; he d. Oct. 2, 1900. *Children:* Bernadine; Perry; m. 2d, May 31, 1902, Donald D. Jaggers. *Children:* Marguerite; David Carlton.

308 JAMES M.[9] MOSES, son of DAVID B. (307), is the editor of the Marshall, Mich., *Expounder and Chronicle:* m. May 6, 1880, Catherine Otis, b. July 18, 1857, in Rockford, Mich.

    CHILDREN: Frank K., b. July 3, 1883.

  Frank K. is associated with his father in conducting the newspaper at Marshall, Mich.

309 REUBEN G.[9] MOSES, son of JONAH (306), was a soldier enlisting at Hudson, Mich. (see soldier list), is a merchant and postmaster of Cuylerville, N. Y., m. Lydia E. Fredenburgh.

CHILDREN: Ferren G., b. 1869; Maude M., b. 1878; Jennie E., b. 1880; Byron E., b. 1882.

Ferren G., m. Nellie Dennis. *Children:* Theodore Moses, b. 1899.

310 REUBEN[7] MOSES, son of ZEBULON (304), removed from Lima, N. Y., to Cuba, N. Y. His widow survived him there, "living with and for her children," for thirty-three years. He m. Aug. 22, 1804, Lucinda Stevens, who was b. May 15, 1788; d. at Cuba, Mar. 15, 1870.

CHILDREN: Anson G., b. Oct. 17, 1805, d. Jan. 25, 1868; Patty, b. Mar. 24, 1807, d. July 2, 1863; Mary G., b. July 24, 1808, d. Apr. 7, 1878; Alfred, b. June 2, 1810, d. 1895; Samuel S., b. Apr. 5, 1812, d. Mar. 3, 1895; Phoebe R., b. Dec. 11, 1814, d. Jan., 1891; Calvin C., b. Feb. 11, 1816; Editha Hester, b. Sept. 19, 1819, d. Feb. 13, 1891; William B., b. July 14, 1821, d. July 18, 1821; Francis, b. May 2, 1822, d. Oct. 27, 1888; Richard B., b. Dec. 7, 1825, d. Feb. 10, 1894; Sarah Adelia, b. Apr. 17, 1829, d. Feb. 26, 1885.

311 ANSON GEORGE[8] MOSES, son of REUBEN (310), was a contractor and builder in New York City, later resided in Cuba and Olean, N. Y., removed to Rockford, Ill., in 1853; m. in New York City, Apr. 17, 1828, Mary Ann Bowen; she was b. in Philadelphia, Feb. 2, 1811, survived her husband 22 years, and died at Great Bend, Kans., Jan. 28, 1890.

CHILDREN: Mary Louise, b. at New York, Apr. 7, 1828; Lucinda P., b. at New York, June 2, 1830, d. at Turtle Point, Pa., Jan. 7, 1875; Frances T., b. at New York, Oct. 22, 1831; Adeline M., b. at Cuba, N. Y., Dec. 14, 1832; Reuben Henry, b. Sept. 14, 1834, d. Mar. 29, 1837; Anson Frederick, b. at Cuba, N. Y., Sept. 17, 1836, Theodore W., b. at Olean, N. Y., July 30, 1840, d. Dec. 4, 1869; Mary Ann, b. at Olean, N. Y., Mar. 26, 1842, d. Apr. 21, 1849; George Nelson, b. at Olean, N. Y., Apr. 15, 1844; Emma Jane, b. at Olean, N. Y., Apr. 28, 1846; Laura A., b. at Olean, N. Y., Mar. 7, 1848; Charles Alonzo, b. at Olean, N. Y., June 14, 1851; Edward Russell, b. at Olean, N. Y., Mar. 30, 1853.

Lucinda P., m. at Olean, N. Y., Erastus H. Nichols. He died from wounds received while in the Civil War.

Emma Jane, m. at Sedalia, Mo., Mar. 31, 1870, D. W. McKenzie, resides at Bozeman, Mont. *Children:* Blanche, b. in 1873; Reuben Henry, b. in 1875, resides in Chicago; Channell, b. Nov. 14, 1887, resides in Bozeman.

312 MARY LOUISE[9] MOSES, dau. of ANSON G. (311), m.

Feb. 24, 1847, Rufus L. Whitney; he was a soldier, 146th Ill. Inf.; removed in 1869, to Scandia, Kans., where he d. Mar. 14, 1904.

CHILDREN: Marie Louise, b. at Olean, Mar. 27, 1848, m. Charles Isbell; LeRoy, b. at Olean, June 13, 1850; Lee, b. at Olean, Sept. 13, 1852, m. Alice Keeler; George, b. 1854, d. 1875; Frankie, b. at Pecatonica, Ill., in 1856, m. John Cullers.

313 FRANCES T.[9] MOSES, dau. of ANSON G. (311), m. at Perry, N. Y., Nathaniel D. Birdsall, who died Jan. 8, 1894; she resides at Los Angeles, Cal.

CHILDREN: all b. Castile, N. Y; Clarence E., b. 1855, m. Nellie Van Hooten; Mary Jane, b. 1857, m. James Hinchcliff; Addie Lydia, b Dec. 14, 1860, m. Edwin Coleman.

314 ADELINE M.[9] MOSES, dau. of ANSON G. (311), m. 1st at Pecatonica, Ill., Dec. 25, 1857, Henry Eastey. He was a soldier, Ill. Cav., and d. in 1868; m. 2d, Nov. 26, 1872, Jonathan F. Tilton. He was a soldier 10th Ind. Inf., removed in 1870 to Great Bend, Kans.

CHILDREN, by 1st m.: Frank Henry, b. at Winnebago, Ill., Sept 27, 1858, m. Julia Stock; Estella A., b. at Pecatonica, Ill., Mar. 10, 1862, m. Harvey E. Dean.

315 ANSON FREDERICK[9] MOSES, son of ANSON G. (311), was Sergeant in 1st Ill. Cav. during Civil War; killed while acting as special deputy marshal at Sedalia, Mo.

316 REUBEN HENRY[9] MOSES, son of ANSON G. (311), was 1st Sergeant in 1st Ill. Cav. and First Lieutenant in 146th Ill. Inf. in the Civil War. He was ten years county clerk of Pettis Co., Mo.; is at present cashier of the Citizens National Bank, Great Bend, Kans.; m. 1st, at Washington, Ind., Aug. 23, 1865, Frances A. De La Meter. She d. June 15, 1890; m. 2d, at Sedalia, Mo., Oct. 7, 1891, Louise Stock.

CHILDREN: all b. at Sedalia, Mo.; George B., b. July 8, 1874, d. Sept. 1, 1874; Charles F., b. Aug. 27, 1876; Reuben Henry, Jr., b. Sept. 12, 1878; Frank A., b. Apr. 7, 1881; Frances A., b. June 4, 1890; Louise. b. Aug. 1, 1894.

317 CHARLES F.[10] MOSES, son of REUBEN HENRY (316), resides at St. Louis, Mo.; m. at Kansas City, Mo., Apr. 7, 1905, Ida Roënitz.

318 REUBEN HENRY[10] MOSES, son of REUBEN HENRY

(316), is cashier of the U. S. Zinc Co., Pueblo, Col.; m. at Pueblo, Col., Oct. 7, 1900, Susie Cobb.

CHILDREN: Mildred Odell, b. Aug. 24, 1901.

319 FRANK A.[10] MOSES, son of REUBEN HENRY (316), is Asst. Cashier Citizens National Bank, Great Bend, Kans.

320 THEODORE W.[9] MOSES, son of ANSON G. (311), was killed Dec. 4, 1869, while arresting "Moonshiners" in Camden Co., Mo., while in service as U. S. Revenue Marshal.

321 GEORGE NELSON[9] MOSES, son of ANSON G. (311), was Orderly Sergt. in 146th Ill. Inf. in Civil War. In 1872 piloted the first herd of cattle through Great Bend, Kansas, and assisted in laying out the town. Was the first Sheriff of Barton Co., Kans.; was three times Mayor of Great Bend, and once Mayor of Gunnison, Colo.; m. at Geat Bend, June 23, 1873, Ida A. Mitchell. Resides at Great Bend, Kans.

322 LAURA A.[9] MOSES, dau. of ANSON G. (311), m. Dec. 7, 1865, Channel P. Townsley; resides in Great Bend, Kans.

CHILDREN: Channel P., b. Jan. 20, 1867, at Sedalia, Mo., m. Lois Kilmer, resides in London, Eng.; Florence Evelyn, b. Oct. 14, 1869, m. Edwin S. Leland, resides in Brooklyn, N. Y.; Laura Emma, b. Dec. 12, 1870, d. Apr. 11, 1874; Theodora Alice, b. Mar. 8, 1872, d. June 19, 1872; Jessie Stuart, b. May 25, 1874, d. Oct. 17, 1874; George Leopold, b. Feb. 22, 1877, d. Aug. 11, 1877; Edward Moses, b. Jan. 20, 1879, d. July 29, 1879; William Lawrence, b. Apr. 4, 1881; Charles Reuben Francis, b. July 15, 1884 (resides at Brooklyn, N. Y.); Laura, b. Oct. 31, 1891), (resides at Brooklyn, N. Y.).

William Lawrence Townsley, is the Editor of the GREAT BEND, KANS., TRIBUNE.

323 CHARLES ALONZO[9] MOSES, son of ANSON G. (311), is a contractor and builder at Chicago, Ill.; m. 1st, at Great Bend, Kans., Jan. 6, 1887, Jessie M. Culver; she d. Dec. 11, 1893; m. 2d, at La Grange, Ill., 1898, Emma Roenitz.

CHILDREN: Ruth, b. Aug. 23, 1888; Marian, b. May 27, 1900.

324 EDWARD RUSSELL[9] MOSES, son of ANSON G. (311), is chairman of the Executive Committee of the National Irrigation Congress, and of the Trans-Mississippi Congress; President of the Inter-State Irrigation Congress; President of the Citizens National Bank, Great Bend, Kans., and President of the Mutual Mfg.

Co., Neosho, Mo.; resides at Great Bend, Kans.; m. at Great Bend, Kans., Nov. 17, 1879, Serepta I. Newell.

CHILDREN: Edward Russell, Jr., b. Aug. 20' 1880; resides at Great Bend, Kans.; Grace, b. Dec. 10, 1883.

325 PATTY[8] MOSES, dau. of REUBEN (310), m. Aug. 15, 1824, John Lowing, and removed from Cuba, N. Y., to Crawford Co., Penn.

CHILDREN: Lucinda, b. Dec. 4, 1825, m. Parley Carpenter; William Edwin, b. Jan. 15, 1832, d. May 5, 1905.

326 MARY S.[8] MOSES, dau. of REUBEN (310), m. Erastus H. Willard. He and his oldest son were physicians of some note at Friendship, N. Y.

CHILDREN: Alexis Edwin, b. Nov. 19, 1831; Almira P., b. Apr. 29, 1833; Caroline P., b. July 14, 1834, d. May 21, 1861; Daniel B., b. Mar 1, 1836, d. Apr. 24, 1850; Erastus W., b. Oct. 22, 1838; Mary G., b. Nov. 30, 1840; Ambrose P., b. Feb. 26, 1843; Viola L., b. Aug. 10, 1844; Franklin C., b. March 5, 1846, d. Aug. 14, 1846; Florence A., b. June 12, 1847; Terrence M., b. Aug. 7, 1849, d. Sept. 11, 1849; Laura N., b. Oct. 5, 1850.

327 ALFRED[8] MOSES, son of REUBEN (310), m. at Cuba, N. Y., Nov. 3, 1830, Catherine Perine; moved to Ill., and again to Tehama, Cal.

CHILDREN: George R., b. Aug. 8, 1833, d. at West Jordan, Utah, in 1905; Lucinda M., b. Sept. 27, 1836; Charlotte A., b. July 10, 1840; Lucetta A., b. Sept. 11, 1842; Lucretia, b. Dec. 24, 1849; Henry D., b. Mar. 1838, d. ——.

George R., had one dau. living at Granger, Utah, and two sons, Reuben and Lewis, in Idaho.

Lucetta A., resides at Traer, Iowa; has three children.

Lucretia, resides at Wyaconda, Md.; has fourteen children, all living in 1906

Henry D., d. at Laporte, Iowa, in the "eighties," and left four sons and one daughter.

328 SAMUEL S.[8] MOSES, son of REUBEN (310), moved with his parents to Cuba, N. Y., and resided in the town until his death; m. at Friendship, N. Y., Oct. 26, 1834, Lucetta Taylor, b. Jan. 25, 1813, at Salem, Mass.

CHILDREN: Calvin H., b. July 29, 1835, d. at Eldred, Pa., Dec. 15, 1891; Reuben H., b. Apr. 28, 1837; John T., b. Mar. 6, 1839; Eunice A., b. Nov. 14, 1845; Franklin T., b. Nov. 16, 1847; Samuel E., b. Dec. 2, 1852, d. at Cuba, N. Y., Sept. 11, 1872.

Reuben H., resides at Mt. Morris, N. Y.; m. Lucinda Moses.
Franklin T., resides at Union City, Pa.; m. Livonia Wilkinson.

329 EUNICE A.[9] MOSES, dau. of SAMUEL S. (328), resides at Eldred, Pa. To her untiring efforts the writer is indebted for important data relating to her own and collateral branches of the Zebulon Moses group; m. Dec. 2, 1868, Francis N. Burnham, who was b. Nov. 14, 1838, and d. July 26, 1881.

CHILDREN: Cecil, b. Sept. 8, 1869, drowned in the Allegheny river near his home, Nov. 16, 1888; Reuben, b. Mar. 17, 1871; George, b. May 21, 1878.

330 CALVIN H.[9] MOSES, son of SAMUEL S. (328), m. Elizabeth Consalus.

CHILDREN: Effie Lucetta, Flora, Archie, Harry, Reuben.

331 JOHN T.[9] MOSES, son of SAMUEL S. (328), resides at Cuba, N. Y., m. Lovina A. Beebe.

CHILDREN: Elmer Samuel, Vernon Henry, Carl John, Edgar A., Reuben R.

332 PHOEBE R.[8] MOSES, dau. of REUBEN (310), m. Mar. 1834, Josiah Clark Burnham; they lived and died at Eldred, Pa.

CHILDREN: Henry C.; Francis N.; Dwight H.; Martha Helen, d. at Postville, N. Y., Nov. 1891.

Henry C., resides at Fairport, Md.

Francis N., was 1st Lieut. 58th Pa. Reg. in the Civil War; was an Associate Judge of McKean Co., Pa., at time of his death, at Eldred, July 25, 1881.

333 CALVIN C.[8] MOSES, son of REUBEN (310). From a newspaper article in 1906, published on his 90th birthday, it appears that for 40 years he engaged in lumbering and rafting. In 1847 he was elected Justice of the Peace of Eldred, Pa., and after the war was continuously re-elected, the present Commission expiring 1907. He was a Captain of the 58th Penn. Inf. In 1863 was made prisoner, and for 20 months suffered the horrors of southern prison pens. He was one of the comrades who dug the famous tunnel through which many escaped from Libby prison. Let it be noted that this patriot enlisted at the age of 45, and took his two eldest sons with him.

He m. at Richmond, Pa., Jan. 30, 1838, Emily A. Haight.

CHILDREN: William E.; Calvin J.; Harriet M.; Albert R.; Emily D., d. at Eldred; Mary Lucinda; Rose Elizabeth, b. May 24, 1862; Myrtle E., b. Apr. 13, 1866, d. Feb. 1896.

William E., was a 1st Sergt. Penn. Reg. in 1863, and Lieutenant N. C. Colored Reg., Apr. 29, 1864; was buried at Soldiers' Home, Erie, Pa.

Calvin C., was a soldier Penn. Reg. from 1861 to Jan. 24, 1866. Is now living at Shingle House, Pa.

Harriet M., resides at Port Allegany, Pa.

Albert R., resides at Muncy, Ind.

Myrtle E., was the wife of William Wirths, Findlay, Ohio.

334 EDITHA HESTER[8] MOSES, dau. of REUBEN (310), m. at Cuba, N. Y., John M. Wright, and removed to Eldred, Pa.

CHILDREN: William A., of Olean, N. Y.; Edick, of Eldred, Pa.; John, of Allegany, N. Y.

335 FRANCIS[8] MOSES, son of REUBEN (310), resided at Friendship, N. Y., Cuba, N. Y., and Smithport, Pa., m. 1st, June 23, 1844, Emeline Egleston, she d. Feb. 19, 1852; m. 2d, Mary Sortor, Sept. 30, 1853.

CHILDREN: Lafayette L., b. June 14, 1845; d. at New Hudson, N. Y., May 10, 1884; Francis S., b. Aug. 9, 1846; James R., b. Nov. 12, 1848. By 2d marriage; Ida E.; William H., living at Ord, Neb.; Clarence, living at Walnut, Ill.

Lafayette L., was a soldier in Civil War.

Francis L., was a soldier; resides at Kalispell, Mont.

Ida E., m. a Mr. Stroup, resides at Ord, Neb.

336 RICHARD[8] MOSES, son of REUBEN (310), was a soldier of the Civil War, resided thereafter at Eldred, Pa.; m. Emily E. Knapp.

CHILDREN: Alfred George, living at Port Allegany, Pa.; Richard Frank, living at Eldred, Pa.; three other children said to have died in youth.

337 SARAH ADELIA[8] MOSES, dau. of REUBEN (310), m. at Cuba, N. Y., Jan. 28, 1845, Enos W. Van Ness.

CHILDREN: John, now living at Olean, N. Y., and Mrs. Adelbert (Moses) Moot. Her husband is a prominent lawyer of Buffalo, N. Y.

338 LUTHER[7] MOSES, son of ZEBULON (304), was closely associated with his father in his first holding, in 1791, of land on which the village of Lima now stands; was a soldier of the War of 1812, participating in several engagements. He m. 1811, Sally Phillips; she d. 1861.

CHILDREN: Ogilvie, b. Aug. 8, 1812, d. Nov. 29, 1865; Wilber, b. Sept. 3, 1814, d. Mar. 6, 1899; Lewis, b. Feb. 9, 1819, d. Dec. 21, 1885.

339 OGILVIE[8] MOSES, son of LUTHER (338), resided in Lima, N. Y., m. Nov. 1, 1836, Cynthia H. Beaman.

CHILDREN: Mary O., b. Sept. 30, 1838, d. Nov. 20, 1873; Urial B., b. Jan. 21, 1843; Jane E., b. Oct. 24, 1852, d. Jan. 12, 1859.

Mary O., m. Erwin Bloomer.

340 URIAL B.[9] MOSES, son of OGILVIE (339), resides in Lima, retired; m. Nov. 25, 1863, Augusta J. Briggs.

341 WILBER[9] MOSES, son of LUTHER (338), was a farmer and hotel keeper in Kansas; m. Harriet Warner.

CHILDREN: A. W. and Wilber, d. when young; Sarah Jane m. Frank Stevens; Harriet, m. Horace Bronson, had one son (all dead); Olive B., m. Robert Johnson (one son), live in Penn.; Carrie, m. M. King.

342 LEWIS[9] MOSES, son of LUTHER (338), resided in Lima, N. Y., m. 1st, Caroline M. Hicks, she d. 1859; m. 2d, Celia A. Green. The County History states that, "he was well known for his many excellent qualities."

CHILDREN: Lewis H., b. Aug. 18, 1846; Irving, b. Dec. 28, 1848; Edward O., b. 1867, d. 1887; Frank, b. 1875; Luther, b. 1879.

343 LEWIS H.[10] MOSES, son of LEWIS (342). A sketch in the History of Livingston Co., N. Y., is quoted in part:

"Lewis H. Moses, Supervisor of the town of Lima, resides on the old homestead three miles southeast of the village of Lima. A portion of this land comprises the half section originally taken from the Government during latter part of the eighteenth century. . . . He was educated at the Genessee Wesleyan Seminary. . . . He served the town of Lima four years as Justice of the Peace, and the past nine years he has occupied the responsible office of Supervisor." May the title to the old Zebulon Moses homestead continue in the Moses name for other centuries. (Z. M.)

Lewis H. m. in 1869, Alice B. Harden, she d. in 1901.

CHILDREN, all residents of Lima: Caroline E., b. Mar. 9, 1871; Fred I., b. Nov. 22, 1879; James G., b. Sept. 23, 1881.

344 IRVING[10] MOSES, son of LEWIS (342), resides in Lima, N. Y., m. 1st, Ella Brice, she d. 1900; m. 2d, Mary S. Babcock.

345 DANIEL[7] MOSES, son of ZEBULON (304), resided in Granger, N. Y.; m. 1822, Phoebe ——.

CHILDREN: Francis, b. 1834, d. 1855, Ashbell, b. 1828, d. 1850; Luther, b. 1831, d. 1863; Aziza, b. 1836; Washington, b. Jan. 9, 1834.

Ashbel, was a "forty-niner," and d. in California.
Luther, d. a prisoner of war at Andersonville, Ga. (see Soldier List).
Aziza, resides in Granger, N. Y. *Children:* Ervin L. and Oren, both reside in Nunda, N. Y.

346 WASHINGTON[8] MOSES, son of DANIEL (345), resides in Dalton, N. Y.; m. Jan. 8, 1863, Ellen Parker.

CHILDREN: reside at Dalton, N. Y.; Grant E., b. May 26, 1868; E. Walter, b. Oct. 4, 1872.

347 KATHERINE[7] MOSES, dau. of ZEBULON (304). After Zebulon's death, his widow, Hannah, lived with her daughter Katherine (Hardy); and the family Bible record, from which important data has been gleaned, was handed down to her youngest daughter, Clarissa Jane (Swick). Katherine Moses m. Manning Hardy.

CHILDREN: Henry M., b. Jan. 5, 1821; Marianna C., b. May 5, 1822; Sarah L., b. Feb. 1, 1824; Susan, b. June 21, 1826; Rachel Ann, b. Apr. 30, 1829; David M., b. June 8, 1831; Louisa, b. July 28, 1833; Clarissa Jane, b. Apr. 8, 1837.

Clarissa Jane, m. Phineas Swick, and had *Children:* Ninna, b. Feb. 10, 1863; and Manning, b. Apr. 8, 1865.

Page 87, No. 141 JONAH[6] MOSES, son of ZEBULON (20). See personal paragraph in Vol. 1. In addition to the association at Rutland, Vt., of Jonah with "Zebulon, Jr.," therein stated, and the wide intervals in birth dates shown on page 60, attention is also called to the names in the family of "Zebulon, Jr." (See other pages of this volume.) Zebulon, the second, named a son by his first marriage, Jonah, and Zebulon's first son named his first son, Jonah, and his second son, Erastus. This circumstantial evidence is quite as convincing as the traditions and statements handed down in families, and which have frequently to be accepted by genealogists. The writer has, therefore, no hesitation in *definitely* placing Jonah (141), and the father of Erastus (142), as the brother of Zebulon, the second.

Jonah was a soldier of the Revolution in 1779 (see Moses Soldier List). He was in Col. John Ashley's Berkshire Co., Mass., Reg., and his company marched to Conn. Berkshire Co., Mass., adjoins Vermont, and the Moses name does not again appear in the County. Jonah's military service was less than two months and his sojourn in the County was probably connected with his emigration from Simsbury, Conn., to Rutland, Vt.

Page 88, No. **143** JOHN[8] MOSES, son of ERASTUS[7] (142). From the Chicago *Evening Post* of July 6, 1898.

"DEATH OF EX-JUDGE MOSES.

"Ex-Judge John Moses died at his residence 3803 Rhodes Avenue, Sunday. Interment was at Winchester, Ill. John Moses was born in 1825, and came to Naples, Ill., in 1837. He served as county judge of Scott County and at the breaking out of the war was appointed private secretary of Governor Yates. Mr. Moses in 1881 began his historical work, 'Illinois, Historical and Statistical.' The work occupied the greater part of his attention for eleven years. Mr. Moses was the author of a history of Chicago, which he compiled with the aid of Major Kirkland. He was elected secretary and librarian of the Chicago Historical Society in 1886."

He took a deep interest in the genealogical researches connected with the volume of this book published in 1890, and the writer holds in grateful remembrance the correspondence and personal intercourse of that and succeeding years. Judge John Moses stands at the head of the Moses family in literary achievement, and has reflected great and lasting honor on the name. The magnificent

"HISTORY OF ILLINOIS,"

(1316 pages) will be his monument.

See also personal sketch on page 88 of Vol. 1. He d. July 3, 1898. His widow, Mrs. Sallie M. Moses, now resides in Minneapolis, Minn. She has for many years been engaged in literary pursuits, and is at present Asst. Editor of the Northwestern Agriculturalist.

CHILDREN of John Moses: by 1st marriage, Caroline, b. Mar. 17, 1850; Richard H., b. Apr. 26, 1851, d. at Spokane, Wash., Mar. 25, 1899; John F., b. Oct. 28, 1853; Charles K., b. July 31, 1855; Louis, b. Apr. 1857, deceased: by 2d marriage, Mabel L., b. May 14, 1860, d. May 11, 1894; Sadie A., b. July 17, 1862, d. Nov. 1888; Henry W., b. June 14, 1866, d. Oct. 8, 1890; Philip G., b. Aug. 1, 1869; Dorothy, b. Mar. 18, 1872, d. May 19, 1905.

Mabel L., m. Mar. 4, 1883, James R. Paul, of Evanston, Ill.

348 CAROLINE[9] MOSES, dau. of JOHN (143), m. Apr. 25, 1872, at Winchester, Ill., James Monroe Walker, M.D., and resides in Denver, Colo.

CHILDREN: James Frederick, b. Aug. 8, 1881; Stanley Moses, b. Oct. 1, 1887.

James Frederick, graduated at West Point in 1905, is now 2d Lieut. U. S. A., stationed at Fort Williams, Portland, Me.

Stanley Moses, is connected with a copper mining Co. in Mexico.

349 JOHN F.[9] MOSES, son of JOHN (143), resides in Hunter, Okla.; m. Nov. 25, 1888, Inez A. McMillan, in Red Cliff, Colo.

CHILDREN: Mabel A., b. Oct. 18, 1889; Sadie I., b. Mar. 6, 1892; John Frederick, Jr., b. Apr. 14, 1895; Ellen, b. Apr. 26, 1902.

350 CHARLES K.[9] MOSES, son of JOHN (143), resides in Winchester, Ill.; m. Sept. 29, 1886, Marina Ellen Antrobus.

CHILDREN: John Frederick, b. Mar. 25, 1888; Mary Louisa, b. Jan. 17, 1890, d. Mar. 12, 1890; Caroline, b. Aug. 11, 1891; Claude and Maude (twins), b. July 4, 1894.

351 PHILIP G.[9] MOSES, son of John (143), resides in Chicago, Ill.; m. Aug. 4, 1896, Jeanne Fraser Donald of Forfarshire, Scotland.

CHILDREN: Marjorie J.; Donald P.

Page 53, No. 10 JOSHUA[4] MOSES; see Norfolk, Conn., Records, for deed July 2, 1772, from "Joshua, the elder to son Joshua," also purchase of lands in Norfolk, in 1769, by the elder Joshua.

A granddaughter of Joshua Nelson Moses (the last of the Joshuas), Mrs. Louisa Waugh Pendleton, now residing at Winsted, Conn., has in her possession the old Moses family Bible, printed in 1734, and has kindly permitted a copy to be made of the family record therein.

The first entry is evidently in the handwriting of the Joshua who first made a permanent settlement in Norfolk. It reads, "father Moses, his Deth in the year 1773 — Joshua Moses his bibel wich is entailed to him and his heirs." The following entries may be used to check with the names of children recorded on page 53 as *children* of the first Joshua (b. Oct. 3, 1689). Hannah and Mary, b. Jan. 14, 1719; Rachel, b. July 10, 1725; Joshua, b. Feb. 23, 1727, d. Aug. 8, 1820; Othniel, b. Aug. 22, 1730; John, b. Sept. 5, 1841. The Bible entries will be further used in the paragraphs immediately following.

Page 85, No. **139** JOSHUA[5] MOSES, of Norfolk, b. in Simsbury, Conn., Feb. 23, 1727. Although not a descendant of his resides in Norfolk in 1906, there were "four Joshuas of successive generations," on what is yet known as "Moses Hill," and these are "buried in the South End Cemetery." (See Hist. of Norfolk, Conn.). Joshua Moses, 2d, bought land of Joseph Mills, May 7, 1759, and built a log house just south of the Thomas Moses place [now owned by Dr. Frederic Dennis and named "Tamarack Lodge."] After building, Joshua returned to Simsbury, married Abigail Terry, and brought her to Norfolk on horseback, she on a pillion.

CHILDREN (from family Bible): Joshua, b. May 5, 1762, d. Aug. 8, 1820; Abigail (Parmer), b. Oct. 25, 1765, d. Mar. 27, 1841; Thomas, b. July 19, 1768, d. Sept. 24, 1850; Jesse, b. July 3, 1771, d. Mar. 31, 1860; Ruth, b. Mar. 24, 1774; Jonah, b. Oct. 25, 1777; Jonathan, b. May 16, 1780. (See personal paragraphs in Vol. 1.)

352 JOSHUA[6] MOSES, son of JOSHUA (139), resided "on hill," in Norfolk, was b. in 1762, and d. in 1820; m. Elizabeth Balcom, she d. Nov. 30, 1832, aged 72. From Norfolk Records see distribution of the estate of Joshua Moses on June 13, 1822, to Elizabeth, his widow.

CHILDREN (family Bible): Betsey, b. July 10, 1787, d. June 19, 1802; Abigail, b. Dec. 16, 1789, d. Mar. 7, 1790; Aaron, b. June 30, 1791, d. Dec. 3, 1791; Clarissa, b. May 11, 1793, d. Sept. 8, 1875; Sarah, b. July 19, 1797, d. June 18, 1850; Joshua N., b. June 10, 1801, d. Apr. 13, 1853.

Clarissa, m. Samuel Johnson.
Sarah, m. Daniel Hotchkiss.

353 JOSHUA NELSON[7] MOSES, son of JOSHUA (352), lived on his father's old homestead in Norfolk until middle life; m. May 15, 1823, Eliza Brown of Salisbury, Conn. She was b. Jan. 30, 1802, d. May 18, 1884.

CHILDREN: Elizabeth, b. Apr. 21, 1824, d. June 16, 1891; Louisa, b. Mar. 17, 1828, d. 1884; Sarah, b. May 18, 1834, d. July 29, 1864.

Elizabeth, m. Jan. 1, 1852, Baldwin Frisbie.
Louisa, m. June 5, 1850, W. W. Waugh. *Children:* Louisa Waugh, now Mrs. Pendleton of Winsted, Conn., and owner of the very old Joshua Moses family Bible, an heirloom, which has been inherited by her as descendant of the last Joshua of Norfolk.
Sarah, m. Mar. 4, 1857, Joseph Hakes.

354 THOMAS[6] MOSES, son of JOSHUA (139), spent his life on his father's old homestead at Norfolk, Conn. He was b. July 19, 1768, d. Sept. 24, 1851, and m. 1st, Nov. 24, 1791, Abigail

Brown, who was b. Aug. 17, 1769, and d. Feb. 16, 1823; m. 2d, Nov. 11, 1839, Caroline Brown.

CHILDREN: Salmon, b. Dec. 14, 1792, d. Nov. 27, 1874; Thomas, Jr., b. Aug. 16, 1794; Ralph, b. Jan. 13, 1797, d. unmarried in North Carolina, July 24, 1819; Benjamin, b. Dec. 6, 1798, d. Oct. 5, 1832; Hiram, b. Sept. 19, 1800, d. June 5, 1885; Betsy, b. Oct. 1, 1803, d. Sept. 1899; Julia, b. Oct. 8, 1805, d. June 21, 1844; Eunice, b. Mar. 27, 1808, d. Apr. 6, 1861; Abigail, b. Oct. 12, 1818, d. July 24, 1842; Ruth, b. July 24, 1812, d. June 24, 1853.

Thomas, moved to Ohio, and then to Crawford Co., Pa., where he died within a few years of 1885. He m. Rhoda Sturtevant and had seven children. One son Ralph, who died in Iowa, left sons Elmer and Emet now living in Ashtabula, Ohio, and another son, name unknown, who lives in Iowa. One of Thomas'7 seven children, Hiram, moved to Michigan.

Abigail, m. Lorin Foote and removed to Morgan, Ashtabula Co., Ohio, and died there.

Betsey, m. Mar. 24, 1830, Halsey Hurlbert, and moved to Seville, Ohio, and died there, leaving *children:* William, Mary, and Julia.

Ruth, m. 1837, Harlow Royce, a leather merchant of New York. She d. years ago.

Eunice, m. Mar. 24, 1830, George Brown, and moved to Lorain Co., Ohio.

Julia, m. June, 1836, Nathaniel Oviatt, and moved to Ohio.

355 BENJAMIN[6] MOSES, son of THOMAS (354), m. 1831, Clarissa Manley; resided in Norfolk, Conn. (See page 86 as to the administration, Oct. 12, 1832, of his estate, on account of a widow, Clarissa, and a minor child, Abigail, one year old.)

CHILDREN: Abigail, b. 1832, d. 1906.

Abigail, m. Hiram P. Lawrence, and resided in Winsted, Conn.

356 SALMON[7] MOSES, son of THOMAS (354), was educated at Hamilton, N. Y., College, and had a large practice as a physician at Hoosick Falls, N. Y. An interesting letter from him is published in the History of Norfolk, Conn. He was a zealous churchman, reading service for several years in the schoolhouse, until funds were provided to build the present St. Mark's Episcopal Church of Hoosick Falls. He m. Feb. 18, 1823, Sarah Haswell.

CHILDREN: Robert Haswell, b. Jan. 27, 1824, d. Oct. 7, 1838; Harriet Haswell, b. Mar. 4, 1826; Sarah Julia, b. July 6, 1830, d. Sept. 13, 1902; Thomas Salmon, b. June 23, 1828, d. April 28, 1902; Elizabeth Tweedale, b. Aug. 11, 1833; Cynthia Haswell, b. Jan. 12, 1838; Mary, b. July 4, 1841; Charles Arthur, b. July 10, 1847.

Sarah Julia, m. Moses Brown, and since death of her husband resides at Brooklyn, N. Y. She had one child (deceased).

Charles Arthur, resides at Pasadena, Cal., m. Sarah Elizabeth Johnston. *Children:* Charles Arthur and Ella E.; both died young.

357 THOMAS SALMON MOSES, son of SALMON (356), resided at Bennington, Vt., m. Mary Ann Whitehead of Hoosick Falls, N. Y.

CHILDREN: Janie; Maria; Louise; Frances; Kate; Harriet; Martha; Alice; Thomas S.; Walter.

Janie, m. S. J. Niles of Bennington, Vt. *Children:* Lois; Walter.

Maria Louise, m. Fred Peters of Hoosick, N. Y. *Children:* Marion; Mildred; Mary.

Frances, m. William Phillpot of Hoosick Falls, N. Y. *Children:* Ella; Edward Tibbits; Harrison.

Kate, m. Wm. Stevens of Waloomsac, N. Y. *Children:* Ruth; Jenette.

Harriet, m. D. Fullam of Springfield, Vt.

Martha, m. Charles Prebble of Hoosick Falls, N. Y. *Children:* Guy; Gertrude; Ruby.

358 THOMAS S. MOSES, son of THOMAS SALMON (357), resides at Eagle Bridge, N. Y., m. Mary Robertson.

CHILDREN: Winona; Forest; Lloyd; Anna.

359 WALTER MOSES, son of THOMAS SALMON (357), resides at Bennington Centre, Vt., m. Zoe Hills.

CHILDREN: Paul; Frank.

360 HARRIET HASWELL MOSES, dau. of DOCTOR SALMON (356), m. Garret B. Fonda.

CHILDREN: Sarah E., resides at Boston, Mass.; Henry resides at Bennington, Vt.; Shepard resides at Schenectady, N. Y.

361 DR. HIRAM[7] MOSES, son of THOMAS (354), was a physician practicing in Petersburg, N. Y., m. Mar. 30, 1828, Abalina Worthington; she d. July 6, 1877.

CHILDREN: Hiram Moses, Jr., b. Feb. 14, 1829, Aaron Thomas, b. July 14, 1831, d. Sept. 30, 1895; Charles J., b. June 28, 1834; Adelbert A., b. Mar. 24, 1837; Solon W., b. Mar. 5, 1842, d. Apr. 1, 1899.

Adelbert A., resided in Petersburg, N. Y., m., 1856, Harriet A. Lewis.

Solon W. (see Moses soldiers of New York in Civil War), resided in Princeton, Ill., m., 1868, Mary S. Corey.

362 DR. HIRAM[8] MOSES, JR., son of HIRAM (361), is a practicing physician at Petersburg, N. Y., m. Sept. 17, 1860, Philena Collard.

CHILDREN: Carrie, b. July 3, 1863; Estelle, b. Nov. 10, 1876, d. Aug. 10, 1880.

Carrie, m. Dec. 3, 1884, F. B. Finch, residence at Petersburg, N. Y.

363 AARON THOMAS[8] MOSES, son of HIRAM (361), lived in Petersburg, N. Y., m. Oct. 18, 1850, Deborah Hartshorn.

CHILDREN: Elizabeth; Charles A.; Ruth; Sanford H.; William; Fred.

364 CHARLES J.[8] MOSES, son of HIRAM (361), resides at Eagle Mills, N. Y., m. May 1, 1863, Mary M. Hewitt.

CHILDREN: Jennie A., b. Sept. 11, 1864; Solon W.; Frank; Carl; Gladys.

Jennie A., m. Albert A. Dunham, resides at Eagle Mills, N. Y.

365 JONATHAN[6] MOSES, son of JOSHUA (139), b. May 16, 1780, d. Sept. 18, 1841; m. Sept., 1803, in Norfolk, Conn., Abigail Plumly, b. Feb. 11, 1787, d. Oct. 13, 1853.

CHILDREN: Alonzo, b. May 16, 1805, d. Oct. 11, 1885; Charles, b. Nov. 11, 1806, d. Jan. 13, 1875; Harlow, b. Dec. 17, 1808, d. Sept. 7, 1900; Coleman, b. Feb. 1, 1811, d. Dec. 3, 1831; Rachel, b. Feb. 21, 1813, d. Oct. 28, 1841; Lucy, b. Apr. 14, 1816, d. Nov. 18, 1846; Louisa, b. June 7, 1818, d. Feb. 1, 1901; Caroline, b. Aug. 30, 1820, d. April 7, 1860; Celestia, b. Sept. 10, 1825, d. Oct. 15, 1827; Martha, b. Sept. 10, 1827, d. Nov. 6, 1905; Clarissa, b. April 21, 1822, d. Jan. 13, 1856; Halsey H., b. July 12, 1830.

Harlow, lived in Morgan after he was five years old, and on the same farm on which he died in Sept., 1901, nearly ninety-two years old. He left no children.

Rachel, m. J. T. St. John.
Lucy, m. Henry S. Clark.
Louisa, m. Andrew Griffing.
Martha, m. A. M. Tinker.
Clarissa, m. James Lawrence.

366 HALSEY H.[7] MOSES, son of JONATHAN (365). Educated at Austinburg, Ohio, Institute; practiced law thirty-five years in Ohio, ten years in Ashtabula Co., ten at Warren, Trumbull Co., and fifteen at Youngstown, Mahoning Co. He is widely known for his great legal work,

"MOSES ON MANDAMUS,"

published in 1866, which is regarded as authority and is constantly quoted in all the courts of the United States. He was an unsuccessful candidate for Congressional honors against James A. Garfield. He has retired from the practice of law and is leading an ideal life, a portion of each year at Pasadena, Cal., and at other times at Wayne, Nebraska, near which place, on a farm of eight hundred acres, he and his son Franzi E. are engaged in the breeding of blooded stock; m. Mar. 24, 1852, Mary Jane Murdock, she was b. Mar. 24, 1829.

CHILDREN: Franzi E., b. Mar. 27, 1857; Hosmer C., b. Dec. 1, 1862; Berenice A., b. May 7, 1861, d. Jan. 14, 1889; Harlow E., b. Feb. 27, 1853, d. Oct. 29, 1858.

Hosmer C., m. 1st, Dec. 7, 1886, Elizabeth Wilson; m. 2d, Mary DeLaney; lives at Rock Creek, Ohio.

Berenice A., m. May 22, 1883, William E. Hawley. *Children:* Melvin M.

367 FRANZI E.[8] MOSES, son of HALSEY H. (366), has a great breeding farm near Wayne, Neb.; m. Nov. 9, 1879, Martha Johnson.

CHILDREN: Halsey S., b. Oct. 13, 1880; Edith, b. Sept. 18, 1882; Mertie, b. Nov. 25, 1884; Irving, b. Sept. 3, 1880.

368 ALONZO[7] MOSES, son of JONATHAN (365), a farmer. Lived and died in Morgan Co.

CHILDREN: Philip A., b. Nov. 2, 1837, at Rock Creek; Sophia Phoebe Langton, b. Nov. 8, 1841, resides Youngstown, Ohio; Agnes Inez, b. Jan. 23, 1848, d. July 3, 1896.

Philip A.[8], m. July 5, 1886, Sarah J. Crowill. *Children:* three who died young, and Charles Russell[9] Moses, b. July 1, 1882; m. Sept. 22, 1903, Adda Horne; resides at Youngstown, Ohio.

369 CHARLES[7] MOSES, son of JONATHAN (365), a farmer, lived and died in Morgan Co.

CHILDREN: Henry.

370 HENRY[8] MOSES, son of CHARLES (369), resides in Dorset, Ohio.

CHILDREN: Herbert, Jefferson, Ohio; Albert, Dorset, Ohio; Hattie Graham, Dorset, Ohio; William, Dorset, Ohio; James, Ashtabula, Ohio.

371 RUTH[6] MOSES, dau. of JOSHUA (139), m. Nathan Sturdevant. They lived in Rome, Ohio, for many years and died there.

CHILDREN: Hiram; Moses; Reuben; Abigail; all dead. Moses Sturdevant left a son Albert.

372 JONAH[6] MOSES, son of JOSHUA (139), b. in Norfolk, Conn., Oct. 25, 1777, d. Nov. 8, 1866; m. about 1805, Sarah Smith, of Norfolk, Conn., migrated to Guilford, N. Y., 1811.

CHILDREN: Mary P., b. Mar. 30, 1806, at Norfolk; Asher C., b. Nov. 3, 1807; Albert G., b. May 29, 1810, d. Nov. 5, 1898; Lucy C.,

b. June 21, 1812, at Guilford, d. June 16, 1856; Ralph, b. Feb. 3, 1814, d. May 19, 1815; Hiram P., b. July 7, 1818, d. Dec. 16, 1891; Rufus A., b. July 18, 1822.

Mary P., m. Mar. 16, 1826, John Reynolds.

Asher C., a lawyer; twice married; has had five daughters.

Lucy C., m. Dec. 28, 1837, W. S. Throop; had one daughter living at Poultneyville, N. Y.

Hiram P., m. July 13, 1848, to Sylvia Cooper; no children.

Rufus A., m. Eliza Pepper; living at Sodus, N. Y.; has one daughter.

373 ALBERT G.[7] MOSES, son of JONAH (372), was a farmer at Guilford, N. Y.; m. Dec. 24, 1834, Caroline Beverly.

CHILDREN: Mary L., b. July 4, 1837; Jonah, b. Nov. 19, 1842.

Mary L., resides Guilford, N.Y.; m. about June 15, 1851, Martin Van Buren Windsor; *children:* one daughter.

374 JONAH[8] MOSES, son of ALBERT G. (373), owner Guilford Mills, Guilford, N. Y.; m. at Bovina, N. Y., May 7, 1867, Nancy Jane Erkson.

CHILDREN: Mary E., b. June 28, 1868; Sarah E., b. Aug. 8, 1871; Wealthy H., b. Feb. 1, 1874; Albert Jonah, b. Dec. 16, 1877; Jesse, b. Apr. 15, 1880; Helen, b. Nov. 2, 1882; Margaret B., b. Dec. 13, 1891.

Mary E., m. Dec. 31, 1891, Ernest B. Day; resides Haynes, N. Y. *Children:* two boys.

Sarah E., m. Oct. 6, 1904, Hayden L. Moore; residence, San Juan, P. R. *Children:* one son.

Wealthy H., m. Feb. 16, 1898, Clarence J. Barber; residence, Guilford, N. Y.

Helen, m. Feb. 21, 1906, Willard B. Phettleplace; residence, Norwich, N. Y.

375 JESSE[6] MOSES, son of JOSHUA (139), m. Esther Brown, b. in So. Manchester, Ct., June, 1774, settled in Caanan, Conn., and lived in Norfolk, Conn.

CHILDREN: Giles, b. Apr. 26, 1789; Achsa, b. Dec. 9, 1797; Roxylana, b. Apr. 22, 1804; James, b. Feb. 28, 1806; Julian, b. Apr. 11, 1810; Fidelia, b. Jan. 13, 1813; Annie; Phebe; Parnell.

Giles, d. at Big Cottonwood, Utah, about 1870.

376 FIDELIA[7] MOSES, dau. of JESSE (375), m. Joshua Benedict, d. about 1860; she still resides in Salt Lake City, Utah.

CHILDREN: Ann Eliza, b. about 1845; Mary, b. about 1848; Garrie, b. about 1854, d. about 1872.

377 JAMES[7] MOSES, son of JESSE (375), m. 1st, Roxy M. Terry; m. 2d, Eliza ———; he resided in Utah.

CHILDREN by 1st m.: Jane (Petit); a son, d. young; by 2d m.: Martha, b. about 1840; Eliza, b. about 1844 (Newman); Jesse Tilton, b. May 9, 1848; James, b. about 1850, d. about 1881; Fred F., b. about 1854.

378 JESSE TILTON[8] MOSES, son of JAMES (377), resided at Big Cottonwood, at Smithfield, and Salt Lake City, Utah; m. May 9, 1848, Phoebe Arabell Woodruff.

CHILDREN: Sarah Eliza, b. Apr. 18, 1876, d. Feb. 16, 1877; Jesse Tilton, b. Jan. 28, 1878; Sylva Arabel, b. Aug. 24, 1880; Wilfred Newton, b. May 18, 1882; James Julian, b. July 29, 1885, d. Aug. 6, 1885; David Courtney, b. July 6, 1886, Clarence Frederick, b. Apr. 15, 1891; Elmer Woodruff, b. June 5, 1894; Ethel Woodruff, b. June 5, 1894, d. Mar. 20, 1895; Phoebe Esther, b. Jan. 20, 1896; Harry Brown, b. Mar. 11, 1898; May Woodruff, b. June 14, 1901; Brigham Woodruff, b. Nov. 22, 1903, d. Nov. 23, 1903.

379 JULIAN[7] MOSES, son of JESSE (375), was for many years a minister; he was the first man who taught school in Utah. He was later in life a Justice of the Peace, and owned a large farm. He d. at East Mill Creek, Utah, April 12, 1892. He m. 1st about 1835, Barbara Matilda Neff; m. 2d about 1856, Ruth Ridge.

CHILDREN, by 2d marriage: Julian Neff, b. Dec. 29, 1857, d. Nov. 27, 1875; Barbara Matilda, b. Dec. 3, 1859; Sarah Elizabeth, b. Mar. 18, 1862; Esther Brown.

380 BARBARA MATILDA[8] MOSES, dau. of JULIAN (379), m. Aug. 4, 1881, Horace M. Cummings. He is a highly educated man, and is Supt. of the Church Schools, Temple Street, Salt Lake City, Utah. The writer is indebted to him for the history of the Utah Moses families.

CHILDREN: Horace, b. May 26, 1882; Julian, b. Mar. 15, 1884; William Ridge, b. Aug. 23, 1888, d. Nov. 29, 1888; Ruby, b. Jan. 18, 1890, d. Nov. 29, 1891; Victor Clyde, b. Oct. 9, 1891; Norma, b. Apr. 14, 1893; James Rulon, b. June 14, 1896; Lorenzo John, b. June 3, 1900; Harold, b. Sept. 30, 1905.

Horace, m. June 21, 1906, Florence Dye.

381 SARAH ELIZABETH[8] MOSES, dau. of JULIAN (379), m. Jan. 14, 1886, Christian Neilson, resides at Big Cottonwood, Utah.

CHILDREN: Julian Neff, b. June 10, 1886; Ruth, b. July 23, 1887, d. Sept., 1891; Christian, b. Jan. 11, 1889; Marie, b. Sept.

1892; Clarence, b. May, 1893; Jesse, b. Mar., 1896; Irone, b. Feb. 20, 1898; Vivian, b. Feb. 22, 1899; Esther, b. Aug., 1901; Horace C., b. July, 1903; Mabel, b. July, 1904, d. about May, 1905; Lyle, b. Mar., 1905.

382 ESTHER BROWN[8] MOSES, dau. of JULIAN (379), m. Jan., 1904, Albert Swain, of Salt Lake City.

CHILDREN: Julian Moses, b. Oct. 1905.

CONTINUATION OF CHAPTER V.

JOHN MOSES OF PORTSMOUTH. N. H., AND SOME OF HIS DESCENDANTS.

When the first volume of this work was sent to the press, the writer was well aware, that the searching of the records of Portsmouth, of Exeter, and of Epsom, for names of other descendants of John Moses of Sagamore Creek, had been neglected. As stated on page 117, very little could be obtained by correspondence with old men then living in Portsmouth; and the traditions and statements of several Moses men of great age (see page 115), as to the genesis of the Maine group of the Moses family, prove now to have been erroneous. During the sixteen years that have elapsed since the former publication, the writer has made numerous notes and extracts from private letters and from the great libraries at Washington, giving pointers for further investigation. When a decision was reached, in the spring of 1906, to publish a second volume, four months was allotted to active correspondence, and within that time much valuable material relating to New Hampshire and Maine families has been received from William H. Moses of Tilton, N. H., who, in addition to other data, procured and furnished the writer at his own expense, copies of 400 Vital Records from all towns of New Hampshire, showing births, marriages, and deaths in the Moses families, during a period of about one hundred and fifty years. Theodore W. Moses has contributed the results of much labor in recording the lineage of the Exeter families. Howard N. Moses, M.D., of Salina, Kansas, kindly volunteered to combine the old Maine material with the new, which he almost entirely collected. He then furnished the rearranged text in typewritten printer's copy (series 600), thus making a record easily understood and saving the writer much valuable time. To John M. Moses of Strafford, N. H., the writer is under obligations for the results of much searching in the city of Portsmouth. The last named correspondent belongs to a genealogical society, and writes that he has had the valuable aid of his relative, Miss Albertina Cate, also a genealogist. By his permission copious extracts have been made from the material he has kindly presented, thus furnishing many items and new discoveries relating to the earlier generations. Many of the Moses names he has unearthed from parish records, deeds, tax lists, etc., are not herein mentioned, because their connection with the main line is obscure, and for the further reason that there are at the present day no known male descendants from the men bearing the rejected names, who would be interested in the argument for, or against, a connection. Such arguments, if lengthy or involved, can have the space required in such periodicals as the Boston Transcript, where they should be looked for. The writer has rejected hundreds of Moses names from all parts of the country because the circumstantial evidence as to connections with the two main lines was not, in his opinion, sufficient.

400 JOHN[1] MOSES, of Sagamore Creek, Portsmouth, N. H.

As shown on page 95, in the deed to him of land in Cascoe Bay, he settled in this country as far back as 1639.

It appears that John Moses deeded this same land on July 3, 1669, to his two sons-in-law, Joseph Walker, and Thomas Creber. From York deeds, and from Maine Hist. and Gen. Recorder, is also quoted the record, dated Dec. 13, 1721, showing that one-half of the same property was conveyed by Alice Shortridge and son Richard, as heirs of John Moses, she being the only surviving child of Thomas Creber. We know that Joseph Walker's wife was named Elizabeth from Portsmouth Records, May 20, 1674: "Laid out to Joseph Walker 28 acres—joins corner bound tree of Caleb Becks 13 acres, thence 112 rods, bordering along by his father Moyses land and Henry Becks land . . . of which 28 acres, is 15 acres given to him by his father Moyses, which was due to him from the town in 52 and 13 acres, given by the town unto Joseph Walker's wife, *Elizabeth.*"

The wife of John Moses mentioned in agreement, page 99 of Moses history, it now appears, was previously a widow Jones. Her oath was taken as Ann Moses, executrix of John Jones' estate, Sept. 17, 1667. She had deposed as Ann Jones, Aug. 5, 1661. As John Jones died after Sept. 2, 1666, we can place the second marriage of John Moses at about 1667. We also know something about his span of life, for the N. H. Prov. Court papers, records his deposition, Oct., 1696, stating his then age at 70.

From N. H. Prov. Deeds we glean other items: Aug. 15, 1651, an exchange of a little point of land, (an acre,) adjoining Ambrose Lane's saw mill on Sagamore Creek:—this was about opposite the Moses place. On Nov. 28, 1668, John Moses and wife, Ann, for love, etc., deed to son-in-law, Thomas Creber, seaman, 12 acres. On Mar. 5, 1664, John Moses, (no wife signs,) for love, etc., deeds to son-in-law Joseph Walker, tracts of marsh land up the creek, and branch creek, to the southwest.

See pages 93 to 100 for other facts concerning John Moses, the Ancestor of the Line.

Referring to the contract with his son, Aaron, for future support, dated 6th January, 1679, there has also been found a contract of a similar character, made the same day by near neighbors, Henry and Ann Beck, with their son Thomas. Francis Hucking witnessed both contracts. Both instruments contain the words "supposed son." The papers appear to have been drawn by a lawyer, and we may presume that this strange expression was a legal phrase now obsolete.

Also referring to the picture, page 98, of the old homestead, the title for which has remained in the Moses name for 260 years, and around which so many fond associations cluster, it is feared that unless some of the public spirited Moses descendants of the Portsmouth line shall be willing to invest in, and preserve the property, it may soon pass into the hands of strangers.

CHILDREN of John[1] Moses: By his first wife, a son, Aaron, b. ——, d. June 1713; a daughter, name unknown; a daughter Elizabeth; a daughter Sarah.

It is barely possible that Sarah may have been born after the second marriage.

Elizabeth, m. before 1662, Joseph Walker. *Children* (perhaps not all): George; Elizabeth.

Daughter (name unknown), m. before 1665, Thomas Creber, a seaman. *Children:* Moses, d. without issue; Alice, who m. May 16, 1687, Richard Shortridge.

Sarah. On the strength of the conjectures of A. D. Moses and of Brewster, Sarah is mentioned on page 103, as possibly married to Timothy Waterhouse. The will of Timothy Waterhouse names his wife as "Ruth." Her family name is uncertain. We cannot say that Sarah was ever married, or that she ever received her wedding portion of five pounds.

401 AARON[2] MOSES, son of JOHN (400). See personal sketch, page 102. After his death in 1713, his widow Mary was

sion copious extracts have been made from the material he has kindly presented, thus furnishing many items and new discoveries relating to the earlier generations. Many of the Moses names he has unearthed from parish records, deeds, tax lists, etc., are not herein mentioned, because their connection with the main line is obscure, and for the further reason that there are at the present day no known male descendants from the men bearing the rejected names, who would be interested in the argument for, or against, a connection. Such arguments, if lengthy or involved, can have the space required in such periodicals as the Boston Transcript, where they should be looked for. The writer has rejected hundreds of Moses names from all parts of the country because the circumstantial evidence as to connections with the two main lines was not, in his opinion, sufficient.

400 JOHN[1] MOSES, of Sagamore Creek, Portsmouth, N. H.

As shown on page 95, in the deed to him of land in Cascoe Bay, he settled in this country as far back as 1639.

It appears that John Moses deeded this same land on July 3, 1669, to his two sons-in-law, Joseph Walker, and Thomas Creber. From York deeds, and from Maine Hist. and Gen. Recorder, is also quoted the record, dated Dec. 13, 1721, showing that one-half of the same property was conveyed by Alice Shortridge and son Richard, as heirs of John Moses, she being the only surviving child of Thomas Creber. We know that Joseph Walker's wife was named Elizabeth from Portsmouth Records, May 20, 1674: "Laid out to Joseph Walker 28 acres—joins corner bound tree of Caleb Becks 13 acres, thence 112 rods, bordering along by his father Moyses land and Henry Becks land . . . of which 28 acres, is 15 acres given to him by his father Moyses, which was due to him from the town in 52 and 13 acres, given by the town unto Joseph Walker's wife, *Elizabeth.*"

The wife of John Moses mentioned in agreement, page 99 of Moses history, it now appears, was previously a widow Jones. Her oath was taken as Ann Moses, executrix of John Jones' estate, Sept. 17, 1667. She had deposed as Ann Jones, Aug. 5, 1661. As John Jones died after Sept. 2, 1666, we can place the second marriage of John Moses at about 1667. We also know something about his span of life, for the N. H. Prov. Court papers, records his deposition, Oct., 1696, stating his then age at 70.

From N. H. Prov. Deeds we glean other items: Aug. 15, 1651, an exchange of a little point of land, (an acre,) adjoining Ambrose Lane's saw mill on Sagamore Creek:—this was about opposite the Moses place. On Nov. 28, 1668, John Moses and wife, Ann, for love, etc., deed to son-in-law, Thomas Creber, seaman, 12 acres. On Mar. 5, 1664, John Moses, (no wife signs,) for love, etc., deeds to son-in-law Joseph Walker, tracts of marsh land up the creek, and branch creek, to the southwest.

See pages 93 to 100 for other facts concerning John Moses, the Ancestor of the Line.

Referring to the contract with his son, Aaron, for future support, dated 6th January, 1679, there has also been found a contract of a similar character, made the same day by near neighbors, Henry and Ann Beck, with their son Thomas. Francis Hucking witnessed both contracts. Both instruments contain the words "supposed son." The papers appear to have been drawn by a lawyer, and we may presume that this strange expression was a legal phrase now obsolete.

Also referring to the picture, page 98, of the old homestead, the title for which has remained in the Moses name for 260 years, and around which so many fond associations cluster, it is feared that unless some of the public spirited Moses descendants of the Portsmouth line shall be willing to invest in, and preserve the property, it may soon pass into the hands of strangers.

CHILDREN of John[1] Moses: By his first wife, a son, Aaron, b. ——, d. June 1713; a daughter, name unknown; a daughter Elizabeth; a daughter Sarah.

It is barely possible that Sarah may have been born after the second marriage.

Elizabeth, m. before 1662, Joseph Walker. *Children* (perhaps not all): George; Elizabeth.

Daughter (name unknown), m. before 1665, Thomas Creber, a seaman. *Children:* Moses, d. without issue; Alice, who m. May 16, 1687, Richard Shortridge.

Sarah. On the strength of the conjectures of A. D. Moses and of Brewster, Sarah is mentioned on page 103, as possibly married to Timothy Waterhouse. The will of Timothy Waterhouse names his wife as "Ruth." Her family name is uncertain. We cannot say that Sarah was ever married, or that she ever received her wedding portion of five pounds.

401 AARON[2] MOSES, son of JOHN (400). See personal sketch, page 102. After his death in 1713, his widow Mary was appointed administratrix of his estate. In 1733 his son James was appointed to close up its settlement. The inventory showed 97¾ acres, besides marsh.

In addition to:

CHILDREN: James; Joseph; Josiah; Mark; Martha; Hannah; Abigail; and Sarah, mentioned on page 103; a son Aaron; and a daughter Elizabeth (Moses) Smith; are mentioned as having died without issue previous to winding up the estate Sept. 10, 1734.

On account of Brewster's statement that Timothy Waterhouse married a Miss Moses, it has been surmised that Aaron might have had a daughter Ruth. No such daughter is mentioned in the settlement of his estate, and Ruth Waterhouse was living at the time.

Aaron's widow, as stated on page 96, married John Sherburne Oct. 20, 1720. He was probably a cousin, and not, as stated on page 96, a brother of Aaron's first wife Ruth Sherburne, for that brother of Ruth died in 1698. For the reason that Aaron's widow omitted the son Aaron, and daughter Elizabeth, in *her* will (see page 101), it is assumed that they were the children of Aaron's first wife. *or dead*

402 JOSIAH³ MOSES, son of AARON (401), see page 104. He lived at first on part of Thomas Creber's place which he sold in 1727-8 and removed to Islington Creek, where he was living as late as 1761. He m. Nov. 12, 1719, Abigail Nelson of Portsmouth.

CHILDREN, according to North and South Church records: Abigail, bap. Dec. 4, 1720; George, bap. July 5, 1722; Mary, bap. Apr. 9, 1724; Nathaniel, bap. May 15, 1726; Daniel, bap. Mar. 31, 1728, was living in 1756.

Nathaniel, had a daughter Catherine, bap. June 13, 1756.

George, founder of the Scarborough, Maine, branch; see (600).

403 JOSEPH³ MOSES, son of AARON (401), was a soldier in Fort William and Mary in 1708. Mention is made in Prov. Papers of N. H., Vols. 4 and 5, of payments to Joseph Moses; in 1724, for "Joyners Work on Castle boat," and in 1746, "In full for work done at ye battery at Jerrys Point to be paid out of ye money in Ye Treasury for Defence of Ye Government." He was by trade a joiner in Portsmouth. See page 104 for his first and second marriage, and page 97 as to the two chapters given by Brewster in his "Rambles" to "Doctor Joe," and his son and grandson. He also mentions "Madam Moses who kept a school in the Joseph Moses house about the period of the Revolution." She was doubtless the third wife and widow. Although more than one hundred and thirty years have passed since the death of Joseph

Moses, his stories and peculiarities are yet talked over in Portsmouth, and only recently another author, Thomas Bailey Aldrich, in Chapter VI of his "Old Town by the Sea," gives yet other tales and traditions about him.

The stories, as related, do not appear to justify this lasting fame. It is probable that Joseph Moses was more a humorist than a wit, and as most observers know, the entertaining manner, and the subtle irresistible comicality of the humorist, very frequently cannot be reported or reproduced, unless by some gifted contemporary writer, himself a humorist. He was of the style of men known as "Characters," who are seldom found outside of pioneer communities. His strong individuality attracted prominent men who desired his company. His wives were religious, of fair social standing; his children were baptized, and Brewster concedes that the son, Samuel, a barber, "did those things which led to the spiritual good of his fellows." On Jan. 11, 1773, the sons, Samuel and Theodore, petition against the establishment of theatres in Portsmouth. The records contradict the idea of straitened circumstances which is somewhat implied in the above-named books. He owned a lot 146 feet by 53 feet in the heart of the city, bounded by Congress, Fleet, and Brier streets, and he was one of the original proprietors of Barrington. His house was small, as were most of the houses of the Colonial period. It was, however, of a character to make it suitable for a school subsequent to his death. Also, see State Papers of N. H., Vol. 18: "Joseph Moses, on Sept. 9, 1745, subscribed 13 shillings to support of French prisoners at Portsmouth," which is evidence that he possessed a philanthropic nature. He m. 1st, Aug. 17, 1712, Rebecca Ayres; and 2d, before 1725, Hannah ———; both wives were members of North and South Churches. He m. 3d, Aug. 10, 1759, Eleanor Lang (N. Ch.), presumed to be the widow of Joseph Lang, and the daughter of John Jackson, who calls her in his will of June 3, 1776, "my daughter Elinor Moses."

CHILDREN: Joseph Moses, b. (Pierce's Record) Sept. 9, 1713; Peletiah, bap. (S. Ch.), Mar. 6, 1725-6; Theodore, bap. (S. Ch.), Feb. 4, 1728-9; Hannah, bap. (S. Ch.), Oct. 26, 1729; Samuel, bap. (S. Ch.), Aug. 31, 1735; Hunking (N. H. Deeds, 67); Katharine, died before Sept., 1791; Love, and another daughter bap. (S. Ch.) Mar. 19, 1737-8; he had a daughter Elizabeth, d. before Sept., 1791. Compare Rock. Deeds, 130-480, with N. Ch. record of marriage of John Thomas, and Elizabeth, Apr 27, 1753.

appointed administratrix of his estate. In 1733 his son James was appointed to close up its settlement. The inventory showed 97¾ acres, besides marsh.

In addition to:

CHILDREN: James; Joseph; Josiah; Mark; Martha; Hannah; Abigail; and Sarah, mentioned on page 103; a son Aaron; and a daughter Elizabeth (Moses) Smith; are mentioned as having died without issue previous to winding up the estate Sept. 10, 1734.

On account of Brewster's statement that Timothy Waterhouse married a Miss Moses, it has been surmised that Aaron might have had a daughter Ruth. No such daughter is mentioned in the settlement of his estate, and Ruth Waterhouse was living at the time.

Aaron's widow, as stated on page 96, married John Sherburne Oct. 20, 1720. He was probably a cousin, and not, as stated on page 96, a brother of Aaron's first wife Ruth Sherburne, for that brother of Ruth died in 1698. For the reason that Aaron's widow omitted the son Aaron, and daughter Elizabeth, in *her* will (see page 101), it is assumed that they were the children of Aaron's first wife.

402 JOSIAH³ MOSES, son of AARON (401), see page 104. He lived at first on part of Thomas Creber's place which he sold in 1727-8 and removed to Islington Creek, where he was living as late as 1761. He m. Nov. 12, 1719, Abigail Nelson of Portsmouth.

CHILDREN, according to North and South Church records: Abigail, bap. Dec. 4, 1720; George, bap. July 5, 1722; Mary, bap. Apr. 9, 1724; Nathaniel, bap. May 15, 1726; Daniel, bap. Mar. 31, 1728, was living in 1756.

Nathaniel, had a daughter Catherine, bap. June 13, 1756.

George, founder of the Scarborough, Maine, branch; see (600).

403 JOSEPH³ MOSES, son of AARON (401), was a soldier in Fort William and Mary in 1708. Mention is made in Prov. Papers of N. H., Vols. 4 and 5, of payments to Joseph Moses; in 1724, for "Joyners Work on Castle boat," and in 1746, "In full for work done at ye battery at Jerrys Point to be paid out of ye money in Ye Treasury for Defence of Ye Government." He was by trade a joiner in Portsmouth. See page 104 for his first and second marriage, and page 97 as to the two chapters given by Brewster in his "Rambles" to "Doctor Joe," and his son and grandson. He also mentions "Madam Moses who kept a school in the Joseph Moses house about the period of the Revolution." She was doubtless the third wife and widow. Although more than one hundred and thirty years have passed since the death of Joseph

Moses, his stories and peculiarities are yet talked over in Portsmouth, and only recently another author, Thomas Bailey Aldrich, in Chapter VI of his "Old Town by the Sea," gives yet other tales and traditions about him.

The stories, as related, do not appear to justify this lasting fame. It is probable that Joseph Moses was more a humorist than a wit, and as most observers know, the entertaining manner, and the subtle irresistible comicality of the humorist, very frequently cannot be reported or reproduced, unless by some gifted contemporary writer, himself a humorist. He was of the style of men known as "Characters," who are seldom found outside of pioneer communities. His strong individuality attracted prominent men who desired his company. His wives were religious, of fair social standing; his children were baptized, and Brewster concedes that the son, Samuel, a barber, "did those things which led to the spiritual good of his fellows." On Jan. 11, 1773, the sons, Samuel and Theodore, petition against the establishment of theatres in Portsmouth. The records contradict the idea of straitened circumstances which is somewhat implied in the above-named books. He owned a lot 146 feet by 53 feet in the heart of the city, bounded by Congress, Fleet, and Brier streets, and he was one of the original proprietors of Barrington. His house was small, as were most of the houses of the Colonial period. It was, however, of a character to make it suitable for a school subsequent to his death. Also, see State Papers of N. H., Vol. 18: "Joseph Moses, on Sept. 9, 1745, subscribed 13 shillings to support of French prisoners at Portsmouth," which is evidence that he possessed a philanthropic nature. He m. 1st, Aug. 17, 1712, Rebecca Ayres; and 2d, before 1725, Hannah ———; both wives were members of North and South Churches. He m. 3d, Aug. 10, 1759, Eleanor Lang (N. Ch.), presumed to be the widow of Joseph Lang, and the daughter of John Jackson, who calls her in his will of June 3, 1776, "my daughter Elinor Moses."

CHILDREN: Joseph Moses, b. (Pierce's Record) Sept. 9, 1713; Peletiah, bap. (S. Ch.), Mar. 6, 1725-6; Theodore, bap. (S. Ch.), Feb. 4, 1728-9; Hannah, bap. (S. Ch.), Oct. 26, 1729; Samuel, bap. (S. Ch.), Aug. 31, 1735; Hunking (N. H. Deeds, 67); Katharine, died before Sept., 1791; Love, and another daughter bap. (S. Ch.) Mar. 19, 1737-8; he had a daughter Elizabeth, d. before Sept., 1791. Compare Rock. Deeds, 130-480, with N. Ch. record of marriage of John Thomas, and Elizabeth, Apr 27, 1753.

Peletiah, was apprenticed to a shoemaker when about sixteen.

Hannah, m. before Mar. 3, 1755 (when her father deeded her husband part of home lot), Christopher Faxon, a tailor of Portsmouth and Lee.

Hunking, probably died before Aug. 26, 1767.

Elizabeth, m. Apr. 27, 1753, John Thomas of Portsmouth, tailor, and had *children*, Elizabeth and Joseph; Rock. Deeds 130.

Katharine, m. Elisha Pike, blacksmith, of Portsmouth, and had a daughter Catherine. Rock. Deeds 130.

404 SAMUEL[4] MOSES, son of JOSEPH (403). Potter mentions him as a soldier, Invasion of Canada in 1760. His father, in deed to him of Aug. 12, 1772, calls him a "periwig maker." Brewster relates, that Samuel the barber placed a stone in the pavement in front of his shop on which was inscribed his initials, S. M.; and these letters stand in the pavement at date of this writing. A barber of the time of the Revolution had a trade not easily learned. Wigs were common, and long hair, then in vogue, was elaborately dressed. A good barber was also a dentist and a minor surgeon; and his shop was a rendezvous for the choice spirits of the town. John Paul Jones was undoubtedly among them during his stay in Portsmouth, of five months in 1777 fitting out the "*Ranger*," and again for over a year in 1781-2, preparing the frigate "*America*," which he was to command.

His father's house lot was sold by Samuel Moses on May 27, 1783 (Exeter Deeds 115-119), to Nathaniel Dean, who erected the building shown on page 185 of "Portsmouth, Historic and Picturesque." His father, Joseph, left no will and the record shows Samuel only, as "signing out" on the estate, prior to 1813. He and Theodore, and a Thomas, signed the Association Test (page 97), Aug. 14, 1776. He m. Anna ——.

CHILDREN (Perhaps not all): Samuel; Theodore, b. Sept. 20, 1766, d. Sept. 10, 1862; Joseph, b. Apr. 17, 1776 (see 514).

405 SAMUEL[5] MOSES, son of SAMUEL (404), succeeded his father as a barber. He m. Jan., 1784, Mary How of Portsmouth.

CHILDREN: Thomas, b. ———, d. 1856; John and George, taxed in Portsmouth in 1823 as "sons of Samuel."

Thomas; Brewster in his Rambles mentions Thomas. He is also mentioned in the Portsmouth Directory of 1839, and is not taxed after that year.

John and *George* do not appear on tax lists after 1833.

406 THEODORE[4] MOSES, son of JOSEPH (403), was a barber, and so called by his father in deed to him of May 5, 1761.

He is mentioned in New Eng. Hist. and Gen. Coll. as a Ruling Elder of the Ind. Cong. Church in 1777. His will, with an unusually religious preamble, names as Executors, his brother Samuel, and Joseph Walton, of Stratham. He m. Hannah ———, and seems to have died without issue. The N. Ch. records the marriage, Jan. 25, 1785, of Joseph Walton and Hannah Moses, and Exeter Deeds 184-243, shows that Theodore's widow is "now Hannah Walton."

407 DANIEL^4 MOSES, son of JOSIAH (402), was a mariner, and resided on the north side of Deer St., Portsmouth (N. H. Deeds). He m. a sister of Robert Ham. (Rock. Deeds 203-480.)

CHILDREN (perhaps not all): William, bap. (N. Ch.), Oct. 9, 1857, buried (S. Ch.), Feb. 20, 1795—(Exeter Deeds 145).

408 MARK^3 MOSES, son of AARON (401); (see paragraph, pages 104 and 109). He lived in Portsmouth, Greenland, and later in Epsom, N. H., to which town he removed between Oct. 17, 1758, and Oct. 9, 1762. His residence was about half a mile northeast of the present railroad station. He m. 1st, Oct. 29, 1724, Martha Williams, b. Nov. 18, 1702, dau. of Paul Williams of Kittery, Me. He m. 2d, March 12, 1735, Jane Wallace, dau. of William Wallace, of Greenland, N. H. She was living in 1780. He d. Feb. 2, 1789, aged 86. He left no will. He had deeded his land to his son James.

CHILDREN: Samuel, bap. (S. Ch.), Mar. 26, 1726; Elizabeth, bap. (S. Ch.), June 1, 1729; Aaron, b. 1742, d. at Gilmanton, Mar. 20, 1816; William, b. 1748 (was bap. and owned the Covenant at the age of 20 in 1768), d. 1828, in Chichester; Sylvanus, b., not at Epsom, Aug. 25, 1754, d. Jan., 1832; James, b. Feb. 27, 1758, d. Aug. 17, 1819; Jenny, (probably named for her mother,) was bap. in the Epsom Cong. Church, Dec. 18, 1763, and the same day owned the Covenant, showing that she was not then a child. In the same church, Feb. 23, 1772, Samuel Moses was bap. and owned the Covenant and is entered on the record, "a man 34 years of age." It is likely that the Samuel, b. in 1826 d. in infancy; this is all the more probable from the dates of Samuel's marriage and birth dates of some of his children.

409 WILLIAM^5 MOSES, son of DANIEL (407), was a truckman; lived in his father's house on Deer St., (Rock. Deeds 145,) m. May 15, 1777, at Greenland, Margery Grove (or Grover); she was buried (S. Ch.) Dec. 15, 1813, aged 62.

CHILDREN (S. Ch. records): Daniel, bap. Oct. 12, 1783,

buried Dec., 1786; William, bap. Oct. 17, 1784; Martha Simpson, bap. Feb. 19, 1786; Sarah Ham, bap. Oct. 12, 1786.

Sarah Ham, m. M. J. De Rochefort (Rock. Deeds 203-480).

William. If he lived to be of age was not taxed in Portsmouth.

410 JOHN[4] MOSES, son of JAMES (see pages 104 and 105 for personal items) was bap. (S. Ch.) Nov. 4, 1716; was with Capt. Meserve in the Crown Point Expedition. He m. Feb. 3, 1739-40 (Pierce's Record) Sarah Beck, dau. of Samuel Beck.

CHILDREN (all bap. S. Ch.): Aaron, bap. Nov. 9, 1740; James, bap. Nov. 4, 1744; Martha, bap. Dec. 7, 1746; George, bap. Mar. 4, 1749-50; Phœbe and Mary, bap. Nov. 2 and 5, 1758; Daniel, bap. Sept. 29, 1760; Hannah, bap. Oct., 1765; probably, Joshua.

Joshua, whose record of service with John Paul Jones and in the navy will be found on later pages, may have been a son. The intervals between the above-mentioned baptisms, the fact that Sarah, wife of John, had a brother Joshua, and that no Joshuas are found in contemporary Moses families, the occupation of the shipwright John and his association with naval vessels, also the patriotic spirit of the family, as shown in the military services of John, the father, and of Daniel, who would have been a brother, are all circumstances lending the weight of evidence to the conjecture.

411 DANIEL[5] MOSES, son of JOHN (410), was a soldier of the Revolution, and was also in the Navy. (See his fine record in the Moses soldier list.) Both he and his widow had government pensions, and from her statement it appears that he m. August, 1789, Polly Cuth at Wendell (now Goshen), and that after the war they lived in Portsmouth and Wendell until 1810, when they removed to Orange and Plainfield, Vermont. Her pension affidavit is dated 1843 from Barre, Vt., where they had then resided about twenty-five years.

412 AARON[6] MOSES, son of NADAB (see page 106 for marriage and full list of children): Aaron[7] d. Mar. 27, 1848; Mary d. 1891, James d. about 1903:

Mary, m. 1st, Thomas Hoit; 2d, ———— Jackson.

James, m. Apr. 12, 1838, Sarah A. Frost. She died about 1865.

Leonard, m. May 28, 1837, Caroline Frost; she d. Nov. 21, 1902.

Abigail W., resides in Newington.

Thomas, was a sea captain.

Charles, was a jeweler in Providence, R. I.

Susan, m. Mar. 30, 1856, Berne Bixby, now a widow in Providence.

Elvira, m. Mar. 30, 1856, Nathaniel Paul, now a widow in Providence, R. I.

William, removed to California; married.

413 AARON[7] MOSES, son of AARON (412), was a carpenter of Portsmouth, m. Sept. 28, 1831, Jane Frost of New Castle; she d. Apr. 29, 1893.

CHILDREN: John William, b. Dec. 31, 1832; Joseph S., b. Oct. 1, 1834, d. Jan., 1836; Harriet A., b. Oct. 6, 1835; George W., b. Sept. 4, 1837, d. 1855; Anna M., b. Apr. 8, 1840, d. Mar., 1862; Catherine A., b. Mar. 4, 1843, d. Jan. 19, 1865.

Harriet A., m. Alpheus Green, resides in Providence, R. I., has dau. Alice.

Catherine A., m. William Marvin, has dau. Mattie.

414 JOHN WILLIAM[8] MOSES, son of AARON (413), formerly lived in Boston. For twenty-five years he has had the whole of Marvin's Island, Portsmouth Harbor, for a residence. He has improved the place and made it exceedingly lovely, until it is the admiration of all beholders. He m. Mary Franklin Hayes in Yarmouth, N. S.

CHILDREN: Albert, d. in infancy; Ella, d. in infancy.

415 ALFRED D.[7] MOSES, son of LEVI (see paragraph, p. 107), m. 1st, Jan. 20, 1839, Charlotte Grover of York, Me.; m. 2d, Julia Ann Moses.

CHILDREN: Marie L.; Charlotte E.; Henry Howard, d. aged 7 mo.; Clara Abbie, b. May 30, 1874.

Marie L., m. ——— Heald.

Charlotte E., m. Thornton Bottom, of Portsmouth.

416 SAMUEL WALLACE[7] MOSES, son of JAMES (see paragraphs on pages 106-7). He at one time published for several years,

"THE NEW HAMPSHIRE GAZETTE"

(the "oldest newspaper in America." See N. E. H. and G. Reg., Vol. 26, p. 134); m. Oct. 12, 1834, Olive Ann Cate.

CHILDREN: Mary C.; Frederick F.; Harriet O., b. Jan. 12, 1842, d. ———; Eliza E. M., b. Dec., 1843, d. ———; Samuel W.

Mary C. A., m. Apr. 29, 1858, Robert N. Bodge. *Children:* Fred H., d. young.

Harriet O., m. Edwin W. Foster. *Children:* Elizabeth M., m. Frank W. West; Annie G., m. I. R. Davis; Carrie, m. George McPhetus; Eva L., m. Allen Tobey.

417 SAMUEL W.[8] MOSES, son of SAMUEL W. (416), is a

merchant of Portsmouth; m. 1st, Eva L. Nutter, she d. Aug. 24, 1878; m. 2d, Apr. 23, 1901, Lilla L. Joy.

CHILDREN: Mabel L., b. Apr. 1, 1876, d. Jan. 14, 1878.

418 FREDERICK FERNALD[8] MOSES, son of SAMUEL W (416), is a merchant of Portsmouth, m. Dec. 2, 1863, Georgine Webster.

CHILDREN: Frank W., b. Feb. 16, 1865, d. Mar. 3, 1895; Georgine H.; Helen, b. Nov. 20, 1875, d. Feb. 21, 1880; Julia Dearborn.

Georgine H., m. Jan. 20, 1892, Thomas F. Flanigan of Portsmouth. *Children*: Barbara H. W.

Julia Dearborn, m. July 4, 1906, Harry Prescott Chase, M.D., of Exeter, N. H.

419 FRANK W.[9] MOSES, son of FREDERICK F. (418); m. about 1888, Pauline Holmes of Boston, a grandniece of Oliver Wendell Holmes.

CHILDREN: Georgine M.; Olive B.; Dearborn W.

420 JAMES[3] MOSES, son of AARON (401). See pages 103-4. His will is dated June 3, 1772; proved, Feb. 24, 1779. S. Ch. gives baptisms of:

CHILDREN: Mary, Aug. 4, 1715; John, Nov. 4, 1716; Aaron, June 14, 1719; Sarah, Sept. 10, 1721; George, May 31, 1724; Martha, Aug. 14, 1726; Ruth, May 3, 1730; Dorothy, June 30, 1734; Abigail, Jan. 3, 1736.

421 JOSEPH J.[6] MOSES, son of MARK, lived in Epsom and Manchester, N. H. (see p. 111); m., Apr. 9, 1829, Hannah Cate, b. July 27, 1804, d. Aug. 31, 1878, dau. of John and Molly (Towle) Cate of Epsom.

CHILDREN: Elizabeth G., b. Mar. 26, 1836.

422 ELIZABETH G.[7] MOSES, dau. of JOSEPH J. (421), m. Mar. 29, 1857, Sherburn D. Cass, now of Lee, N. H.

CHILDREN: Myrtta E., b. Jan. 19, 1866, m. Aug. 3, 1889, D. H. Hill.

423 DEARBORN B.[6] MOSES, son of MARK (see page 111), m. Feb. 13, 1839, Sally H. Locke, b. Mar. 29, 1812, d. Sept. 5, 1886, dau. of William and Sally Hoyt Locke of Northwood, N. H.

CHILDREN: Sarah L., b. Nov. 25, 1841; Mary E., b. Apr. 13, 1848, d. Aug. 21, 1848.

Sarah L., m. June 19, 1869, James H. Tripp, of Epsom. *Children:*

PORTSMOUTH LINE. 207

Walter H., b. Apr. 24, 1875, who m. Oct. 12, 1898, Alice M. Fowler, and has children, Harold J. and Russell F.

424 MARK S.[6] MOSES, son of MARK, resides at Epsom; m. 1st, May 28, 1835, Elvira Dolbear, b. June 12, 1815, d. Sept. 26, 1853, dau. of John and Sally (Sherburne) Dolbear of Epsom; m. 2d, Jan. 1, 1854, Mary A. Towle, dau. of Robey and Abigail Nelson Towle of Barnstead, N. H.

CHILDREN: John M., b. Aug. 2, 1855; Cyrus S., b. Aug. 28, 1860, d. Apr. 30, 1864.

425 JOHN M.[7] MOSES, son of MARK S. (424), resides at Northwood, N. H. He graduated at Dartmouth College in 1878. He assisted in compiling the Towle genealogy, and contributes to periodicals. His valuable aid in collecting material relating to the Moses families of Portsmouth has been acknowledged elsewhere.

426 WILLIAM WARREN[8] MOSES, son of HIRAM W. (p. 113), m. July 4, 1897, Mary A. Tilton.

CHILDREN: Malcolm Harold, b. Dec. 21, 1898.

427 AARON[4] MOSES, son of JAMES (420), (see personal, page 105), was a soldier and shipwright, m. Elizabeth Fernald (N-H. Deeds 53). From S. Ch. it appears she covenanted May 5, 1745, and the same day was bap. Katharine and Dorothy, " daughters of Elizabeth;" Molly "dau. of Aaron " bap. Aug. 22, 1756; Dorothy "dau. of Elizabeth " bap. July 27, 1766. See page 105 for son Nadab.

428 SYLVANUS[4] MOSES, son of MARK (408) (see paragraph, page 110). His daughter, *Sarah*, m. 2d, John Girard. From Rock. Co. Records: "On May 6, 1820, Sylvanus and wife Mariam Moses, of Epsom, deed all the land I own, where I now live, valued at $2000, to John B. Girard, Confectioner, and wife Sarah, seamstress, both of Montreal, for support in old age."— She, Mariam Moses, d. 1840.

429 JOHN[5] MOSES, son of SYLVANUS (428), lived at Stafford Blue Hills, N. H., and died somewhere about 1876.

CHILDREN (probably others): John; David, b. ———, d. about 1852; Daniel; Noah.

430 DAVID[6] MOSES, son of JOHN (429). From Vital Records of N. H. and from County Records, it may be said that he lived in

Chichester, and had lands in Loudon, "adjoining Pembroke." Lydia (Jones) Moses, his widow, in 1852, had his estate settled ($1808.48).

CHILDREN: Noah Jones, b. May 29, 1849; David; James F.; Daniel F., b. about 1840; William Franklin; Joseph W.; Lydia A.; Sarah, d. young; John S., b. about 1848.

Noah Jones, resides at Concord, N. H. He m. Nov. 18, 1873, Martha Richardson Holt, dau. of Gilman Holt.

John S., m. Gertrude Merrill, and resides in Concord, N. H. *Child*, Mary.

431 DAVID[7] MOSES, son of DAVID (430), lives at the old homestead in Chichester; m. Sarah Davis.

CHILDREN: Frank.

432 DANIEL F.[7] MOSES, son of DAVID (430). The Vital Records of N. H. give the names of both of his parents, and his residence in 1898, as Pembroke; m. 1st, Mary Browne; 2d, Mar. 31, 1883, Mary J. Simpson; she d. in 1897, and wills all to her husband, Daniel F. Moses of Pembroke; m. 3d, Feb. 28, 1898, Lura M. Ash.

CHILDREN: Mary; Lizzie; and Frank S. d. Apr. 1, 1884, aged 21.

433 JAMES F.[7] MOSES, son of DAVID (430), m. Ella Davis

CHILDREN: George; Melvin J.; Carrie.

George, m. Julia Beauregard.
Melvin J., m. Sept. 14, 1903, Lilian Green.
Carrie, m. ——— Piggot.

434 WILLIAM FRANKLIN[7] MOSES, son of DAVID (430), m. Mar. 24, 1875, the widow Emily Davis.

CHILDREN: William; Edward; Fred; Clara.

Clara, m. ——— Grover, and resides in Chelmsford, Mass.

435 JOSEPH W.[7] MOSES, son of DAVID (430), resides in Concord, N. H.; m. 1st, the widow Sally Locke; 2d, ——— Jacobs.

436 LYDIA[7] MOSES, dau. of DAVID (430), m. John Nelson of Concord, N. H.

CHILDREN: Sarah Jane; Letitia Anne.

Sarah Jane, m. George H. Sawyer of Concord.
Letita Anne, m. Frederick H. Kelsey.

437 DAVID[5] MOSES, son of SYLVANUS (428), resided at different times in Epsom, Concord, Chichester, and Stewardstown; m.

Mehitable Rand. On Feb. 14, 1823, they deed to John Keyar 110 acres in N. E. corner of Concord. The date of his death may be inferred from Inventory Oct. 20, 1828, of Estate of David Moses of Chichester ($1597.94).

CHILDREN (from Vital Records of N. H.): Willard, b. in Epsom, 1809, d. at Colebrook, N. H., July 3, 1882; John, b. July 12, 1817, d. at Colebrook, Oct. 8, 1894.

Willard, m. 1st, Jan. 7, 1833; Eliza Fletcher; m. 2d, Feb. 21, 1875, Eliza Lapham (a widow).

438 MARIAM[5] MOSES, dau. of SYLVANUS (428), m. in 1810, Capt. Mark French of Epsom.

CHILDREN: Mark Moses French, b. Apr. 20, 1811; and another son.

439 ELIJAH[5] MOSES, son of SYLVANUS (428), was taxed in Epsom from 1815 to 1830; m. July 25, 1813, Ruth Pecker, of Epsom. They had six children, none living.

440 WILLIAM[4] MOSES, son of MARK (408), was the first settler on Bear Hill in Chichester, N. H. The records show that he bought land in 1774 and 1778; in 1779 and 1782 he signed petitions for election of Representative and for division of the town; on March 10, 1784, he was chosen tything man; on March 11, 1808, he was certified as belonging to the Freewill Baptist Society of Pittsfield (which adjoined Chichester). His will, a copy of which is in the writer's possession, was dated June 3, 1828, and leaves his property to his wife, Mehetable, and his "two sons" Samuel and William, and to the son of his deceased daughter Sally. He reserved $\frac{1}{3}$ of an acre for a burying ground "never to be disposed of."

He m. Mar. 16, 1780 (Vital Records), Mehetable Blake.

CHILDREN: Samuel, had his poll tax abated in 1811, and was therefore born before 1790, d. before 1860; William, said to have died unmarried on the home place; Sally.

Sally, m. Nov. 17, 1803, Benjamin Mason. *Children:* William.

441 SAMUEL[5] MOSES, son of WILLIAM (440), with his brother, William, lived on the home place in Chichester. On Sept. 15, 1847, they both join in a deed to John Shaw of some of the land formerly belonging to their father, William. He m. April 26, 1821, Clarissa, dau. of Simeon Hilliard, of Chichester.

CHILDREN: William (Vital Record), b. about 1823, and d. at Warren, N. H., Oct. 8, 1884.

442 WILLIAM[6] MOSES, son of SAMUEL (441), lived on the home place until about 1863, when he removed to Warren. He m. 1st, Dec. 20, 1842, Nancy Fellows, of Chichester; m. 2d, Sept. 28, 1883, in Warren, N. H., Belle F. Wolcott.

     CHILDREN: Jonathan (deceased); Sarah; Clara; John B., b. 1851; Ellen A., b. June 15, 1853; Mary Frances; Willie H., b. 1855; Lucy M., b. July 20, 1862.

Sarah, m. George Head, and resided in Warren.
Clara, m. Charles Head, and resided in Warren.
John B., m. Sept. 24, 1873, Viola Merrill of Warren.
Willie H., m. Sept. 25, 1875, Laura G. Ellsworth of Wentworth.

443 SAMUEL[4] MOSES, son of MARK (408). He lived in Greenland, N. H., in 1758, and soon after settled in Epsom on the farm, where his nephew, Mark[6], afterward resided. Here he buried his wife, Bridget. In 1800 he sold this place to his brother James, a wife, Susanna, joined in deed. He is not taxed in Epsom after 1800, but is referred to in a deposition, Dec. 24, 1802.

He m. 1st, April 9, 1760, Bridget Weeks, daughter of Jedediah Weeks, of Greenland; she renewed her church covenant at Epsom, Oct. 16, 1763; m. 2d, Susanna ———.

     CHILDREN (probably not all):

The names of the children of Samuel come from two sources: 1st, from Josiah Moses of Ticonderoga, N. Y., now 89 years old. He writes June 28, 1906, that his grandfather's name was Samuel of Epsom, his father's name, William, and that his father's brothers were: Ebenezer; Samuel; Theodore; Sylvanus; John; James; and David. 2d, From the Records of the Epsom Cong. Church which run from 1761 to 1774 only: Entries are found of the baptism of "*children of Samuel and Bridget Moses*," as follows: Abigail and Martha on Oct. 16, 1763; Ebenezer on Aug. 19, 1764; Joshua Weeks, bap. in private Nov. 12, 1770; Samuel, Joseph, and James were baptized in private Feb. 5, 1774; Sylvanus, bapt. Dec. 18, 1774.

These are not dates of birth. From gravestone inscriptions at Hopkinton, N. Y.: William Moses was born Aug. 10, 1777, d. Mar. 16, 1853. From a Family Bible, James was b. Nov. 26, 1772, d. May 6, 1866. — From other sources: Samuel, b. before 1774, d. about 1835.

Martha, m. in Epsom, June 9, 1785, Samuel Moulton.
Joshua Weeks, m. (See Vital Records), while residing at Pembroke,

N. H., on Nov. 13, 1794, Polly Piper. He and Joseph petition for incorporation of a Baptist Society at Meredith in 1797.

John: Was taxed in Epsom 1805, not taxed in 1806, and reappears on the Epsom tax list for the years 1814 and 1816.

Joseph: Was taxed in Epsom for 1805 only. Joseph Moses and wife, Comfort, deed land in Meredith about 1809. On Jan. 30, 1810, John Harper deeds land in Meredith to Joseph Moses: Witness to deed, Ebenezer Moses.

444 EBENEZER[5] MOSES, son of SAMUEL (443), m. April 24, 1788, Betty Brigham of Pembroke, N. H. On Oct. 29, 1794, Ebenezer Moses, of Pembroke, deeds land to Obed Shattuck: On Aug. 15, 1808, a deed is recorded from Nathaniel Folsom to Ebenezer Moses, both of Meredith. The rapid preparation of this volume has not permitted the searching of the records of Meredith for descendants of Ebenezer and Joseph.

445 SAMUEL[5] MOSES, son of SAMUEL (443), resided in Epsom, m. Oct. 4, 1792, Abigail Robertson, who d. about 1840.

CHILDREN: Betsey; Martha; Susan; Anna Morrill, b. 1797, d. about 1866; Charlotte; John; Sarah; Samuel, Jr., b. about 1808, d. Nov. 1847; Thomas; Mary; Harriet; Flora, d. when 17 years old; Abigail.

Betsey, m. 1810, William Fellows of Chichester.
Martha, m. July 7, 1816, Benjamin Morrill of Concord.
Susan, m. July 18, 1816, Amos Ames of Epsom. *Children:* Charles; Thomas.
Charlotte, m. —— Richardson.
John, went to sea at 15, and was never heard from.
Sarah, m. —— Gilman of Boston.
Thomas, m. Judith Dooley, resided in Gloucester, Mass.
Mary, m. —— Richardson, of Portsmouth. *Children:* Priscilla.
Harriet, m. Nov. 28, 1834, John Lear of Epsom.
Abigail, m. May 7, 1840, Samuel McConnell, of Pembroke.

446 ANNIE MORRILL[6] MOSES, daughter of SAMUEL (445), m. 1st, July 18, 1818, David Hilliard, of Chichester; m. 2d, Jacob Morse and lived in Western New York.

CHILDREN: by first marriage, Mary A., who m. Mar. 28, 1836, Solomon Yeaton, of Epsom, and now resides in Lowell. By second marriage, Thomas Jefferson, Benjamin Willis, Frances, Oliver Perry, Samuel.

447 SAMUEL[6] MOSES, son of SAMUEL (445), resides at Northwood, N. H.; m. Dec. 11, 1836, Mary Trickey.

CHILDREN: Thomas (dead); Benjamin Willis, b. 1839; James E.; Elizabeth C. (Haines), resides in Concord.

448 BENJAMIN WILLIS[7] MOSES, son of Samuel (447), was a soldier of the 12th N. H. Reg. in the Civil War. He m. 1st, Dec. 4, 1865, Ruth Maria Staples; 2d, Oct. 31, 1887, Mrs. Susan E. Griffin.

Children: George, lives in Northwood; Frank, Elizabeth. *Frank*, resides in Plastow, N. H., m. May 19, 1901, Hattie Reynolds. *Elizabeth*, m. John Kelley.

449 WILLIAM[5] MOSES, son of Samuel (443), removed shortly after his marriage from Epsom to Barnston, the province of Quebec, Canada. He returned to the United States during the War of 1812, and resided first at Chittenden, Vt., where his first wife died, and afterward at Hopkinton, N. Y., where he is buried. He m. 1st, at Epsom, 1799 (Vital Records of N. H. and Family Bible), Sally Robinson, b. in Epsom, 1777; m. 2d, Ruth Stoddard; she died at Hopkinton May 17, 1834; m. 3d, Betsey Roberson.

Children: by his first wife. Samuel, b Sept 18, 1801, d. Oct. 9, 1891; David; Theodore; Ebenezer; Lorenzo; William; Sally.

By his second wife: Thompson; Josiah, b. in Pitsford, Rutland Co., Vt., Jan 13, 1817; Polley; Susan; Ruth; Lucy; Charles.

By his third wife: John; Betsey; Irena; Haldy; Lorenzo.

450 JAMES[5] MOSES, son of Samuel (443), removed shortly after his marriage from Epsom, N. H., to Knowlton, in the Province of Quebec, Canada; afterward, in 1831, removed again to New York, leaving one son, William, in Canada, and then, in 1841, to Ohio, where he died. He m., according to Family Bible (date not given), Dorothy Rowell, b. Mar. 13, 1769, d. June 27, 1857; he m., according to the Vital Records of N. H., on Dec. 15, 1796, Dolly Rowell: (Dolly was the name of their second daughter, and Dorothy was the name of their fifth daughter).

Children: Sarah, b. Dec 15, 1794; Dolly, b. 1797, died young; Harriet, b. Mar. 12, 1799; Elizabeth, b. Oct. 24, 1801; Abraham, b. Jan. 27, 1805, d. in Kansas, 1876; Dorothy, b Nov. 12, 1807, d. about 1884; James R., b. Sept. 24, 1809, d. Oct. 18, 1887; William, b. Aug. 4, 1811, at Knowlton, Canada, d. 1862; Enoch, b. Sept. 4, 1813, d. Sept. 4, 1893; perhaps a daughter, Phylena.

Dorothy, m. a Higbee, and had five sons, one of them named Abraham.

451 JAMES[6] MOSES, son of James (460), m. Jane Boyce.

Children (perhaps not all): Thomas; Enoch R ; Valentine; Ebenezer (lived at Beatrice, Neb.).

452 ENOCH[6] MOSES, son of JAMES[5] (450), m. Caroline Moses, a distant relative.

CHILDREN: several, among whom Reuben was the oldest, and Enoch the youngest.

Enoch, resides in Fenton, Ohio, and has two daughters.

453 SARAH[6] MOSES, dau. of JAMES (450), m. 1st, Valentine Mock, Province of Quebec, Canada; m. 2d, Israel Lewis.

CHILDREN: Dorothy; James; Christiana; Hester; Valentine; Joseph; Phylena.

454 HARRIET[6] MOSES, dau. of JAMES (450), m. William Williams of Shefford, Province of Quebec.

CHILDREN: William; James; Julia; Jane; Melissa; Caroline.

455 ELIZABETH[6] MOSES, dau. of JAMES (450), m. 1st, Kingsbury; and 2d, ——— Parmer.

CHILDREN: William; Lucy; Elizabeth; Mary; Charles M. (Parmer).

456 ABRAHAM[6] MOSES, son of JAMES (450), died in Kansas; m. Eliza Abbott.

CHILDREN: Sarah (m. a Patison); Kimble; Sidney G., Drakes Creek, Ark.; James (killed by Indians in 1881); Sophia; William; Franklin; Viola (m. ——— Hale).

Sophia, m. ——— Moore, resided in Cowley Co., Kansas, and had nine children.

William, was an engineer, lived at Garret, Ind., and had ten children.

Franklin, was a soldier of the Civil War, resides at Pleasant Bend, Ohio, has children: Myrtle May, b. 1871; Howard, b. 1877; Charles A., b. 1879.

457 WILLIAM R.[6] MOSES, son of JAMES (450), lived in Knowlton, Canada, m. Euphemia Barr.

CHILDREN: Ellen, b. 1836; James, b. 1838; Amanda, b. 1840; William, b. April 16, 1842; Sarah, b. 1852.

Amanda, m. George Robb of Cowansville, Province of Quebec. Children: William; Malcolm; George; Nettie A.; Myrtle.

Sarah V., m. Andrew Jones and resides in Knowlton, Prov. of Quebec.

458 ELLEN[7] MOSES, dau. of WILLIAM R. (457), m. Sept. 11, 1855, Amos A. Mooney, resides South Craftsbury, Vt.

CHILDREN: Euphemia V.; William B.; James R.; Lulu C.; Florence E.; Howard A.; Lucius S. H.; Maude G.; Ethel L.

459 WILLIAM[7] MOSES, son of WILLIAM (457), is a merchant and President of a bank at Alexandria, Minn. Is also an officer in other banks; m. 1st, in 1865, Martha Ralston, by whom he had no children; m. 2d, in 1873, Mary Morrison.

CHILDREN: William John Barr, b. June 27, 1874; Charles Wesley, b. Dec. 5, 1876.

460 WILLIAM JOHN BARR[6] MOSES, son of WILLIAM (459), resides at Alexandria, Minn. He graduated at Hamline University, St. Paul, Minn., and also took special courses at the University of Minnesota, and the Chicago University. Is by profession an author and contributes to periodicals of New York and other cities.

461 CHARLES WESLEY[8] MOSES, son of WILLIAM (459), is a merchant and resides at Drayton, North Dakota; m. Robina Halcrow, in 1902.

CHILDREN: Charles William[9], b. Aug. 10, 1904; Dorothy Elizabeth, b. Aug. 29, 1906.

462 WILLIAM[6] MOSES, son of WILLIAM (449), was a banker and resided in Wisconsin.

463 THEODORE[6] MOSES, son of WILLIAM (449), resided in Canada but died in Flint, Mich. He m. Jerusha Peck.

CHILDREN: William H.; Lorenzo; Renaldo; Theodore; Mary; Sarah; Lecta; Lucinda; Maria; Alice.

Theodore, has one child named Evart.

William H., lived at Nicollet, Minn., and now resides at Prospect, Marian Co., Ohio.

464 SAMUEL[6] MOSES, son of WILLIAM (449), resided at Euclid, Jerome, and Richmond, in Ohio; m. Sept. 18, 1823, Sally Stoddard, who was b. May 14, 1800, at Morristown, Vt.

CHILDREN: Renaldo, b. May 22, 1824; Caroline, b. Nov. 13, 1825, d. Sept. 20, 1861; William, b. June 17, 1827; Lorenzo, b. Mar. 26, 1830, d. at Richmond, Apr. 25, 1906; Sally Ann, b. Oct. 6, 1831, d. Oct. 5, 1891; Julia, b. Nov. 13, 1833; James, b. May 17, 1835, d. Oct. 13, 1862; Esther, b. Dec. 10, 1836, d. Jan. 30, 1837; Polly P., b. Oct. 1, 1840.

James, resided in Indiana; volunteered in 1862, and received his death wound at the battle of Perryville. He m., 1835, Margaret Headley at Richwood, Ohio. *Children:* John; Sarah.

Lorenzo, was a soldier of the Civil War in the 16th Ohio Inf., was taken prisoner while making a charge at Vicksburg, was paroled, exchanged, and served at the front until 1865.

William, resided at the Dalles, Or.; m. Hannah Thackeray. They had four children. Only one grew to manhood — Samuel, who married and died before he was thirty.

465 RENALDO[7] MOSES, son of SAMUEL (464), resided at Richwood, Ohio. He m. 1st, —— Hurd; m. 2d, Nancy E. ——, who survives him and now resides in Bellingham, Wash.

CHILDREN, by the 1st wife: William Henry, b. June 11, 1849, at Richwood, Ohio; Jaspar Newton, b. Jan. 8, 1852. By the 2d wife: Albert J.; Frank W.

Albert J., d. about 1890 in Idaho, after a varied career as a ranchman, and sheriff, in Kansas and in the State of Washington. He and his brother, Frank W., were men of huge physique.

Frank W., is a teacher of stenography, and resides in Napa, Cal.; is married and has one son, b. about 1900.

466 WILLIAM HENRY[8] MOSES, son of RENALDO (465), m. at Richwood, O., Helen Elizabeth Barney, née Turney. Both are now residing at Indianapolis, Ind. Helen E. Moses was born Jan. 27, 1863, at Columbus, O. Since 1899, she has been National Secretary of the Christian Woman's Board of Missions, and since 1898 she has been editor of the "Missionary Tidings." She is widely known as a speaker and organizer, and has been very successful in her chosen work.

Their *children* are: Jaspar Turney, b. May 28, 1880, at Richwood, O.; Alwin Raymond, b. Nov. 23, 1885, at Richwood, O.

467 JASPAR TURNEY[9] MOSES, son of WILLIAM HENRY (466), was educated in the public schools of Topeka, Kans., and graduated from Butler College, Indianapolis, in 1903. Was a reporter on the Indianapolis *News,* Editorial Reader for the Bobbs Merrill Pub. Co., and Assistant Editor of *"Madame."* Since 1905 he has been President of the Christian Institute, a large American College at Monterey, Mexico.

He m. Dec. 26, 1905, Katherine Elliott, at Newcastle, Ind.

468 ALWIN RAYMOND[9] MOSES, son of WILLIAM HENRY (466), was educated in the Indianapolis High School. Is the Estimator for the Brown-Ketcham Iron Works, Indianapolis.

469 JASPAR NEWTON[8] MOSES, son of RENALDO (465), m. 1882, Sallie Wilson, at Springfield, O.

CHILDREN: Minnie Louise, b. 1885; Helen, b. 1889; Ross, b. 1892.

470 ENOCH R.[7] MOSES, son of JAMES[6] (451), was a soldier, and resided at Douglass, Ill.; m. Mar. 21, 1858 (?), Deborah A. Woolsey.

CHILDREN: Luther R., Blue Springs, Neb.; Charles W., Lexington, Okla.; Orris C., Fairfax, S. Dak.; James H., Fairfax, S. Dak.; David E., Fairfax, S. Dak.; Louise, d. Oct. 1905 at Gilson; also three sons residing at Douglass, Ill.; Sanford D.; Frank; Woolsey B.

Louise, m. ——— Taylor, and had one son b. about 1901.

471 JOSIAH[6] MOSES, son of WILLIAM (449), is still living at the age of 89, at Ticonderoga, N. Y. He states that his father had twenty-two children, nineteen of whom he enumerates.

Success in making the New Hampshire connection for the large number of descendants of William[5] and James[5], is due very largely to the recollections of the venerable Josiah, which have been verified by fortunate discoveries in the N. H. records.

He was m. 1st, Mar. 16, 1847, in Hopkinton, N. Y., to Clarissa Wetherell, who was b. Aug. 16, 1823, and d. in Hopkinton, N. Y., Feb. 4, 1880; m. 2d, Feb. 16, 1881' in Norfolk, N. Y., to Edna Wright.

CHILDREN: Theron J., b. Dec. 22, 1847, d. Sept. 23, 1849; Eugene C., b. in Lawrence, June 3, 1849, d. Sept. 6, 1877; Emergene, b. Aug. 12, 1852, d. 1869; Frances M., b. Mar. 5, 1855, d. in Muscatine, Iowa, Sept. 25, 1890; Merton W., b. July 20, 1864; Mattie A., b. Sept. 12, 1866, d. Sept. 20, 1867.

Eugene C., m. Jan. 1, 1877, Clista Sanford.

Frances M., m. 1st, Sept. 5, 1876, Clark A. Chittenden; m. 2d, Feb. 14, 1893, at Muscatine, Iowa, J. C. Shipley.

Merton W., m. May 4, 1892, at Hopkinton, N. Y., Nettie E. Fuller; resides at Ticonderoga, N. Y.

472 THOMPSON[6] MOSES, son of WILLIAM (449), with his family resided at Lyons, Iowa, about 1870. No further information.

473 SYLVANUS[5] MOSES, son of SAMUEL (443), d. in 1859, at the age of 87. He resided at Tunbridge, Vt.; m. Sallie Borden.

CHILDREN: Joseph, b. Mar. 21, 1822, d. 1863; John; Samuel; Jonathan, b. 1828; Martha; Lydia; Sallie.

Samuel, m. *Children* (perhaps others): Rosette.

John, d. at age of 77 at Tunbridge. No issue.

474 JOSEPH[6] MOSES, son of SYLVANUS (473), was a soldier of the 12th Vt. Inf., and d. at Wolf Run Shoals, Va. He m. Mar. 20, 1843, Eleanor Pearl.

CHILDREN: Esther, b. Mar. 18, 1844; Sarah, b. Nov. 29, 1845; Norman, b. July 1, 1849; William, b. Dec. 20, 1851; Mary, b. Jan. 12, 1855; Pearl, b. July 13, 1858.
Esther, has resided in So. Royalton, Vt., and Northfield, Vt.
Mary, resides in Bridgeport, Conn.
William, resides at South Royalton, Vt.; m. Jennie Dewey.

475 NORMAN[7] MOSES, son of JOSEPH (474), resides at South Strafford, Vt.; m. Jan. 8, 1882, Nellie Harper.

CHILDREN: Nettie, b. May 21, 1874; Forrest, b. Oct. 17, 1875; William, b. Feb. 21, 1878; Joseph, b. Feb. 10, 1884; Ella, b. Mar. 7, 1888; Mary, b. Nov. 28, 1890; George, b. Oct. 23, 1892; John, b. Aug. 4, 1895; Grover, b. Feb. 27, 1898; Hazel, b. Oct. 19, 1900; Scott, b. Nov. 29, 1902; Grace, b. Mar. 21, 1906.
Nettie, resides at Royalton, Vt.

476 PEARL[7] MOSES, son of JOSEPH (474), resides at Tunbridge, Vt.; m. Mar. 26, 1879, Melissa Cleveland.

CHILDREN: Cora; Guy; Wyona; Perley; Hattie; Lena; Lee.

477 JONATHAN[6] MOSES, son of SYLVANUS (473), resided at Tunbridge, Vt.; m. 1st, ———— ; m. 2d, at age of 63, on June 7, 1891, at Bath, N. H. (Vital Records), Mary Barney, a widow.

CHILDREN: Samuel; Orra; Sylvanus.
Sylvanus, resided at Haverhill, N. H.; m. 1st, Emma Barney; 2d, Emma Jerome. Vital Records show that in 1899 eight children had been born to him.

478 ORRA[7] MOSES, son of JONATHAN (477), at one time resided at Post Mills, Vt.; m. ————.

CHILDREN: Jonathan; Lydia; John; Emma; Orin; Eva; Hattie; Nettie; Flora.

479 THEODORE[5] MOSES, son of SAMUEL (443), resided in or near Charleston, Vt.; moved to Michigan; had a daughter Jane. Norman Moses, now living at South Strafford, Vt., was ten years old when his grandfather Sylvanus died. He writes, "I had also a great uncle Theodore Moses."

480 JAMES[7] MOSES, son of WILLIAM R. (457), resided in Manitoba; m. Minerva Green.

CHILDREN: Carrie E., b. Feb. 14, 1865; William R., b. Mar. 14, 1867; Clarence, b. 1870, d. 1874; Edith M., b. July 4, 1873.
Edith M., m. June 12, 1895, B. Richardson. *Children:* Muriel, d. 1902; Doris A., b. Mar. 2, 1903; Phylis M., b. Apr. 6, 1905.

481 WILLIAM R.[8] MOSES, son of JAMES (480), resides in Kirksville, Mo. Is Dist. Manager Mutual Life Ins. Co.; m. 1887, A. L. Rounds.

CHILDREN: Genevieve K., b. Jan. 14, 1888; E. Agnes, b. June 2, 1892; Eugene McKenzie, b. May 14, 1899.

482 THEODORE[5] MOSES, son of SAMUEL (404), removed from Portsmouth to Newmarket in 1779, and eight years thereafter to Exeter, where he became prominent, founding a successful business, which was greatly enlarged and extended in other cities by his sons and grandsons. Brewster, in his "Rambles," prints an interesting letter written by Theodore in his 93d year, and Bell, in his ."History of Exeter," publishes a biographical sketch of him, in connection with the activities which he created. The ."History of the Exeter, N. H., Baptist Society," states that, "a century ago the firm were hatmakers, a great industry at the time of Theodore Moses." He, Theodore, was a selectman of Exeter in 1830.

He m. at Stratham, Nov. 1789, Deborah Emery, who was born Nov. 22, 1769, and d. Oct. 20, 1846.

CHILDREN: Theodore Bland, b. Nov. 15, 1790, d. Apr. 7, 1871; John Folsom, b. Sept. 10, 1792, d. Dec. 24, 1877; Susan Thurston, b. Aug. 27, 1784, d. Aug. 3, 1850; Samuel Tenney, b. Jan. 20, 1798, d. Oct. 26, 1842; George Washington, b. Jan. 7, 1800, d. 1856-7; Charles C. P., b. May 17, 1802, d. 1883; William Pitt, b. Aug. 9, 1804, d. Apr. 2, 1863; Ann Ayers, b. Oct. 2, 1807, d. July 3, 1881; Abigail F., b. Feb. 11, 1810, d. Jan. 3, 1881; Elizabeth Mary, b. June 25, 1813, d. 1897 or '98; Mary Elizabeth, b. June 25, 1813, d. Aug. 24, 1891.

Elizabeth Mary, m. Elbridge G. Lane, of Exeter. *Children:* Ellen; Lucius; Deborah; Elbridge, Jr.

Mary Elizabeth, m. Jeremiah L. Merrill, of Exeter. *Child:* Joseph W.

483 THEODORE BLAND[6] MOSES, son of THEODORE (482), resided at Somersworth and Great Falls, N. H., where he was Treasurer of the Great Falls Manuf. Co. He m. Nov. 15, 1814, Mary Smith, who was b. Nov. 18, 1792, d. Apr. 20, 1876.

CHILDREN: Hannah, b. Dec. 11, 1815, d. Sept. 15, 1883; Theodore Bland, Jr., b. Mar. 12, 1817, d. Apr. 6, 1893; Charles Smith, b. Apr. 25, 1819, d. July 25, 1834; Lucius Manlius, b. Apr. 21, 1822, d. Jan. 24, 1890; Thomas Gibbs, b. Feb. 8, 1825, d. Feb. 28, 1841; William Pitt,

PORTSMOUTH LINE. 219

b. Dec. 15, 1826, d. Sept. 15, 1905; Mary Burley; Horace Hardy, b. Feb. 17, 1831; Kirke White, b. Nov. 28, 1833; Annie Ayers.

Mary Burley, m. 1st, Howard Moses (a cousin); he d. about 1857-8, willing his property to his wife; m. 2d, Albert Hastings.

Annie Ayers, m. —— Archibald.

484 THEODORE BLAND[7] MOSES, son of THEODORE BLAND (483), resided at Clarendon Hills, Boston, Mass., was a civil engineer. He m. 1st, Mary Moody Brazier; m. 2d, June 27, 1844, Frances Lafayette Bouvé, daughter of Ephraim and Lydia (Cushing) Bouvé. She was b. Dec. 1822, d. Feb. 9, 1905.

CHILDREN: by 2d wife, Theodore Bland, b. Nov. 22, 1847; Lilla Bouvé; Charles Smith, b. Dec. 12, 1851.

Theodore Bland, m. ——.
Charles Smith, m. Mary Adelaide O'Brien.

485 LUCIUS MANLIUS[7] MOSES, son of THEODORE BLAND (483), was a Captain for years in the merchant marine service, and died at Chicago, Ill.; m. 1st, Aug. 14, 1849, Mary Wingate Titcomb, b. May 14, 1825, d. Aug. 9, 1861; m. 2d, Adeline Gower.

CHILDREN: by 1st marriage, Lucia Gray; Thomas Gibbs, b. July 21, 1856; Frank Deming, b. Feb. 23, 1858; Illinois Mary; by 2d marriage, Kirke White; Walter Farrington.

Lucia Gray, m. Samuel P. Cook of Woonsocket, R. I.
Frank Deming, resides in Trenton, N. J.
Thomas Gibbs, resides in Chicago. *Children:* William Pitt, b. Sept. 7, 1881, and m. Elizabeth Martin; Mary Titcomb; Thomas Rupert, b. July 24, 1889.

486 HORACE HARDY[7] MOSES, son of THEODORE BLAND (483), is a surveyor, and resides at Boston, Mass.; m. Cornelia Simmons.

CHILDREN: Alice; Clara; Cornelia; Mary.

487 WILLIAM PITT[7] MOSES, son of THEODORE BLAND (483), was in the Civil War (Lieut. and Q. M. 9th N. H.,) (see Moses Soldier List), resided at Berwick, Me., and Great Falls, N. H., where he succeeded his father in the Great Falls Manuf. Co.; m. Mar. 20, 1855, Fannie Blake of Somersworth, N. H.

488 KIRKE WHITE[7] MOSES, son of THEODORE BLAND (483), was Lieut. 23d Me. Inf., Civil War. (See Soldier List.) Is a manufacturer at Lawrence, Mass.; m. 1st, Francis Abby Lewis; she d. Sept. 9, 1884; m. 2d, Emma Frances Lathrop.

F

CHILDREN: by 1st marriage, Genevieve; Kirke White, Jr., b. Mar. 18, 1859; Bertha Archibald; by 2d marriage, Frances Moses.

Kirke White, Jr., m. Lillian D. Hubbard; *Children*: Kirke Lewis, b. June 1, 1885.

489 CHARLES C. P.[6] MOSES, son of THEODORE (482), was a manufacturer, and resided at Dover and Newmarket, N. H.; m. May 21, 1829, Hannah M. Wiswall.

CHILDREN: Howard; Sarah; Cornelia.

Howard, m. Mary Burley Moses, his cousin. He d. 1857-8, willing his property to his wife.

490 WILLIAM PITT[6] MOSES, son of THEODORE (482), was a wool merchant and lived and died at Exeter; m. Nov. 14, 1839, Abigail K. Leavitt.

CHILDREN: Eugenia, b. about 1841, d. Aug. 10, 1890.

491 ABIGAIL F.[6] MOSES, dau. of THEODORE (482), lived and died at Exeter; m. Luke Julian.

CHILDREN: Elizabeth; George N.

George N., was a Captain in the 13th N. H. Reg. during the Civil War. Howard M. Moses, son of the Rev. Theodore, of Harmony, Me., and later of Exeter, was a soldier in his second cousin's company.

Elizabeth, m. Col. Freeman Connor, one of the original Ellsworth Zouaves.

492 JOHN FOLSOM[6] MOSES, son of THEODORE (482), lived and died at Exeter, N. H.; was a successful wool merchant; was a Sergeant in Capt. James Thom's Company, in the War of 1812; was a Representative in the State Legislature in 1849, 1850, 1851; a most devout religious man, devoted to the poor, the sick, and to criminals. The following summary, perpetuated in the form of a memorial tablet in the Baptist Church at Exeter, tells his life:

"In blessed memory of,
JOHN FOLSOM MOSES,
1792-1877.

Sixty-nine years a faithful member; Sixty-two years a deacon of the church; A founder of the Sunday School in Exeter, and for fifty years Superintendent in this parish."

He m. 1st, Dec., 1815, Mary Smith Pearson, daughter of Major Edmond and Dorothy Swasey Pearson, b. June 10, 1790, d. Aug. 10, 1844; m. 2d, Aug. 24, 1847, Abigail Cleaveland Boyd, dau. of William and Ruth Shaw Boyd, b. Oct. 3, 1812, d. May 18, 1878

CHILDREN: by 1st marriage, James Coleman, b. Nov. 21, 1817, d. June 24, 1870, at Knoxville, Tenn.; Deborah Ann, b. Oct. 16, 1819; John Leese, b. May 9, 1822, d. Apr. 2, 1887; Dora Pearson, b. Aug., 1824; Samuel Dodge, b. Oct. 17, 1826, d. Dec. 18, 1873; Henry Clay, b. 1828, d. Sept. 19, 1900; Mary Jones, b. 1830; Isaac Dodge, b. 1832, died 1858, at Knoxville, Tenn.

CHILDREN: by 2d marriage, Charles Orne, b. May 5, 1849, d. June 14, 1882; Theodore William, b. Jan. 26, 1851; Joseph Walker, d. in infancy; Katherine Williams, b. Jan. 4, 1856.

Deborah Ann, m. Elijah Frank Rickee; *Children:* Susan; James; Mary Frances; Deborah Moses; John.

Dora Pearson, m. Joseph Walker; *Children:* Edward Walton; Lillie; Frank.

Mary Jones, m. Samuel Rickee; *Children:* Frank; Isaac; Henry; Mary; Charles.

493 JAMES COLEMAN[7] MOSES, son of JOHN FOLSOM (492), was a merchant and lived and died at Knoxville, Tenn. He m. Susan Wells (Park) Baker, a widow, who d. Mar. 7, 1894.

CHILDREN: John Folsom, d. Nov. 7, 1857; Mary Jones; Frank Armstrong, b. June 19, 1845; Charles Howard, b. Oct. 2, 1847; Fannie Pearson; James Coleman, Jr., d. Sept. 3, 1852; William Everett, b. Mar. 3, 1853; Henry Leese, b. Nov. 1, 1855, d. Apr. 16, 1903.

Charles Howard, m. Bettie M. Brown; *Children:* Lina; Susie W.; Bettie O.

Fannie Pearson, m. Eberia Grainger of England.

Henry Leese, m. Lizzie Grant; *Children:* Frank Armstrong; Ethel.

494 JOHN LEESE[7] MOSES, son of JOHN FOLSOM (492), lived and died at Knoxville, Tenn.; held the degree of A.B. (Waterville College), now Colby University; President of the Board of Trustees of the University of Tennessee, Knoxville; Treasurer of Knoxville and Kentucky R. R., now Southern R. R.; m. Jan. 14, 1847, Susan, dau. of John and Malinda (White) Williams, who d. July 3, 1877.

CHILDREN: John William, d. Dec. 23, 1877; Thomas Lanier, b. Dec. 13, 1849; Leese; Theodore (d. young); Edmund Pearson, b. July 24, 1857; James; Mary.

Leese, married, had one son.

Mary, m. a Mr. Branson.

495 SAMUEL DODGE[7] MOSES, son of JOHN FOLSOM (492), was a Physician and Surgeon; A.B., Williams College; M.D., University of Virginia; was in the Civil War under General Lee; practiced medicine in Knoxville, where he died; m. 1st, Sally

Armstrong; m. 2d, Bettie Overton, dau. of A. J. and Betty Lewis Brown.

CHILDREN: Sally; Lewis Minor, b. June 21, 1870.

Lewis Minor, served in the Spanish War (Va. Reg.).

496 HENRY CLAY[7] MOSES, son of JOHN FOLSOM (492), born and died at Exeter, N. H.; was a wool merchant with office at Boston; was trustee of Robinson Female Seminary at Exeter; Representative to State Legislature 1864-65; m. Lucy Ann, dau. of Ira B. and Elizabeth (Huntress) Hoitt.

CHILDREN: Ella; Lewis; Dora, b. about 1853, d. Mar. 25, 1881; Herbert Henry, b. Dec. 21, 1855.

Herbert Henry, m. Dec. 22, 1887, Katherine F., dau. of Alva and Mary (Gerrish) Wood. *Children:* Dora; Paul, b. Dec., 1893.

497 CHARLES ORNE[7] MOSES, son of JOHN FOLSOM (492), was a wool merchant, and lived and died at Exeter, N. H.; was a Representative to the State Legislature in 1880; m. Harriet Naylor, dau. of John and Mary (Warren) Butler.

CHILDREN: John Edward, d.; Charles Orne, b. 1872, d. Mar. 10, 1893; Katherine.

498 THEODORE WILLIAM[7] MOSES, son of JOHN FOLSOM (492), was educated at Phillips Exeter Academy, and Harvard University, where he was graduated with degree of A.B.; studied abroad at University in Vienna; is an Educator, has been much identified with music, both professionally and otherwise, in New York, and elsewhere. Resides at Norfolk, Conn.

499 FRANK ARMSTRONG[8] MOSES, son of JAMES COLEMAN (484), was an Ensign of the 63d (Confederate) Tenn. Inf., was wounded at Drurys Bluff, Va., May 16, 1864, at which battle his regiment was confronted by the 13th N. H. Reg., in which regiment his cousin, George N. Julian (see 491), was a Captain. Resides at Knoxville, Tenn.; m. Oct. 20, 1870, Elizabeth M. Mitchell.

CHILDREN: James Coleman, b. June 20, 1871; Lida Mitchell (who m. Frank Atlee).

500 WILLIAM EVERETT[8] MOSES, son of JAMES COLEMAN (492), was instructor of chemistry at the University of Tenn., resides at Knoxville, Tenn.; m. Annie M. Partin.

CHILDREN: Henry Maxwell; William Everett; Samuel Dodge; Margaret; Charles Howard.

Henry Maxwell, m. Beulah Montgomery. *Children:* Katherine.

501 WILLIAM EVERETT, JR.,[9] MOSES, son of WILLIAM EVERETT (500), holds the degree of LL.B., University of Tenn.; and resides at Knoxville, Tenn.

502 THOMAS LANIER[8] MOSES, son of JOHN LEESE (494); is Supt. of State School for Deaf Mutes, at Knoxville, Tenn.; m. 1st, Katie, dau. of Rev. Thomas C. and Delia Lottridge Teasdale; she d. Dec. 11, 1901; m. 2d, July 22, 1903, Jane Lee, dau. of John Graham and Annie (White) Lee.

CHILDREN by first marriage: Delia Lottridge; John Leese; Katie Love; by second marriage: Graham Lee.

503 EDMUND PEARSON[8] MOSES, son of JOHN LEESE (494), is an educator; resides at Raleigh, N. C.; is Supt. of the Board of Education. Has published works on educational subjects; is a teacher, historian, A.B. and A.M., University of Tenn.; m. Carrie Emerson, dau. of Thomas and Mary (Atkinson) Dosser.

CHILDREN: Susan; Herbert; Carrie; Mary; Mildred; Edward; Elizabeth.

504 ABIATHAR[5] MOSES, son of AARON, son of MARK (p. 111), had no son Sanborn as stated in Vol. 1.

CHILDREN: John; William, b. in Plymouth, N. H., 1808, d. Feb. 14, 1875; Isaac, b. either in Gilmanton or Plymouth, lived and died in Campton, N. H.; Olive, who m. her cousin, Nathaniel Moses (see p. 112).

505 WILLIAM[6] MOSES, son of ABIATHAR (504), resided in Campton, N. H. He engaged in the freighting business, running several six horse teams from Boston to Plymouth, N. H.; and as the railroad crept slowly up the Merrimack Valley, continued his teams from the moving terminal, until, Plymouth reached, he extended his business to North Woodstock, N. H. He was a Representative of the town of Campton in the N. H. Legislature. He retired in 1865, and resided thereafter with his son, Thaddeus, at Meredith, N. H.; m. Abigail, dau. of William Keniston; she was b. Oct. 5, 1806.

CHILDREN: Stephen T., b. Oct. 27, 1832; Thaddeus Stillman, b. Jan 28, 1835, d. at Meredith, Jan. 13, 1902; Robert S., b. Mar. 17, 1839; Lydia A., b. Apr. 17, 1840.

Stephen T., m. Orinda D. Bragdon; Children: Fannie, who m. Hiram Gordon and resides at Lowell, Mass.

506 THADDEUS STILLMAN[7] MOSES, son of WILLIAM

(505); at the age of eighteen he started in the tin and stove business at Plymouth. In 1860 he removed to Meredith, N. H., continuing and greatly enlarging the business. He held offices in Meredith as follows: Chairman Board of Selectmen, 1870-71; Town Treasurer, ten years; Member Board of Education, four years; Representative in the Legislature, 1878-9; Member Convention to revise the State Constitution in 1876; State Senator, 1888-9; he was for many years a Deacon of the First Baptist Church; he m. Feb. 22, 1862, Emily S., dau. of Aaron Currier of Plymouth.

CHILDREN: William Hammond, b. Sept. 3, 1863; Geneva Ardella, b. Mar. 12, 1867; Chester Stillman, b. Mar. 15, 1872; Mina Maud, b. Oct. 14, 1881.

507 WILLIAM HAMMOND[8] MOSES, son of THADDEUS STILLMAN (506), was for several years in business with his father; was Town Treasurer of Meredith for one year, and Chairman of the Board of Education for several years. In 1890 he started in the woolen business at Tilton, N. H., and is now President and Treasurer of the Tilton Mills, manufacturers of fancy cassimeres, tweeds, cheviots, and dress goods. He is also President and Treas. of the Tilton Electric Co.; Treas. of the Aqueduct Co.; Director in the Manchester, N. H., National Bank; and in the Concord and Montreal R. R.; is Trustee of the Lona Savings Bank of Tilton; of the Park Cemetery Assn., and of the Tilton Seminary. He is also a Member of the Democratic State Committee of N. H. He m. June 11, 1890, Mabel T., dau. of Alpha J. Pillsbury.

CHILDREN: Hazel Pillsbury, b. Oct. 2, 1893; Marjorie, b. May 22, 1897.

508 GENEVA ARDELLA[8] MOSES, dau. of THADDEUS STILLMAN (506), m. Oct. 19, 1889, Frederick L. Hawkins, M.D. They reside at Meredith.

CHILDREN: Helen Emily, b. Mar. 5, 1891; Ruth Charlotte, b. Sept. 9, 1893; Marguerite, b. July 22, 1896; Frederick Lewis, b. Aug. 14, 1898, d. Apr. 14, 1900.

509 ROBERT S.[7] MOSES, son of WILLIAM (505), resides at Meredith, N. H.; m. Sept. 1867, Sarah F. Mills.

CHILDREN: Hattie E., b. July 5, 1868; Flora B., b. Oct. 4, 1873; Millie M., b. Jan. 30, 1883.

510 LYDIA A.[7] MOSES, dau. of WILLIAM (505), m. Apr. 17, 1867, William R. Kimball, and resides at Plymouth, N. H.

CHILDREN: Edith A., b. Oct. 8, 1869; Addie O., b. July 9, 1871; William A., b. July 14, 1876.

511 EDWARD[7] MOSES, son of LEVI (p. 107); particulars concerning him and his descendants have been furnished writer by Mrs. Lucy J. Moses of Brooklyn, N. Y. He was b. Oct. 27, 1813, d. May 18, 1864, entered Navy in 1861, as Acting Master, was in command of the Ship *"Fernandina"* at the time of his death. He m. Sept. 25, 1844, Elizabeth A. Mills, in New York City.

CHILDREN: Augusta M., b. July 28, 1845; Edward Frost, b. Jan. 25, 1847, d. at Fall Brook, Cal., Sept. 3, 1893; Harry Wolf, b. Jan. 8, 1849, d. Dec. 30, 1869; Sarah Elizabeth, b. Mar. 12, 1851.

Augusta M., m. Willard Arnaud, of Boston, Mass.

Harry Wolf, was drowned with all on board the Ship *"Santee,"* at Skipperen Bay, South coast of Ireland.

Sarah Elizabeth, m. James Hillis, New York City.

512 EDWARD FROST[8] MOSES, son of EDWARD (511), was an architect and building contractor of Portsmouth, N. H.; m. July 6, 1871, Lucy Jean Fish.

CHILDREN: Mabel Gertrude, b. Nov. 9, 1872, (now Mrs. W. G. Gove of Brooklyn, N. Y.); Frances L., b. Dec. 20, 1878, d. Feb. 17, 1880.

513 ISABEL[7] MOSES, dau. of DAVID BOYNTON MOSES (page 113), m. Duplessis M. Helm, who d. Dec. 30, 1889. She now resides at Ossining, formerly Sing Sing, N. Y.

CHILDREN: David Boynton, b. Aug. 21, 1872; Jeanette I., b. Apr. 5, 1876; Florence A., b. Aug. 5, 1878; William Lloyd, b. Nov. 19, 1887.

514 JOSEPH[5] MOSES, son of SAMUEL (404). The parentage of Joseph is conclusively proved: William Moses, born 1835, of Tracy, Minn., gives Samuel as the father of Joseph: Joseph Moses of Northfield, Minn., states concerning his grandfather: "There was a Theodore Moses, hatter, at Exeter, N. H., a brother of Joseph, who was also a hatter, and who was one of the first settlers of Harmony, Me. His wife named the town of Harmony on account of the peace and harmony in it." The brothers, Theodore of Exeter and Joseph of Harmony, both found their wives in Stratham, N. H.; the Rev. Theodore, son of Joseph, spent the close of his life in Exeter, near his uncle Theodore, and the relationship was acknowledged. Fortunately most desirable data as to the family of Joseph has been furnished from the Town Records of Harmony, Me.: Joseph Moses was b. in Portsmouth, N. H., April 17, 1776; Martha Moses, wife of Joseph Moses, was b. in Stratham, N. H., Jan. 4, 1775.

CHILDREN: Joseph and Benjamin d. at birth, Dec., 1800; John Wiggin, b. Feb. 20, 1802; Joseph, b. Apr. 16, 1804; Nancy, b. Jan. 30, 1806; Martha Jane, b. June 30, 1808; Benjamin Shepard, b. Sept. 14, 1810, d. Dec. 28, 1903; Theodore, b. Nov. 18, 1812; Arvilla and Lavina (twins), b. Nov. 21, 1814; Arvilla d. Apr. 7, 1836; Samuel Newell, b. Feb. 11, 1817, d. Dec. 27, 1821.

515 BENJAMIN SHEPHERD[6] MOSES, son of JOSEPH (514), resided in Wellington, Me., Guilford, Me., Monson, Me., and Tracy, Minn.; m. Dec. 15, 1833, Sarah Herring, b. at Guilford, Me., July 6, 1811, d. Nov. 18, 1901.

CHILDREN: William Shepherd, b. July 8, 1835; Marilla, b. Sept. 23, 1836, d. Jan. 20, 1905; Webster W., b. Oct. 9, 1838; Leonard H., b. Mar. 27, 1840, d. at Fayette, Wis., Jan. 12, 1864; Maria L., b. Dec. 10, 1841; James G. B., b. Nov. 2, 1843; Charles T., b. Aug. 5, 1846; Lucy E., b. Aug. 17, 1847, d. Dec. 26, 1895; Hiram Stacey, b. May 27, 1851.

Maria L., m. Sept. 2, 1863, Edwin R. Harkness; *Children:* Amelia, b. June 18, 1864, at Zumbretta, Minn., m. James M. Clark.

516 WILLIAM SHEPHERD[7] MOSES, son of BENJAMIN SHEPHERD (515) was a soldier in the Civil War in Minn. Reg.; resided at Deerfield, Minn.; m. 1st, Nov. 22, 1866, Mary E. Chapin, she died at Morristown, Minn., May 7, 1877; m. 2d, Nov. 22, 1877, Anna E. Evans.

CHILDREN: Webster C., b. Aug. 9, 1867; Flora, b. Nov. 17, 1868, d. Jan. 4, 1897; Minnie, b. June 17, 1870, d. June 12, 1881; Edward, b. Jan. 12, 1872, d. June 12, 1881; Abbie, b. Jan. 31, 1874; Jasper, b. June 11, 1875, d. June 9, 1881; Mary, b. Apr. 17, 1877, d. Sept. 22, 1877.

Webster C., m. Nov. 17, 1896, Dora Christenson; *Children:* Homer A. Moses, b. Sept. 13, 1902.

Abbie. m. June 26, 1901, William Whisler of Williams, Iowa; *Children:* Hazel, b. July 20, 1902; William Moses, b. Feb. 12, 1904; Blanche, b. July 16, 1905.

517 MARILLA[8] MOSES, dau. of WILLIAM SHEPHERD (516), m. Sept. 15, 1857, George Sook of Deerfield and Rockford, Minn.

CHILDREN: Sarah M., b. Nov. 5, 1861, d. Oct. 4, 1864; Della M., b. Sept. 16, 1863, d. Apr. 19, 1896; Emery S., b. Apr. 4, 1867; George Webster, b. Apr. 26, 1869, Alvin M., b. Dec. 23, 1871, d. Apr. 9, 1897; Robert H., b. July 29, 1873, d. May 8, 1875.

Della M., m. May 31, 1894, Charles M. Nowland: *Children:* Rosalia M., b. Jan. 15, 1895; Adelbert M., b. Mar. 24, 1896; Pearl, b. Mar. 24, 1896, d. Apr. 19, 1896; Sarah V., b. Nov. 11, 1900; Henry Clay, b. May 6, 1904.

518 WEBSTER W.[8] MOSES, son of WILLIAM SHEPHERD (516), was a soldier in the Civil War, enlisted in Ill. Reg., but his Co. was a part of famous Kansas "Jayhawkers" Reg.; resided at Bureau, Ill., Rochester, Minn., and Tracy, Minn.; m. Mar. 19, 1865, Nancy Mowry.

CHILDREN: Edwin Ralph, b. Sept. 26. 1866, d. Sept. 29, 1866; Eugene Willifred, b. Oct. 10, 1867; Amelia Lois, b. Dec. 9, 1869, d. May 29, 1880; Jessie Mae, b. Nov. 5, 1875; Robert Shepherd, b. Apr. 16, 1878, d. June 1, 1880; Webster Lloyd, b. Feb. 11, 1881; Francis Willard, b. Sept. 4, 1890.

Jessie Mae, m. Sept. 7, 1897, M. G. R. Donaldson; *Children:* Dale Moses, b. Oct. 4, 1899; Mary Doris, b. Jan. 30, 1901; Ruby Mae, b. Dec. 13, 1902; Lawren Russell, b. May 13, 1903; Jessie Rosamond, b. Feb. 24, 1906.

519 EUGENE WILFRED[9] MOSES, son of WEBSTER W. (518), resided in Windom, Slayton, and Tracy, Minn.; m. Sept. 17, 1889, Edith E. Greenfield.

CHILDREN: Lois Edith, b. Sept. 23, 1890; Mildred Jeanette, b. Mar. 27, 1893; Grace, b. Aug. 23, 1895; Clarence Eugene, b. Mar. 20, 1897; Blanche Vivian, b. May 27, 1901; Robert, b. Dec. 29, 1902, d. Jan. 18, 1904.

520 WEBSTER LLOYD[9] MOSES, son of WEBSTER W. (518), resides at Tracy, Minn.; m. June 29, 1904, Lucile May Ingham.

CHILDREN: Gerald Eugene, b. Dec. 22, 1905.

521 LEONARD HATHAWAY[8] MOSES, son of WILLIAM SHEPHERD (576), is now living at Northfield, Minn. He was a soldier of the 37th Wis. Inf. in 1864, serving fourteen months until the close of the War. His college course interrupted, he later took part of the course at Wheaton College and a two-years' course at Seabury Divinity School. For twenty-five years he was pastor at various Congregational Churches in Minn. and Ill. His insistance sent all of his children to Carleton College in Minnesota, where all but two graduated. He m. 1st, Mar., 1862, Almeda Cook, who d. Jan. 12, 1864; m. 2d, Oct. 29, 1865, Urena J. Denison.

CHILDREN: Lura M., b. June 10, 1863, d. Jan. 10, 1894;

Albert Curtiss, b. Faribault, Minn., Sept. 23, 1866; Lurton D., b. Apr. 7, 1870, d. Aug. 10, 1899: Nina Leona, b Faribault, Dec. 7, 1874; Elva Urena, b. Rose Creek, Minn., Mar. 4, 1880; Elliott Leonard, b. Mar. 4, 1880.

Lura M., left Carleton College before graduation, and m. Nov. 30, 1889, George W. Brown. *Children:* Harold P., b. Jan. 12, 1893, at Villard, Minn

522 ALBERT CURTISS[9] MOSES, son of Rev. LEONARD HATHAWAY (521), graduated 1889, A.B. from Carleton College, Northfield, Minn., and in 1892, B.A. from the Chicago Theological Seminary, his alma mater the same year conferring on him the degree of Master of Arts. He is life president of his Seminary Class. Between 1892 and 1903 he filled the pastorates of Congregational Churches at Shopiere, Wis., Byron, Ill., and Harvey, Ill., and the latter year he entered Yale University, devoting one year to the study of sociology and the modern labor movement. While at Yale he acquired the degree of M.A. In 1894 he became the pastor of the Green Street Congregational Church, Chicago, Ill. He m. Dec. 23, 1891, Julia E. Kellogg, b. at Minerva, N. Y.

523 LURTON D.[9] MOSES, son of Rev. LEONARD HATHAWAY (521), left Carleton College at the close of the junior year to enter business. He m. Oct. 28, 1891, Adele M. Downing.

CHILDREN: Laila Floris, b June 1, 1892; Curtis, b. May 8, 1895; Helen Leona, b at Northfield, Minn., July 12, 1898.

524 NINA L.[9] MOSES, dau of Rev. LEONARD HATHAWAY (521), graduated at Carleton College; m. June 14, 1900, Marion Leroy Burton; for three years Principal of Windom Institute, Montevideo, Minn.; is (1906), completing his term at the Yale Divinity School.

CHILDREN: Theodosia, b. Aug. 4, 1901; Paul Leonard, b. Nov. 1, 1905.

525 ELVA URENA[9] MOSES, dau. of Rev. LEONARD HATHAWAY (521), graduated at Carleton College; m. Aug. 18, 1904, Howard W. Brubaker, who holds the degree of Ph.D. of the University of Penn. and is now a professor in the Whitman College, Walla Walla, Wash.

CHILDREN: Leonard H, b. Dec. 20, 1905.

526 ELLIOT LEONARD[9] MOSES, son of Rev. LEONARD HATHAWAY (521), is a graduate of Carleton College, and of Hartford, Conn., Seminary; he is pastor of the Middleton, Mass.,

Cong. Church; m. Aug. 1, 1906, at Medford, Mass., Harriet Norma Roberts.

527 JAMES G. B.[7] MOSES, son of BENJAMIN SHEPHERD (515), was a soldier in the Civil War, in a Minn. Reg.; has resided at Owatonna, and Jackson, Minn.; m. Nov. 7, 1871, Lavinia H. Martin.

CHILDREN: Bertrand A., b. Mar. 14, 1874; Gertrude M., b. Jan. 18, 1876; Millie M., b. Dec. 25, 1878; Ernest B., b. Jan. 25, 1881; Cora L., b. Nov. 19, 1885; Roy R., b. Oct. 18, 1889; Gaylord M., b. Aug. 24, 1896

Gertrude M., m. May 30, 1895, Arthur E. Greenfield; *Children:* Gerald, b. June, 1897; Mildred, b. Jan. 4, 1904.

Millie M., m. Mar. 30, 1900, Peter Thomson; *Children:* Roy, b Feb. 8, 1901; Earl. b. Apr. 4, 1903

Cora L., m. July 16, 1902, William Plum; *Children:* Bannon, b. Feb. 3, 1903; Alva, b. Oct. 13, 1904.

Ernest B., m. Jan. 8, 1902, Bertha R. Erickson; *Children:* Lillian, b. Dec. 21, 1902.

Bertrand A., of Fairmount and Jackson, Minn., m. Oct. 9, 1894, Ada E. Thompson. *Children:* Howard L., b. Feb. 22, 1896; Hazel L. E., b. Sept. 1, 1897.

528 CHARLES TORREY[7] MOSES, son of BENJAMIN SHEPHERD (515), was a soldier in the Civil War in Minn. Reg.; resided at Warsaw, Minn., and Jonesboro, Ind.; m. 1st, Nov. 26, 1872, Esther Durham; m. 2d, May 1, 1890, Susie Spencer.

CHILDREN: Edith, b. Feb. 3, 1874; Walter, b Oct. 12, 1875; Mattie L, b. Sept. 18, 1877; Hazel Ella, b. Apr. 22, 1893, d. June 4, 1893.

529 LUCY E.[7] MOSES, dau. of BENJAMIN SHEPHERD (515), m. Nov. 29, 1868, John M. Wardell, of Faribault, and Tracy, Minn.

CHILDREN: William John, b. June 19, 1870, d. Dec. 20, 1877; Frederick J., b. Dec. 19, 1871, d. Mar., 1881; Samuel Truman, b. Feb. 8, 1873; Ezra Steele, b. Aug. 29, 1874; Florence, b. Sept. 25, 1876; John M., b. June 25, 1880; Eva Bessie, b. Dec. 17, 1883.

530 HIRAM STACY[7] MOSES, son of BENJAMIN SHEPHERD (515), resided at Tracy, Minn., m. Sept. 30, 1874, Alice E. Youngs.

CHILDREN: Hiram C., b. Dec. 14, 1878, d. Mar. 27, 1880; Mabel Grace, b. June 2, 1882; Minnie Mae, b. Mar. 23, 1887.

Mabel Grace, m. Oct. 1904, John Hopping.

Minnie Mae, m. Aug. 30, 1905, Albert Johnson.

531 THEODORE[6] MOSES, son of JOSEPH (514), was a Free Will Baptist minister; removed from Harmony, Me., and officiated at different towns in New Hampshire, residing finally at Exeter, N. H., the home of his Uncle Theodore. He m. (Vital Records of N. H.), Jan. 19, 1840, Abigail G. Colcord of Exeter. As a widow, she was for many years a member of the Baptist Church of Exeter, and it appears probable that the Rev. Theodore died there.

CHILDREN: Howard M., b. 1841, at Harmony, Me.; Theodore; Mary.

Howard M., was a soldier in the Civil War in the Company of his second cousin, Capt. George N. Julian, of Exeter (see Moses Soldier List).

W. E. Moses, of Northfield, Minn., reports that Howard and his brother, Theodore, were lately living about nine miles from Minneapolis, Minn.

Mary, m. and resided at Malden, Mass.

532 JOSEPH[6] MOSES, son of JOSEPH (514), d. in Maine; m. ——.

CHILDREN: Elias, b. Apr. 3, 1828, d. in California, 1898; Henry, b. 1836; Joseph, b. Mar. 14, 1833; Martha, b. 1842; Mary Elizabeth, b. 1846, d. 1889.

Elias, was a very successful banker of Minneapolis, Minn., and also was largely interested in lumbering. He had three children; all dead; m. Lydia Cobb; one son, Herbert, b. 1859, d. 1865.

Henry, lives in Pasadena, California; m. 1869, Martha Balch. Children: Helen; Maud.

Martha, lives in California; m. Royal Plummer in 1870.

Mary Elizabeth, m. W. Neil in 1866, and resided in California.

533 JOSEPH[7] MOSES, son of JOSEPH (532), resided at Northfield, Minn.; is a lumberman; m. 1858 at Shelbyville, Ill., Mary Tolly.

CHILDREN: John Henry, b. Apr. 10, 1857; d. Dec. 14, 1876; William Elias, b. Jan. 15, 1860; Edward B., b. 1863, d. 1865; Royal H., b. 1883; Joseph, b. 1888.

Royal H., is a graduate of Carleton College, Minn.: m. 1906, Daisy Kelly.

534 WILLIAM ELIAS[8] MOSES, son of JOSEPH (533), is a lumberman and merchant at Northfield, Minn.; m. Mar. 12, 1890, Elizabeth Gress.

CHILDREN: Herbert W., b. Dec. 15, 1890; Donald F., b. Mar. 12, 1894; Mary Elizabeth, b. Oct. 14, 1898.

535 JOHN WIGGIN[6] MOSES, son of JOSEPH (514), resided at Wellington, Me., m. Sarah, dau. of Ichabod Goodwin. She was b. Sept. 3, 1803, d. at Stetson, Me., Jan. 19, 1864. The names of children come from different sources. There may not be as many but all are given.

CHILDREN: John W., Jr., b. in Harmony, Me., 1828, d. 1891; Cyrus, b. 1830, d. 1899; Colby, b. 1836; Newell, b. 1838; Joel, b. 1837, d. 1898; Freeman, b. 1840; Bradford; Oliver; Elvira; Sarah.

Newell, resides in Hutchinson, Minn.
Bradford, has three daughters.
Oliver, resides in Wellington, Me., on the old homestead.
Freeman, resides in Athens, Me.
Joel, m. Julia, dau. of Joseph Parsons, of Marshfield, Mass.

536 COLBY^7 MOSES, son of JOHN WIGGIN (535), is a hotel keeper at Minneapolis.

CHILDREN: Elmer, b. 1851 (resides at Minneapolis), Sadie, b. 1868 (m. to Harry Leigh).

537 CYRUS^7 MOSES, son of JOHN WIGGIN (535), was a contractor, Minneapolis.

CHILDREN: Flora, b. 1860; Della, b. 1868 (now Mrs. Williams); Grace, b. 1870.

538 JOHN W.^{7} MOSES, son of JOHN WIGGIN (535), resided in Corrunna, Me.

CHILDREN: Addie, b. 1860; Isa John, b. 1864.
Addie, m. Frank Folsom, of Anoka, Minn. *Children:* Chester; Lillian.

539 ISA JOHN^8 MOSES, is a hotel keeper at Herman, Minn., m. June 15, 1885, ―――.

CHILDREN: Berenice Chester, b. May 13, 1886; George Freeman, b. Mar. 12, 1888; Joyce R., b. Jan. 3, 1891; Addie R., b. Oct. 31, 1895.

ADDITIONS AND CORRECTIONS.

PAGE 105. MARTHA^4 MOSES, m. 1st, Daniel Lang of Portsmouth:
CHILDREN: Daniel; Moses; Catherine; Martha; Sarah.
For 2d marriage see p. 105.

PAGE 106. LEONARD^7 MOSES, m. May 28, 1837, Caroline Frost.

PAGE 106. AARON^7 MOSES, (son of AARON,) m. Sept. 29, 1831, Jane Frost.

PAGE 106. ELVIRA^7 MOSES, m. Mar. 30, 1856, Nathaniel Pond of Wakefield, N. H.

PAGE 106. SAMUEL W.^{7} MOSES, d. June 16, 1882.

PAGE 106. MARTHA J.^{7} MOSES, d. Oct. 20, 1890.

PAGE 106. JAMES^7 MOSES, son of JAMES, d. Apr. 4, 1887.

PAGE 106. WILLIAM[7] MOSES, d. Jan. 11, 1892.

PAGE 107. ANGELIA STREETER[7] MOSES, m. Jan. 4, 1830, Benjamin Carr of Salem, Mass.

PAGE 110. SALLIE T. COCHRAN, d. Sept. 24, 1901.

PAGE 110. ELIZABETH (SHERBURNE) MOSES, d. Nov. 3, 1826.

PAGE 110. BETSEY S. MOSES, d. April 28, 1869.

PAGE 110. SARAH MOSES, d. April 1771.

PAGE 110. BETSEY (CATE) MOSES, d. Aug. 29, 1848.

PAGE 110. ELIJAH MOSES, d. Jan. 1829, at Epsom, N. H.

PAGE 111. BETSEY[5] MOSES. In list of children, insert comma after Sarah, to read Sarah, *and* Jane.

PAGE 111. MARY[5] MOSES, dau. of JAMES, m. James (not John) Morrison.

PAGE 111. AARON[6] MOSES, (son of AARON,) went to Vermont.

PAGE 112. DAVID BOYNTON[6] MOSES, d. Sept. 17, 1893.

PAGE 112. WILLIAM[6] MOSES, d. Feb. 24, 1896, at Brooklyn, N. Y.

PAGE 113. HIRAM W.[6] MOSES, d. Dec. 22, 1893; had a son George W. Moses, b. Feb. 21, 1836, d. Jan. 21, 1841.

PAGE 113. ISADORA[8] MOSES, m. 1st, Alvah S. Rand, Oct. 4, 1883; m. 2d, Walter L. Clough, Jan. 12, 1895.

PAGE 113. WILLIAM WARREN[8] MOSES, m. July 4, 1898.

PAGE 113. SUSAN RANLET[8] MOSES, b. Feb. 2, 1878, m. July 23, 1902, John W. Pearl, of Worcester, Mass.

The Scarborough Maine group of the Moses Family which follows has been compiled by Howard N. Moses, M.D. of Salina, Kansas, to whom I am indebted for his great interest in this section of the book.

600 GEORGE[4] MOSES, son of JOSIAH (402), was the founder of the Maine or Scarborough group of the family, and the discovery by Mr. J. M. Moses of the deed records, which prove it, adds more than one hundred years of American lineage to all of the said group. Records of deeds Vols. 30, 39, 40, 49, and 64 recite that: "Josiah Moses, tanner, wife Abigail, and George Moses, cordwainer, " owned two small lots on Islington Creek, Portsmouth. They mortgage and redeem these lots. George finally owning one of them. On Oct. 4, 1754, "George Moses of Scarborough, York Co., Mass., cordwainer, and wife Frances," convey the other lot and the house in which Josiah then lived. George Moses removed from Portsmouth and settled on a farm owned by Joseph Prout on Scottow's Hill, Scarbough, Maine (then Mass.), in 1754. Scottow's Hill was a land mark and was used in the early surveys, it is but a short distance from the sea, and from the site of the original Moses home, vessels may be seen passing to and from the harbor.

CHILDREN: In the North Parish records of *Portsmouth* are found the following baptismal dates (not birth dates). It is presumed that children were baptized at ages to suit the convenience of parents. The records read as follows: "Mar. 22, 1747, bap. George son of George; On Apr. 16, 1749, bap. child of George; On Feb. 3, 1750-51, bap. Ann, dau. of George; On July 12, 1752 or 3, bap. a child of George; On Oct. 15, 1775, bap. Nathaniel, son of George. "At *Scarborough*, the record of George's children has been handed down as: Mary; Sarah; George; Anna; Katherine; Daniel (Dunstan, Scar. Ch. Rec.), bap. June 30, 1754, d. Feb. 8, 1824; Josiah, bap. (Dunstan Ch. Rec.), June 27, 1756, d. May 19, 1839; Nathaniel, b. Oct. 13, 1758, d. about 1840. (An error of a year in birth dates, or the duplication of the name of a dead child is not unusual in old records.)

From Second Cong. Ch. Rec., Scarborough, (among others) find:
Mary, m. Mar. 12, 1767, Thomas Babb.
Sarah, m. Sept. 28, 1769, Samuel Waterhouse.
Anna, m. Jan. 20, 1774, James Harmon.
Katherine, m. July 6, 1777, John Milliken.

601 GEORGE[5] MOSES, son of GEORGE (600), Private in Revolution (see Moses Soldier Record). He m. (2d Cong. Ch., Scar.) Aug. 27, 1772, Anna Harmon.

CHILDREN: William (Bible Rec.), b. Dec. 29, 1772, d. Sept. 29, 1829; John (Dunstan Ch. Rec.), bap. Dec. 9, 1787; Anne; Abigail, Aphia; Josiah, d. young; (Dunstan Ch. Rec.) says a dau. Nabby, bap. Dec. 7, 1788.
Anna, m. (1st) David Fenderson; (2d) —— Moulton.
Abigail, m. Jacob Whitney.
Aphia, m. May 6, 1817, Phineas Rice.

602 DANIEL[5] MOSES, son of GEORGE (600), Sergeant in Revolution, (see Moses Soldier Record). He m. (2d Cong. Ch., Scar.) Jan. 23, 1777, Lydia Coolbroth (she bap. Apr. 12, 1777). Resided Windham, Maine.

CHILDREN: (Births from Scar. Town Rec.), Daniel, b. Sept. 29, 1777; Sarah, b. Oct. 25, 1780; Lorane, b. July 23, 1782, d. Sept. 11, 1839; James, b. July 21, 1785; Abigail, b. Jan. 10, 1787; Martha, b. Mar. 5, 1789, d. about 1875; James, b. Mar. 17, 1791; Elizabeth, b. Feb. 28, 1793; Lavina, b. Sept. 1, 1795; Eunice, b. Nov. 17, 1798.

Lorane, m. Aug. 28, 1808, Nathaniel Libby, (he d. Apr. 22, 1826) of

Scarborough as his 2d wife. *Children:* Edward; Freeman; Mary; David; Sally; Ansel.

Martha, m. John Libby, (he b. Nov. 7, 1791, d. June 1842,) his third wife. CHILDREN: Edmund; Abigail.

603 JOSIAH[5] MOSES son of GEORGE (600), Private in Revolution (see Moses Soldier Record). He m. (1st), (1st. Cong. Ch. Rec.) July 1, 1779, Sarah Ringe; (2d) Oct. 4, 1787, Elizabeth (Harmon) Libby, wid. of Daniel Libby of Scarborough, (she b. 1759, d. Dec. 18, 1835). Resided Standish, Maine.

CHILDREN: Sarah, b. Sept. 13, 1788; Daniel, d. Aug., 1828; Josiah, b. Aug., 1799, d. Feb. 22, 1860; William, d. July 19, 1828; Mehitable, d. May 9, 1861.

Sarah, m. Deacon William Cummings (he b. June 20, 1777). *Children:* Esther; Catharine; Simon; Lucy; Abbie; Esther; Moses.

Mehitable, m. May 22, 1823, Joseph Libby (he b. 1795). *Children:* Marshall; Sarah; William; Jane; Mary; Martha.

Daniel and William met death by an explosion in a powder mill at Gambo. Daniel made an effort to save his brother, received injuries which resulted in his death several weeks later.

604 NATHANIEL[5] MOSES, son of GEORGE (600), Private in Revolution (see Moses Soldier Record). A local antiquarian writes: "Uncle Nat" lived to be very old and he used to amuse the old timers with descriptions of his share in the unfortunate Bagaduce (Penobscot, 1779) expedition, how they swam the rivers and slept in the trees to save themselves from being eaten by the bears and wolves. He m. (2d Cong. Ch. Rec.) Nov. 28, 1782, Elizabeth, dau. of Edward Milliken (she b. Sept. 10, 1766, d. Feb. 19, 1863), she was a sister of Ann who m. William (605). Resided in Scarborough on Scottow's Hill.

CHILDREN: (Births from Scar. Town Rec.) Rebecca, b. Dec. 19, 1783; Sally, b. Dec. 29, 1785, d. about 1864; Benjamin, b. Jan. 16, 1788; Elizabeth, b. Dec. 16, 1789, d. about 1874; Silas, b. Jan. 16, 1792; Rufus, b. June 28, 1795, d. Feb. 8, 1893; Hannah, b. Aug. 11, 1798; William Vaughan, b. Jan. 30, 1801, d. Dec. 15, 1878; Oliver, b. May 12, 1803, d. Feb. 11, 1882; Phebe, b. Jan. 25, 1807; Ebenezer, b. Aug. 10, 1809, d. Feb., 1879.

Rebecca, m. —— Fickett.
Sally, m. Simeon Nash.
Elizabeth, m. John Strout.
Hannah, m. —— Nash, Raymond, Maine.
Phebe, m. —— Nash, Raymond, Maine.

605 WILLIAM[6] MOSES, son of GEORGE (601), resided Scarborough and Buxton, Maine, removed to Eaton, N. H., 1822. He m. Jan. 31, 1796, Anne Milliken, (she b. Dec. 31, 1774, d. July 30, 1856,) she later m. Samuel Berry, Buxton, Me.

CHILDREN (Bible): Cyrus, b. Sept. 2, 1796, d. Feb. 11, 1885; Abraham, b. Dec. 6, 1798, d. Oct. 27, 1800; Frances, b. Jan. 24, 1801, d. June 13, 1870; William, b. June 14, 1804, d. Aug. 7, 1880; George, b. Nov. 4, 1806, d. June 30, 1899; Mary Fenderson, b. May 10, 1809, d. Sept. 12, 1901; Horace, b. Aug. 17, 1811, d. Apr. 26, 1880; Edward, b. Feb. 9, 1814, d. Nov. 29, 1905; Eliza Ann, b. Jan. 30, 1817, d. Mar. 26, 1902.

Frances, m. about 1820, 1st, Tristram Ayer, Saco, Me. (he b. Feb. 19, 1799, d. about 1864); 2d, Samuel Came, Buxton, Me. (he b. Feb. 15, 1798, d. Mar. 29, 1870). *Children:* Mary A.; William; Sarah E.; John L.; Maria G.; Lyman G.; Frances J.; Charles H.

Mary Fenderson, m. 1st, James Huntress, Effingham, N. H.; 2d, 1860; Nathaniel Cross Thurston, Freedom, N. H. (he b. May 16, 1820, d. Nov. 26, 1875).

Eliza Ann, m. William Berry, Buxton, Me. (he son of Samuel Berry who m. as his last wife Mrs. Ann Milliken Moses). *Children:* Edward; Orrin Mansel; Freedom; Frederick; Jenny.

606 JOHN[6] MOSES, son of GEORGE (601), lived on the old homestead Scarborough. He m. Aug. 20, 1809, Olive (Harmon) Milliken (she d. July 7, 1872).

CHILDREN: Ann, b. Dec. 17, 1810, d. Mar. 31, 1826; Alice, b. Dec. 17, 1810, d. Feb. 24, 1816; Bethsheba, b. Feb., 1813; Miranda, b. Mar. 20, 1820, d. Dec. 1, 1832.

Bethsheba, m. David Meserve, lived on homestead.

607 CYRUS[7] MOSES, son of WILLIAM (605), farmer and shoemaker, resided at Eaton, Freedom, N. H., Parsonsfield, Saco, and Standish, Maine. He m. Mar. 20, 1819, Eunice Underwood (she b. Apr. 2, 1798, d. June 23, 1891).

CHILDREN: Martha J., b. Jan. 22, 1820, d. Feb., 1905; Abram, b. Mar. 24, 1821, d. Sept. 2, 1905; Tryphena, b. Dec. 9, 1822, d. Dec. 19, 1862; David W., b. Dec. 18, 1824, d. infancy-cholera; John, b. May 7, 1826, d. young; Thomas Gannett, b. Mar. 7, 1829; William C., b. Mar. 20, 1831; Eliza Ann, b. Nov. 18, 1832, d. Aug. 20, 1887; Alonzo, b. Feb. 5, 1836.

Martha J., m. Dec. 10, 1842, James Benson, Parsonsfield, Me. Resided Wakefield, N. H.

Tryphena, m. 1850, Maj. Josiah Libby (he b. Oct. 17, 1825). *Children:* Alphanzo; Nettie; Mary; Clarence; William D.

Eliza Ann, m. May 1, 1853, John H. Larkin, Bangor, Me. Resided Limington, Maine.

608 WILLIAM[7] MOSES, son of WILLIAM (605), farmer, lived on old Berry farm, Beech Ridge, Scarborough. He was always known as "Captain Moses," having held that position and later Colonel in the Maine State Militia. He m. 1st, Mary L. Berry (she b. 1807, d. Nov. 26, 1829); 2d, June 1st, 1831, Adeline, dau. of Daniel Harmon, Scarborough (she b. 1804, d. Oct. 13, 1841); 3d, July 31, 1843, Ann Berry, sister of Mary the first wife (she b. 1817, d. Mar. 10, 1876).

CHILDREN: Joseph Almond, b. Dec. 10, 1828, d. Sept. 13, 1882; John Francis, b. Mar. 27, 1832, d. Sept. 20, 1899; Mary Berry, b. Oct. 27, 1835, d. Aug. 13, 1890; William Austin, b. Apr. 10, 1838, d. Jan. 22, 1884; Horace Wilson, b. Oct. 15, 1839.

Mary Berry, m. Mar. 10, 1862, Frank Wilson Butler, North Scarborough, Me. *Children:* George W.; Annie L.; William F.; Rose H.; Horace F.; Eugene B.; Perley C.

609 GEORGE[7] MOSES son of WILLIAM (605), farmer, lived at Freedom, N. H. To Uncle George, the compiler owes much of the early family history. His father's Bible records, in his possession, have entered largely into the writing of the Scarborough branch. He m. Feb. 11, 1830, Elizabeth Wilkinson, Eaton, N. H. (she b. Sept. 1, 1808, d. Sept. 15, 1876).

CHILDREN: Anne E., b. May 14, 1831; Mary J., b. Oct. 31, 1834; William Ransaellar, b. Aug. 21, 1840; Rosanna Frances, b. Sept. 16, 1843; Wesley George, b. Sept. 16, 1845; Olen Edward, b. Aug. 19, 1849, d. June 28, 1904.

Anne E., m. Jan. 1, 1855, Job Allard (he d. Apr. 24, 1859); 2d, Jan. 24, 1875, Charles Beach (he d. May 24, 1903), resides Freedom, N. H. *Children:* Loren J.; George Wesley; Alta Ann; Fred Russell; Arthur Maynard.

Mary J., m. Oct. 7, 1860, Alonzo Pease, Freedom, N. H. *Children:* Albion B.; Bessie M.; Lewis.

Rosanna Frances, m. Sept. 1, 1867, Elisha S. Hayes, Charlestown, Mass. *Children:* Arthur B.; Wilber F.

610 HORACE[7] MOSES, son of WILLIAM (605), resided Eaton, N. H., Scarborough, Maine, and Freedom, N. H. He m. Nov. 17, 1834, Pelina Young (she b. June 8, 1816, d. Dec. 21, 1883).

CHILDREN: Edwin, b. Sept. 28, 1835; Isaac, b. June 27, 1839, d. Feb. 22, 1842; Adaline, b. May 5, 1841, d. Mar. 13, 1842; Mary A., b. Feb. 17, 1843; Alvira, b. Jan. 17, 1845, d. Apr. 9, 1861; William Isaac, b. Aug. 1, 1847, d. Sept. 2, 1899; Clarissa, b. Apr. 29, 1849; Eliza Frances, b. Feb. 11, 1856.

Mary A., m. June 30, 1861, John L. Sargent, Freedom, N. H.

Clarissa, m. July 1, 1874, Morris D. Stevens, Freedom, N. H. Resides Wolfboro, N. H.

Eliza Frances, m. Dec. 25, 1879, George D. Tyler, Freedom, N. H. *Children:* Charles Francis; resides Wolfboro, N. H.

611 EDWARD[7] MOSES, son of William (605). Soldier Seminole Indian War, 1835-6. Settled in Indiana, returned to Maine, was surveyor and bridge contractor, Scarborough, Me. Since 1899 resided at Melrose, Mass. He m. Nov. 29, 1837, Mary Ann Milliken, Scarborough (she d. June 6, 1902).

CHILDREN: Simon Milliken, b. 1840, d. Mar. 2, 1906; Edward Augustus, b. Aug. 9, 1843; James K. Polk, d. infancy; James Thomas, b. Sept. 19, 1849.

Edward Augustus, resides Melrose, Mass.

612 ABRAM[8] MOSES, son of CYRUS (607), resided Saco, Maine. He m. Dec. 3, 1842, Mary Ann Foss, Saco, Me. (she b. Jan. 31, 1823, d. Sept. 5, 1887).

CHILDREN: Georgia Ann, b. Aug. 23, 1844, d. Aug. 13, 1846; Mary Ann, b. May 19, 1847, d. June 18, 1871, Ellen Augusta, b. July 22, 1849, d. June 2, 1897; Charles Malcolm, b. Aug. 25, 1851; Cordelia Ada, b. May 31, 1859.

Mary Ann, m. Nov. 1868, James P. Barrows, resided Saco, Maine.

Ellen Augusta, m. Dec. 31, 1885, Edmond H. Shaw, resided Portland, Me.

Cordelia Ada, m. Apr. 12, 1883, Albion Boothby, resides Saco, Maine. *Child:* Adelia May.

613 THOMAS GANNETT[8] MOSES, son of CYRUS (607), educated at Thornton Academy. Resided at Standish, moved to Buxton about 1860. Licensed to preach by the York and Cumberland Christian Conference, Dec., 1862. Ordained at Kittery, Maine, June 15, 1863. Pastorates, Lubec, Eastport, Me., and Franklin, N. H. He was New England Missionary, residence Skowhegan, 1893-5. Pastor at York and Eastport, Me., until 1904, when he retired from active service. He m. (1st) Dec. 1, 1850, Ruth Sprague Smith, Standish, Me. (she b. Apr. 26, 1827, d. Jan. 6, 1878); (2d) June 6, 1880, Florence Della Higgins, Eastport, Me. (she b. Aug. 5, 1852).

CHILDREN: Luella Adelaide, b. June 15, 1852; Elbridge Franklin, b. May 28, 1853; Charles Thomas, b. Oct. 10, 1855; William Herbert, b. Sept. 8, 1858; John Winfield, b. Nov. 9, 1860; George Higgins, b. Feb. 9, 1869; Cyrus Arthur, b. June 17, 1889, d. Jan. 30, 1890.

Luella Adelaide, m. Oct. 7, 1883, Andus T. Capron.

614 WILLIAM C.[8] MOSES, son of CYRUS (607), mechanic,

resided Saco, later Buxton, Maine. He m. (1st) Eliza Milliken (she d. July 3, 1880); (2d) Apr. 16, 1883, Lucy (Townsend) Hall (she d. May 1893); (3d) Sept. 11, 1894, Ellen Buck.

CHILDREN: Lydia Frances, b. Dec. 7, 1854; Martha Jane, b. May 22, 1857, d. Oct. 12, 1874; Florence A., b. May 11, 1859; Hattie E., b. July 3, 1861, d. 1862; Willis H., b. Aug. 9, 1862; Linwood, b. Sept. 28, 1885.

Lydia Frances, m. (1st) William Harmon; (2d) Ernest Harmon.
Children: Jennie; Ethel.

Florence A., m. Jan. 15, 1881, Thomas Seavy, Saco, Me. *Children:* Walter L.; Mildred E.

Willis H., m. Bessie Fellows, residence New Jersey.

615 ALONZO[8] MOSES, son of CYRUS (607), resides old farm Standish, Me. Served in Civil War, m. Nov. 30, 1854, Hannah E. Burnham.

CHILDREN: Eva Ella, b. Feb. 2, 1855, d. Oct. 7, 1857; Orianna, b. Aug. 25, 1856; Ida E., b. May 25, 1858.

Orianna, m. Feb. 17, 1874, Charles F. Boulter, Standish, Me. *Children:* Bertha M.; Susie E.; Ella M.; Millard G.; Roy E.; Alton G., Percy R.; Pearl R.; William F.

Ida E., m. Eben S. Burnham, Limington, Me. *Children:* Alonzo E.; Hattie B.; G. Rudolph; Mildred E.

616 CHARLES MALCOLM[9] MOSES, son of ABRAM (612.) Collector of Customs, Portland, Maine. Resided Saco, now living in Portland. He m. Jan. 17, 1872, Lillian J. Deering, Saco, Me. (she b. Mar. 22, 1852).

CHILD: Catherine Miriam, who m. June 14, 1904, Paul S. Hill. Resides Washington, D. C. *Child:* Paul Stanley, b. Sept. 23, 1906.

617 ELBRIDGE FRANKLIN[9] MOSES, son of THOMAS GANNETT (613), clerk, Portland, Maine. He m. Oct. 30, 1887, Marian Fish.

CHILDREN: George, b. Dec. 1889; Inez.

618 CHARLES THOMAS[9] MOSES, son of THOMAS GANNETT (613), packing and canning, resided Portland, Eastport, and Corrina, Maine. He m. Etta Hinkley, Portland, Me.

CHILDREN: Maude Hinkley, b. Oct. 13, 1876; Ruth Smith, b. Feb. 7, 1878; Charles Thomas, b. Oct. 1881; Cora Bement, deceased; Luella Adelaide, b. 1885; George; Julius Tillotson, b. May 28, 1895.

Maude Hinkley, m. Oct. 12, 1904, Charles Ellis Jones, Newport, Me.

Ruth Smith, m. Dec. 31, 1902, John S. Williams, Newport, Me. *Children*: Lenore Moses; Ivan.

Luella Adelaide, m. Oct. 31, 1906, C. Russell Hutchins, Corrina, Me.

619 WILLIAM HERBERT[9] MOSES, son of THOMAS GANNETT (613), resides Eastport, Me. He married Lucy Lawrence.

CHILD: Marion.

620 JOHN WINFIELD[9] MOSES, son of THOMAS GANNETT (613), canner at Pittsfield, Maine. He m. Cora Bement, Dexter, Maine.

CHILDREN: John, who d. 1905; Frank; Alma; Warren; Walter.

621 GEORGE HIGGINS[9] MOSES, son THOMAS GANNETT (613), graduated from Phillips Exeter Academy 1887; Dartmouth College 1890. At different times since 1890 has been private secretary to the Governor of New Hampshire. Managing Editor and President of Company "CONCORD MONITOR AND STATESMAN." Author of

"JOHN STARK";
"NEW HAMPSHIRE MEN."

He m. Oct. 3, 1893, Florence Abby Gordon (she b. May 11, 1870), Franklin, N. H.

CHILD: Gordon, b. Oct. 5, 1900.

622 CHARLES THOMAS[10] MOSES, son of CHARLES THOMAS (618), canner at Corrina, Maine. He m. June 3, 1906, Mollie Knowles, Corrina, Me.

623 JOSEPH ALMOND[8] MOSES, son of WILLIAM (608), served in Civil War, merchant in Portland, Maine. He m. Dec. 1, 1860, Clara Knapp, Standish, Me. (she b. Dec. 3, 1839).

CHILD: Alice Clara, b. June 1, 1868, m. Nov. 23, 1898, Richmond Wheeler, Oakland, Cal. Resides Salinas, Cal.

624 JOHN FRANCIS[8] MOSES, son of WILLIAM (608), farmer Scarborough, Maine. Lumbering at Hudson, Wis. Settled at Elmsville, New Brunswick, later Calais and Old Orchard, Maine. He m. July 13, 1858, Helen C. Dyer, Elmsville, N. B., at Hudson, Wis. (she b. May 7, 1835, d. Jan. 28, 1900).

CHILDREN: Effie Adeline, b. Apr. 1, 1859; Horace William, b. Aug. 26, 1860; Frank Lafayette, b. July 26, 1862; Evelyn Jane, b. Jan. 26, 1864; Howard Milton, b. Sept. 12, 1865, d. May 2, 1866; Ina Helen, b. Aug. 6, 1867; Prentice Dyer Grant, b. May 20, 1869; Jessie Edna, b. Oct. 29, 1871, d. July 11, 1903; Willard Washington, b. Feb. 14; 1874; Mildred May, b. Apr. 7, 1876.

Effie Adeline, m. Feb. 28, 1881, Alvin F. Jordan, Cape Elizabeth, Me.

Resides Portland, Me. *Children:* Chester Arthur; Frank Lawrence; Carrie Edna; Harold Clayton; Gladys Alma.

Evelyn Jane, m. Jan. 26, 1898, Edwin B. Carter, West Scarborough Me.

Children: Lawrence Weston; Helen Dorcas; Mildred Evelyn; Benjamin Edwin.

Ina Helen, educated Woman's College, Baltimore, Missionary to Peru, South America, m. June 14, 1900, Rev. Thomas A. Cullen of Edinburg, Scotland, at Lima, Peru, S. Amer. At present engaged in mission work, Washington, D.C. *Children:* Paul Thomas; Philip Lewis.

Jessie Edna, educated Armour Institute, Chicago, Kindergarten. She m. June 22, 1897, Samuel M. Griffin, Canton, Pa. Resided San Francisco, Cal. *Children:* Raymond Earl; Frances Helen.

Prentice Dyer Grant, mechanic, residence Illinois.

Mildred May, educated Armour Institute, Chicago. Kindergarten teacher, Somerville, Mass.

625 WILLIAM AUSTIN[8] MOSES, son of WILLIAM (608), steelsmith, Scarborough (Beech Ridge), Maine. He m. Mar. 10, 1860, Shuah B. Pillsbury, Saco, Me.

CHILD: Sarah Adeline, b. Jan. 24, 1865, d. Nov. 19, 1898. She m. Feb. 23, 1884, John P. Moses (639).

626 HORACE WILSON[8] MOSES, son of WILLIAM (608), cooperage, creamery, and produce merchant, Geneseo and Chicago, Ill., and Philadelphia, Pa. Was instrumental in introducing modern methods of packing and shipping produce. Patentee of machinery for the manufacture of cooperage stock, etc. Later interested in stock raising in Kansas. In 1884 was Prohibition candidate for Representative. Retired, now living at Ottawa, Kan. He m. Jan. 31, 1870, Ellen Maria Nelson, Portland, Maine (she b. Mar. 27, 1848).

CHILDREN: Howard Nelson, b. Dec. 19, 1873; Harry Sherman, b. Aug. 17, 1876, d. Oct. 19, 1900; Nellie Gertrude, b. Dec. 27, 1880, d. Apr. 25, 1882; Drusilla Adeline, b. Nov. 15, 1884.

Drusilla Adeline, educated Ottawa University, Secretary to the President of Ottawa Univ., Ottawa, Kansas.

627 HORACE WILLIAM[9] MOSES, son of JOHN FRANCIS (624), sailor, Old Orchard, Me., later merchant, S. Dakota and Illinois. He m. Apr. 5, 1883, Nellie Kopp, Sheffield, Ill.

CHILDREN: Ethel May, b. Mar. 24, 1884; Frank Lafayette, b. Oct. 21, 1885; Leslie Forest, b. Sept. 20, 1887.

Ethel May, m. Dec. 11, 1902, Gus. A. Rohman, Moline, Ill. *Child:* Lester Lawrence.

Frank Lafayette, and *Leslie Forest,* reside Seattle, Wash.

628 FRANK LAFAYETTE[9] MOSES, son of JOHN FRANCIS (624), merchant, m. Dec. 4, 1888, Hortense Parkman, Aledo, Ill. Residence same.

629 WILLARD WASHINGTON[9] MOSES, son of JOHN FRANCIS (624), service in Spanish American War, Philippines, and China, m. Mar. 28, 1906, Mary E. Collings, Watkins, Oregon. Residence same.

630 HOWARD NELSON[9] MOSES, son of HORACE WILSON (626), physician, graduated Knox College (B.S.), Galesburg, Ill.; Pre-medical course University of Wisconsin, Madison; graduated 1899, Rush Medical College (University of Chicago). Member of American Medical Association, Secretary Salina Hospital, Salina, Kansas. He m. Sept. 10, 1901, Lizzie Deborah Smith, Adrian, Mo. (she b. May 6, 1878).

CHILD: Horace[10] Smith, b. Nov. 25, 1906.

631 WILLIAM RANSAELLAR[8] MOSES, son of GEORGE (609), farmer, resides old farm, Freedom, N. H., m. Oct. 1, 1864, Hattie E. Mears.

CHILDREN: George Eben, b. Nov. 23, 1865; Fred Leslie, b. Feb. 11, 1870; Walter Orion, b. May 1, 1873.

632 WESLEY GEORGE[8] MOSES, son of GEORGE (609), shoe manufacturer, Lynn, Mass. He m. July 3, 1873, Susan G. Walsh.

CHILD: Garnet Edna, b. May 9, 1874, m. July 12, 1905, Frank A. Bacheller.

633 OLEN EDWARD[8] MOSES, son of GEORGE (609), resided Haverhill, Mass., m. Mar. 11, 1875, Delia M. Jenkins.

CHILD: Eva Belle, b. Mar. 18, 1877, m. Dec. 19, 1899, Gilbert Day.

634 GEORGE EBEN[9] MOSES, son of WILLIAM RANSAELLAR (631), rubber manufacturer, Chelsea, Mass. He m. Aug. 12, 1891, Rose A. Towle, Freedom, N. H.

CHILD: Florence Eva, b. June 6, 1892.

635 FRED LESLIE[9] MOSES, son of WILLIAM RANSAELLAR (631), salesman, resides Somerville, Mass. He m. Jan. 11, 1899, Ada Gilmore.

636 WALTER ORION[9] MOSES, son of WILLIAM RANSAELL-

LAR (631), rubber manufacturer, Chelsea, Mass. He m. May 10, 1899, Carrie Gray.

637 EDWIN[8] MOSES, son of HORACE (610), carpenter and farmer, Scarborough, Gorham, Me., later Illinois and Michigan. Living at South Windham, Me. He m. Feb. 20, 1856, Rosanna Hunnawell (she b. Aug. 8, 1835, d. Jan. 24, 1902).

CHILDREN: Herbert Gregson, b. Feb. 26, 1860; John Princent, b. Jan. 18, 1863; Edward Horace, b. July 9, 1868; Frank Ossesmus, b. Jan. 23, 1870.
Herbert Gregson, resides Stroudwater, Maine.
Edward Horace, resides Boston, Mass.
Frank Ossesmus, salesman, resides South Windham, Me.

638 WILLIAM ISAAC[8] MOSES, son of HORACE (610), carpenter and farmer, Freedom, N. H., m. Nov. 20, 1870, Sarah Jane Wilkinson (she d. June 27, 1902).

CHILDREN: Angie, b. Aug. 15, 1872; Ellen Frances, b. June 25, 1875; Mabelle S., b. Jan. 2, 1881.
Angie, m. Aug. 7, 1892, Winslow H. Brown. *Children:* Della J.; Ernest W.; Archie D.; resides Freedom, N. H.
Ellen Frances, m. Sept. 28, 1897, Roy F. Gray, Freedom, N. H.
Mabelle S., m. Nov. 13, 1901, Carl D. Sawyer, Freedom, N. H.

639 JOHN PRINCENT[9] MOSES, son of EDWIN (637), m. Feb. 23, 1884, Sarah Adeline, dau. of William Austin Moses (625); 2d, Oct. 8, 1901, Etta J. Falsom. Resided Westbrook, Scarborough, Gorham, Me., and Boston, Mass.

CHILDREN: Iva L., b. June 6, 1885; Herbert A., b. Mar. 4, 1887; Iza W., b. Apr. 27, 1889.

640 SIMON MILLIKEN[8] MOSES, son of EDWARD (611), service in Civil War, Brigade wagon master, ranked as one of Butler's staff officers. Was taken prisoner, confined in Andersonville prison for five months, escaped, was captured by bloodhounds and taken to Libby prison, after confinement for four months made escape, was again captured and taken to Florence, S. C., and imprisoned, where he again made his escape, joining Hatch's troops after the evacuation of Charlestown. He m. Jan. 2, 1867, Elisa J. Babb, resided, Melrose, Mass.

641 JAMES THOMAS[8] MOSES, son of EDWARD (611), merchant, Charlestown and Somerville, Mass. He m. Feb. 21, 1874, Mary B. Lord, Freedom, N. H.

CHILD: Herbert Albion, b. May 13, 1875.

642 HERBERT ALBION[9] MOSES, son of JAMES THOMAS (641), hardware salesman, Boston, Mass., m. June 25, 1902, Hattie M. Page, Somerville, Mass.

CHILD: Mildred Frances, b. Dec. 13, 1905.

643 JOSIAH[6] MOSES, son of JOSIAH (604), farmer, known for his physique, lived at Standish, Maine. He m. June 6, 1821, Lydia Parker (she b. Oct. 1797, d. June 30, 1879). It is said by those who knew him that Josiah had a strong resemblance to Lyman Beecher, the famous divine.

CHILDREN: Orrin P., b. Aug. 2, 1822, d. Dec., 1891; Marshall, b. June 26, 1824, d. Oct. 2, 1906; Elizabeth, b. Sept. 26, 1826; Margaret, b. Sept. 21, 1832; William, b. Dec. 15, 1828, d. Jan. 15, 1858; Alonzo J., b. Sept. 22, 1834.

Elizabeth, m. Charles Edgecomb (he b. Oct. 6, 1822), Livermore, Me. *Children:* Charles Fred; Edwin E.; Ella F. Resides Waterville, Maine.

Margaret, m. Caleb G. Carver (he b. Dec. 6, 1830, d. Dec. 19, 1890), Leeds, Maine. *Children:* two d. infancy; an adopted dau. Jennie, who m. John Fogg.

644 ORRIN P.[7] MOSES, son of JOSIAH (643), carpenter and builder, Portland and Standish, Me. He m. 1849, Sarah Allen (she b. Aug. 13, 1829, d. July 13, 1888).

CHILDREN: Alvarez, b. Oct. 19, 1850, d. Nov., 1874; Abbie, b. Apr. 3, 1852, d. May, 1905; Lydia, b. Jan. 16, 1854; Sarah Margaret, b. Oct., 1856, d. Dec., 1888; Elizabeth F., b. Sept. 6, 1861; Thomas, b. Dec. 15, 1857; William, b. Dec. 14, 1859; Lillian, b. Aug. 28, 1863, d. May 28, 1885; Josiah, b. Aug. 1, 1865; Daniel, b. Nov. 16, 1867, d. Sept. 14, 1906; Alonzo, b. Nov. 14, 1870.

Abbie, m. Feb. 25, 1880, Fred Cash, South Windham, Maine. *Children:* Daniel; Eva, b. 1886; Alvarez, d. Feb., 1904.

Lydia, m. Henry M. Irish. *Children:* George H.; Eva; Albert N.; Velma.

Elizabeth F., m. Frank Riggs, Westbrook, Maine. *Children:* Frank Elmer, b. June 20, 1888; Arthur, b. Feb. 22, 1891; Ruth E., b. Aug. 2, 1897.

Sarah Margaret, m. Sept. 29, 1879, Charles C. Libby (he b. Apr. 24, 1857), Windham, Maine. *Children:* Fannie (Nash), b. 1883; Beatrice.

Josiah, farmer, resides Standish, Maine.

Alonzo, m. Cynthia Perry, of Warren; carpenter, resides at Monument Beach, Mass.

Daniel M., Resides Monument Beach, Mass., m. Katherine Perry. *Children:* Lillian, b. 1892; Maud C., b. 1897; Orrin L., b. 1899.

645 MARSHALL H.[7] MOSES, son of JOSIAH (643), merchant and manufacturer, Portland and N. Gorham, Maine. He

m. Nov. 26, 1850, Adeline D. P. Higgins, Thorndike, Maine (she b. Sept. 29, 1829). Observed Golden Wedding 1900.

CHILDREN: George H., b. Dec. 21, 1851; Charles A., b. May 31, 1854; Frank, b. May 8, 1856, d. young; Edward M., b. Feb. 2, 1861; Ella F., b. Aug. 11, 1865; Addie M., b. July 15, 1872.

Ella F., m. 1897, Edwin W. Sadler, Gorham, Me. *Children:* Elizabeth F.; Hilda A.; Virginia A. Resides Deering, Me.

Addie M., m. 1893, Joseph B. Manchester, North Gorham, Maine. *Children:* Hazel M.; Doris E.; Charles N.; Mattie M.; Josephine.

646. ALONZO J.[7] MOSES, son of JOSIAH (643), m. 1st, Susan Richards (she d. Jan. 3, 1884); 2d, Annie Kenny of South Portland, Maine (she d. 1886); 3d, Lillian Macy, Providence, R. I.

CHILD: Frank Alonzo, b. Dec. 1885, electrician, N. Gorham, Me.

647 ALVAREZ[8] MOSES, son of ORRIN P. (644), resided Standish, Maine. He m. Mar. 28, 1873, Alice Manchester, Windham, Maine.

CHILD: Clifford Alvarez, b. Sept. 7, 1874, resides N. Windham, Me.

648 THOMAS[8] MOSES, son of ORRIN P. (644), carpenter, m. Mar. 22, 1882, Mary Lord.

CHILDREN: Ralph C., b. 1884; Kathleen C., b. 1892.

649 WILLIAM[8] MOSES, son of ORRIN P. (644), carpenter and builder, Portland, Maine. He m. Jan. 4, 1887, Ella W. Jordan, Cape Elizabeth, Me. (she b. Mar. 22, 1864).

CHILDREN: Howard, b. Aug. 1, 1888; Marcia, b. Jan. 21' 1891; Warren, b. Apr. 11, 1893; Helen, b. June 9, 1895.

650 GEORGE H.[8] MOSES, son of MARSHALL H. (645), camp proprietor, North Gorham, Maine. He m. 1st, Anna Strout, Raymond, Me. (d. July 3, 1880; 2d, Alice Johnson, Bridgeton, Me. (she d. Feb. 1895).

CHILDREN: Mamie S. (Colley), b. Jan. 7, 1876; Ethel M., b. May 19, 1886; Cora F., b. May 1, 1888; Katherine L., b. Sept. 1893; Emily I., b. Apr. 1892; Alice, b. Feb. 14, 1895.

651 CHARLES A.[8] MOSES, son of MARSHALL H. (645), mechanic, contractor, Cumberland Mills, Maine. He m. 1st, 1875, Sarah F. Leslie, b. 1856, Gray, Me. (she d. Jan. 2, 1877); 2d, Oct. 22, 1884, Celia M. Bradeen, Westbrook, Me.

CHILD: Mina A., b. Oct. 14, 1885.

PORTSMOUTH LINE.   245

652 EDWARD M.[8] MOSES, son of MARSHALL H. (645), carpenter and builder, North Gorham, Maine.   He m. Fanny Mabry (she d. Jan. 7, 1902).

CHILDREN: Harland J., b. Feb. 18, 1887; Wilbur M., b. Oct. 1, 1890; Russell Walcott, b. July 22, 1893; Marion L., b. Feb. 11, 1889; Leland H., b. Nov. 19, 1897; Harry E., b. Aug. 30, 1895, d. in infancy.

653 BENJAMIN[6] MOSES, son of NATHANIEL (604), resided Durham, Maine. He m. Feb. 7, 1813, Catherine, dau. of Samuel and Abigail Libby (she b. Dec. 28, 1793).

CHILDREN: Alvena, d. about 1865; Webster; Christopher, b. Oct. 15, 1825; Amanda; Hannah Nash, b. Feb. 22, 1832, d. June 19, 1906; Cynthia E., b. Aug. 13, 1837; Catherine; Abigail; Eliza.

Cynthia E., m. Dec. 13, 1857, Charles S. Kilby. *Children:* William J.; Henry M.; John W.; Cynthia E.; Emma O.; Dorcas S.

Amanda, m. —— Trask, Fulton, Cal.

Hannah Nash, m. Nov. 6, 1853, George Brewer, Freeport, Maine. *Children:* Georgia A.; Alvena Moses; Sumner Grant; Katie Phoebe.

654 SILAS[6] MOSES, son of NATHANIEL (604), lived on old farm, Scottow's Hill, Scarborough, Me.   Served in War of 1812. He m. (1st) Sept. 5, 1816, Deborah Harmon (she b. 1800); (2d) Dec. 31, 1837, Grace Waterhouse (she b. 1794, d. June 14, 1846); (3d) Mary Ann Abbott (she later m. Simeon Nash, Raymond, Me.).

CHILDREN: Abram True, b. Oct. 29, 1817; John Simpson Harmon, b. 1819, d. Nov. 22, 1863.

655 RUFUS[6] MOSES, son of NATHANIEL (604), blacksmith and veterinarian. Resided Durham, Maine. For fifty years (since about 1822) was on Congress Street, Portland, Maine, moved to Cape Elizabeth about 1870. Celebrated 70th anniversary of wedding 1890. He m. Nov. 21, 1820, Margaret Weeks Freeman, Portland (she b. Sept. 5, 1802, d. May 6, 1896), she a sister to Sarah who m. William Vaughn Moses (656).

CHILDREN: Joshua Freeman, b. Feb. 4, 1822, d. Apr. 22, 1903; Margaret F., b. May 16, 1824, d. Sept. 3, 1825; Harriet C., b. Sept. 26, 1826, d. July 9, 1852; Margaret F., b. Sept. 22, 1828, d. Oct. 2, 1840; Elizabeth M., b. Jan. 4, 1832; Andrew J., b. Mar. 13, 1834, d. 1905; Abbie L., b. Jan. 3, 1836, d. Sept. 1, 1836; Alfred C., b. June 20, 1837, d. Sept. 25, 1863; Henry C., b. Sept. 18, 1839, d. Dec. 30, 1853; George W., b. Aug. 4, 1843, d. Jan. 22, 1863; Rufus W., b. Nov. 26, 1846, d. Apr. 26, 1895.

Harriet C., m. Rufus Wood, New York.

Elizabeth M., m. Jan. 1, 1855, John C. Perry, Portland, Maine. *Children:* William H. V.; Harriet A.

656 WILLIAM VAUGHAN[6] MOSES, son of NATHANIEL (604), shipbuilder and banker, Bath, Maine. He m. May 1828, Sarah Freeman (she b. May 18, 1808, d. Sept. 14, 1893). William with his brother Oliver settled in Bath in 1825, where they conducted a hardware store and iron foundry under the firm name of W. V. & O. Moses. In 1844 they started a shipyard and built a number of brigs and barques and in 1850 began building larger merchant ships. In 1856 Oliver withdrew from the firm, his place being taken by the two sons of William V. under the firm name of William V. Moses and Sons. They continued to conduct the shipyards and many large and first class vessels were launched. For many years and up to the time of his death he was President of the Sagadohock National Bank of Bath. It was said of William V. that "his business life was one of success. This was well earned by his invariable attention to his business, his strict integrity and pleasing manners; with a fine physique was added a uniformly cheerful countenance. He had a strong sense of humor which frequently manifested itself in his daily intercourse with his family and friends. In his just and upright walk in life he made no enemies. He lived and died a most respected citizen."

CHILDREN: William F., b. Apr. 18, 1829; Albert T, b. July 13, 1831, d. Jan. 27, 1906; Sarah Eliza, b. Aug. 19, 1833, d. June 10, 1876; Thomas Freeman, b. June 8, 1836; Henry Worcester, b. June 21, 1839, d. Aug. 15, 1869; Frances Ellen, b. Nov. 11, 1842, d. Nov. 24, 1879; George Frederick, b. Oct. 1, 1845; Alice Dike, b. Feb. 1, 1847.

Henry Worcester, a sea captain, d. Hong Kong.

657 OLIVER[6] MOSES, son of NATHANIEL (604), shipbuilder and banker, Bath, Maine. He m. June 9, 1829, Lydia Ham Clapp, Bath, Me. (she b. Aug. 21, 1808, d. May 1, 1886). Oliver came to Bath from Gardner, Me., became associated with his brother William V. in shipbuilding. In 1856 he withdrew from the firm and became interested in railroad promotion. He was instrumental in inducing Bath to invest in the building of the Knox and Lincoln R. R. and was chief manager in its construction. He was an extensive builder of buildings at this time. In 1861 he was instrumental in founding the First National Bank of Bath, the first in the State of Maine. He was a director and its first president, which position he held to his death in 1882, the year the charter expired.

CHILDREN: Francis Oliver, b. Nov. 27, 1831, d. Sept. 16, 1833; Frank Oliver, b. Sept. 19, 1833, d. Mar. 11, 1895; Galen Clapp, b. Aug. 30, 1835; Harriet Sylvester, b. Feb. 5, 1838; Julia Parker, b. Mar. 31, 1840, d. Apr. 9, 1845; Anne Elizabeth, b. Sept. 19, 1842; Wealthy Clapp, b. Aug. 9, 1850.

Harriet Sylvester, m. Oct. 11, 1866, George H. Knight, Portland, Me. (he b. May 22, 1825, d. Sept. 18, 1899). *Children:* George Moses; Marcia Bowman; Pamelia Dyer; Lydia Clapp; Annie Louise; Anna Putnam; Dorothea Clapp.

Anne Elizabeth, m. July 16, 1868, Benjamin F. Harris, Portland, Me. (he b. Dec. 7, 1834). *Children:* Julia Parker; Hattie Moses; Galen Moses; Oliver Moses; Harriet Louise; Galen Moses.

Wealthy Clapp, m. Aug. 9, 1876, John Watson Hinds, Allston, Mass. (he b. July 20, 1846). *Children:* George Clarence; Robert Watson.

658 EBENEZER[6] MOSES, son of NATHANIEL (604), resided Bath, Maine. He m. (1st) 1833, Lydia Todd (she d. June 1834); (2d) Nov. 25, 1835, Eleanor T. Parshley (she d. Apr. 2, 1869); (3d) Nancy Nash, wid. of Josephus Nash.

CHILDREN: Ernestine L., b. Mar. 24, 1834, d. Apr., 1895; Lydia Theresa, b. Oct. 5, 1836; Caroline Gardiner, b. Mar. 19, 1838, d. Jan., 1839; Sarah Augusta, b. Nov. 26, 1839; Charles Edward, b. Nov. 11, 1841, d. Oct. 11, 1862; Frederick Shirley, b. Feb. 11, 1850, d. Oct., 1851.

Ernestine L., m. June 1856, John S. Larrabee (he d. 1876); (2d) 1880, Horace Curtis. *Children:* Carrie May; Theresa A.

Sarah Augusta, m. Oct. 10, 1865, George D. H. Gay (he d. Apr. 26, 1882).

Charles E., died at sea.

659 ALVENA[7] MOSES, son of BENJAMIN (653), resided Durham and Pownal, Maine, later removed to the Western States. He m. Dec. 12, 1839, Rebecca Davis Estes (she b. Aug. 23, 1817).

660 WEBSTER[7] MOSES, son of BENJAMIN (653), resides Pownal, Maine. Held office of Collector and Constable, 1848-50.

CHILDREN: one son, who died; two dau. living.

661 CHRISTOPHER[7] MOSES, son of BENJAMIN (653), m. (1st) Julia Weymouth; (2d) June 16, 1857, Harriet S. Newell.

CHILDREN: Ida, b. Apr. 24, 1853; Nellie, b. Mar. 25, 1858; Harriet J., b. Oct. 11, 1859; George W., b. May 27, 1862; Charles E., b. Feb. 16, 1866.

Ida, m. J. H. Brook, San Francisco, Cal. *Child:* Christopher Allen.

Nellie, m. Oscar Merrill. Durham, Me. *Child:* Leon Merrill.
Harriet J., m. June 15, 1880, Arthur W. Mitchell, Freeport, Me.

662 GEORGE W.[8] MOSES, son of CHRISTOPHER (661), bookkeeper. He m. Dec. 6, 1888, Alice R. Fogg (she b. Feb. 18, 1863).

CHILDREN: Raymond G., b. June 5, 1890; Mildred S., b. Apr. 24, 1899.

663 CHARLES E.[8] MOSES, son of CHRISTOPHER (661), accountant, Malden, Mass. He m. Oct. 17, 1893, Aurie Belle Small (she b. July 2, 1869).

CHILD: Clayton Small, b. Apr. 18, 1902.

664 ABRAM TRUE[7] MOSES, son of SILAS (654), tinplate worker, Waldoborough, Portland, South Paris, and Deering, Maine. He m. Nov. 17, 1840, Margaret Mitchall, Bath, Me.

CHILDREN: Charles Oscar, b. Sept. 23, 1841; Maria, b. Mar. 30, 1843, d. Feb. 13, 1889; Theodore S., b. Nov. 16, 1845; Mary, b. Jan. 29, 1848, d. July 15, 1897; Abbie, b. Sept. 28, 1857, d. 1905.

Maria, m. May 20, 1868, Clifton Stevens, resides Deering, Me. *Children:* Harry Clifton; Hattie Belle.

Mary, m. June 24, 1868, Edward Grant, resides Deering, Me. *Children:* Hattie; Ned.

Abbie, m. Fred Copeland, resides Providence, R. I.

665 JOHN SIMPSON HARMON[7] MOSES, son of SILAS (654), lived on the old farm, Scottow's Hill, Scarborough, Maine. Captain in the State Militia. He m. Nov. 28, 1844, Johanna L. Poland, Peru, Me. (she b. June 26, 1824, d. June 26, 1901.)

CHILDREN: Nathaniel, b. Nov. 27, 1845; Deborah Harmon, b. Nov. 20, 1855.

Deborah Harmon, resides Portland, Maine.

666 CHARLES OSCAR[8] MOSES, son of ABRAM TRUE, β 64), conductor, Portland R. R., resides Deering, Maine. He m. June 20, 1870, Abbie Ballard.

CHILDREN: Charles Dwight, b. Apr. 24, 1871; Margaret Mitchell, b. July 11, 1882, d. July 25, 1884.

667 THEODORE S.[8] MOSES, son of ABRAM TRUE (664), roadmaster, Portland R. R., resides Deering, Maine. He m. Apr. 29, 1868, Abbie Frazier, Gorham, Maine.

CHILDREN: Gertrude S., b. Dec. 25, 1868; Abram True, b. Mar. 6, 1873.

Gertrude S., m. Oct. 5, 1904, George M. Kurtz, Boston, Mass.

668 CHARLES DWIGHT[9] MOSES, son of CHARLES OSCAR (666), horological inspector, Portland, Maine. He m. Oct. 25, 1896, Marion Sturdevant.

669 ABRAM TRUE[9] MOSES, son of THEODORE (667), Portland, Maine, m. June 24, 1893, Agnes McCann, Deering, Me.

CHILDREN: Millicent, b. Sept. 2, 1894; Gladys, b. Mar. 30, 1896.

670 NATHANIEL[8] MOSES, son of JOHN SIMPSON HARMON (665), lives on the old farm, Scottow's Hill, Scarborough, Maine. He m. Jan. 19, 1878, Hattie E. Wing (she b. Oct. 3, 1854).

CHILDREN: Anne Evelyn, b. Apr. 27, 1879; Elvena Rose, b. Oct. 16, 1880; John Simpson Harmon, b. Sept. 16, 1884.

Anne Evelyn, m. July 29, 1896, James E. Purchase, Prince Edward Island. *Children:* Edna Eugene; Charles Edward.

Elvena Rose, m. Apr. 23, 1902, Edgar H. Allen, Portland, Me.

John Simpson Harmon, lives on old farm Scottow's Hill. Drives ox team, which adds antiquity to the old homestead.

671 JOSHUA FREEMAN[7] MOSES, son of RUFUS (655), blacksmith, Portland, Maine, removed to Westbrook 1852 and later to Portland. He m. Oct. 14, 1844, Sarah Elizabeth Gray (she b. July 31, 1822, d. Oct. 3, 1904).

CHILDREN: Helen Freeman, b. Oct. 8, 1847, d. May 22, 1857; Margaret Ella, b. July 28, 1849, d. Dec. 1, 1852; George Warren, b. Aug. 8, 1851; Herbert Franklin, b. July 1, 1855, d. Aug. 11, 1863; Anne Estella, b. Mar. 7, 1858; Emma Isabelle, b. Dec. 9, 1860; Mary Gray, b. Mar. 12, 1865.

Anne Estella and Mary Gray, reside Portland, Maine.

Emma Isabelle, m. June 17, 1890, George G. Clapp, Boston, Mass.

672 ANDREW J.[7] MOSES, son of RUFUS (655), Civil War Service, resided Somerville, Mass. He m. Susan ———.

CHILDREN: Alice; Charles; Margaret; Annie; Frank; William.

Alice, m. James Bowditch.

Margaret, m. ——— Fisher.

Annie, m. E. M. Shedd, Somerville, Mass.

673 ALFRED C.[7] MOSES, son of RUFUS (655), Civil War service. He m. Louise Pierson.

674 GEORGE W.[7] MOSES, son of RUFUS (655), Civil War service. He m. Augusta Stewart.

675 GEORGE WARREN[8] MOSES, son of JOSHUA FREEMAN

(671), resided Winthrop, Mass., now living Portland, Maine. He m. Aug. 29, 1876, Aldora Paine (she b. May 1, 1852), Winthrop, Mass.

CHILDREN: Helen Freeman, b. June 5, 1877; Mary Edith, b. July 19, 1879; Clifford Albert, b. Oct. 26, 1881; George Furber, b. Sept. 3, 1884; Marion Aldora, b. Sept. 2, 1887.

Helen Freeman, m. July 3, 1901, Fred B. Jordan, Portland, Maine. *Child:* Leroy Moses.

676 WILLIAM F.[7] MOSES, son of WILLIAM VAUGHAN (656), shipbuilder, firm of William V. Moses and Sons, Bath, Maine. He m. (1st) July 21, 1856, Elizabeth Randall (she d. July 28, 1857); (2d) Oct. 20, 1864, Frances, dau. of Deacon Samuel W. Larrabee, Portland, Me.

CHILD: Elizabeth, b. June 16, 1857.

677 ALBERT T.[7] MOSES, son of WILLIAM VAUGHAN (656), shipbuilder, firm of William V. Moses and Sons, Bath, Maine. He m. Oct. 12, 1859, Lucy Childs, Bath, Me.

CHILDREN: May D., b. Dec. 18, 1866, d. July 1, 1868; Caroline M., b. Dec. 6, 1868; Louise C., b. Dec. 6, 1872.

Louise C., m. Oct. 20, 1898, Winthrop D. Green.

678 THOMAS FREEMAN[7] MOSES, son of WILLIAM VAUGHAN (656), was graduated from Bowdoin College in 1857; A.M. in 1860; from the Jefferson Medical College, Philadelphia, in 1861. Spent one year abroad in the medical schools of London and Paris. Returning soon after the outbreak of the Civil War he entered the service as Acting Assistant Surgeon, U. S. Army, and was placed in charge of the Hospital Transport "*Euterpe*"; was afterwards in charge of Grace Church Hospital at Alexandria, Va., and attached to U. S. General Hospital "Finley" at Washington, D. C. In the spring of 1864 he was assigned to duty on board the hospital transport "*Connecticut,*" of which he was later appointed Executive Officer. During the Wilderness campaign of General Grant he superintended the transportation of 14,000 wounded men from the front to the Hospitals of Alexandria and Washington. At the close of the war he practiced medicine in Hamilton Co., Ohio, until 1870, when he was appointed Professor of Natural Sciences in Urbana University, Urbana, Ohio, and was elected President in 1886, which office he held until 1894 when he retired on account of ill health. He was a member of the Pension Examining Board at Urbana from 1889 to 1892. Has been a member of the Geological Society of America, Fellow American Association for Advancement of Science, American Academy of Medicine, Anthropological Society of America. Editor and translator of

"UNITY OF NATURAL PHENOMENA",
author of "SPIRITUAL NATURE OF FORCE",
"PRELIMINARY EDUCATION OF THE PHYSICIAN",
"SCIENTIFIC PAPERS UPON GEOLOGY AND ARCHAEOLOGY."

Present residence, Waltham, Mass. He m. May 9, 1867, Hannah Appleton Cranch, Washington, D. C., she a dau. of John and Charlotte Dawes Appleton Cranch and granddaughter of Chief Justice Cranch of the Supreme Court of the District of Columbia.

CHILDREN: John Cranch, b. Feb. 14, 1868; William Vaughan, b. Apr. 20, 1869; Thomas Freeman, b. Aug. 9, 1871, d. Aug. 25, 1872; Charlotte Cranch, b. May 30, 1873; Christina, b. Dec. 25, 1874, d. July 21, 1875; Ethelwyn, b. Dec. 25, 1874, d. July 24, 1875; Earnest Meabry, b. Sept. 24, 1876; Edmund Quincy, b. Jan. 29, 1882; Eliot Brewster, b. July 15, 1892.

679 GEORGE FREDERICK[7] MOSES, son of WILLIAM VAUGHAN (656), ship owner, for some years connected with the Patten Car Works. In 1866 went to Ohio, where he engaged in agriculture, later returned to Maine and became interested in shipping. Residence Portland, Maine, and Washington, D. C.

680 JOHN CRANCH[8] MOSES, son of THOMAS FREEMAN (678), engineer of construction in Boston Bridge Works. Graduated A.B. Urbana (Ohio) Univ. 1885, Univ. of Michigan, B.S. C.E., 1887. Member American Society of Civil Engineers. Author of

"SHOP HINTS FOR STRUCTURAL DRAFTSMEN".

Resides Cambridge, Mass. He m. Aug. 26, 1891, Mary W. Mayhew, Yarmouthport, Mass.

681 WILLIAM VAUGHAN[8] MOSES, son of THOMAS FREEMAN (678), draftsman in General Electric Co., Lynn, Mass. Graduated University of Michigan, B.S., C.E., 1889. Instructor Mechanical Drawing and Machine Design in Harvard University 1893-1901. Resides Swampscott, Mass. He m. June 16, 1895, Mabel B. Snow, Cambridge, Mass.

H

682 ERNEST MEABRY[8] MOSES, son of THOMAS FREEMAN (678), draftsman in Boston Elevated R. R. Co. Graduated B. S., C. E., Harvard University 1897. Resides Waltham, Mass.

683 EDMUND QUINCY[8] MOSES, son of THOMAS FREEMAN (678), Assistant Examiner in U. S. Patent Office, Washington, D. C. Graduated S.B. Harvard University, 1902, George Washington University, B.L. 1905, Master of Patent Law, 1906. He m. June 29, 1905, Emma Lee, Washington, D. C.

684 FRANK OLIVER[7] MOSES, son of OLIVER (657), shipbuilder, Bath, Maine. He m. Oct. 16, 1855, Anna Maria Swanton Larrabee (she b. Feb. 14, 1837, d. Aug. 19, 1896).

CHILDREN: Orville Bowman, b. July 26, 1856, d. Sept. 22, 1901; Emma Pedrick, b. Feb. 17, 1860; Lydia Clapp, b. June 24, 1864; Oliver, b. May 26, 1867.

Emma Pedrick, and Lydia Clapp, reside Bath, Maine.

685 GALEN CLAPP[7] MOSES, son of OLIVER (657), was educated at Bowdoin College, later connected with several manufacturing enterprises, especially of woolen goods. In 1882 he succeeded his father as President of the First National Bank of Bath. Has been a philanthropist, aiding in the building of the Old Ladies' Home, the Y. M. C. A., and erected a library building which he donated to the city of Bath. In 1888 upon the reorganization of the New England Ship Building Co. he became its first President, and is a director in the Bath Iron Works. He m. (1st) June 20, 1860, Susan T. Croswell (she b. 1835, d. 1882), Charlestown, Mass; (2d) Jan. 26, 1884, Emma Hall McIlvain, Philadelphia.

686 ORVILLE BOWMAN[8] MOSES, son of FRANK OLIVER (684), resided, Dresden, Me., Bath, Maine; and Malden, Mass. He m. Nov. 28, 1876, Jane Owen Cate (she b. Jan. 9, 1852), Dresden, Maine. She resides Groton, Conn.

CHILDREN: Frank Oliver, b. July 1, 1877; Sally Pearson, b. Oct. 28, 1881.

687 OLIVER[8] MOSES, son of FRANK OLIVER (684), resides Bath, Me. He m. June 7, 1893, Augusta Plummer, Lisbon Falls, Me. (she b. Feb. 20, 1870).

CHILDREN: Helen Larrabee, b. June 15, 1894; Frances Plummer, b. Nov. 2, 1896; Oliver, b. Apr. 28, 1899.

As the book goes to press, the record of an old Bible is furnished to the writer by Professor Thomas Freeman Moses (678). The reader is referred to pages 109-112 for paragraphs with which the Bible record is connected (see also 408).

RECORD copied from an old family Bible, given (by will), to Mr. Sherburne by his Aunt Jane Moses and now in possession of his widow, Mrs. Iza Sherburne, one of whose daughters is the wife of Rev. Mr. Small of Bridgewater, Mass. The Bible is a leather covered thick quarto, much dilapidated.

Mrs. Sherburne has also the old Moses clock, supposed to be at least 200 years old. It has a tall case, a "moon face," and is exceedingly antiquated in appearance.

The clock was also willed to Mr. Sherburne by his Aunt Jane Moses, who d. Aug. 17, 1869.

MARRIAGES.

James Moses and Elizabeth Shirburn, m. Mar. 9, 1780.

THEIR CHILDREN.

Mark Moses and Betsey Cate, m. June 19, 1802.
James Moses and Betsey Chesley, m. Feb. 26, 1807.
David Sherburn and Betsey Moses, m. Nov. 25, 1807.
James Morrison and Mary Moses, m. May 20, 1814.
John Lake and Sarah Moses, m. Nov. 8, 1814.

BIRTHS.

James Moses, b. Feb. 27, 1758.
Elizabeth, b. July 25, 1759.

THEIR CHILDREN.

Mark, b. Jan. 19, 1781; James, Jr., b. Jan. 7, 1783; Janney, b. Oct. 9, 1784; Betsey, b. Dec. 15, 1785; Betsey S., b. Dec. 15, 1786; Mary, b. Nov. 25, 1788; Sarah, b. Aug. 27, 1792.

CHILDREN OF JAMES MOSES, JR., AND BETSEY CHESLEY.

Hannah, b. Sept. 25, 1807; Lucindy, b. May 4, 1810.

CHILDREN OF MARK MOSES AND BETSEY CATE.

Joseph, b. Oct. 30, 1803; Dearborn, b. Aug. 3, 1805; Mark, Jr., b. July 7, 1808.

CHILDREN OF BETSEY MOSES, who m. David Sherburn. (This Betsey Moses was the grandmother of Mrs. Iza Sherburn's husband.) William, b. Oct. 11, 1808; James Moses Sherburne, b. Dec. 12, 1802; Eliza, b. Mar. 21, 1813; David, b. Oct. 25, 1815; Sarah, b. Mar. 24, 1818; Jane, b. Mar. 22, 1821; William, b. Apr. 8, 1823; Mary Ann, b. Jan., 1827; Lucinda Sherburne, b. Mar. 21, 1829 (is living in Washington, D. C.).

CHILDREN OF MARY MOSES, who m. Morrison. John, b. May 30, 1815; Betsey and James (twins), b. Apr. 10, 1819; Jane Morrison, b. Sept. 6, 1823.

CHILDREN OF SARAH MOSES, who m. Lake. Moses Lake, b. May 23, 1815; Aaron, b. Apr. 4, 1818; James, b. July 19, 1824; Mary Jane, b. Jan. 6, 1826; Sarah Ann, b. Feb. 28, 1829; Lovina, and Orlando, b. Nov. 8, 1833.

DEATHS.

Mark Moses, d. Feb. 2, 1789, aged 86 (see 408).
Janney Moses, d. Apr. 27, 1790, aged 74 (see 408).
Dearborn Blake Moses, d. Apr. 13, 1795, aged 19.
Mark Moses, d. Mar. 15, 1811, aged 30.
James Moses, Jr., d. Oct. 30, 1812, aged 39 (?).
Lucindy Moses, d. Jan. 15, 1812, aged 21 months.
James Moses, d. Aug. 17, 1819, aged 62.
William Sherburn Moses, d. Sept. 8, 1822, aged 14.
Moses Lake, d. Mar. 23, 1822, aged 7.
James Morrison, d. Aug. 5, 1823, aged 36.
Sarah Sherburn, d. Feb. 18, 1826, aged 8.
James Lake, d. Aug. 18, 1824, aged 1 month.
Elizabeth Moses (wife of James Moses), d. Nov. 3, 1826, aged 77.
Jane Moses, d. Aug. 17, 1869, aged 82 years and 10 months.
James Moses Sherburne, d. Nov. 10, 1867, aged 57.

CONTINUATION OF CHAPTER VI.

OTHER EARLY NEW ENGLAND FAMILIES OF THE MOSES NAME.

This book is intended as a history of two family lines only, and the names which follow would not have been here recorded, unless there were some slight probabilities favoring the theory that they belonged to one or the other of these main lines. If sufficient circumstantial evidence could have been found to warrant the connection, such names would have been included in the preceding chapters; but surmises only are not such evidence, and these names are therefore classed under a separate heading.

800 SAMUEL MOSES, b. 1749, d. in Warwick, May 9, 1834: — parents unknown — lived in Royalton, Worcester Co., Mass., and in Warwick, Mass., m. Jan. 30, 1773, at Richmond, N. H., by Rev. M. Ballou, to Lydia Ballou.

Philo and Philander Moses (twins) lived for many years about twenty miles from the writer's birthplace in Central New York. In 1902 Philander P. writes that, "his grandfather Samuel of Warwick when young went whaling voyages at sea and after marriage commenced the tanning boot and shoe business." This statement makes it probable that Samuel lived at the seashore before he appears at Royalton, and we naturally look for him among the numerous Samuels of the Moses sailor family of Salem; there seems however to be none of the name whose birth coincides with the above-named Samuel, who is first found at Royalton, Mass., but not born there. From the letters of Philander P. and from the "Ballous in America," the following genealogical table is made, with the expectation that the connection with the main line will at some time be established.

CHILDREN: Sarah, b. 1774; Royal, b. 1776; Samuel, b. 1778; Anna, b. Sept., 1783; Lydia, b. May, 1786; Ambrose, b. 1788; Levi, b. ——; Mary, b. ——.

Anna, m. 1st, Mr. Chamberlin, 2d, Nathl. Proctor.
Lydia, m. Z. Kingsley.
Mary, m. John Hall.
Ambrose went to Cleveland, and Philander P. states that Ambrose had some sons.

OTHER MOSES FAMILIES.

801 ROYAL MOSES, son of SAMUEL (800), removed to Owego, Chenango Co., N. Y., and had

CHILDREN: Gracie; Laura; Samuel; Philo and Philander P. (twins), b. 1824 at Norwich, N. Y.; Nathan.

Samuel, no children.

Philo, one son, Hartwell E. Moses, resides at Etna, Tompkins Co., N. Y.

Philander P., one son Frederick E., resides at Newark Valley, N. Y.

Nathan, two sons residing at Syracuse, N. Y., Ambrose D. Moses, and Le Grand Moses.

Laura, m. Joel Shaw.

802 SAMUEL MOSES, son of SAMUEL (800), died in Warwick, Mass., Feb. 23, 1870, aged 91, m. 1807, Eunice Sheldon of Rupert, Vt.

CHILDREN: Salina, b. in Dorset, Vt., Jan. 9, 1808; Louisa, b. Jan. 3, 1812; Sheldon C., b. Warwick, Dec. 31, 1814; Abbie S., b. 1820; Eunice I., b. Feb. 28, 1823, d. 1839; Samuel A., b. May 6, 1825.

Abbie S., m. June 6, 1848, Jacob N. Tolman.

Samuel A., a machinist at Worcester, Mass., m. 1861, Eliza T. Loud.

803 SHELDON C. MOSES, son of SAMUEL (802), resides at Mendota, Ill., teacher of music.

CHILDREN: Charles; Frank; Nellie.

Charles, lives in Ill., a musician.

Frank, lives at Worcester, Mass.

Nellie, m. L. Clark, lives in Worcester, Mass.

On page 117 a partial sketch is given of the families and ancestry of John G. Moses, and J. Woodman Moses, of Portsmouth. Careful searching substantiates the statements of these two old men, made sixteen years ago. Dates and details now furnished, give us a line for about one hundred and fifty years.

The argument that this line is part of the Sagamore Creek family, is based on proximity of residence, and the chances that one or several of the second and third generations of the older family may have had sons who did not get a record in family or town archives.

The opposing argument is: that tradition in the families themselves, and as shown in the manuscript of Alfred D. Moses, and the Brewster book, has all along favored the idea of two lines, instead of one, at Portsmouth. Also no claim has been set up at any time, of relationship. (Vide letters to writer in 1889 from J. Woodman Moses, and Capt. John Gilman Moses, even then old men.) The fact that Portsmouth was an important seaport, gives greater possibility for an independent Moses immigrant, and the argument of proximity of residence does not count for as much as it would in an interior town.

804 THOMAS MOSES, of Portsmouth, (parentage not proved,) was a cordwainer. He bought the Drown-Moses place, 36 Vaughn St., Portsmouth, of Joseph Cotton, Nov. 21, 1778 (Rock. Deeds 110-460). The same day he, with his wife Lydia (Weeks), deeded the northern half of it to William Weeks of Portsmouth, cordwainer. A half tone picture of the Drown-Moses house will be found in "Portsmouth Historic and Picturesque." He m. 1st, Lydia Weeks; she was buried (N. Ch.), July 28, 1785; he m. 2d, July 9, 1786, Elizabeth, widow of Nehemiah Rowell. She was buried (N. Ch.), Dec. 11, 1792, aged 41. He d. apparently early in 1789, aged 37.

CHILDREN: Benjamin, b. between Aug., 1774, and Feb. 1775, d. 1849-50; Mary, b. 1776, d. Feb. 14, 1857; Thomas, b. June 3, 1779, d. June 21, 1856; William, b. 1780, drowned Dec. 22, 1837; John, b. May 21, 1787, d. at sea.

805 BENJAMIN MOSES, son of THOMAS (804), was a trader and cordwainer. He had his father's half of the house 36 Vaughn St. In 1803 he had a grocery store near the upper town wharf. He m. 1st, in May, 1795, his stepmother's daughter, Sally Rowell; m. 2d, Apr. 14, 1805, Anna Coleman of Newington. She d. Feb. 16, 1837, aged 66.

CHILDREN: Benjamin; Elizabeth; Nehemiah, b. 1800 or 1802, d. Apr. 22, 1879; Sarah Ann, d. ———; Sarah Ann 2d, d. 1890; Lydia Weeks, b. May 28, 1808, d. June 13, 1904; Joseph Coleman, b. 1810, d. Feb. 24, 1900; John Woodman, b. Mar. 16, 1813, d. May 12, 1903.

Benjamin, m. Dec. 4, 1818, Abigail Ricker. *Children:* William and Abbie, who lived in Auburn, N. Y. They left no children. (This William is probably the editor and printer, William Moses of Auburn, N. Y., whom the writer visited about 1889, and could not then connect.)

Elizabeth, m. Oct. 30, 1822, John Fitzgerald of Portsmouth. She was a widow for many years.

Sarah Ann 2d, m. Aug. 23, 1831, Daniel Vaughn of Portsmouth. *Children:* Major Daniel Vaughn of Cambridge, Mass.

Lydia Weeks, united with North Church Nov. 24, 1829, lived and died at homestead, 36 Vaughn St.

Joseph Coleman, m. Jane ———; lived at Metuchen, N. J. The New York papers of Feb. 25, 1900, noticed his death at 90 years. *Children:* James; Josephine, m. ——— Jackson, and had children.

OTHER MOSES FAMILIES.

806 THOMAS MOSES, son of THOMAS (804), was a boat builder of Portsmouth; m. Oct. 18, 1804, Mrs. Elizabeth Grant. She was b. Oct. 25, 1773, in Kittery, Me., and was a daughter of John Trot of London, Eng.

CHILDREN: Mary M., b. Oct. 3, 1805, d. Mar. 4, 1845; Thomas Palmer, b. Feb. 8, 1808, d. Nov. 22, 1881; William T., b. Apr. 5, 1810, d. July 13, 1834; John Nelson, b. Dec. 29, 1811, d. Dec. 17, 1837; Eliza D., b. Jan. 2, 1814, d. Apr. 2, 1893; Susan W., b. Aug. 22, 1817, d. July 23, 1875.

Mary M., m. Rev. Tobias Ham Miller.

William T., was at the time of his death second officer of the brig "*Beta*" of Boston, then in Chinese waters.

John Nelson, was at the time of his death, Clerk to the Naval storekeeper at Fort Foster, Florida.

Eliza Darling, m. Oct. 24, 1837, Henry H. Ham, of Portsmouth. *Children:* Margaret Elizabeth; Mary Harriet; Susan Frances; Mary Horatio; Anna Louise; Emma Walter.

Susan Wingate, m. Thomas Christie.

807 WILLIAM MOSES, son of THOMAS (804), was a sailmaker of Portsmouth; m. Feb. 17, 1803, Mrs. Elizabeth Dame, born a Sanborn.

CHILDREN: William, b. 1805, d. Oct. 29, 1882; John Gilman, b. 1807, d. Aug. 15, 1893; Abbie, b. 1810; Martha Twing, b. 1811, d. Mar. 6, 1893.

William, was a sailmaker of Portsmouth; m. Apr. 20, 1839, Eliza Brewster. *Children:* Tryphena Moses of Portsmouth.

Abbie, m. John Hanscom, resided in Portsmouth. *Children:* Martha A., who m. 1st, Gustavus Ackerman, 2d, ——— Kingsbury; Mary L., who m. Thomas Neil of Portsmouth and had Neil *children:* Caroline G , Jennie S., and Mary T.; John who was a sea captain and d. in Calcutta; Jackson M., d. in S. Boston; Caroline E., who m. 1st, Louis Whiten, and 2d, Col. Stone, both of Boston.

Martha Twing, lived in Portsmouth.

808 NEHEMIAH MOSES, son of BENJAMIN (805), was a draper and tailor in Portsmouth, and lived at the corner of Court and Roger streets. He was Ensign of the Rockingham Guards in 1839; Selectman of the City in 1836, and again in 1841. He m. 1st, April 28, 1823, Elizabeth Green; she d. in July, 1835, aged 28. He m. 2d; Feb. 2' 1846, Mary Abbie Moses, dau. of Levi; she d. July 20, 1863, aged 40.

CHILDREN by first marriage: Henry (left a daughter); Benjamin Franklin; Sarah Elizabeth, who d. young, as did several others.

OTHER MOSES FAMILIES.

By second marriage: Wallace Rowell; Elizabeth H.; Mabelle; Fred G., b. Sept. 25, 1852, d. Feb. 7, 1890.

Benjamin Franklin, m. July 10, 1854, Hannah Mugridge; he lives in the South, and has a large family, — one son a Methodist minister.

Wallace Rowell, m. Clara Nelson of Portsmouth; resides at West Palm Beach, Florida, and has *children:* Sarah, and Elwyn, both married.

Elizabeth H., lives in Brooklyn, N. Y.; is a widow.

Mabelle, m. Samuel Poole of Boston.

Fred G., m. Mary Dwyer. *Children:* Lena, resides in Portsmouth.

809 JOHN WOODMAN MOSES, son of BENJAMIN (805), was a draper and tailor of Portsmouth; m. 1st, Jan. 31, 1836, Mary Nelson Nutter of Portsmouth; she d. Mar. 23, 1883, aged 67: m. 2d, Jan. 3, 1884, Mrs. Caroline Black Dunn: she d. July 12, 1903.

CHILDREN: John Henry; Mary Elizabeth; Annie M.

John Henry, m. May 19, 1864, Delia H. Wells of Portsmouth. He resides at Roxbury, Mass. *Children*: George; Charles.

Mary Elizabeth, m. Mar. 2, 1865, John Davis Whitcomb; resides at Medford, Mass.

Annie M., m. Jan. 16, 1866, William W. Cotton, of Portsmouth: *Children:* Mrs. Mary (Cotton) Tufts; Mrs. Gertrude (Cotton) Wilmington. Both reside in Somerville, Mass.

810 THOMAS PALMER MOSES, son of THOMAS (806), was a musician, artist, and poet. A landscape is mentioned which he painted in North Carolina, where he lived for a number of years after his marriage. He returned to Portsmouth and was a noted teacher of music and Church organist. He made his mark in the community, and was very popular with his friends.

Like most musicians, he had rivals, and apparently he did not forget them. He was another Moses "Character," and this is probably best shown by quoting the title page of his volume of poems, published in 1850, which the writer found in the Library of Congress.

"Sketch of the Life of Thomas P. Moses, Teacher of Music, and also some remarks upon the doings of Pharisees, Hypocrites, and Defamers of Character, with the addition of a few short Poems.

Near the margin of the renowned translucent river, Piscatauqua, two miles off the sea girt shore, stands the humble dwelling within whose sheltering chambers on 17 Feb. between the years 1808 and 1816, glimmered forth my spark of life, to flicker, blaze, grow dim and expire amid commingling elements of this sublunary planet. My father, still living, is a ship carpenter and boat builder. He was left an orphan at seven years."

He m. about 1871, Nellie M. Franklin. He d. Nov. 22, 1881: his widow resides in Boston, Mass.

811 CAPTAIN JOHN GILMAN MOSES, son of WILLIAM (807), followed the sea, advancing from cabin boy to Captain. At one time he commanded the "*City of New York,*" one of the largest vessels sailing to Europe. He was afterward Commander and sole owner of the "*Judah Truro,*" a noted merchant ship. After he had given up active life, and until he was eighty, he often crossed the ocean for pleasure. He was a noted man on the streets of Portsmouth up to the day of his death, and he leaves a pleasant and lasting memory. He m. Mary E. Furness, who survived him, and d. May 27, 1902, age 80.

SOLDIERS OF THE MOSES NAME.

On page 120 see the allusion to the "bird of Mars" in the ancient coat of arms of the English Moses family and to the Moses heraldic motto, "Dum spiro spero" (While I breathe I hope).

CONNECTICUT SOLDIERS IN THE COLONIAL WARS.

From Col. Hist. of Conn. and Windsor, Conn., Manuscript Records:

JOHN MOSES: — In Capt. John Mason's Mounted Dragoons in King Philip's War.

His sons WILLIAM MOSES } at Storming of Narragansett Fort Dec. 19, THOMAS MOSES } 1675; were "wounded that they dyed."

From Conn. Hist. Collections, Vol. X.:

ASHBEL MOSES (1757): Col. Lyman's Reg. — Capt. Israel Putnam.

OTHNIEL MOSES (1757): Col. Lyman's Reg. — Capt. Israel Putnam.

ANDREW MOSES: Col. Lyman's Reg. — Farmington Company.

Andrew Moses died in 1761 in Capt. Fitch's Ind. Co.

JONAS MOSES (1757 and 1762): Col. Lyman's and Col. Whiting's Regs.

EZEKIEL MOSES — Col. Lyman's Reg.

ZEBULON MOSES — Col. Lyman's Reg.

ZEBULON MOSES Jr. — Col. Lyman's Reg.

HUGH MOSES (1760); Conn. Reg. of Provincials.

JOHN MOSES — Col. Whiting's Reg.; New Haven Co.

LIEUT. TIMOTHY MOSES (1759); Col. Lyman's Reg.

ABEL MOSES (1757); 4th Reg.

AARON MOSES (1757); 4th Reg.

ELISHA MOSES (1757); 4th Reg.

SERGT. ISAAC MOSES (1757); 4th Reg.

HAMAN MOSES (1757); 4th Reg.; Whitings, Norwich Co.

CONN. IN THE REVOLUTION; ADJUTANT-GENERAL'S REPORT.

ABRAHAM MOSES, 18th Militia.

REUBEN MOSES, 18th Militia; also in Col. Hooker's Reg.

ENSIGN AARON MOSES, 18th Militia.

ABEL MOSES, Wadsworth Brigade.

ASA MOSES, Col. Hooker's Reg.

DARIUS MOSES, Col. Hooker's Reg.

ASHBEL MOSES, Col. Belden's Reg.

SERGEANT AARON MOSES, Lexington Alarm.

BENONI MOSES, Lexington Alarm.

ENAM MOSES, Col. Shelden's Light Dragoons.

EZEKIEL MOSES, 5th Conn. Line.
JESSE MOSES, Wadsworth Brigade, Wallingford Company.
ISAIAH MOSES, Wadsworth Brigade, Wallingford Company.
JONAS MOSES, 6th Conn.
MARTIN MOSES, 7th Conn.
MICHAEL MOSES, 18th Reg. Col. Phelps.
OTHNIEL MOSES, Col. Wolcot's Reg.
SEBA MOSES, Col. Belden's Reg. and Col. Moreley's Reg.
SHUBAEL MOSES, in 3d Reg., also in 18th Reg.

CONN. HIST. COLL., VOL. 8.

DANIEL MOSES. Col. Huntington's 17th Continental Reg.; Capt. Bissell's Company.
ABEL MOSES, Gen'l Wooster's Reg.
ABNER MOSES, Col. Swift's 2d Reg.

CONNECTICUT MILITIA; WAR OF 1812; ADJUTANT-GENERAL'S REPORT.

BARNABAS MOSES, Command of Webster,
COLLIN MOSES, Command of Phelps,
JOSHUA MOSES, Command of Deming,
MARTIN MOSES, Command of Phelps,
NATHAN MOSES, Command of Hadley,
ERASTUS MOSES; enlisted Middletown 25th Inf. Command of Ketcham. (See Register of Army, War of 1812.)

MASSACHUSETTS SOLDIERS AND SAILORS IN WAR OF REVOLUTION.

JOSIAH MOSES, Capt. Libbes Co., Col. Fogg's Reg.; aged 21; arrived at Fishkill, June 16, 1778.
BENJAMIN MOSES, Salem, aged 42 years; 1st Lieutenant Capt. Benj. Ward, Jr., Co. July 11, 1775; "defense of sea coast"; also Master brigantine "*Tyrannicide,*" Com. by Capt. John Fisk; engaged Oct. 27, 1776; also same vessel engaged Jan. 1, 1777: engaged Feb. 20, 1777; also 2d Lieutenant brig. "*Tyrannicide*", Mar. 10, 1777; also 2d Lieutenant ship "*Pilgrim*" (privateer); also in descriptive list of officers and crew of ship "*Junius Brutus*" June 15, 1780.
BENJAMIN MOSES, JR., Boy, brig. "*Tyrannicide:*" engaged Feb. 20, 1777; dischg. Aug. 29, 1777.
DANIEL MOSES, Scarborough, Col. Ed. Phinney's 31st Reg.; also Col. Mitchel's Reg.; also Col. Reuben Fogg's 3d Cumberland Co. Reg.; also Col. Francis Reg.; also Col. Thomas Marshall's Reg.; also Sergt. 4th Co. Col. Marshall's Reg. (10th) Continental Army.
DAVID MOSES, Harwich; Col. Aaron Willard's Reg. 1777; Dischg. Fort Edward.
DAVID MOSES; Sandwich, Col. Nath. Freeman's 1st Barnstable Co. Reg.
JOHN MOSES; Haverhill; Under Gen'l Paterson; mustered Oct 25, 1780.
JOHN MOSES, Col. Ashley's Berkshire Co. Reg.; entered service Aug. 17, 1777; dischg. Aug. 20, 1777.

JOSEPH MOSES (?), also given on same roster JONAH; Col. John Ashley's Berkshire Co. Reg.; service in 1779.

JOSHUA MOSES, Landsman sloop "*Providence*," commanded by Capt. John Paul Jones. In list of officers and men entitled to prize in ship "*Alexander*," captured Sept. 20, 1776; also a marine on ship "*Alfred*", commanded by Capt. John Paul Jones; in list of men entitled to prize shares in the ship "*Mellish*" and brig "*Active.*"

GEORGE MOSES, Boston, Col. Nath. Wade's Reg. 1778.

GEORGE MOSES, aged 44, Salem; list of 6 months men returned by Gen'l Paterson Oct. 25, 1780.

GEORGE MOSES, Salem; in 10th and 11th Mass. Reg. in 1780.

GEORGE MOSES, Scarborough, Capt. Knight's Co. July 18, 1775; also Capt. Benj. Larrabee's Co., Col. Mitchel's Reg.; marched July, 1779; dischg. Sept. 12, 1779.

GEORGE MOSES, list Feb. 11, 1779; men detached from Col. Jabez Hatch's Reg. (Boston) to serve at Providence.

JOSIAH MOSES, Scarborough, Capt. Wm. Crocker's Co. Mar. 1, 1776, to Aug. 31, 1776; also Col. Mitchel's Reg. Aug. 31, 1776, to Nov. 23, 1776; also in Continental Army. 9 mos. in 1778; aged 21 years; at Fishkill June 25, 1778.

MOSES MOSES, Nantucket; also given Edgartown and Sandwich. In 3d Plymouth Co. Reg.; also Col. Wigleworth's Reg.; also Col. Brook's Reg. Continental Army; also Col. Alden's Reg. reported died Dec. 31, 1777.

SAMUEL MOSES, Mashpee (also given Sandwich), Col. Brewer's Reg., Feb. 22, 1777; also Col. Sprout's Reg. Continental Army, Feb. 16, 1777, to Apr. 1, 1779; reported died Apr. 1, 1779.

SAMUEL MOSES, Col. Woodbridge's Reg.; enlisted Aug. 22, 1777, dischg. Nov. 29, 1777, at Saratoga.

SAMUEL MOSES, Col. Jacob Gerrish's Reg. of Guards; Nov. 11, 1777, to Apr. 3, 1778; Rolls dated Camp at Winter Hill.

SAMUEL MOSES, Sailor, ship "*Eagle*," commanded by Capt. Wm. Groves, June 17, 1780.

THOMAS MOSES, Col. Edmund Phinney's Reg.; garrison Fort George; enlisted Dec. 1, 1778; reported died July 23, 1779.

WILLIAM MOSES, Capt. Pope's Co., Col. Wm. Shepard's 4th Reg.; roll May, 1781.

NATHAN MOSES, Scarborough, Col. Jona. Mitchell's Maine Reg., July 9, 1779, to Sept., 1779; on the Penobscot or Bagaduce Expedition. (Note. This should read NATHANIEL, who was the brother of Daniel Moses, a soldier in the same Regiment. This is confirmed by the History of Scarboro, Me., page 205.)

FROM 3D REP. D. A. R. LIST OF MASS. CITIZENS WHO LOANED money to the Government during the Revolution.

  BENJAMIN MOSES, Salem; JOSEPH MOSES, Salem.

New Hampshire Colonial Wars.

From Military History of New Hampshire by C. E. Potter; List of Soldiers at Fort William Henry, 1708, Capt. Walton.

JAMES MOSES,
JOSEPH MOSES.

In Regiment for Crown Point Expedition, Col. John Hart, Capt. John Pickering of Portsmouth.

JOHN MOSES, April to Oct., 1758.

In Regiment for Invasion of Canada:—(Cut through Wilderness to Green Mountains, then to Crown Point) Col. John Goffe and Capt. George March.

SAMUEL MOSES, enl. Mar. 8, 1760; dischg. Oct. 23, 1760, "at No. 4."
JOHN MOSES, enl. Apr. 2, 1760; dischg. Nov. 27, 1760.

New Hampshire State Papers; Revolutionary Rolls.

LIEUT. MOSES, Col. Wyman's Reg., Capt. Chandler's Co.
WILLIAM MOSES, Col. Bartlett's Reg. Roll sworn to in Exeter; also with Col. Daniel, Fort Sullivan.

The STATE PAPERS, Vol. 8, contains the names of 8199 men who signed the ASSOCIATION TEST. John Farmer, who compiled the list, states: "Had the cause in which these men pledged their lives and fortunes failed, it would have subjected every individual who signed, to the pains and penalties of treason; to a cruel and ignominious death."

Signers in Epsom:

MARK MOSES, SAMUEL MOSES, SILVANUS MOSES.

Signers in Lee:

TIMOTHY MOSES.

Signers in Portsmouth:

THOMAS MOSES, AARON MOSES, JOHN MOSES, SAMUEL MOSES, THEODORE MOSES, NADAB MOSES, JAMES MOSES.

Vermont; Revolutionary Rolls.

ASA MOSES, Col. Thos. Lee's Reg. 1781.
ELNATHAN MOSES, Col. Thos. Lee's Reg. 1781.
JOHN MOSES, Col. Thos. Lee's Reg. 1781.
SHUBAEL MOSES, Col. Thos. Lee's Reg. 1781.
JOHN MOSES; in three Companies, 1778–1779 and 1780.
JOHN MOSES, JR.; in three Companies, 1778–1779 and 1780.
SHUBAEL MOSES, Col. Allen's Reg. 1780.
ZEBULON MOSES, Col. Allen's Reg. 1780.

New York: Col. and Rev. Wars.

From Report of State Historian, Vol. 2; Muster Rolls of men under command of Capt. Robert Rea of New York, Dec. 20, 1763.

JACOB MOSES.

MOSES SOLDIER LIST.

"Revolutionary Rolls" page 214.
JOHN MOSES, Col. Crane's Westchester Co. Reg.
JOSEPH MOSES, Col. Malcom's Levies.

MAINE: COLONIAL WARS.

From the History of Scarborough.
THEODOSIUS MOSES; in Capt. George Berry's Co., 1747.

VOLUNTEER ARMY REGISTER.

OFFICERS of the Union Army Civil War.

KIRK W. MOSES, 1st Lieut. 23d Maine Inf., Sept. 29, 1862; Capt. 30th Maine Inf., Dec., 1863.
WILLIAM PITT MOSES, 1st Lieut. and R. Q. M. 9th N. H. Inf., Nov., 1862.
HARVEY J. MOSES, 2d Lieut. 91st N. Y. Inf., Apr. 15, 1865.
ROBERT H. MOSES, 1st Lieut. and Adjutant 122d N. Y. Inf., July 9, 1864; Brevet Captain Oct. 19, 1864.
THOMAS MOSES, 1st Lieut. 16th N. Y. Battery, Jan. 2, 1865.
LUCIUS MOSES, Capt. 122d N. Y. Inf., 1862, dischg. Feb. 24, 1863.
ISRAEL MOSES, Lieut. Col. 72d N. Y. Inf., dischg. Oct. 20, 1862.
CALVIN C. MOSES, Captain 58th Penn. Inf., dischg. Mar. 16, 1865.
DAVID MOSES, 2d Lieut. 52d Penn. Inf., mustered out on expiration of service May 1, 1865.
ELMER MOSES, Capt. 125th Ohio Inf., dischg. Jan. 5, 1865.
ALBERT J. MOSES, Capt. 28th Ill. Inf., resigned Nov. 4, 1865.
JOHN W. MOSES, 2d Lieut. 60th Ill. Inf., resigned Oct. 14, 1864.
REUBEN H. MOSES, 1st Lieut. 146th Ill. Inf., Sept. 17, 1864.
JOHN MOSES, 1st Lieut. 2d Kansas Inf.; missing among 19 officers August, 1862.
T. W. MOSES, 1st Lieut. and R. Q. M. 14th Missouri Cav., resigned Dec. 8, 1862.
THOMAS MOSES, JR., Capt. 2d Col. Cav., Mar. 3, 1863.
WILLIAM E. MOSES, Capt. 14th U. S. Heavy Art., resigned Apr. 4, 1865.

NEW HAMPSHIRE IN THE CIVIL WAR: ADJUTANT-GENERAL'S REPORT:

9th Inf. Lieut. and Quartermaster, WILLIAM PITT MOSES, born Exeter, appointed 1862, mustered out 1865; residence Roxbury, Mass.
12th Inf., DANIEL F. MOSES, b. Chichester, enl. 1862, aged 24, residence Loudon.
12th Inf., WILLIS MOSES, b. Epsom, enl. 1862, aged 21, residence Northwood.
1st Art., DAVID P. MOSES, b. Alexandria, enl. 1864, aged 21.
13th Inf., HOWARD M. MOSES, b. Harmony, Me., enl. 1862, aged 21, residence, Exeter.
8th Inf., JAMES E. MOSES, b. Epsom, enl. 1861, aged 19, residence, Northwood.
15th Inf., JAMES F. MOSES, b. Chichester, enl. 1862, aged 23, residence, Concord.

4th Inf., JOHN H. MOSES, b. Nashua, enl. 1861, aged 18, residence, Oakland, Cal.

7th Inf., JOHN P. MOSES, b. Barrington, enl. 1861, aged 35.

18th Inf., WILLIAM F. MOSES, b. Chichester, enl. 1864, aged 21, died 1879, at Pembroke.

16th Inf., WILLIAM S. MOSES, b. Alexandria, enl. 1862, aged 24, residence, New Liberty.

Navy: Acting Master EDWARD MOSES, b. Portsmouth, aged 48, served on U. S. S. *"Fernandina."*

Navy: LEVI MOSES, b. Portsmouth, enl. 1861, aged 30, as seaman on U. S. S. *"Princeton"* and *"Flag"*; drowned at sea from the *"Flag"* Sept., 1861.

MAINE IN THE CIVIL WAR; ADJUTANT-GENERAL'S REPORT.

LIEUT. KIRKE W. MOSES; 23d Inf.
ALONZO MOSES; 17th Inf.
ANDREW J. MOSES; 17th Inf.
ELI N. MOSES, 22d Inf.
SIMON M. MOSES; 12th Inf.
GEORGE S. W. MOSES; 17th Inf.
ALFRED L. MOSES; 1st. Inf.
WILLIAM MOSES; 6th Inf.

CONNECTICUT MEN IN WAR OF REBELLION: ADJUTANT-GENERAL'S REPORT.

1st Heavy Art., CHARLES MOSES, Canton; Aug., 1864, to July, 1865.

10th Inf., GEORGE A. MOSES, Monroe; Nov., 1864, to June 6, 1865.

24th Inf., SERGT. GEORGE M. MOSES, Middletown; Sept., 1862, to Sept., 1863.

6th Inf., HENRY MOSES, New Britain; Aug., 1861, died Oct. 4, 1862.

12th Inf., JAMES O. MOSES, Canton; Nov., 1861, to Apr., 1862.

10th Inf., LINUS A. MOSES, New Haven; Aug., 1862, to June, 1865.

25th Inf., MARCUS MOSES, Simsbury; Aug., 1862, to August, 1863.

21st Inf., PHILIP MOSES, Hartford; Aug., 1862, to Sept., 1862.

27th Inf., WILLIAM W. MOSES, New Haven; Sept., 1862, to July, 1863.

1st Cav., WILLIAM A. MOSES, New Haven; Nov., 1861, to Oct., 1863.

VERMONT IN WAR OF REBELLION; ADJUTANT-GENERAL'S REPORT.

ALONZO D. MOSES, 9th Inf.; enl. Dec., 1863, at Hartford; dischg. Sept., 1864.

JOSEPH MOSES, 12th Inf., enl. Aug., 1862, at Tunbridge; dischg. Mar., 1863.

MICHAEL MOSES, 2d Art., enl. Dec., 1862, at New Orleans, La.; trans. to 1st Art., Mar., 1865.

SERGT. RUFUS L. MOSES, 3d Inf.; enl. Dec. 1863, at Randolph; mustered out July, 1865.

SILAS MOSES, 1st Cav.; enl. Aug., 1862, at Huntington, prisoner, and dischg. April, 1863.

Rhode Island in War of Rebellion: Adjutant-General's Report.

Ashley O. Moses, 7th Inf., Aug., 1862, at Cranston.

Massachusetts—War of Rebellion—Adjutant-General's Report.

James Moses, 5th Inf., 23d, 24th and 40th Inf., enl. May, '61, age 21, at Beverly. In the 40th Inf., to June, 1865.

George Moses, 5th Inf. and 50th Inf.; July, 1861, age 20, at South Reading. In 50th Inf., to Aug. 1863.

George Moses, Regular Army, Mar., 1864, in Signal Corps.

John F Moses, 50th Inf., Sept., 1862, age 27, at South Reading; d. July 4, Baton Rouge, La.

John Moses, 5th Cav., Jan., 1864, age 22, at Gardner.

Caton Moses, 5th Cav., May, 1864, age 25, at Cambridge; to Oct., 1865.

Rinaldo P. Moses, 11th Inf., Apr., 1864, age 26, at Leominster; to July, 1865.

John Moses, 19th Inf., two enlistments; Feb., 1862, age 34, at Haverhill; to June, 1865.

John E. Moses, 23d Inf. and Veteran Reserve Corps, Sept., 1861, age 30, at Beverly; to Nov., 1865.

George F. Moses, 39th Inf., Aug., 1862, age 19, at Milton; to Mar., 1865.

John A. Moses, 59th Inf., Dec., 1863, age 32, at Beverly; to July, 1864.

New York—War of the Rebellion—Adjutant-General's Report.

Sergt. Mark E. Moses, 22d Cav., enl. 1863, age 24, at Rochester, prior service in 23d Inf.

Edgar P. Moses, 1st Dragoons, enl. July, 1862, age 23, at Groveland, N. Y., dischg. 1864.

Philip Moses, 1st Vet. Cav., enl. Sept., 1863, age 18, at Buffalo; killed Mar. 10, 1864, at Cabletown, W. Va.

Francis F. Moses, 9th Art. and 2d Art., enl. Feb., 1864, age 18, at Canadea, N. Y., mustered out Sept., 1865.

Lafayette Moses, 9th Art. and 2d Art., enl. Feb., 1864, aged 19, at Canadea, N. Y., mustered out Sept., 1865.

Hiram Moses, 6th Art., enl. Dec., 1863, age 35, at Stockholm; mustered out Aug., 1865.

John Moses, 14th Art. and 6th Art., enl. age 29, at Binghamton, mustered out Aug., 1865.

Alexander Moses, 14th Art., no descrip., borne on Reg. return April, 1865.

D. Moses. 14th Art., no descrip., borne on Reg. return April, 1865.

Lewis Moses, 14th Art., enl. Jan., 1864, age 18, at Cattaraugus; mustered out July, 1865.

Sprague Moses, 14th Art., enl. Jan., 1864, age 21, at Chautauqua; mustered out Aug., 1865.

George S. Moses, 16th Art., enl. Dec., 1863, age 25, at Plattsburg, dischg. May, 1865.

MOSES SOLDIER LIST.

LIEUT. THOMAS MOSES, 16th Battery, enl. Dec., 1861, age 23, at Binghamton; mustered out as 1st Lieut. Nov., 1864.

WILLIAM MOSES, enl. Aug., 1862, aged 21, mustered out July, 1865.

JOSEPH C. MOSES, 23d Battery, enl. Sept., 1861, age 39, Warren Co.; mustered out Aug., 1865.

HENRY C. MOSES, 1st Eng., enl. age 21, at Paterson, N. J.; mustered out June, 1865.

SOLON W. MOSES, 2d Inf. and 10th Inf., enl. Sept., 1861, age 21; mustered out Aug., 1862.

GEORGE A. MOSES, 5th Inf., enl. July, 1862, age 26, at New York City.

MICHAEL MOSES, 12th Inf., enl. Dec., 1861, age 18, at Batavia.

JOEL P. MOSES, 16th Inf., enl. Oct., 1861, aged 36, at Potsdam, wounded and mustered out 1863.

MARCUS E. MOSES, 23d Inf. and 22d Cav., enl. May, 1861' age 22, at Elmira; mustered out 1863.

JACOB MOSES, 31st Inf., enl. June, 1861, aged 30, at New York City, dischg. July, 1861.

ISAAC F. MOSES, 40th Inf. enl. Sept., 1861, age 22, at New York City; dischg. Sept., 1864.

HERMAN MOSES, 48th Inf., trans. from Ind. L. Inf. 1864' wounded 1864, and dischg. Mar., 1865.

SERGT. AUGUSTUS F. MOSES, 49th Inf., enl. Aug., 1861, age 23, at Clymer, mustered out Oct., 1864.

GEORGE MOSES, 52d Inf., enl. Oct., 1861, age 42, at New York City, killed at Fair Oaks, June, 1862.

HENRY MOSES, 54th Inf., enl. 1861, age 38, at Hudson City, N. J., mustered out Oct., 1864.

LIEUT.-COL. ISRAEL MOSES, 72d Reg., June, 1861, age 38; mustered out Oct., 1862, as surgeon.

WILLIAM MOSES, 79th Inf., trans. from 45th Penn.

MARSHALL S. MOSES, 81st Inf., enl. Dec., 1861, age 26, at Morrisville, wounded 1864, dischg. 1864.

JOHN C. MOSES, 83d Inf., enl. May, 1861, age 31, at New York City, hosp. steward U. S. Army.

LUTHER MOSES, 85th Inf., enl. Sept., 1861, age 29, at Granger, died at Andersonville 1864.

LIEUT. HARVEY J. MOSES, 91st Inf., enl. Oct., 1861, aged 23, at Glenns Falls; mustered out July, 1863.

SAMUEL B. MOSES, 96th Inf., enl. Nov., 1861, age 18, at Warrensburg, mustered out Jan., 1865.

SERGT. WALLIS MOSES, 104th Inf., enl. Nov., 1861, age 21, at Geneseo.

HIRAM E. MOSES, 111th Inf., enl. July, 1862, age 44, at Sodus; mustered out Aug., 1865.

CAPT. LUCIUS MOSES, 122d Inf., enrolled 1862, aged 24, at Syracuse, dischg. Feb., 1863.

CAPT. ROBERT H. MOSES, 122d Inf., enrolled July, 1862, age 18, at Marcellus; commissioned 1st Lieut. with rank from May, 1864, Adjutant with rank from Sept. 1864. Capt. not mustered, Aug. 2, 1865, with rank from June 16, 1865.

LEWIS MOSES, 146th Inf., enl. Aug. 1862, age 35, at Florence, trans. Nov., 1864, to Vet. Res. Corps.

MICHIGAN VOLUNTEERS IN THE CIVIL WAR; ADJUTANT-GENERAL'S REPORT.

GEORGE W. MOSES, 6th Inf., enl. Dec., 1863, at Jackson, dischg. Mar. 27, 1864.

HENRY MOSES, 15th Inf., enl. Jan., 1864, at Monroe, Aug., 1865.

ELISHA A. MOSES, 16th Inf., enl. Jan., 1862, age 24, at Mundy, dischg. April, 1863.

BYRON MOSES, 23d Inf., enl. July, 1862, age 39, at Watertown.

REUBEN MOSES, 30th Inf., enl. Dec., 1864, age 20, at Hudson; to June, 1865.

JABEZ H. MOSES, 2d Cav., enl. Aug., 1862, age 25, at Hillsdale, to March, 1863.

ANDREW F. MOSES, 3d Cav., enl. Sept., 1861, age 18, at Lafayette, dischg. May, 1862.

JUDSON J. MOSES, 3d Cav., enl. Sept., 1861, age 19, at Paw Paw, dischg. Nov., 1862; residence, Arlington, Mich.

CHARLES E. MOSES, 5th Cav., enl. Aug., 1862, age 18, at Allegan, died at Andersonville Sept., 1864.

THOMAS MOSES, 1st Sharpshooters, enl. Jan., 1865, age 18, at Detroit, to July, 1865.

PENNSYLVANIA — IN THE REVOLUTION.

From the Archives of Pennsylvania.

Vol. 23. ENSIGN TOBIAS MOSES, of a German Company of Northampton Co. of 1778–1782, known as "Rangers on the Frontier."

Vol. 11. HENRY MOSES, Paying war taxes.
ADAM MOSES, " "
JACOB MOSES, " "
PETER MOSES, "
JOHN MOSES,
MICHAEL MOSES, "
SAMUEL MOSES, " "

The writer has considerable material showing emigration to Pennsylvania in Colonial days of Moses families of German and Swiss extraction belonging to the Lutheran faith. Many of the descendants of this sturdy and patriotic stock have made successful business and professional careers. A few instances are given in outline, as starting points for a future genealogist.

Mr. William E. Moses, an Attorney of Denver, Colo., and Washington, D. C., communicates the following:

"Great-grandfather, Jacob Moses," (See foregoing list,) "was a native of

Germany, born 1739. He was a man of affairs, a reading man, an ardent student of the Bible; he affiliated with the Lutheran Church. He lived at East Berlin, Pa., and had eight children.

"Grandfather, John Moses, b. 1772, removed to Ohio 1801, settled near Somerset; had fourteen children.

"Father, Jacob Creth Moses, b. in Adams Co., Pa., 1795, and d. in Brown Co., Ill. *Children:* John Calhoun; Howard A.; Joseph H.; Susan A.; Elizabeth R.; Anthony H.; and William E."

John G. Moses, Editor Daily News, Westchester, Pa., writes that he is descended from the Adam Moses of the Revolution, and gives his line. Silas Moses of New Florence, Pa., states that his great-grandfather, Adam, had three brothers; William, Michael, and Samuel, who came with him to this country. (See foregoing list.) Capt. H. S. Moses, of Canton, Ohio, states that his original ancestor was a French Huguenot from Alsace, who settled in Franklin Co., Pa., in 1750.

Mr. E. B. Moses of the Watkins Banking Co., and the Gulf Land Co. of Lake Charles, La., gives his chain of descent from the Peter Moses, mentioned above in the Penn. Archives, and states that Peter was a brother of Jacob Moses.

The writer is well aware that the foregoing, summarized from a portion of his notes, does not come strictly within the scope and plan of this work. He makes no claim, however, that all of the names in the Moses Soldier List are descendants of John of Plymouth, and John of Portsmouth, though a large majority were such descendants.

The Adjutant-General's Reports of Pennsylvania, Ohio, Illinois, Indiana, and some other states, contain many names of Moses men in the Civil War: they would have been published in this list, but for the labor involved. In the Reports for the said states, the names are alphabetically arranged by companies, and not by regiments. Nearly 1500 company rosters would have to be examined in the Ohio Adjutant-General Report alone.

APPENDIX.

American Genealogical Works usually give, not only the histories of families in this country and their derivation, but also some account of notable families across the sea who bear the same name and whose records date back of the first emigration to America.

Reference is accordingly made herein to some such Moses families of the British Isles, also to some of their descendants who have in more recent years become residents of the United States and have achieved distinction therein.

The writer has, in a few instances, been asked for assurances as to the purely Anglo-Saxon strain of the early Moses families, but there need be no doubt upon this point on the part of any one who can trace descent from ancestors living in Great Britain before the time of the Commonwealth. Those curious about such matters are referred to the 360 year period described on pages 596 and 598 of Vol. 8 of the American Encyclopedia. Also to Chambers Miscellany, Vol. 9, No. 153.

In this work will be found the names of several men who have distinguished themselves in literature or in college and professional life. It is gratifying to find that as far back as the days of the Stuarts there was a William Moses, Master of a College, a founder of scholarships, and of fame sufficient to have entitled him to a biographer.

From Memorials of Cambridge by Thomas Wright and Rev. H. Longueville, 1845, Vol. 1, p. 16, Pembroke College, England. "Sergeant Moses, Master of the College under the Protectorate, founded several exhibitions of fifty pounds a year for scholars from Christ's Hospital which are held along with others allowed by the Governor."

Privileges of the University of Cambridge together with Observations on its History, Antiquities, Structure, and Biography. By George Dyer London, 1824, Vol. 1, pp. 43, 109.

"Mr. William Moses who founded several good scholarships for youths (coming from Christ's Hospital — proceeded A. M. 1647, and was admitted the thirtieth), Master 1654. He was ejected by the Uniformity, yet he seems to have been a loyalist from a copy of ouses of his in the Congratulation to Charles at the Restoration. He afterwards took to the law and died a rich old Sergeant L. C."

Architectural History of the University of Cambridge, by Robert Willis, M.A., Cambridge, 1886, Vol. 1, p. 144:

"Mr. Sergeant Moses whose proceedings in reference to the matter are best described in the words of his biographer Dr. Sampson.

'After the displacing of Mr. Vines and death of Mr. Simson who succeeded, the fellows unanimously chose him for their Master which yet came under a great contest at Whitehall.

'For the then called Protector would needs have imposed upon them another. But the Fellows by representation of his worth and serviceableness to the College gained their point and got a revocation of his order.

'In the five years of his Mastership he bestirred himself for ye advancement of his College as if it had been his only business and proper estate. He brought to some issue and settlement ye estate of Sir Robert Hitcham wch had been so long contested for, got the moneys received from it into the College hands, raised that building wch bears his name.

"That old and withered face of that ancient and pious foundation he repaired and made it look young again. The building over the library which was ready to tumble down and the walls of the College which were so decayed, rueful and illfavored that they would rather affright students from them than bring them thither, he brought to this pleasant aspect that they have ever since had.

"By his interest and acquaintance he procured many hundred pounds to be layd out upon them. And all this at a time when Universities and Colleges were devoted to ruin in the desires of some and the apprehensions of most men."

A Note to above extract. "Memorials of Mr. Sergeant Moses, Master of Pembroke Hall who died Oct. 30, 1688, aged 66, by Henry Sampson. MS. in Pembroke College Lodge. He was Master from 1654 to 1660. The Society was at this time said to flourish "sub dispencione Mosaica—Dr. Ainslee, p. 93."

The following is from Professor J. F. Bethune Baker, dated Pembroke College, Cambridge, England, May 15, 1905, in answer to the writer's numbered queries.

"Sergeant William Moses:

(1) Born in 1622, baptized Aug. 15, 1622, in the parish of St. Saviour's, Southwark.

(2) Father, John Moses, "a Taylor"; mother, daughter of Mr. Crow, Rector of Stoke, near Guilford in Surrey.

(3) His money would be all of his own making.

Father and mother died when he was three, and he was brought up until eleven by the grandfather, Mr. Crow, who placed him in Christ Church

Hospital, whence he came up to Pembroke and by his own merits won scholarships and patrons who provided for him.

As Fellow, and Tutor, and Master, he would be in the way of saving something, but the chief part of his wealth must have come after he retired from Cambridge. When he was ejected at the Restoration and in middle life, he began the study of Law and evidently rapidly made a large practice. He became *Solicitor* and *Counsel* to the *East India Company*. So that though always a liberal giver he left behind him about 8,000 pounds, according to Dr. Sampson, who says that an estate of that value might devolve on the College and Christ's Hospital; but I believe the College received only 1,700 pounds, most of which was to be used for scholarships for boys from Christ's Hospital. I don't know what the school received. There were also legacies to "divers of his kindred and friends."

(4 and 5). Can be judged from the fact that he was made Fellow originally by the Earl of Manchester's Commission of 1644, the only one of the Fellows appointed who was a Pembroke man. So probably his political sympathies were with the Commonwealth. He remained Fellow all through and was elected Master by the Fellows, (all of whom were nominees of the Cromwell party,) and accepted as such by Cromwell, though he had intended to appoint some one else (probably knowing little of Moses).

At the restoration he was ejected. But Sampson says he had always argued for the Episcopal form of government as most suitable to Scripture and antiquity. He also declared he was pious and devout, although "the multitude of his business and the Debonairite and francness of his Conversation and some bodily infirmities gave occasion to some that knew him little to misjudge him in some of these things."

Professor Baker adds: "The life" is a short one and in English, —very racy and quaint at times."

From Professor Carl Kinsley of the Chicago University, who was at Cambridge during the summer of 1905, I am advised: "The College (Pembroke College, Cambridge University) is just *now* putting in a MEMORIAL WINDOW in honor of WILLIAM MOSES, whose title of Sergeant merely meant that he was a barrister."

On pages 179 and 180, Vol. 39, of the Dictionary of National Biography, is found an abridgment of the foregoing. Quotation is made from the latter part of the article which gives a fuller account of the remarkably successful career of Sergeant William Moses after he was removed from the Mastership of Pembroke College, Cambridge University:

"At the Restoration Laney was reinstated. Moses was not in orders, and was disinclined to enter the ministry of the Established Church though he was averse to Presbyterianism and in favor of moderate Episcopacy. His deeply religious mind was cast in a puritan mould; Baxter was very desirous to have him appear as one of the Commissioners, Mar. 25, 1661, to the Savoy Conference, but could not prevail.

"His own health led Moses to have some practical acquaintance with medicine, and he was the friend of several leading physicians. But after hesitating as to his future vocation he turned to the law and became Counsel to the East India Company. He was a 'very quick and ready man.' Charles II took particular notice of him when he pleaded for the Company before the Privy Council.

"The Lord Chancellor, Henage Finch, the first Earl of Nottingham (q. v.), said, that had he taken earlier to the law he would easily have been at the head of his profession. He was made a Sergeant-at-law on 11 June, 1688, died 'a rich batchellor' in the same year and left considerable benefactions to his college. A short Latin poem by him is included in Academiæ Cantabrigiensis, Cambridge, 1660, a congratulatory collection on the restoration of Charles II."

From the same volume:

"Miles Mosse or Moses; 1580–1614; a divine, educated at Cambridge University: proceeded D.D. between 1595 and 1603."

He published several books; one a "Catechism 1590, which is now only known by an answer by Thomas Rogers (q. v.), entitled Miles Christianus — a Defense written against an Epistle prefixed to a catechism made by Miles Moses."

Also on same page:

"Alexander Mosses: born 1793, Liverpool, England; an artist." A full column of the Dictionary is given to a description of his celebrated paintings.

That the Moses family was located in the County of Kent, before the year 1600, is proved by the following quotation from Mass. Hist. Society, Vol. 6, p. 57. "Dexter's List of English Exiles in Amsterdam 1597-1625."

"Moyses, Timothy, (from Penshurst, Kent,) married July 6, 1613, Merriweather, Elizabeth, (from Ingoldswells, Lincolnshire). From the autographic signatures in the Amsterdam Marriage Records dated July 6, 1613."

In early days the name was sometimes spelled "Moises," and again "Moysis," (see pages 89 and 95 of this work).

From Dict. of Natl. Biography, London, Vol. 28:

"HUGH MOISES, 1722–1806. In 1787 was presented to the rectory of Greystoke, and was succeeded by his nephew, Rev. Edward Moises. In 1801 was chaplain to his old pupil, Lord Eldon, who had just been raised to the woolsack. In 1810 a fine mural monument executed by Flaxman, was erected to his memory; the expenses, 400L, were defrayed by subscription among his pupils"

From Vol. 39, p. 248:

"DAVID MOYSIE — MOISE — MOYSES or MOSEY; Author of the Memoirs

APPENDIX. 275

of the Affairs of Scotland 1577-1603. Was a Writer and Notary Public; was Clerk of the Privy Council, 'giving continewale attendance upon his Hienes at Court,' afterwards in the office of Kings Secretary. In 1584, he obtained a grant under privy seal of 32 L. of certain lands for his son, David, for his 'help and sustentation at the scolis and education in Vertew and guid lettres'.

"The Memoirs are the record of an eye witness and are in two manuscripts, were printed in 1755, and edited for the Bannatyne Club, Edinburgh, 1830."

From "List of Pilgrims to America, 1600 to 1700," by John Camden Hotten: Among those "acknowledging the Supremacy of the Church of England in 1635, emigrating from Gravesend to St. Christopher, is *Matthew Moyses*, aged 17."

Same book, page 169: "List of living and dead in Virginia, Feb. 16, 1623. Att ye Colledge Land, (29 names, among them) *Thedor Moises*." P. 202, "Muster of inhabitants in Virginia Colledg Land, Henrico, taken 23, Jan., 1624, *Theodor Moyses;* came in the London Marchannt."

From N. E. Hist. and Gen. Reg., Vol. 2, "Passengers for Virginia, 1635, *James Moyses*, aged 28."

Comments by writer: In "British Family Names," by Barber, will be found the names of men who came with William the Conqueror, and are recorded in Domesday Book. A *Moyses* is among them, and it is likely that the name, of Norman French origin, was, in succeeding centuries, slightly changed in spelling, but no more so than with other names found in the same Domesday Book, or with English words in general. Take Chaucer's poems as originally printed, and note the wide variation from the present spelling.

In a table of "Derivation of Family Names," Barber gives, "Moyse from Moissac, a local name in France." In early days, even in this country, the names of our own progenitors were sometimes written in the *public records*, "Moises," "Moysis," "Mosses," and also "Moyses." See pages 89, 95, and 100, also paragraph, No. 400.

Many inquiries have been made since the first volume of this book was published in 1890, concerning the Moses crest (see p. 119). In 1892, a very large illustrated work was published in Edinburgh, entitled, "Fairbairn's Book of Crests of Families of Great Britain and Ireland."

On pages 112, and 113, of Vol. 1, will be found a list of over 300 English families having a cock for a crest. (See the many forms of these crests in large plates 89, 90, and 91.) The "*Cock regardant, (looking behind,)*" is illustrated in No. 9, of Plate 91, Vol. 2, and is described as the crest of the Byers, Byres, Greive, Moses, Kimberlee, and Tame families.

Extracts from letters 1892-3 to Zebina Moses, from Rev. Richard G. Moses, Rector of Grace Church, Merchantville, N. J.:

"We belong to a family which has lived in the parish of Meavy, Devonshire, England, and the immediate neighborhood, for many generations. I have a distinct remembrance of my grandfather's brother, Richard Moses, who was for a long time one of the Churchwardens of that parish and who told me that the parish register contained the names of several successive generations of the family, as far back as the Commonwealth period. He knew nothing of the older books, but the parish being a small one, the book in use fifty years ago covered a very long period of time. . . . . In Walker's Sufferings of the Clergy, a book relating to the tribulations of the Church during the supremacy of the Long Parliament and Cromwell's Triers of Charles I, mention is made of the maltreatment of the rector or vicar of Meavy by some of his parishioners, among them one *Richard Moses* was prominent.

"When Charles II was restored, the vicar prosecuted Richard Moses at the Devon assizes for assault, and Richard like a prudent man acknowledged his faults and was let off, at the vicar's intercession I believe, with a fine.

"This was in 1660, and the probabilities evidently favor the opinion, that the Moses family were of some local standing and not newcomers at that date.

"Extract from 'WALKER'S SUFFERINGS OF THE CLERGY,' describing an occurrence at Meavy, Devonshire, in which one of my family figures. Walker, the author, was a clergyman at Exeter, who died about 1730:

"'Joseph Shute, rector of Meavy, Devon, sixty years old, formally dispossessed of his living under the Parliament and Protectorate, but according to accounts, much harassed by the parishioners opposed to him. The most notorious affair occurred on a Sunday, when the greater part of the parish conspired to keep him out of the church. Mr. Shute attempted to get in by the great door, and was pushed back from the porch by one *Richard Moses*, which fall was like to have killed him. Then he went and preached upon the cross, and alluded to the conspiracy against Paul as being like to the conduct of the parishioners. (Vide Acts XXIII, 12-14). After the King's return he brought his action against Richard Moses, and out of his religious nature forgave him upon easy terms.'

"The inference from this statement that Richard Moses was a leading opponent of the rector is a just one, and agrees with family traditions which ascribe to us permanent residence in the parish and ownership of land of some sort. My grandfather's younger brother, also named Richard, was a churchwarden of Meavy parish for many years, and he repeatedly told me about this Richard Moses of the Commonwealth period and his behavior towards his parson. The rector had a book, he said, which related this story, but he could not tell me the name of it. After my curiosity was excited, I had no difficulty in ascertaining that the record was in Walker's book narrating the persecution of the Episcopal clergy during the civil war and the Protectorate. Walker was an Exeter clergyman, and was likely to be well informed concerning Devonshire matters. I suspect that the Rev. Joseph Shute was of the stamp of the Vicar of Bray, celebrated in the famous old song, and as the rural folk were intensely royalist in their feeling throughout the West of England, it may be that Richard Moses was a stalwart royalist and churchman rather than a Puritan. Certainly the family had no connection, or tradition of connection, with any other religious belief and profession than that of the church of England, in my grandfather's time. He, George Moses, son of John, died in 1855, aged seventy-three years. He was born at Meavy in 1782, and was the second son of John Moses, of Meavy, whose death at an advanced age I distinctly remember. I think he was upwards of ninety, and therefore might have been only two generations later than the Commonwealth Richard Moses of Meavy. The parish registers of Meavy Church I have not personally searched, but my great-uncle, the late churchwarden, informed me that the rector had told him often that the family was mentioned in the oldest extant records. In the churchyard the gravestones bearing the name are numerous, although I do not remember seeing any of earlier date than the eighteenth century. The moor country storms, and the mosses growing on the stones, make havoc of the inscriptions in a very little while. My last visit was in the summer of 1870, when I spent a week in the neighborhood. My great-uncle Richard was then living and showed me the site of the cross and other noteworthy spots. . . . . I met, and afterwards corresponded with two persons of the name besides yourself. The first was a very aged woman, over 90 years, living at Lymington, Hampshire, England. She told me that she was born in the Isle of Wight, not far from Lymington, which is on the Solent between the Isle of Wight and the main land. Her husband had been dead many years. A few years later I received a letter from a clergyman of the Church of England, making inquiries concerning my family history, but as he came from Ireland we were both satisfied that there was nothing but the name in common to us. . . . . Meavy is a village on the edge of Dartmoor, about ten miles north of Plymouth, Devon. Near by are the parishes of Walkhampton, Sheepster, Shaugh, Buckland, and Monarchorum. The last named parish indicates that there were church lands in the neighborhood."

*INDEX TO VOL. II.

MOSES NAMES.

Aaron, 189, 199, 200, 204, 205, 206, 207, 231, 232, 261, 264.
Aaron T., 191, 192.
Abbie, 226, 243, 248, 257, 258.
Abbie L., 245.
Abbie R., 166.
Abbie S., 256.
Abby, 156.
Abel, 155, 261, 262.
Abigail, 153, 167, 189, 190, 200, 206, 210, 211, 233, 245.
Abigail F., 218, 220.
Abigail W., 204.
Abiathar, 223.
Abner, 160, 161, 262.
Abraham, 212, 213, 235, 261.
Abram, 235, 237.
Abram T., 245, 248, 249.
Achsa, 194.
Adam, 269, 270.
Addie, 231.
Addie R., 231.
Adeline M., 179, 180.
Adeline, 158, 236.
Adelaide, 158.
Adelbert A., 191.
Adrian, 163.
Adrian L., 164.
Agnes, 176, 218.
Agnes A., 159.
Agnes J., 193.
Alan, 172.
Albert, 161, 169, 193, 205.
Albert C., 228.
Albert G., 193, 194.
Albert J., 194, 215, 265.
Albert P., 170, 171.
Albert R., 183.
Albert T., 246, 250.
Alexander, 267, 274.
Alfred, 161, 179, 182.
Alfred C., 245, 249.
Alfred D., 205, 256.
Alfred G., 184.

Alfred L., 266.
Alice, 157, 191, 214, 219, 235, 249.
Alice C., 239.
Alice D., 246.
Alice R., 157.
Alma, 239.
Almira, 157.
Alonzo, 173, 192, 193, 235, 238, 243, 266.
Alonzo D., 266.
Alonzo J., 243.
Alvarez, 243.
Alvena, 247.
Alvira, 236.
Alwin R., 215.
Amasa, 169, 170, 213.
Amasa Foster, 170.
Amanda, 245.
Ambrose, 255.
Ambrose D., 256.
Amelia A., 227.
Amoret, 155.
Andrew, 261.
Andrew F, 269.
Andrew J., 169, 245, 249, 266.
Andy, 168.
Angelia S., 232.
Angie, 242.
Ann, 158, 233, 236.
Ann A., 218.
Ann Eliza, 164.
Anna, 191, 233, 255.
Anna C., 178.
Anna M., 205, 211.
Anne, 233.
Anne E., 236, 249.
Anne Estelle, 249.
Annie, 194, 249.
Annie A., 219.
Annie M., 259.
Anson F., 179, 180.
Anson G., 179.
Anthony H., 270.

*Map Index page 144. Index of Family Histories recording Moses alliances page 298.

Aphia, 233.
Archie, 183.
Ardolissa, 173.
Arnold Henry, 278.
Artemus, 169.
Arthur A., 163.
Arthur C., 172.
Arthur E., 163.
Arthur H., 151.
Arvilla L., 226.
Asa, 149, 165, 168, 169, 261, 264.
Asa Benoni, 169, 170.
Asa L., 165.
Ashbel, 157, 158, 185, 186, 261.
Asher C., 193.
Ashley O., 267.
Auria, 164.
Augusta M., 156, 225.
Augustus F., 151, 268.
Augustus L., 173, 174.
A. W., 185.
Azariah W., 160, 161.
Aziza, 185, 186.
Barnabas, 157, 262.
Barbara M., 195.
Benjamin, 153, 190, 226, 234, 245, 257, 262, 263.
Benjamin F., 258.
Benjamin S., 226.
Benjamin W., 211, 212.
Benoni, 154, 169, 261.
Bessie, 168.
Bernard, 163, 164.
Bernie O., 168.
Berenice A., 193.
Berenice C., 231.
Bertha A., 220.
Bertha M., 164.
Bertrand A., 229.
Betsey, 149, 154, 189, 190, 211, 212, 232, 253.
Betsey L., 175.
Betsey M., 173, 174.
Betsey S., 232, 253.
Betty O., 221.
Bethsheba, 235.
Beulah F., 162.
Bildad, 145.
Blanche V., 227.
Bradford, 231.
Bradley E., 152.
Brigham W., 195.
Byron, 269.
Byron E.,
Caleb, 146, 154.
Calvin C., 179, 183, 265.
Calvin H., 182, 183.

Calvin J., 183.
Candace T., 174.
Carl, 192.
Carl J., 183.
Caroline, 187, 188, 192, 214.
Caroline A., 173, 174.
Caroline E., 185.
Caroline H., 152.
Caroline G., 247.
Caroline M., 250.
Carrie, 152, 185, 191, 208, 223.
Carrie E., 218.
Carrie M., 173.
Cassius M., 172.
Catharine, 171, 200, 245.
Catharine A., 205.
Catherine M., 170, 174, 238.
Caton, 267.
Celia, 175, 176.
Celestia, 192.
Charles, 152, 166, 173, 177, 178, 192, 193, 204, 212, 249, 256, 259, 266.
Charles A, 156, 179, 181, 192, 213.
Charles B., 157.
Charles C. P., 218, 220.
Charles D., 248, 249.
Charles E., 247, 248, 269.
Charles F., 180.
Charles H., 221, 222.
Charles J., 191, 192.
Charles K., 187, 188, 278.
Charles M., 237, 238.
Charles O., 221, 222, 248.
Charles R., 152, 164, 176, 193.
Charles S., 218, 219.
Charles T., 191, 226, 229, 237, 238, 239.
Charles W., 162, 173, 174, 214, 216.
Charlotte, 155, 211.
Charlotte A., 174, 182.
Charlotte C., 251.
Charlotte E., 164, 205.
Chauncey, 166.
Chloe, 176.
Chester S., 224.
Christina, 251.
Christopher, 245, 247.
Clara, 159, 208, 210, 219.
Clara A., 163, 205.
Clarence, 184, 218.
Clarence E., 227.
Clarence F., 195.
Clarenda R., 156.
Clarissa, 189, 192, 236.
Clarissa H., 157, 158.

INDEX.

Clifferd A., 250.
Claude, 188.
Clayton L., 171.
Clayton S., 248.
Clyda Yorke, 151.
Clyde E., 166.
Cora, 217.
Cora B., 238.
Cora E., 159, 165.
Cora L., 229.
Colby, 231.
Coleman, 192.
Collin, 262.
Cordelia, 155, 161.
Cornelia, 219, 220.
Curtis, 238.
Curtis Lee., 162.
Cyrus, 231, 235.
Cryus A., 237.
Cyrus S., 207.
Cynthia, 172.
Cynthia E., 245.
Cynthia H., 190.
Daniel, 147, 148, 177, 185, 203, 204, 207, 233, 234, 243, 262.
Daniel F., 208, 265.
Daniel R., 163.
Darius, 167, 267.
David, 145, 207, 208, 209, 210, 212, 262, 265, 274.
David B., 178, 232.
David C., 195.
David E., 216.
David P., 265.
David W., 235.
Dearborn, 263.
Dearborn B., 206, 254.
Dearborn W., 206.
Deborah Ann, 221.
Deborah H. 248.
Deborah, 149, 154.
Delia L., 223.
Della, 159, 231.
Dennis, 150.
DeWitt S., 158, 159.
Dolly, 212.
Donald F., 230.
Donald P., 188.
Donna, 172.
Dora, 222.
Dora P., 221.
Dorcas, 169, 172.
Dorothy, 187, 206, 207, 212.
Dorothy E., 214.
Dorothy M., 151, 171.
Drusella A., 240.
Ebenezer, 210, 211, 212, 234, 247.

E. B., 270.
Edgar, 158.
Edgar A., 183.
Edgar P., 267.
Edith, 159, 193, 218, 229.
Edith G., 278.
Editha H., 179, 184.
Edmund P., 221, 223.
Edmund Q., 251, 252.
Edna M., 157.
Edward, 208, 223, 225, 226, 235, 237, 266, 274.
Edward A., 237.
Edward B., 230.
Edward F., 225.
Edward H., 242.
Edward L., 153.
Edward O., 185.
Edward R., 179, 181, 182.
Edward W., 171.
Edwin, 178, 236, 242.
Edwin D., 162.
Edwin L., 170, 171.
Edwin P., 157.
Edwin R., 227.
Effie A., 239.
Effie L., 183.
Elbridge F., 237, 238.
Eleazer, 153.
Elias, 230.
Elihu, 172, 173, 174.
Elihu B., 175.
Elinor, 172.
Eliot B., 251.
Eli N., 266.
Elizur, 167.
Elijah, 209, 232.
Elisha, 261.
Elisha A., 269.
Eliza, 158, 195, 245.
Eliza A., 174, 175, 235.
Eliza D., 258.
Eliza E., 205.
Eliza F., 236.
Elizabeth, 156, 157, 166, 173, 189, 192, 199, 200, 201, 202, 203, 212, 213, 223, 232, 233, 234, 243, 250, 257.
Elizabeth C., 211.
Elizabeth F., 243.
Elizabeth G., 157, 158, 206.
Elizabeth H., 259.
Elizabeth M., 163, 218, 219, 245.
Elizabeth R., 270.
Elizabeth T., 190.
Ella, 205, 217, 22.
Ella B., 164.

Ella E., 191.
Ella L., 173.
Ellen, 152, 188, 213, 242.
Ellen A., 210, 237.
Elliot L., 228.
Elmer, 165, 231.
Elmer E., 170.
Elmer S., 183.
Elmer W., 195.
Elnathan, 264.
Elvena R., 249.
Elvira, 204, 231.
Elva M., 228.
Elwyn, 259.
Emeline, 149.
Emerson, 164.
Emergene, 216.
Emily, 157.
Emily D., 183.
Emily E., 162.
Emma, 165, 217.
Emma I., 249.
Emma Jane, 179.
Emma L., 170.
Emma P., 252.
Enam, 261.
Enoch, 212, 213.
Enoch R., 212, 216.
Erastus, 178, 186, 187, 262.
Ernest B., 229.
Ernest C., 151.
Ernest H., 170.
Ernestine L., 247.
Ernest M., 251, 252.
Ervin, 186.
Estelle, 191.
Esther, 157, 177, 195, 196, 214, 217.
Esther J., 178.
Ethelwyn, 251.
Ethel, 168, 221.
Ethel A., 170.
Ethel E., 157.
Ethel M., 171, 240.
Ethel May, 171.
Ethel W., 195.
Eugenia, 220.
Eunice, 190, 233.
Eunice A., 182, 183.
Eunice I., 256.
Eugene C., 216.
Eugene M., 218
Eugene W., 227.
Eva, 217.
Eva Belle, 241.
Eva E., 238.
Evart, 214.

Evaline, 176.
Evelyn J., 239.
Evelyn L., 151.
E. Walter, 186.
Ezekiel, 261, 262.
Fanny, 155, 169.
Fanny P., 221.
Fannie, 223.
Ferdinand, 168.
Ferren G., 179.
Fidelia, 194.
Flora, 183, 211, 217, 226, 231.
Flora A., 166.
Flora B., 162, 224.
Flora E., 166.
Florence C., 178.
Florence, 238.
Florence E., 241.
Floretta, 157.
Forest, 191, 217.
Frank, 166, 185, 191, 192, 208, 216, 239, 249, 256.
Frances, 191, 220, 235, 242.
Frances A., 180.
Frances E., 151, 246.
Frances L., 151, 225.
Frances M., 216.
Frances P., 252.
Frances T., 180.
Francis, 179.
Francis, 184, 185, 267.
Francis H., 165.
Francis O., 247.
Francis S., 184.
Francis T., 179.
Francis, W., 227.
Frank A., 180, 181, 221, 222.
Frank D., 162, 219.
Frank E., 152, 176.
Frank F., 160.
Frank K., 178.
Frank L., 239, 240, 241.
Frank N., 152.
Frank O., 242, 247, 252.
Frank S., 171.
Frank W., 206, 215.
Franklin, 150, 156, 157, 165, 213.
Franklin T., 182, 183.
Franzi E., 193.
Fred, 159, 168, 170, 192, 208.
Fred A., 143, 151.
Fred C., 151.
Fred F., 195.
Fred G., 259.
Fred I., 185.
Fred L., 241.
Frederic C. S., 156.

INDEX. 285

Frederick E., 151, 256.
Frederick E., 162.
Frederick F., 205, 206.
Frederick H., 167.
Frederick S., 247.
Freeman, 231.
Galen C., 247, 252.
Garnet E., 241.
Gaylord M., 229.
Geneva A., 224.
Geneveive, 220.
Genevieve K., 218.
George, 156, 159, 170, 173, 200, 202, 204, 206, 208, 212, 217, 232, 233, 235, 236, 238, 259, 263, 267, 268, 277.
George A., 164, 170, 266, 268.
George C., 166.
George E., 168, 241.
George F., 164, 231, 246, 250, 251, 266, 267.
George H., 151, 168, 237, 239.
George Geminy, 166.
George L., 152, 176.
George M., 266.
George N., 179, 181.
George P., 180.
George R., 182.
George S., 266, 267.
George W., 205, 218, 232, 245, 247, 248, 249, 268.
George W., 175.
Georgia A., 237.
Georgine H., 206.
Georgine M., 206.
Gerald, 170.
Gerald E., 227.
Gerald L., 168.
Gertrude E., 164.
Gertrude H., 157.
Gertrude M., 229.
Gertrude S., 248.
Giles, 194.
Gladys, 192, 249.
Gordon, 239.
Green, 182, 217, 227, 231.
Gracie, 256.
Grace M., 170.
Graham L., 223.
Grant E., 186.
Grover, 217.
Guy, 150, 217.
Haldy, 212.
Halsey H., 192, 193.
Haman, 261.
Hannah, 167, 188, 200, 201, 202, 203, 204, 218, 234, 253.

Hannah A., 154.
Hannah Maria, 154.
Hannah N., 245.
Harlow, 192.
Harlow E., 193.
Harold A., 162.
Harriet, 159, 174, 185, 191, 211, 212, 213.
Harriet A., 175, 205.
Harriet C., 245.
Harriet H., 190.
Harriet J., 247.
Harriet M., 183.
Harriet N., 156, 157.
Harriet O., 205.
Harriet S., 247.
Harriet W., 160.
Harrison, 156.
Harry, 165, 166, 168, 183.
Harry B., 195.
Harry S., 240.
Harry W., 225.
Hartwell E., 256.
Harvey, 152.
Harvey J., 265, 268.
Harvey W., 165, 166.
Haskell, 156.
Hattie, 166, 217, 238.
Hattie A., 154.
Hattie B., 224.
Hattie G, 193.
Hattie L., 170.
Hazel, 217.
Hazel E., 229.
Hazel L. E., 229.
Hazel P., 224.
Hector, 165.
Helen, 166, 194, 206, 230.
Helen C., 151.
Helen E., 157.
Helen F., 249, 250.
Helen L., 228, 252.
Helen P., 157.
Henrietta A., 163.
Henry, 143, 144, 152, 154, 166, 173, 193, 230, 258, 266, 268, 269.
Henry C., 221, 222, 245, 268.
Henry D., 182.
Henry H., 152, 205.
Henry M., 222.
Henry W., 187, 246, 278.
Herbert, 193, 223, 230.
Herbert A., 171, 242, 243.
Herbert F., 249.
Herbert G., 242.
Herbert H., 222.

Herbert W., 230.
Herman, 268.
Hiram, 150, 168, 170, 190, 191, 267.
Hiram C., 229.
Hiram E., 268.
Hiram P., 194.
Hiram S., 226, 229.
Hiram W., 232.
Horace, 235, 236.
Horace A., 152.
Horace C., 162, 164.
Horace H., 219.
Horace W., 236, 239, 240.
Homer A., 226.
Hosmer C., 193.
Howard, 213, 220.
Howard A., 270.
Howard L., 229.
Howard M., 230, 239, 265.
Howard N., 197, 232, 240, 241.
Hoyt, 155.
Hugh, 261, 274.
Hunking, 201, 202.
Ida, 247.
Ida E., 184, 238.
Ida F., 170.
Ilinois Mary, 219.
Ina E., 239.
Inez, 238.
Irving, 155, 185, 193, 212.
Ira, 177.
Irwin H., 173.
Isa John, 231.
Isaac, 223, 236.
Isaac D., 221.
Isaac F., 268.
Isaac, 172, 261.
Isaiah, 262.
Isabel, 225.
Isadora, 232.
Israel, 265, 268.
Iva L., 242.
Iza W., 242.
Jabez F., 265, 269.
Jabez H., 155, 156, 157.
Jabez H., 269.
Jacob, 254, 268, 269, 270.
Jacob Creth, 270.
James, 193, 194, 195, 200, 203, 204, 205, 206, 210, 212, 213, 214, 216, 217, 221, 231, 233, 253, 254, 257, 264, 267, 274.
James C., 221, 222.
James E., 165, 211, 265.
James F., 155, 167, 208.
James G., 185, 229.
James G. B., 226.
James H., 216.
James J., 195.
James K. P., 237.
James M., 178.
James O., 266.
James R., 184, 212.
James T., 237, 242.
James W., 157.
Jane, 157, 195, 217, 232, 253, 254.
Jane Amelia, 149.
Jane E., 165, 185.
Janet, 158.
Janie, 191.
Janney, 253, 254.
Jaspar, 226.
Jaspar T., 215.
Jay A., 168.
J. E., 164.
Jenney, 159, 203.
Jennie, 166.
Jennie A., 192.
Jennie E., 179.
Jennie G., 170.
Jaspar N., 215.
Jesse, 154, 161, 189, 194, 262.
Jessie Mae, 227.
Jesse Tilton, 195.
Jessie, 170.
Jessie E., 239.
Jessie F., 160.
Jessie L., 165.
Jessie M., 162.
Joel, 231.
Joel P., 168, 268.
John, 143, 144, 145, 149, 154, 155, 161, 167, 168, 187, 197, 198, 199, 202, 204, 206, 207, 208, 209, 210, 211, 212, 214, 216, 217, 223, 233, 235, 239, 257, 261, 262, 264, 265, 267, 269, 270, 272, 277.
John A., 267.
John B., 210.
John Bingham, 150, 151.
John C., 155, 172, 251, 268, 270.
John E., 151, 175, 222, 267.
John F., 187, 188, 218, 220, 221, 236, 239, 267.
John G., 256, 258, 260.
John H., 230, 259, 266.
John L., 221, 223.
John M., 197, 207, 232.
John N., 173, 174, 258.
John O., 176.
John P., 242, 266.
John Robert, 278.

INDEX. 287

John S., 208.
John Shapleigh, 278.
John S. H., 245, 248, 249.
John T., 182, 183.
John V., 171.
John W., 205, 221, 226, 230, 231, 237, 239, 259, 265.
Jonah, 177, 178, 186, 189, 193, 194, 243, 263.
Jonathan, 168, 189, 192, 210, 216, 217.
Jonas, 261, 262.
Joseph, 149, 153, 200, 201, 202, 210, 211, 216, 217, 225, 226, 230, 253, 263, 264, 265, 266.
Joseph A., 236, 239.
Joseph C., 257, 268.
Joseph H., 270.
Joseph J., 206.
Joseph S., 205.
Joseph W., 208, 221.
Josephine, 257.
Joshua, 146, 154, 188, 189, 204, 262, 263.
Joshua F., 245, 249.
Joshua Nelson, 188, 189.
Joshua W., 210.
Josiah, 200, 203, 210, 212, 216, 232, 233, 234, 243, 262, 263.
Joyce R., 231.
Judson J., 269.
Julia, 157, 190, 214.
Julia D., 206.
Julia P., 247.
Julia W., 177.
Julian, 194, 195.
Julian N., 195.
Juliette, 157, 164.
Julius T., 238.
J. Woodman, 256, 257.
Katherine, 177, 186, 201, 202, 207, 222, 233.
Katherine W., 221.
Kate, 191.
Katie L., 223.
Kenneth R., 151.
Kimball, 213.
Kirke L., 220.
Kirke W., 219, 220, 265, 266.
Lacy, 168.
Lafayette, 267.
Lafayette L., 184.
Laila F., 228.
Laura, 176, 256.
Laura A., 179, 181.
Laura M., 169.
Lauren N., 165.

Lavina, 178.
Lawrence, 216.
Lecta, 214.
Lee, 217.
Leese, 221.
Le Grand, 256.
Lena, 217, 259.
Lena A., 168.
Leonard, 204, 231.
Leonard H., 226, 227.
LeRoy H., 170.
Leslie F., 240.
Levi, 155, 205, 225, 255, 266.
Levi Rose, 159, 160.
Lewis, 182, 184, 222, 267, 268.
Lewis H., 185.
Lida M., 222.
Lila 159.
Lily H., 154.
Lilla B., 219.
Lillian, 159, 170, 229, 243.
Lina, 221.
Lincoln E., 171.
Linus A., 266.
Linwood, 238.
Lizzie, 208.
Lloyd, 191.
Lois E., 227.
Lorane, 233.
Lorenzo, 212, 214.
Loren N., 165.
Loren S., 165.
Louisa, 189, 192, 256.
Louise, 180, 191, 216.
Louise C., 250.
Louise E., 168.
Louis, 187.
Louis A., 174.
Louis Bingham, 150.
Louis H., 160.
Louis M., 222.
Love, 201.
Lucy, 159, 192, 212.
Lucy C., 193.
Lucy E., 226, 229.
Lucy M., 210, 278.
Lucia G., 219.
Lucian, 155.
Lucius, 155, 265, 268.
Lucius C., 161.
Lucius H., 164.
Lucius Lawrence, 161.
Lucius M., 218, 219.
Lucetta A., 182.
Lucinda, 214, 253, 254.
Lucinda M., 182.
Lucinda P., 179.

Lucretia, 149, 168, 182.
Luella A., 237, 238.
Lula I., 165.
Lura, 227.
Lurton D., 228.
Luther, 152, 173, 175, 186, 177, 184, 185, 186, 268.
Luther R., 216.
Lydia, 208, 216, 217, 243, 255.
Lydia A., 208, 223, 224.
Lydia B., 170.
Lydia C., 252.
Lydia F., 238.
Lydia L., 159, 160.
Lydia T., 247.
Lydia Weeks, 257.
Lyman T., 150.
Mabel, 170.
Mabel A., 188.
Mabel G., 225, 229.
Mabel L., 187, 206.
Mabelle, 259.
Mabelle S., 242.
Madge, 156.
Malcom, 154.
Malcom H., 207.
Mandana, 168.
Marcus, 266.
Marcus E., 268.
Margaret, 171, 222, 243, 245, 249.
Margaret B., 194.
Margaret E., 249.
Margaret I., 150.
Margaret M., 248.
Margery, 152.
Margery D., 174.
Margery J., 188.
Maria, 178, 191, 214, 248.
Maria L., 226.
Marie L., 205.
Marianna C., 174.
Marian, 181.
Marion, 239.
Marion A., 250.
Marion E., 151.
Marilla, 226.
Marjorie, 224.
Mark, 200, 203, 210, 253, 254, 264.
Mark E., 267.
Mark S., 207.
Marshall, 243.
Marshall H., 243.
Marshall R., 159.
Marshall S., 158, 268.
Marshall S., 268.
Martin, 154, 155, 156, 157, 159, 262.

Martin L., 174.
Martha, 154, 191, 192, 195, 200, 204, 206, 210, 211, 216, 230, 231, 233, 235.
Martha A., 151, 155, 173, 174.
Martha J., 231, 226, 238.
Martha S., 204.
Martha Twing, 258.
Mary, 143, 144, 148, 149, 159, 161, 188, 190, 200, 204, 206, 208, 211, 214, 217, 219, 221, 223, 226, 230, 232, 233, 248, 253, 255, 257.
Mary A., 157, 236, 237, 278.
Mary Ann, 179.
Mary Abby, 258.
Mary B., 219.
Mary C., 171, 205.
Mary E., 151, 164, 166, 167, 169, 194, 206, 230, 250, 259.
Mary Elizabeth, 218.
Mary F., 235.
Mary Frances, 210.
Mary G., 179, 249.
Mary J., 221, 236.
Mary L., 183, 194.
Mary Louise, 179, 180, 188.
Mary M., 178, 258.
Mary O., 185.
Mary P., 193, 236.
Mary S., 182.
Mary T., 219.
Maryette, 170.
Matthew, 274.
Mattie, 229.
Mattie A., 216.
Maude, 188, 230.
Maude C., 243.
Maude H., 238.
Maude M., 179.
May, 178.
May D., 250.
May W., 195.
Melvin J., 208.
Mehitable, 234.
Mertin J., 168.
Merton W., 216.
Mertie, 193.
Michael, 266, 268, 269, 270.
Miles, 274.
Mildred, 223.
Mildred E., 170.
Mildred F., 243.
Mildred L., 168.
Mildred O., 181.
Mildred J., 227.
Mildred S., 248.

Millicent, 249.
Millard F., 169, 170.
Millie M., 224, 229.
Mina M., 224.
Minnie, 226.
Minnie L. 216.
Minnie Mae, 229.
Miriam, 209.
Miranda, 235.
Molly, 207.
Moses, 263.
Muriel C., 151.
Myron, 164, 169.
Myron L., 169.
Myrtle, 213.
Myrtle E., 183.
Myfred M., 168.
Nadab, 204, 207, 264.
Nancy, 160, 226, 233.
Nathan, 157, 256, 262, 263.
Nathaniel, 200, 223, 233, 234, 248, 249.
Nehemiah, 257, 258.
Nellie, 176, 247, 256.
Nellie H., 167.
Nellie G., 240.
Nelsen D., 178.
Nettie, 217.
Newell, 231.
Nina L., 228.
Ninna M., 162.
Noah, 207.
Noah J., 208.
Noel H., 155.
Norman, 217.
Ogilvie, 184, 185.
Olen E., 236.
Olin E., 241.
Oliver, 231, 234, 246, 252.
Oliver E., 164.
Olive, 172, 223.
Olive B., 185, 206.
Orator, 158.
Oren, 169, 186.
Orianna, 238.
Orin, 217.
Ormenta, 154.
Orpha Ann, 159.
Orson E., 170.
Orson P., 170.
Orra, 147, 217.
Orrin, 176.
Orrin J., 152, 176.
Orrin L., 243.
Orrin P., 243.
Orris C., 216.
Orville B., 252.

Oscar, 159.
Oscar F., 162.
Oscar Greenman, 155.
Oscar Lea, 151.
Othniel, 154, 155, 172, 175, 188, 261, 262.
Ovid, 178.
Owen, 168.
Owen T., 178.
Ozial H., 156.
Patty, 179, 182.
Parnell, 194.
Parrizade, 157.
Paul, 191, 222.
Pearl, 217.
Peletiah, 201, 202.
Penelope, 154.
Perley, 217.
Peter, 269, 270.
Phebe, 194, 234.
Philip, 266, 267.
Philip A., 193.
Philip G., 187, 188.
Philander, 255, 256.
Philena, 212.
Philo, 255, 256.
Philo P., 173, 175.
Phoebe, 177, 204.
Phoebe E., 195.
Phoebe R., 179, 183.
Pluma, 158.
Polly, 160, 161, 172, 212.
Polly P., 214.
Prentice, D. G., 239.
Rachel, 147, 188, 192.
Ralph, 154, 190, 194.
Randolph, 163.
Raymond G., 248.
Rebecca, 234.
Renaldo, 214, 215.
Reuben, 172, 177, 179, 182, 183, 213, 261, 269.
Reuben G., 178, 179.
Reuben H., 179, 180, 182, 183, 265.
Reuben R., 183.
Rhoda, 154, 172.
Richard, 154, 158, 167, 184, 276, 277.
Richard A., 164.
Richard B., 179.
Richard F., 184.
Richard G., 276, 278.
Richard George, 278.
Richard H., 187.
Richard J., 158, 159.
Richard P., 149.

Richard Schuyler, 151.
Richard W., 165, 166.
Richmond W., 239.
Renaldo P., 267.
Robert, 227.
Robert A., 163.
Robert E., 165.
Robert H., 150, 190, 265, 268.
Robert S., 223, 224, 227.
Rollin, 166.
Rolly, 168.
Rosanna F., 236.
Rose E., 183.
Rosetta, 216.
Ross, 216.
Roxana, 172, 173, 175, 178.
Roxana C., 156.
Roxana M., 174.
Roxalana, 194.
Royal, 255, 256.
Royal H., 230.
Roy R., 229.
Rufus, 168, 234, 245, 266.
Rufus A., 194.
Rufus W., 245.
Ruth, 181, 189, 190, 192, 193, 200, 206, 212.
Ruth A., 156.
Ruth S., 238.
Sadie, 187, 231.
Sadie E., 155.
Sadie I., 188.
Salina, 149, 256.
Sallie M., 187.
Sally, 209, 212, 216, 222, 234.
Sally Ann, 214.
Sally P., 252.
Salmon, 190.
Samuel, 144, 153, 177, 178, 211, 201, 202, 203, 206, 209, 210, 212, 214, 215, 216, 217, 255, 256, 263, 264, 269, 270.
Samuel A., 175, 256.
Samuel B., 268.
Samuel D., 221, 222.
Samuel E., 182.
Samuel N., 226.
Samuel S., 179, 182.
Samuel T., 218.
Samuel W., 205, 231.
Sanborn, 223.
Sanford E.,
Sanford H., 192.
Sarah, 149, 153, 175, 189, 199, 200, 207, 208, 210, 211, 212, 213, 214, 217, 220, 231, 232, 233, 234, 253, 255, 259.

Sarah A., 168, 179, 184, 240, 247, 257.
Sarah B., 156.
Sarah E., 194, 195, 225, 246, 258.
Sarah H., 204.
Sarah J., 185, 178, 190.
Sarah L., 206.
Sarah M., 243.
Scott, 217.
Schuyler, 143, 151.
Seba, 147, 262.
Selah, 159.
Seldon, 161.
Selina, 155.
Senator, 158.
Seril, 158.
Sevilla, 157.
Seward E., 171.
Seymour D., 166.
Sibyl, 150, 162, 178.
Sidney, 156.
Sidney B., 156.
Sidney G., 213.
Silas, 168, 234, 245, 206, 270.
Simon M., 237, 242, 266.
Sheldon C., 256.
Shubael, 150, 262, 264.
Sophia, 213.
Sophia P. L., 193.
Sophronia, 158.
Solon W., 191, 192, 268.
Sprague, 267.
Stephen T., 223.
Susan, 204, 211, 212, 223.
Susan A., 270.
Susan R., 232.
Susan T., 218.
Susan W., 258.
Susie, 168.
Susie W., 221.
Sylvanus, 203, 207, 210, 216, 217, 264.
Sylvester, 173.
Sylvia, 150.
Sylvia A., 195.
Thaddeus S., 223.
Thedor, 274.
Theodor, 274.
Theodore, 179, 201, 202, 203, 210, 212, 214, 217, 218, 221, 225, 226, 229, 230, 264.
Theodore B., 218, 219.
Theodore S., 248.
Theodore W., 179, 181, 197, 221, 222.
Theodosia, 154.
Theodosius, 265.

INDEX. 291

Theron J., 216.
Thomas, 143, 144, 146, 189, 190, 202, 204, 211, 212, 243, 257, 258, 261, 263, 264, 265, 268, 269.
Thomas Freman, 246, 251, 253.
Thomas G., 218, 219, 235, 237.
Thomas L., 221, 223.
Thomas P., 258, 259.
Thomas R., 219.
Thomas S., 190, 191.
Thompson, 212, 216.
Timothy, 148, 149, 261, 264, 274.
Tobias, 269.
Tryphena, 235, 258.
Urial B., 185.
Valentine, 212.
Vernon H., 183.
Wallace, 168.
Wallace R., 259.
Walter, 191, 229, 239.
Walter C., 157.
Walter F., 219.
Walter L., 166.
Walter O., 241.
Warren, 239.
Washington, 185, 186.
Wealthy C., 247.
Wealthy H., 194.
Webster, 226, 247.
Webster C., 226.
Webster L., 227.
Webster W., 227.
Wells, 177.
Wesley G., 236, 241.
Willard, 158, 209.

Willard W., 239, 241.
William, 145, 146, 152, 159, 170, 192, 193, 203, 204, 208, 209, 210, 212, 213, 214, 215, 216, 217, 223, 225, 232, 233, 234, 235, 236, 243, 244, 246, 249, 257, 258, 261, 263, 264, 266, 268, 270, 271, 272, 273.
William A., 171, 236, 240, 266.
William B., 179.
William C., 235, 237.
William E., 183, 221, 222, 223, 230, 265, 269.
William F., 208, 246, 250, 266.
William G., 270.
William H., 184, 197, 214, 215, 224, 237, 239, 278.
William I., 236, 242.
William J. B., 214.
William L., 160.
William P., 218, 219, 220, 265.
William R., 213, 218, 236, 241.
William S., 226, 254, 266.
William T., 258.
William V., 234, 246, 251.
William W., 155, 207, 232, 266.
Wilfred N., 195.
Willie H., 210.
Wilbur, 161, 184, 185.
Willis, 265.
Willis H., 169, 238.
Willis S., 155.
Woolsey B., 216.
Wyona, 191, 217.
Zebina, 149, 150, 276.
Zebulon, 149, 177, 186, 261, 264.

OTHER NAMES.

Abbe, 176.
Abbott, 156, 213, 245.
Ackerman, 258.
Adams, 149, 151, 154.
Alden, 143.
Allard, 235.
Allen, 165, 176, 243, 249.
Ames, 157, 211.
Andrews, 148.
Antrobus, 188.
Archibald, 219.
Armstrong, 222.
Arnaud, 225.
Ash, 208.
Atkins, 167.
Atlee, 222.
Avery, 156, 173.
Ayer, 235.

Ayres, 201.
Babb, 233, 242.
Babcock, 185.
Bailey, 149.
Baker, 221, 272, 273.
Bakes, 151.
Balch, 230.
Balcom, 171, 189.
Baldwin, 156.
Ballard, 248.
Ballou, 255.
Barnard, 154.
Barney, 215, 217.
Barrows, 237.
Barber, 165, 194.
Barnes, 159, 176.
Barnard, 167.
Barr, 213.

Bartlett, 175.
Bates, 167.
Beach, 236.
Beaman, 185.
Bean, 153.
Beauregard, 208.
Beck, 198, 199, 204.
Beckwith, 163.
Beebe, 164, 183.
Benedict, 149, 194.
Benson, 154, 178.
Bentley, 178.
Berri, 169.
Berry, 235, 236.
Beverly, 194.
Bidwell, 167.
Bingham, 150.
Bird, 278.
Birdsall, 180.
Birge, 157.
Bissell, 147.
Bixby, 204.
Blake, 209, 219.
Blodgett, 162.
Bloomer, 185.
Bodge, 205.
Bonner, 156.
Bonson, 235.
Booth, 178.
Boothby, 237.
Borden, 215.
Bottom, 205.
Boulter, 238.
Bouve, 219.
Bowditch, 249.
Bowen, 179.
Boyce, 212.
Boyd, 220.
Bradeen, 244.
Bragdon, 223.
Branson, 221.
Brazier, 217.
Breer, 162.
Brewer, 245.
Brewster, 258.
Bregenzer, 173.
Brice, 185.
Briggs, 151, 164, 185.
Brigham, 211.
Brockway, 161.
Brook, 247.
Brooks, 177, 178.
Bronson, 185.
Brown, 153, 165, 189, 190, 194, 221, 228, 242.
Browne, 208.
Brubaker, 228.

Buck, 238.
Buckland, 172.
Buckley, 167.
Bump, 169.
Burnham, 183, 238.
Burton, 228.
Butler, 236.
Buttars, 175.
Byers, 275.
Caley, 176.
Came, 235.
Campbell, 175.
Capron, 237.
Care, 155.
Carpenter, 182.
Carr, 232.
Carroll, 153.
Carter, 240.
Carver, 243.
Cash, 243.
Cass, 206.
Cate, 197, 205, 206, 252, 253.
Chamberlin, 255.
Chambers, 161.
Chaffee, 168.
Chapin, 226.
Chase, 206.
Cheesborough, 173.
Cheever, 153.
Chesley, 253.
Chittenden, 216.
Childs, 250.
Christenson, 226.
Christie, 258.
Clapp, 246, 249.
Clark, 154, 156, 168, 192, 226, 255.
Clarke, 149.
Cleveland, 217.
Clough, 232.
Cobb, 181, 230.
Colcord, 230.
Coleman, 257.
Collard, 191.
Collins, 155.
Collings, 241.
Colman, 173, 180.
Colton, 259.
Colvin, 161, 164.
Cotton, 257.
Coningham, 172.
Connor, 220.
Consalus, 183.
Cook, 145, 152, 219, 227.
Cooke, 153.
Coolbroth, 233.
Cooley, 157, 165.

INDEX.

Cooper, 194.
Copeland, 248
Corey, 191.
Coughlan, 171.
Cranch, 251.
Crane, 154, 174.
Craven, 166.
Creber, 198, 199, 200.
Cromwell, 276.
Croswell, 252.
Crowell, 193.
Cullen, 240.
Cullers, 180.
Culver, 181.
Cummings, 195, 234.
Currier, 174, 224.
Curtis, 247.
Cushing, 219.
Cuth, 204.
Dalton, 153, 154.
Dame, 258.
David, 172.
Davis, 205, 208.
Dawes, 173.
Day, 194.
Dean, 180, 202.
Delaney, 193.
De La Meter, 180.
Denison, 227.
Dennis, 179, 189.
Derring, 238.
De Rochefort, 204.
Dewey, 217.
Dexter, 239.
Dickson, 162.
Dille, 174.
Dobson, 165.
Dolbear, 207.
Dongan, 151.
Donald, 188.
Donaldson, 277.
Dooley, 211.
Doolittle, 159.
Dorman, 172.
Dosser, 223.
Downing, 228.
Drown, 257.
Dunckler, 153.
Dunham, 192.
Dunbar, 176.
Dunn, 259.
Durham, 229.
Dwyer, 259.
Dye, 195.
Dyer, 239.
Dygert, 171.
Eastey, 180.

Eastman, 144.
Edgecomb, 243.
Egleston, 184.
Elling, 175.
Elliott, 215.
Ellworth, 210.
Emery, 218.
Erickson, 229.
Erkson, 194.
Estes, 247.
Evans, 226.
Falsom, 242.
Faxon, 202.
Fellows, 163, 210, 211, 238.
Fenderson, 233.
Fernald, 207.
Fickett, 234.
Finch, 191, 274.
Firmin, 160.
Fish, 175, 225, 238.
Fisher, 156, 249.
Fitzgerald, 257.
Flanigan, 206.
Fletcher, 209.
Fogg, 248.
Folsom, 211, 231.
Fonda, 191.
Foote, 190.
Ford, 149.
Foss, 237.
Foster, 160, 170, 205.
Fowler, 207.
Franklin, 259.
Frazier, 248.
French, 209.
Fredenburgh, 179.
Freeman, 245, 246.
Frisbie, 167, 189.
Frost, 204, 205, 231.
Fullam, 191.
Fuller, 216.
Furness, 260.
Gawne, 173, 174.
Gay, 247.
Geminy, 166.
Giles, 153.
Gilman, 211.
Gilmore, 241.
Girard, 207.
Goodrich, 177.
Goodwin, 160, 230.
Gordon, 223, 239.
Gorham, 150.
Gove, 225.
Gower, 219.
Grainger, 221.
Granger, 175.

294 INDEX.

Graham, 149, 162.
Grant, 221, 248, 258.
Gray, 242, 249.
Green, 161, 185, 205, 208, 217, 250, 258.
Greenfield, 227, 229.
Greive, 276.
Gress, 230.
Griffin, 212, 240.
Griffing, 192.
Grove, 174, 203, 205, 208.
Haight, 183.
Haines, 211.
Hakes, 189.
Halcrow, 215.
Hale, 213.
Hall, 238, 255.
Ham, 203, 258.
Hanscom, 258.
Hansen, 170.
Harden, 185.
Hardy, 186.
Harkness, 226.
Harman, 178.
Harmon, 233, 236, 238, 245.
Harper, 211, 217.
Harrington, 176.
Harris, 247.
Hart, 176.
Hartshorn, 192.
Haskell, 155.
Hastings, 156, 219.
Haswell, 190.
Hawkins, 224.
Hawley, 193.
Hayes, 205, 236.
Head, 210.
Headley, 214.
Heald, 205.
Heath, 148.
Hebard, 151.
Hebart, 170.
Helm, 225.
Hendershott, 175.
Heriff, 165.
Herring, 155, 226.
Hewitt, 192.
Hicks, 185.
Higgins, 237, 244.
Higbee, 212.
Hill, 206, 238.
Hilliard, 209, 211.
Hillis, 225.
Hills, 191.
Hinchcliff, 180.
Hinds, 247.
Hinkley, 238.

Hitcham, 272.
Hitchcock, 157.
Hoadley, 146.
Hoit, 204, 222.
Holcomb, 147.
Holcomb, 167.
Holley, 169.
Holms, 205.
Holt, 208.
Holton, 178.
Hopping, 229.
Horne, 193.
Hotchkiss, 189.
Houghtaling, 159.
How, 202.
Hubbard, 220.
Hucking, 199.
Hutchins, 238.
Hughes, 158.
Hull, 174.
Humphreys, 158.
Hunnawell, 242.
Huntington, 147.
Huntress, 235.
Hurd, 215.
Hurlbut, 190.
Ingham, 227.
Irish, 243.
Istrell, 180.
Jacobs, 164, 208.
Jackson, 150, 201.
Jaggers, 178.
Jenkins, 241.
Jerome, 217.
Johnson, 146, 160, 166, 1 193, 229, 244.
Johnston, 149.
Johnstone, 191.
Johns, 154.
Jones, 161, 165, 198, 2 238.
Jordan, 239, 244, 250.
Joslin, 158.
Joy, 206.
Jucker, 171.
Judd, 176.
Julian, 220.
Kaeser, 160.
Keeler, 180.
Kehoo, 153.
Kellar, 159.
Kelley, 212, 230.
Kellogg, 228.
Kelsey, 208.
Keniston, 223.
Kenny, 244.
Keyer, 209.

INDEX.

Kilburn, 157.
Kilby, 245.
Kilmer, 181.
Kimball, 224.
Kimberlee, 276.
King, 185.
Kingsley, 255.
Kingsbury, 213, 258.
Kinsley, 273.
Knapp, 184, 239.
Knight, 158, 247, 278.
Knowles, 239.
Kopp, 240.
Kridler, 165.
Kurtz, 248.
Lafrinier, 175.
Lake, 253, 254.
Lampson, 168.
Lancaster, 157.
Lane, 199, 218.
Lang, 201, 231.
Lapham, 209.
Larkin, 235.
Larrabee, 247, 250, 252.
Lathrop, 219.
Lawrence, 190, 192, 239.
Levitt, 220.
Lea, 151.
Lear, 211.
Lee, 177, 223, 252.
Leland, 181.
Leslie, 244.
Lewis, 191, 213, 219.
Libby, 233, 234, 235, 243, 245.
Locke, 206, 208.
Lockwood, 162.
Lord, 242, 244.
Loud, 256.
Lowing, 182.
Lynch, 166.
Lyon, 168.
Mabry, 245.
Macy, 244.
Manchester, 244.
Manley, 190.
Manzer, 168.
Martin, 219, 229.
Marvin, 205.
Mason, 175, 209.
Matthews, 163.
Mayhew, 251.
McCann, 249.
McConnell, 211.
McCreery, 162.
McDongall, 170.
McFarland, 161.
McGiving, 164.

McGrath, 175.
McIlrath, 175.
McIlvain, 252.
McKenzie, 179.
McMillen, 188.
McPhetas, 205.
Mead, 166, 169.
Mears, 241.
Merrill, 208, 219, 218, 248.
Meserve, 235.
Messenger, 160.
Michall, 248.
Miliken, 233, 234, 235, 237, 238.
Miller, 155, 258.
Mills, 166, 189, 224, 225.
Mitchell, 181, 222, 248.
Mix, 176.
Mock, 213.
Moissac, 275.
Montgomery, 222.
Mooney, 213.
Moore, 177, 194, 213.
Moot, 184.
Morrison, 214, 253, 254.
Morse, 211.
Moulton, 210, 233.
Mowry, 161, 227.
Mugridge, 259.
Murdock, 157, 193.
Muth, 159.
Mylod, 176.
Nash, 158, 234, 247.
Naylor, 222.
Neff, 195.
Neil, 230, 258.
Neilson, 195.
Nelson, 176, 200, 208, 240, 259.
Neumuth, 151.
Newell, 182, 247.
Newman, 195.
Nicholson, 170.
Nichols, 169.
Nickols, 179.
Niles, 191.
Nowland, 227.
Nutter, 206, 259.
O'Brien, 219.
Osborne, 178.
Otis, 178.
Overton, 222.
Oviatt, 190.
Owen, 146, 147.
Paine, 250.
Page, 243.
Parshley, 247.
Parker, 176, 186, 243.
Parkman, 241.

INDEX.

Parmer, 189, 213.
Parsons, 158, 231.
Partin, 222.
Pattison, 213.
Patterson, 178.
Paul, 187, 204.
Pearl, 217, 232.
Pearson, 220.
Pease, 235.
Peck, 168, 214.
Pecker, 209.
Pender, 178.
Pendleton, 188.
Pepper, 194.
Perine, 182.
Perkins, 174.
Perry, 243, 246.
Peters, 191.
Pettibone, 147.
Phettleplace, 194.
Phelps, 169.
Phillips, 184.
Phillpot, 191.
Pierson, 249.
Piggot, 208.
Pike, 202.
Pillsbury, 224, 240.
Pinney, 172.
Piper, 211.
Plum, 229.
Plumly, 192.
Plummer, 230, 252.
Poland, 248.
Pond, 170, 231.
Pool, 259.
Porter, 157.
Powers, 168.
Prebble, 191.
Price, 162.
Pritchard, 158.
Purchase, 249.
Purdy, 156.
Ralstone, 214.
Rand, 209, 232.
Randall, 250.
Ream, 165.
Reynolds, 157, 194, 212.
Rhodes, 159.
Rickee, 221.
Ricker, 257.
Richards, 161, 172, 244.
Richardson, 155, 211, 218.
Rice, 158, 233.
Ridge, 195.
Riggs, 243.
Ringe, 234.
Robertson, 191, 211.

Robb, 213.
Roberson, 212.
Robinson, 212.
Roberts, 154, 162, 229.
Robley, 165.
Roenitz, 180, 181.
Rohman, 240.
Rose, 159, 176.
Rounds, 218.
Rowell, 212, 257.
Royce, 190.
Russell, 164.
Sackett, 163.
Sadler, 244.
Samson, 272, 273.
Sanford, 216.
Sargent, 235.
Sartor, 184.
Sawyer, 208, 242.
Scott, .149, 150.
Scripture, 150.
Seager, 150.
Seavy, 238.
Shattuck, 219.
Shattuck, 152.
Shaw, 237, 256.
Shaweeker, 165.
Shedd, 249.
Sheldon, 256.
Sherbourne, 200, 253, 254.
Shethar, 171.
Shiply, 215.
Shortridge, 198, 199.
Shute, 276, 277.
Simmons, 219.
Simpson, 208.
Small, 248, 253.
Smith, 162, 193, 200, 218, 237, 241.
Snow, 251.
Sook, 226.
Spencer, 229.
Spring, 174.
Stafford, 152.
Staples, 212.
Stevens, 147, 153, 179, 181, 185, 237, 248.
Stewart, 249.
Stickney, 169.
St. John, 154, 192.
Stock, 180.
Stockman, 174, 175.
Stockwell, 178.
Stoddard, 212, 214.
Stone, 258.
Streator, 166.
Strong, 159.

INDEX.

Stroup, 184.
Strout, 234, 244.
Sturdevant, 193, 249.
Sturtevant, 190.
Swain, 196.
Swick, 186.
Taylor, 170, 182, 216.
Teasdale, 223.
Templeton, 178.
Terry, 189, 195.
Thackeray, 215.
Thomas, 201, 202.
Thompson, 145, 229, 278.
Thomson, 229.
Thornton, 151.
Throop, 194.
Thurston, 235.
Tilton, 207.
Tinker, 192.
Titcomb, 219.
Tobey, 205.
Tobman, 256.
Todd, 156, 247.
Tolbot, 173.
Tolly, 230.
Tompkins, 156.
Towle, 205, 207, 241.
Townsley, 181.
Trask, 245.
Traver, 162.
Trickey, 211.
Tripp, 206.
Trot, 258.
Truman, 157.
Turney, 215.
Tyler, 237.
Underwood, 235.
Upson, 176, 160.
Van Bryck, 156.
Van Hooten, 180.
Van Ness, 184.
Vaughn, 257.
Very, 153.
Vines, 272.
Wait, 168.
Walker, 155, 172, 187, 198, 199, 221, 276, 277.
Wallace, 203.
Walton, 203, 278.
Walsh, 241.

Wardell, 229.
Warner, 185.
Warren, 174.
Warriner, 159.
Washington, 148.
Waterhouse, 199, 200, 233, 245.
Waugh, 189.
Webster, 206.
Weeks, 210, 257.
Wells, 167, 221, 259.
Werd, 149.
West, 205.
Wetherell, 216.
Weymouth, 247.
Wheeler, 166, 239.
Whisler, 225.
Whitcomb, 159, 259.
White, 149, 165.
Whitehead, 191.
Whiten, 258.
Whitney, 154, 180, 233.
Wilcox, 147, 160.
Wilkinson, 183, 236, 242.
Willard, 182.
Williams, 158, 203, 213, 221, 238.
Willis, 160.
Wilner, 154.
Wilson, 193.
Windau, 159.
Windsor, 194.
Wing, 249.
Wirths, 184.
Wise, 166.
Wiswall, 220.
Wittern 175.
Wolworth, 174.
Wolcott, 210.
Wood, 171, 222, 245.
Woodford, 177.
Woodruff, 195.
Woods, 165, 169.
Woolsey, 216.
Worthington, 191.
Wright, 184, 216.
Yeaton, 211.
Yell, 153.
Yeomans, 159.
Young, 236.
Youngs, 229.
Zelke, 160.

FAMILY HISTORIES RECORDING MOSES ALLIANCES.

Ames Family.
Amidon Family.
Andrews Genealogy.
Benedict Family.
Ballou Genealogy.
Banta Genealogy.
Balch Family.
Bartholomew Family.
Batchelder Genealogy.
Butler, Thomas and Descendants.
Cutter family.
Cochran Family.
Cutter Family in New England.
Crafts Family.
Crane Family.
Driver Family.
Doggett Family, Hictory of.
Edgecomb Family, Ridlon.
Estes Family.
Eddy Family.
Emery Family.
Earl Family.
Fairbanks Genealogy.
Faxon Family, History of.
Field Family.
Gray Family, Granger Family.
Granger Family.
Goodrich Family.
Goodwin Family.
Hart Family.
Hodges Family.
Hoyt Family.
Humphrey Family.
Hakes Family.
Hayes Family.
Kinsman Family.
Larrabee Family, Ridlon.
Libby Family.
Morrison Family.
Maun Family.
Meriwether's The.
McCutcheon Family.
Noble, Descendants of Thos.
Osgood Family.
Prescott Memorial.
Pierce Pedigree.
Phelps Family of America.
Reade of Weymouth.
Ridlons — Saco Valley Settlements.
Rogers, James and Descendants.
Simpson Family.
Streeter Genealogy.
Starkeys, The.
Shafter Memorial.
Sharpless Family.
Slocums of America.
Shattuck Family Starr.
Starr Family.
Sargent Genealogy.
Sears Genealogy.
Stickney Family.
Tracy Family.
Terry Family.
Thurston Family.
Tuttle Family.
Vilas Family.
Wentworth Family.
White Family.
Willey Family.

The "Phelps Family in America" notes Phelps Marriages with MOSES men and women with given names as follows: Aaron; Amy; Abram; Charles; Curtis H.; Dorcas; Elisha; Elizabeth; Harriet; Henrietta; Henry L.; Hoyt; Julia A.; Keziah; Lucius; Lydia; Martha; Martin; Mary; Mortimer; Robert; Sarah; Susanna; Timothy; Zerviah.

This example will point the reader to further sources of information.

CPSIA information can be obtained
at www.ICGtesting.com
Printed in the USA
BVHW05s0647200418
513968BV00009BB/71/P

9 780282 396107